A GUIDE TO WELSH LITERATURE

A GUIDE TO
WELSH LITERATURE
c. 1900–1996
VOLUME VI

Edited by
DAFYDD JOHNSTON

UNIVERSITY OF WALES PRESS
CARDIFF
1998

© 1998, the contributors

British Library Cataloguing in Publication Data

A catalogue record for this book is available from the British Library

ISBN 0-7083-1424-4

Published with the financial support of the Arts Council of Wales

Cover illustration: Ogwyn Davies

Cover design by Olwen Fowler
Typeset at the University of Wales Press
Printed in Wales by Dinefwr Press, Llandybïe

CONTENTS

PREFACE

Whilst the Welsh quite rightly take great pride in the antiquity and vigour of their literary tradition, which is surveyed in the earlier volumes in this series, no period can compare with the twentieth century in terms of quantity or quality of literature. Such an abundant and multifaceted literature as that of this century is not easily sliced and segmented according to the demands of an introductory guide. The principles according to which this volume is organized are a combination of period and form. The opening chapter discusses the literary revival which began towards the end of the nineteenth century and had a crucial influence on the literature of the twentieth. The First World War was in many ways the watershed between the apparent solidity of the Victorian age and the fragmentation of the twentieth century, and a chapter is therefore devoted to the literature which it produced. Since poetry has traditionally been the primary literary form in Welsh, and continues to flourish in new ways as well as old, poetry after the First World War is treated in three distinct periods, although a certain amount of overlap is inevitable. The other three main literary forms, the novel, the short story, and drama, have been given a chapter each. It should, of course, be borne in mind that some authors, such as Kate Roberts and especially Saunders Lewis, figure prominently in more than one chapter. The situation as the century draws to its close is surveyed in the final chapter by one of Wales's foremost contemporary writers.

The definition of literature adopted for the purpose of this volume is quite a narrow one. Because of the sheer quantity of important works which demand attention, it was judged best to concentrate on the mainstream literary forms, poetry, prose fiction, and drama. Other types of prose-writing, such as the essay and autobiography, are not discussed as forms in their own right, but only as they have been used by an author significant for other reasons, such as the essays of T. H. Parry-Williams, discussed in the chapter on poetry between the wars, or the autobiographical writing of D. J. Williams, discussed in the chapter on the short story. One or two writers have perhaps received less attention than they deserve as a result of this policy, such as the historian and essayist R. T. Jenkins, who is mentioned only on account of his two short historical novels.

No attempt has been made to impose any standard approach or interpretation on contributors, and emphases will be seen to vary considerably from chapter to chapter. The only element of uniformity is that all contributions are written for the general reader without assuming any prior knowledge of Wales or its language. This does not aim to be an exhaustive account, but an informative guide which shows both what is excellent and what is distinctive in twentieth-century Welsh literature.

I am most grateful to the contributors for fulfilling such daunting tasks so effectively, and to the Director and staff of the University of Wales Press for their encouragement and support in the making of this book.

Dafydd Johnston

A NOTE ON CONTRIBUTORS

T. Robin Chapman is a teacher of English in Bradford and Honorary Lecturer in Welsh at University of Wales Bangor

T. Gerald Hunter is a Lecturer in Welsh at University of Wales Cardiff

R. M. Jones is a former Professor of Welsh at University of Wales Aberystwyth

Dafydd Johnston is Professor of Welsh at University of Wales Swansea

Robert Rhys is a Lecturer in Welsh at University of Wales Swansea

John Rowlands is Professor of Welsh at University of Wales Aberystwyth

Elan Closs Stephens is Senior Lecturer in Theatre, Film and Television Studies at University of Wales Aberystwyth

Megan Tomos is Administrative Officer of the Association of Welsh Translators

Gerwyn Wiliams is Senior Lecturer in Welsh at University of Wales Bangor

CHAPTER 1

THE LITERARY REVIVAL

DAFYDD JOHNSTON

The literary revival of the early twentieth century is best understood as part of a broader tendency in the history of Welsh literature since the Middle Ages. Both the Renaissance in the sixteenth century and the Neo-classical movement in the eighteenth followed a similar pattern of reaction against the immediately preceding period, which was considered barren and lacking in literary standards, provoking a return to the supposedly higher standards of an earlier age. The Welsh literary tradition can be seen to have renewed itself periodically by turning back upon itself, deriving energy and inspiration from its past. In the case of the twentieth-century revival the debt to the past was multilayered, the primary source of inspiration in the Middle Ages being augmented by an awareness of the classical standards set by the two earlier revivals, particularly in the Welsh Bible and the poetry of Goronwy Owen. That is not to say that the new movement was simply a matter of imitating former glories. Despite a strong traditionalist impulse, this was very much a creative adaptation of tradition in response to contemporary needs.

Before considering the element of reaction against the nineteenth century in detail, it would be as well to recognize the degree of continuity between the two periods, the ways in which the revival at the turn of the century can be seen as the culmination of long-term developments—if only to dispel the simplistic notion of peaks and troughs which the revival model of literary history may suggest. On the most fundamental level, the economic prosperity which the Industrial Revolution brought to Wales undoubtedly laid the foundations for the new flourishing of literature. The two major industries, coal primarily in the south and slate in the north, created new concentrations of population which were crucial centres for the revitalization of Welsh religious and cultural life. It can be no coincidence that both industries reached the height of their prosperity during the last two decades of the nineteenth century, at the very time when a new spirit became apparent in Welsh literature. Wales was of course making a major contribution to the ascendancy of the British Empire in the Victorian era, and the resultant sense of confidence and optimism was evident in the cultural life of the nation. The establishment of such institutions as the University of Wales in 1893 and the National Library and National Museum of Wales in 1907 is a reflection of this new confidence.

The creation of the University of Wales was the culmination of the development of an education system for Wales in the later nineteenth century, with the establishment of elementary schools in 1870, secondary or so-called county schools in 1889, and the first three constituent colleges of the university, Aberystwyth in 1872, Cardiff in 1883, and Bangor in 1884. This development was crucial for the future of Welsh literature, producing both a new breed of educated writer and a new reading public whose literary tastes were much broader than those which had been stimulated by the Sunday School movement. The Welsh language gained status, albeit gradually and often grudgingly, by becoming the object of academic study, and the amateurism associated with the Eisteddfod gave way to a new professional scholarship and criticism which was able to dispel many misconceptions and popular myths propagated by such creative interpreters of tradition as Iolo Morganwg and William Owen Pughe, clearing the way for a sober reassessment of the Welsh literary inheritance.

The demand for education was just one aspect of a broader phenomenon in nineteenth-century Wales, and one which had parallels in a number of other European countries, the ideal of the cultured common people, or *gwerin* (a Welsh term which still retains its positive resonance). The political expression of this ideal was Liberalism, epitomized by the radicalism of the struggle for democratic rights, and paralleled in the religious sphere by the Nonconformist campaign for freedom from the tithes of the Established Church. The strength of Nonconformity was seen to reflect the high-minded spirituality of the Welsh people, as was the supposed reverence for education in Wales. One cherished myth in this respect was that encapsulated by the phrase *gwlad y menyg gwynion* (the land of the white gloves), according to which the crime rate in Wales was so low that judges often had no cases to hear. In fact, the whole ideal of the *gwerin* must be regarded as a myth, not only in the negative sense that it was a distortion of reality, but also in the positive sense of that term as representing the aspiration of a people, their chosen self-image, and an ideal which was of central importance in the literature of the early twentieth century.

The revival can, therefore, be regarded as the culmination of trends in the economic, religious and cultural life of the nation which had been developing throughout the Victorian era. The impetus of these developments was sustained by one of the fundamental beliefs of that era, faith in progress. Progress meant the continual improvement of the human condition and the gradual disappearance of immorality, ignorance and poverty. It was closely tied up with an arrogant belief in the civilizing benefits of British imperialism, and in the Welsh context it gave rise to a sense of a great future in store for the nation, as suggested by the name of the nationalist movement founded in the 1880s, Cymru Fydd (literally 'Wales to be', known in English as Young Wales).

Various forces were undermining this naive optimism by the beginning of the twentieth century, and it was to be terminally shattered by the devastating upheaval of the First World War. Nationalist hopes attached to the Cymru Fydd movement were disappointed when it came to an end in 1896 as a result of tensions between the anglicized south-east and Welsh-speaking areas. Disillusionment with the belief in continual progress was part of a more general reaction against the ideals of Victorian Wales, focusing above all on its supposed materialism.

The most baleful legacy of the nineteenth century was the effects of the Industrial Revolution in Wales. Environmental issues were hardly fashionable at the turn of the century, but the disfigurement of the landscape's natural beauty through industrialization was of great concern to writers of that time. The drawbacks of industry were also becoming apparent through the increasing number of strikes and major disasters, such as that at Senghennydd in 1913 in which 439 men were killed. There was an escapist tendency in the reaction against industrialization, with unspoilt idylls being sought either in the countryside or else in the pre-industrial era of a medieval setting. In this flight from the modern industrial world Welsh writers were doing exactly the same as their English counterparts such as Tennyson and William Morris, but with an added political element in that industry was often perceived as something essentially foreign to Wales, whilst the rural communities were seen as strongholds of Welsh culture and the Middle Ages as a period of heroic independence.

Another aspect of Victorian Wales which provoked a strong reaction was institutionalized Nonconformity. By the late nineteenth century the Nonconformist sects had lost much of their former vitality, and were dominated by a concern for social respectability and a rigidly puritanical morality, a combination which generated much hypocrisy. There was widespread reaction against the self-righteous pietism of the chapels, and the dry, pedantic theologizing of their sermons. It should be emphasized, however, that this did not constitute a rejection of religion itself. Although some writers of the period did flaunt their hedonism in defiance of chapel condemnation of worldly pleasures, they never adopted such a materialistic position as atheism. Indeed, their quarrel was with the very lack of spiritual content in chapel religion. An agnostic questioning was therefore the most common religious attitude in early twentieth-century Welsh literature.

Although the beginning of the new century was undoubtedly a factor in the excited sense of potential which characterized the new literature, nevertheless literary movements do not fit neatly into the chronological framework imposed by a series such as this one. The revival began to gather impetus in the 1880s, its climax was in the first decade of the twentieth century, and it certainly came to an end with the First World War. Two prose-writers whose work was published mainly before 1900, and is therefore discussed in more detail in the previous volume in this series, but who nevertheless merit attention here because of their formative influence on twentieth-century literature, are Emrys ap Iwan and O. M. Edwards.

Emrys ap Iwan was the *nom de plume* of Robert Ambrose Jones (1848–1906), a Methodist minister and essayist who was a trenchant critic of his own denomination. In that and a number of other ways he can be seen as a harbinger of the new movement. It was he who first identified the prose tradition which derived from the Welsh Bible and ran through the seventeenth and eighteenth centuries in the works of such writers as Morgan Llwyd, Ellis Wynne and Theophilus Evans. He was able to use this perception to establish standards by which to criticize the weaknesses of nineteenth-century prose, especially its excessive use of English idioms. An enormous amount of Welsh prose was produced in the Victorian period, but its artistic standards were generally low, and it tended to be judged according to non-literary criteria, such as morality or even denominational interests. In order to restore prose-writing as an art form in its own right Emrys ap Iwan saw the need to identify the distinctive traits of the Welsh language, for he recognized that thought was moulded by language. The Welsh language was therefore essential to the identity of its speakers, shaping their very character, rather than being merely a superficial quirk, as it tended to be regarded then (and often still is even now).

Emrys ap Iwan's appreciation of the importance of language was stimulated by the time he spent on the Continent learning German and French. The lucid prose of French essayists such as Paul Louis Courier served as a model for the clear reasoning style of his own writing. In his openness to European influences Emrys ap Iwan set an example to many twentieth-century Welsh writers, particularly Saunders Lewis, on whom he was a significant influence. This European perspective determined the nature of Emrys ap Iwan's nationalism, which also anticipated the attitudes of later thinkers. In contrast to the sentimental patriotism prevalent in the nineteenth century, which took pride in plucky little Wales's contributions to the British Empire, he chose to emphasize Wales's uniqueness, arguing that the Welsh had a moral duty to preserve those features which distinguished them from the English, above all their language.

Although O. M. Edwards (1858–1920) was ten years younger than Emrys ap Iwan, he in fact shows much less of a tendency to react against the culture of Victorian Wales, and more than any other writer he embodies the element of continuity in the revival. The son of a poor but cultured Merionethshire smallholder, a highly successful academic career took him to Oxford, where he became Fellow and Tutor of History at Lincoln College in 1889. He thus represents the ideal of the Welsh *gwerin*, including their desire to better themselves through education. Unlike some others, O. M. Edwards used his academic success not to escape from his humble background, but rather to promote its virtues in his writings. His most influential work in this respect was as editor of the magazine *Cymru* (Wales), founded in 1891 with the aim of presenting the history and culture of the country in an entertaining manner, emphasizing in particular the achievements of the common people.

In promoting folk culture O. M. Edwards's influence was more immediate than that of Emrys ap Iwan, being in harmony with the popular trends of the time, but it was ultimately less lasting, since its idealistic element is now much more apparent. Edwards's philosophy of history was typical of its age in its interpretation of the inevitable progress of the Welsh *gwerin* from serfdom in the Middle Ages to freedom in the nineteenth century with the achievement of democratic rights and the benefits of education. The crucial elevating factor in that progress was Nonconformity, which Edwards viewed with a much less critical eye than other writers of the twentieth-century revival. His educational ideal was the Sunday School, a co-operative institution working through the medium of the Welsh language to give the common people a spiritual education with no thought of material gain.

O. M. Edwards's prose had quite different stylistic virtues to that of Emrys ap Iwan, but was equally important in re-establishing artistic standards in Welsh writing. Whilst Emrys ap Iwan excelled in the lucid expression of rational thought, Edwards's prose is rich in colour, and has a lightness of touch which is in striking contrast to the sombre utilitarian tomes of the period. Although he never rebelled against chapel religion, as other authors were to do, the elegance and sensuousness of his writing served as an antidote to the defects caused by the dominance of puritanical pietism in Welsh literature. Whether discussing one of the heroes of the Protestant Reformation, recounting his experiences travelling in Europe, or celebrating the beauties of the Welsh countryside, his essays are journalism of the highest order, at once entertaining and edifying.

O. M. Edwards's devotion to Wales received a crucial stimulus from his association with a remarkable generation of Welshmen at Oxford. The Oxford Welsh Society, Cymdeithas Dafydd ap Gwilym, formed in 1886 under the presidency of the Celtic scholar Sir John Rhŷs, made a major contribution to the revival, particularly in setting appropriate linguistic standards for the new literature. In seeking to reform the Welsh commonly written in the nineteenth century, these Oxford men drew not only on their study of the classics of the literary tradition from the Middle Ages onwards, but also on the spoken language of the day, thus combining purity and naturalness. Although initially regarded with some suspicion as 'Oxford Welsh', this literary standard was soon widely accepted, and continues to be a vital foundation for Welsh literature to this day.

The prime mover behind the establishment of linguistic standards was John Morris-Jones (1864–1929). Brought up in Anglesey, he went to Jesus College Oxford in 1883 to study mathematics. His analytical mind was to serve him well when his interest switched to Welsh philology under the inspiration of Sir John Rhŷs, and all his work is characterized by the same spirit of rational enquiry after truth. His position as professor of Welsh at the University College of North Wales, Bangor, to which he was appointed in 1893, gave him the authority to play a leading role in the new movement as both scholar and critic, in addition to the contribution made by his own poetry.

John Morris-Jones's most important work of scholarship is his definitive account of the traditional literary language, *A Welsh Grammar* (1913), based on his analyses of medieval poetry and the prose classics. Like Emrys ap Iwan, one of his main concerns was to rid the language of the corruptions which had taken root since the eighteenth century. The particular target of his purifying zeal was the pseudo-scholarship of the antiquarian William Owen Pughe, whose dictionary of 1803 had introduced a host of inauthentic forms into the language. In addition to his *Grammar*, Morris-Jones's views on the language were published in the quarterly journal which he edited from 1911 to 1920, *Y Beirniad* (The Critic).

He performed an equally effective demolition job on the druidical rituals which had become associated with the National Eisteddfod, exposing them as the fabrications of another eighteenth-century antiquarian, Iolo Morganwg. The Eisteddfod provided John Morris-Jones with an important platform for his endeavours to restore standards of literary criticism in Welsh. His role as frequent adjudicator of strict-metre *awdlau* in the Chair competition gave him the opportunity to urge poets to follow the example set by the medieval bards, both in metrical practices and in use of language. In his view the majority of nineteenth-century Eisteddfod *awdlau* were merely mechanical exercises in the production of *cynghanedd*, entirely devoid of true poetry. His success in raising standards in this field was apparent at the Bangor National Eisteddfod of 1902, when he had the satisfaction of awarding the Chair to T. Gwynn Jones for his magnificent *awdl*, 'Ymadawiad Arthur' (The Departure of Arthur), one of the landmarks of the literary revival.

John Morris-Jones's views on the language and form of poetry were summed up in another authoritative volume, *Cerdd Dafod* (1925), which took as its title the traditional Welsh term for the art of poetry. Based on a lifetime's study of medieval Welsh poetry, it is as definitive as his earlier volume on grammar, and provided a foundation for the flourishing of the strict metres in the twentieth century. The concept of the poetic tradition as an organic entity with an objective existence is one which was developed slightly later, primarily by Saunders Lewis, but it could hardly have arisen at all without the spadework done by John Morris-Jones on the poetic practices which were actually tradited from one generation to the next.

One aspect of *Cerdd Dafod* which has received a great deal of attention, and a certain amount of mockery, is Morris-Jones's views on the appropriate language of poetry. On the principle that 'the language of poetry must be dignified and pure', he states that certain words are simply not to be used in serious poetry. For instance, Welsh has two words for 'cheek', *boch*, used in everyday speech, and *grudd*, which is a literary word. According to Morris-Jones, only the latter is to be used in poetry. He similarly distinguishes between two different words for mouth, and claims that the nose is too undignified to be even mentioned in poetry, unless it be a lampoon or a comic song. This case does show the weakness of his prescriptive approach to poetry as a craft with hard-and-fast rules. However, the real problem lay in the narrowness of his concept of poetry. In this context he clearly means lyric poetry of a particularly elevated and romantic kind, having little to do with the practicalities of everyday life, exactly the sort of poetry which he himself wrote. In such poetry the choice of the precise word was crucial to maintain atmosphere, and indeed an awareness of the connotations of words over and above their literal meaning is essential to poetry of all kinds. The lack of that sensitivity to the effects of words was one of the major defects of nineteenth-century Welsh poetry, and in that respect John Morris-Jones's stricture was timely, even if ultimately too absolute. Although the new spirit of realism from the First World War onwards meant that poets such as T. H. Parry-Williams and Gwenallt were soon breaking Morris-Jones's 'rule', it was partly due to his influence that they were so aware of the power of words in the first place.

Whilst John Morris-Jones's approach to literary form was a Classical one, in line with traditional Welsh poetic theory, his views on the content and function of poetry derived primarily from the Romantic movement, or at least from that degenerate form of Romanticism which was fashionable in the late nineteenth century. He set out his theory in an important article, 'Swydd y Bardd' (The Poet's Function), published in *Y Traethodydd* in 1902. Two of his central principles were that poetry should deal with the concrete rather than the abstract, and that it should not aim to convey any message or teach any moral lesson. The proper matter of poetry was therefore feelings rather than ideas, and the paramount feeling in the literature of the period, including Morris-Jones's own work, was love. He followed Aristotle in holding that literature should deal not with the specific circumstances of a particular time, which is the matter of history, but with general truths which are timeless. This will be seen to be relevant to the use of myth by several poets, most notably T. Gwynn Jones.

John Morris-Jones conceived of poetry as being set apart from normal life, existing on some timeless plane above the unpleasant realities and political concerns of its age. In this he was very close to the doctrine of art for art's sake, the idea that the poetic artefact should be a thing of beauty with no purpose outside itself. His principles were clearly too prescriptive and delimiting, and in fact he patently transgressed against them in his own early poetry, which contained clear moral lessons, as other poets readily did. Nevertheless, as in the case of poetic language, his pronouncements were a necessary reaction to contemporary weaknesses, and they certainly had a beneficial effect on the literature produced in the early twentieth century. As Emrys ap Iwan had already perceived, the fundamental problem with literature in the Victorian era was that it tended to be regarded as a vehicle for other purposes, especially moral ones, and to be judged on non-literary grounds. An emphasis on purely literary criteria was therefore a necessary corrective. A great deal of Morris-Jones's thinking on both the form and function of poetry can actually be seen as a reaction against a specific movement in the late nineteenth century, known as *Y Bardd Newydd* (The New Poet). Mostly Nonconformist ministers, these poets wrote highly abstract works dealing with theological speculations, and had little interest in poetic form. They represent one of the low points in the history of Welsh poetry, and the virtues of poets such as T. Gwynn Jones and R. Williams Parry shine all the more brightly in contrast to them.

John Morris-Jones published one collection of his own poetry, *Caniadau* (Songs), in 1907. It is a varied collection, containing strict-metre compositions, including two *awdlau*, translations from various languages, most notably lyrics by Heinrich Heine and the verses of the Persian poet Omar Khayyam, and a group of his own lyrics on love and nature. The *awdl* 'Cymru Fu: Cymru Fydd' (Wales that was: Wales to be), first published in O. M. Edwards's *Cymru* in 1892, is clearly a response to the political movement Cymru Fydd, sharing its optimism about Wales's future, but arguing that any reform must be based on a knowledge of tradition. This sense of a glorious past and a promising future, in contrast to dissatisfaction with the present, is typical of the revival, and Morris-Jones's acerbic satire on the religious, political and literary life of the country exemplifies the reaction against the Victorian age. So also does his other *awdl*, 'Salm i Famon' (A Psalm to Mamon), attacking the materialism of the age, and the translations of Omar Khayyam, which implicitly reject chapel puritanism by advocating a hedonistic philosophy.

The translations of Heinrich Heine, previously published in magazines in the early 1890s, are one of the most important items in the collection, representing an attempt to stimulate a new sensibility by bringing European lyric poetry into Welsh. John Morris-Jones's own lyrics follow Heine's example of refined feeling concisely and suggestively expressed, using nature as a correlative for human emotion. His best-known poem is 'Cwyn y Gwynt' (The Wind's Lament), in which the wind is imagined to be lamenting a lost love. The following lyric works in exactly the same way, and also illustrates the aestheticism of his work:

Y SEREN UNIG

Y gwridog haul fachludodd,
    Ac yn y nef uwchben
Y gwelir yn tywynnu
    Ryw unig seren wen.

Mi sylwais ar ei llygad
    Yn gloywi yn y nef,
Fel petai ddeigryn disglair
    Yn cronni ynddo ef.

Mi glywaf ddeigr yn llenwi
Fy llygad innau'n awr;
'R wyf innau'n unig unig;
Fy haul a aeth i lawr.

[The blushing sun has set, and in the heavens above a lone white star can
be seen shining. I noticed its eye glittering in the heavens, as if a bright
tear was welling in it. I feel a tear filling my own eye now; I too am all
alone; my sun has gone down.]

Before moving on to the major poets of the early twentieth
century, attention should be paid to some other popular lyricists of
the period, whose work shows the verbal sensibility advocated by
John Morris-Jones, but who belonged in the tradition of
nineteenth-century poets such as Ceiriog and Alun without adding
very much to it. Three who deserve particular mention are Silyn
(Robert Silyn Roberts; 1871–1930), Elphin (Robert Arthur
Griffith; 1860–1936), and Eifion Wyn (Eliseus Williams; 1867–
1926). The fact that all three were from Caernarfonshire, like the
better-known W. J. Gruffydd and R. Williams Parry, demonstrates
the importance of the slate-quarrying district in the revival. The
most accomplished of these three was Eifion Wyn, and he is the
only one who is still well known today. His best work is contained
in the volume *Telynegion Maes a Môr* (Lyrics of Field and Sea),
published in 1906. In simplicity and directness of style and in the
musicality of his verse he is Ceiriog's equal, and his descriptions of
nature have the authenticity of close observation. Like John
Morris-Jones, he was also an accomplished exponent of
cynghanedd, and the discipline of that craft probably underlay his
deft handling of lyric forms.

Silyn enjoyed brief prominence on the Welsh poetic scene at the
very beginning of the twentieth century, publishing a joint-volume
with W. J. Gruffydd in 1900, *Telynegion* (Lyrics), and winning the
Crown ahead of Gruffydd in a controversial competition at the
memorable National Eisteddfod of 1902 in Bangor. His victorious
poem on the love between Tristan and Isolde was published in his
second volume of 1904, after which he wrote very little poetry. An
essential aspect of the Tristan and Isolde story is the connection
between love and death, which was a favourite theme of late-
Romantic writers. It was also central to Elphin's most significant
work, 'Sonedau'r Nos' (Night Sonnets), published in 1909. The

rather morbid sense of fatalism in such a treatment of love is paralleled by an obsession with autumn and decay in the poetry of the period, and this should be weighed against the more obvious optimism and hedonism when considering the emotional range of the new literature.

Thomas Gwynn Jones (1871–1949) epitomizes the twentieth-century revival more fully than any other writer. His long career maps out the development of the movement from its early optimism to its decline into disillusionment, and his restless energy involved him in all forms of literary activity—the novel, the essay, drama, scholarship and criticism, translations from various languages, and above all poetry. He therefore figures in several chapters of this book, but it is the revival at the beginning of the century which is the essential context of all his work.

Like most other Welsh writers of the period, T. Gwynn Jones was from a humble background, the son of a Denbighshire hillfarmer, from whom he learnt *cynghanedd* as a boy. He is unusual, however, in having given up formal schooling at an early age and not having benefited directly from the new education system. His formidable productivity was perhaps actually stimulated by that, since he pursued a career in journalism which nurtured the fluency of his writing and eventually took him to the town of Caernarfon, at that time the principal centre of Welsh literary culture. He subsequently worked at the newly established National Library of Wales, where he had the opportunity to study medieval poetry in manuscript. He was appointed lecturer in the Welsh Department of the University College of Wales, Aberystwyth, in 1913, and was made Professor of Welsh Literature there in 1919.

Like John Morris-Jones, his earliest work was a satirical attack on Victorian ideals, a long poem with the ironic title 'Gwlad y Gân' (The Land of Song), written in the 1890s and published in a volume with the same title in 1902. In that same year T. Gwynn Jones achieved national fame when he won the Chair at the Bangor National Eisteddfod for his *awdl* 'Ymadawiad Arthur', the single most important poem of the Literary Revival, which was published in its final form in his collection *Caniadau* (Songs) of 1934.

'Ymadawiad Arthur' tells the well-known story of Arthur's departure to the Isle of Avallon, and is heavily indebted to Tennyson's *Morte d'Arthur*. The focus, however, is on the predicament of Bedwyr, Arthur's faithful companion, as the survivor faced with an uncertain future. Bidden by the mortally wounded king to cast his sword Caledfwlch (Excalibur) into the lake, Bedwyr cannot bring himself to do so at first, seeing the sword as essential to the future safety of the kingdom. It is by an act of faith that he does finally carry out Arthur's will, and the hand which rises out of the lake to grasp the sword is a reassurance that this symbol of national leadership will be preserved. Before setting off for Avallon Arthur prophesies a period of treachery and shame until he eventually returns to restore national fortunes. The prophecy was clearly written with an awareness of the national revival of which this very poem was a significant manifestation, and in that sense it is self-fulfilling. It is on this point that the Welsh poem differs most substantially from its English model, since Tennyson's Arthur prophesied no national revival, Victorian England being in no need of one.

After Arthur's departure Bedwyr hears a mysterious song describing the Isle of Avallon. These three verses are a potent expression of the optimistic spirit of the revival, and were also arguably the most beautiful piece of *cynghanedd* poetry produced since the Middle Ages. They are in the strict-metre verse form known as *hir-a-thoddaid*, and their elaborate ornamentation is of course entirely lost in the following translation.

> Draw dros y don mae bro dirion nad ery
> Cwyn yn ei thir, ac yno ni thery
> Na haint na henaint fyth mo'r rhai hynny
> A ddêl i'w phur, rydd awel, a phery
>   Pob calon yn hon yn heiny a llon,
> Ynys Afallon ei hun sy felly.

> Yn y fro ddedwydd mae hen freuddwydion
> A fu'n esmwytho ofn oesau meithion;
> Byw yno byth mae pob hen obeithion,
> Yno, mae cynnydd uchel amcanion;
>   Ni ddaw fyth i ddeifio hon golli ffydd,
> Na thro cywilydd, na thorri calon.

> Yno, mae tân pob awen a gano,
> Grym, hyder, awch pob gŵr a ymdrecho,
> Sylfaen yw byth i'r sawl fynn obeithio;
>   Ni heneiddiwn tra'n noddo—mae gwiw foes
> Ag anadl einioes y genedl yno!

[Over the wave there is a lovely country in whose land no complaint lingers, and there neither disease nor old age ever strike those who come to its pure, free breeze, and every heart in that country remains sprightly and cheerful, the Isle of Avallon itself is so.

In that blessed land are old dreams which once soothed the fears of long ages; old hopes live on forever there, and there too is the growth of high purposes; loss of faith will never come to blight this land, nor time of shame, nor heartbreak.

There is the fire of every inspiration to sing, the strength, confidence, and relish of every man who endeavours; it gives energy to anyone who will reform, it is ever a foundation for those who will hope; we will not grow old while it succours us—the true custom and life breath of the nation is there!]

Note in particular the gradual shift from the physical paradise of the first verse, which is the only traditional aspect of T. Gwynn Jones's treatment of Avallon, through the psychological consolation of the second, to the creative spirit of the final verse, the first person plural being introduced at the very end as Avallon becomes a kind of spiritual powerhouse for the nation. Looking beyond the mythological paraphenalia of the story, the central issue of the poem is the continuing inspirational power of the past, which relates directly to the rediscovery of literary tradition by John Morris-Jones and others. Although the melancholy nostalgia of the Celtic Twilight movement clearly influenced T. Gwynn Jones in this and other poems, his work is no mere self-indulgent escapism. He regarded the myths of the Celtic peoples as embodying eternal truths belonging to the race, and he employed them with specific contemporary relevance.

Most of T. Gwynn Jones's major long poems deal with some aspect of the theme of the lost paradise, and although several are discussed in the next two chapters, it is interesting to survey the gradual loss of faith and onset of disillusionment from the high point of 'Ymadawiad Arthur'. Although not to be reached by mortals in this life, Avallon is a very real source of inspiration for Bedwyr as he returns to the struggle. In 'Madog' (1917), the story of the legendary twelfth-century voyager, the existence of such a paradise has become doubtful, but the search itself is seen as worthwhile, representing a rejection of a decadent and self-destructive human society (clearly reflecting T. Gwynn Jones's own response to the First World War). 'Anatiomaros' (1925) depicts the earthly paradise of an early Celtic people living and dying in harmony with the rhythms of the natural world, but any possibility of permanence in such a vision was soon denied by his next long poem, 'Argoed' (1927), which describes how the timeless idyll of a Gaulish tribe deep in a secluded forest is threatened by the presence of the Roman invaders, with the result that the Gauls set fire to their forest rather than succumb to the inevitable corruption of their civilization. To recognize the contemporary significance of this story one has only to read English for Romans. T. Gwynn Jones had come a long way from the optimism of 'Ymadawiad Arthur' a quarter of a century earlier, and his descent into disillusionment was to continue in his last collection, Y Dwymyn (1944), discussed in chapter three. And yet the resort to the past in 'Argoed' is perhaps not entirely in vain, for the suggestion is made that the Gauls' spirit of defiance might serve as an inspiration to the Welsh to resist cultural corruption. Avallon thus continues to play its positive role as a preserver of timeless truths.

The medieval or mythological settings of these long poems gave T. Gwynn Jones plenty of opportunity for the opulent sensuality which characterized the literary reaction against puritanism. This is most prominent in 'Ymadawiad Arthur', where he revels in describing the beauty of the maidens from Avallon in a passage which deliberately echoes medieval love poetry. His aesthetic instinct is apparent in his depiction of the jewelled sword flashing in the air before disappearing like a fire snake into the lake's blackness. Like John Morris-Jones, he saw the creation of beauty as being one of the principle functions of poetry, and that applied to beauty of sound as much as of visual content. Nevertheless, the urge to express truths about the contemporary world kept him far removed from any concept of art for art's sake.

T. Gwynn Jones did also comment more directly on the contemporary world in a group of polemic poems in the realist mode. These display his radical socialist sympathies, as for instance in a scathing portait of a capitalist mineowner, probably provoked by the Senghennydd disaster of 1913. His antipathy towards imperialistic jingoism inspired the harshest realism of all his work, in another poem with an ironic title, 'Pro Patria' (published in Y Beirniad in 1913, and interestingly never included in any of his collections), which deals with an incident of rape by British soldiers during the Boer War. These poems are often marred by melodrama

or sentimentality, and have not stood the test of time as well as his
major mythic works. They are nevertheless important as some of
the first tentative steps towards modernism in Welsh, even before
the impact of the First World War was felt. The Romantic
tendency in T. Gwynn Jones's poetry was ultimately far stronger,
but his realist poems are an indication of the scope of his work, and
a reminder of his ceaseless urge to experiment with form and style.

W. J. Gruffydd (1881–1954) was another writer of prodigious
energy who produced important work in various fields, as scholar,
critic, essayist, poet, dramatist, and not least as editor of the
influential literary journal *Y Llenor*, which he founded in 1922. His
best poetry was published between the wars, and is discussed in
chapter three. Nevertheless, he played a significant role in the
revival at the beginning of the century, having been influenced as a
student by the Oxford Welsh Society, particularly O. M. Edwards,
whose biography he was later to write.

It is in the work of W. J. Gruffydd that the reaction against the
chapel culture of the nineteenth century is seen in its most extreme
form. His early poetry was an extravagant celebration of sensual
experience, and indeed it seems that he failed to win the National
Eisteddfod Crown in 1902 because his interpretation of the story of
Tristan and Isolde was judged to be immoral. His play *Beddau'r
Proffwydi* (The Graves of the Prophets) was part of the new
movement in Welsh drama in the years preceding the First World
War, representing an outspoken attack on chapel hypocrisy. On the
other hand, he made much of the radical tradition of
Nonconformity, which he saw himself as continuing in the uncompromising editorials which he wrote for *Y Llenor*. Like his hero
O. M. Edwards, the ideal of the *gwerin* meant a great deal to him,
although he put rather less emphasis on their high-minded culture,
influenced also by the novels of Thomas Hardy. Some of his most
successful poems celebrate the stoical endurance of the common
people of his native Caernarfonshire, such as 'Y Tyddynwyr' (The
Hillfarmers) of 1911, and 'Thomas Morgan yr Ironmonger' which
is also discussed in chapter three. His autobiography, *Hen Atgofion*
(Old Memories), published in 1936, acknowledges the formative
influence of the slate-quarrying society in which he grew up, and
perhaps indicates that with the passing of the years his rebellion
against the values of the preceding era was tempered by an
awareness of continuity and valued inheritance.

W. J. Gruffydd's poems about the common people represent a significant development in modern Welsh poetry, in that their subject-matter has nothing unusual or exotic about it, nothing intrinsically beautiful or elevated. They thus ran contrary to the kind of lyric poetry promoted by John Morris-Jones, and the kind produced by Gruffydd himself in his early years. The same shift away from the extremes of Romanticism was crucial in the work of another product of the revival, the poet R. Williams Parry.

R. Williams Parry (1884–1956) was brought up in the slate-quarrying village of Tal-y-sarn in Caernarfonshire, and together with his two cousins T. H. Parry-Williams and Thomas Parry formed a remarkable trio which testifies to the high level of culture in their family and region. Influenced by both the criticism of John Morris-Jones and the eisteddfodic poetry of T. Gwynn Jones, he achieved recognition by winning the Chair of the National Eisteddfod in 1910 with his *awdl* 'Yr Haf' (Summer), which was immensely popular for years afterwards, so much so that he became known as 'the Poet of Summer', a title which he himself came to detest. Because Williams Parry soon disowned his famous *awdl*, even producing a parody on it, and also because he went on to produce much more satisfactory poetry in his later years (discussed in chapter three), critics have tended to take a rather dismissive view of 'Yr Haf'. It was, however, a very significant work in its time, crystallizing the mood of the years preceding the First World War and dealing with concerns central to the revival.

R. Williams Parry matched the medieval masters in the melodious ease of his *cynghanedd*, and his mellifluous style is perfectly suited to the lyrical declaration of the joys of youth, love and nature in 'Yr Haf'. It is a self-consciously literary work, echoing above all the great fourteenth-century love poet Dafydd ap Gwilym, as is evident in the following extract:

> Dymor hud a miri haf
> Tyrd eto i'r oed ataf,
> A'th wyddfid, a'th hwyr gwridog,
> A'th awel chwyth haul a chog.
> A thyrd â'r eneth a'r adar yno,
> A sawr paradwys hwyr pêr i hudo
> Hyd ganllaw'r bompren heno bob mwynder;
> A bwrlwm aber i lamu heibio.

I deml yr oed mal yr hydd
Mae'n dod ym min diwedydd,
A phlyged hoff lygaid dydd
Wedi'i gweled, o g'wilydd.
Mae'n dod i'r oed mewn hud a direidi,
Y deilios, chwarddwch yn dlysach erddi;
   Chwi awelon llon y lli, dowch mwyach
I chwythu'n llonnach o eithin llwyni.

[Season of magic and summer's merriment, come to the love-tryst with
me once more, with your honeysuckle, and your rosy sunset, and your
breeze blowing sun and cuckoo. And bring the girl and the birds there,
and the sweet scent of evening paradise to conjure all pleasure along the
bridge's rail tonight; and the bubbling of a stream prancing by.
   Like the hart she comes at close of day to the love-tryst's temple, and
let the lovely daisies bend their heads with modesty on seeing her.
Wanton and bewitching she comes to the tryst, leaves, laugh more
prettily for her sake; you merry sea breezes, come now to blow more
merrily from gorse groves.]

'Yr Haf' no doubt owed its popularity to such passages of
sensuous beauty, but it would be wrong to see it as a mere
celebration of sensual pleasure after the manner of John Morris-
Jones's translations of Omar Khayyam. The joys of summer and
youth are seen primarily from the point of view of one who has lost
them, and the poem's main theme is the transitory nature of human
experience, a concern which runs through all Williams Parry's
work. Despite its title, this is a poem as much about autumn as
about summer, and it is the combination of joy and melancholy
which makes it so typical of its period. The standard Christian
consolation of the afterlife is rejected because it involves an
unacceptable denial of worldly pleasure. The poem's ultimate
position is an uneasy combination of humanist reliance on memory
as the preserver of transient pleasure and an agnostic hope that
what has been lost may somehow be restored in the future, just as
summer is restored by the cycle of the seasons. Although the poem
may be considered unsatisfactory from a philosophical point of
view, it is nevertheless valuable as an expression of the dilemma
caused by the loss of the old certainties of the Christian faith.
   The same humanist standpoint lies behind Williams Parry's elegy
for Hedd Wyn of 1917, the finest of a group of poems com-
memorating men killed in the First World War (see chapter two).

The exuberant Romanticism of the pre-war *awdl* has been replaced by a classical restraint typical of the *englyn* form, but there is the same concern with the termination of human experience. Death is perceived as an obliteration of the senses, and the absence of any Christian consolation of life after death would have been particularly striking in this traditional commemorative *genre*. 'Yr Haf' is also relevant to the well-known sonnet 'Y Llwynog' (The Fox) of 1922. Again, stylistic differences conceal thematic parallels. The Sunday morning walk on the mountain while the church bells call the faithful to worship is a defiance of established religion, whilst the encounter with the fox represents an alternative spiritual experience deriving from nature. This visionary intensity is essentially transitory, as seen in the famous image which closes the poem, 'Digwyddodd, darfu, megis seren wib' (He happened, and was gone, like a shooting star). 'Y Llwynog' is a more successful poem than 'Yr Haf', partly because it is grounded in real experience, but the view of life is fundamentally the same.

Williams Parry's younger cousin T. H. Parry-Williams (1887–1975) stood in a more ambiguous relation to the revival. A brilliant product of the new educational system, he began his poetic career by mastering the strict metres like his cousin, winning both Chair and Crown of the National Eisteddfod on two occasions, in 1912 and 1915. And yet even his earliest work displays a shift away from the Romanticism of the revival and Morris-Jones's ideal of a refined poetic language, most obviously in the harsh realism of his 1915 *pryddest* 'Y Ddinas', discussed in chapter three. His first collection of poems, *Cerddi*, was not published until 1931, and its use of undignified colloquialisms represents a rejection of Morris-Jones's precepts.

Nevertheless, although a stylistic innovator, T. H. Parry-Williams did adhere throughout his career to another of John Morris-Jones's principles, that literature should not aim to convey any moral or political message. Although he held strong personal views, he carefully avoided expressing them in his work. The same is true of another writer of the same generation, Kate Roberts, one of Morris-Jones's pupils at Bangor, who rigidly excluded her political and religious beliefs from her fiction. The socialist poet T. E. Nicholas was one writer who consistently ignored this principle of detachment even before the First World War, but it was not until the work of Saunders Lewis and Gwenallt between the wars that political commitment became the norm in Welsh literature. It is no doubt significant that that commitment coincided with a renewed religious faith which is in clear contrast to the agnostic uncertainty of the generation of writers who had reacted against the former certainties of Victorian Wales.

The spirit of the literary revival was by no means confined to Welsh-language writing. Welsh writing in English is treated in a companion volume in this series, but it is instructive to note here the parallels between the two literatures in the early twentieth century. The publication of Caradoc Evans's collection of short stories, *My People*, in 1915 is often taken to mark the beginning of modern Anglo-Welsh literature, and of course Evans is notorious for his hostility towards Welsh-language culture. What requires emphasis is that his Welsh-language contemporaries were motivated by the same impulse to reject the Nonconformist establishment which he regarded as essential to that culture. It is true that they did not attack it as directly or as viciously as he did. One reason for that is perhaps their reluctance to abandon entirely the ideal of the *gwerin,* which was so intimately bound up with Nonconformity. Another is that they were writing for their own people, unlike Caradoc Evans who was to a large extent pandering to the prejudices of his English readers. The modernism of Evans's idiosyncratic style is in contrast to the more conservative modes of Welsh writing, but nevertheless the differences are of degree and manner rather than of ideological substance.

Another work which has been identified as a key text in the early history of Welsh writing in English is J. O. Francis's play *Change* of 1912, which deals with industrial unrest in Glamorgan. *Change* was part of a new movement in Welsh drama of both languages, including W. J. Gruffydd's *Beddau'r Proffwydi* referred to above, which dealt with social issues of the day (see chapter eight). Like his Welsh-language counterparts (for instance Daniel Owen as early as 1885 in his novel *Rhys Lewis*), Francis was concerned by the challenge which the new socialism presented to the old chapel values. But whereas Welsh-language writers tended to reject industrialization itself, with the result that Welsh literature has paid scant attention to one of the most significant aspects of modern Wales, J. O. Francis and the Anglo-Welsh authors who followed him between the wars accepted their industrial world of south Wales and created vibrant literature out of the conflicts which it produced.

Writers in both languages were responding, some tentatively and others boldly, to a process of rapid change in Welsh society, in which religion and industry were key factors, broadly representing the old and the new. Whereas Anglo-Welsh writers had very little by way of literary models to fall back on, the distinctive response of the Welsh writers discussed in this chapter was the turning back to the literary traditions of the past, thus establishing the tenor for the greater part of the twentieth century. The following chapters will map out the creative tensions between adherence to those traditions and the search for new modes of expression. Whether modern Welsh writers have been pro- or anti-tradition, it has been virtually impossible for them to ignore the literature of the past, and that is perhaps the most pervasive legacy of the revival at the beginning of this century.

FURTHER READING

Geraint Bowen (ed.), *Y Traddodiad Rhyddiaith yn yr Ugeinfed Ganrif* (Llandysul, 1976).

Hazel Davies, *O. M. Edwards* (Cardiff, 1988).

W. Beynon Davies, *Thomas Gwynn Jones* (Cardiff, 1970).

W. J. Gruffydd, *Owen Morgan Edwards: Cofiant, Cyfrol 1, 1858–1883* (Aberystwyth, 1938).

Gwynn ap Gwilym (ed.), *T. Gwynn Jones* (Llandybïe, 1982).

Allan James, *John Morris-Jones* (Cardiff, 1987).

Bedwyr Lewis Jones, *R. Williams Parry* (Cardiff, 1972).

R. Gerallt Jones, *The Welsh Literary Revival of the Twentieth Century* (1967).

R. M. Jones, *Llenyddiaeth Gymraeg 1902–1936* (Llandybïe, 1987).

Thomas Gwynn Jones, *Emrys ap Iwan: Cofiant* (Caernarfon, 1912).

Saunders Lewis, *An Introduction to Contemporary Welsh Literature* (Wrexham, 1926).

Alan Llwyd (ed.), *R. Williams Parry* (Llandybïe, 1979).

Alun Llywelyn-Williams, *Y Nos, y Niwl, a'r Ynys* (Caerdydd, 1960).

Derec Llwyd Morgan, *Barddoniaeth Thomas Gwynn Jones* (Llandysul, 1972).

Kenneth O. Morgan, *Rebirth of a Nation: Wales 1880–1980* (Oxford, 1981).

T. J. Morgan, *W. J. Gruffydd* (Cardiff, 1970).

Idem, 'Dechrau'r Ganrif', *Ysgrifau Beirniadol*, 4 (Dinbych, 1969), 116–52.

Thomas Parry, 'The Welsh Renaissance of the Twentieth Century', in A. J. Roderick (ed.), *Wales Through the Ages*, ii, 209–14.

CHAPTER 2

THE LITERATURE OF THE FIRST WORLD WAR

GERWYN WILIAMS

' "Lest we forget" say the war memorials; but in Nineties Britain the
First World War is largely forgotten and its battlefields lie
unvisited, its dead ignored.' The words belong to Elspeth Barker,
reviewing in 1993 Sebastian Faulks's *Birdsong* in the *Independent on
Sunday*. Typically metropolitan in outlook, it is assumed that the
view through London windows is representative of Britain as a
whole. *Hon oedd fy ffenestr* (This was my window) stated Waldo
Williams in 'Preseli' and had the said critic been aware of his poem
it might have provided her with a timely piece of advice: that a
uniform perspective is suspect and that various viewpoints, all
equally valid, exist. Looking at the mid-1980s to mid-1990s through
a Welsh window, the terrain is certainly different to the one
outlined in the opening description.

First World War studies have enjoyed a minor revival in recent
years. In 1989 *Gwaedd y Bechgyn* (The Cry of the Lads), an
unprecedented anthology of over two hundred poems dealing with
the war, was published; the collection ranged from poems written
by experienced combatants to responses by present-day poets.
Dewi Eirug Davies considered the fate of religion in Wales during
the war in *Byddin y Brenin* (The King's Army, 1988) whilst military
aspects came under the scrutiny of David Pretty in *Rhyfelwr Môn*
(Anglesey's Warrior, 1989), his compelling study of the Kitchener-
like character, Owen Thomas, who played a major part in
persuading Welshmen to take up arms. Alan Llwyd's exhaustive
biography of Hedd Wyn, the soldier-poet killed in action in the
battle for Pilkem Ridge, appeared in 1991; the tale itself attracted
international attention in 1994 when *Hedd Wyn* was nominated for
an Oscar as the Best Foreign Film. My own studies of First World
War poetry and prose appeared in 1993 and 1996, and an edition
has been published of the English-language letters sent by Saunders
Lewis to his future wife, Margaret Gilcriest, amongst them a

substantial number from the war-torn continent where Lewis served as an officer with the South Wales Borderers.

This random list is not a case of self-congratulation but an attempt to establish that Welsh literature concerning the First World War needs to be evaluated on its own terms. Although names as resonant as Wilfred Owen, Isaac Rosenberg, Robert Graves and Edmund Blunden cannot easily be dismissed, it should be emphasized at the outset to the reader more familiar with English-language war literature that a study of Welsh literature written in response to the same war is not a matter of confirming a cultural inferiority complex or a study of a poor relation. As I myself learned, having approached the field still haunted by 'Futility' and 'Break of Day in the Trenches' and 'Lamentations', it is best to tackle it positively with as few preconceptions as possible. For the time being the comparative approach to literature may be set aside.

I referred above to a recent 'minor revival' in First World War studies; yet some would argue—native Welsh critics at that—that as far as its literature is concerned it has always been a non-starter. As early as 1916 the Anglican J. Vyrnwy Morgan set the agenda for future debate:

> As to the effect of the war on Welsh literature, both prose and poetic, there is nothing of importance to relate. It has not, as yet, produced any ballads or battle-songs for the Welsh soldiers; there are no Welsh war lyrics . . . It is calculated that there are in Wales about three thousand Welsh bards, or rather poetic experimentalists; like all modern poets they think more of freedom than of fighting for it.

W. J. Gruffydd, who had been a lieutenant on a mine-sweeper between 1915 and 1918, referred in *Y Llenor* in 1930 to the absence of Welsh prose dealing with the war as compared to the torrent of volumes which were currently flooding the English-language market: 'No one has written anything similar in Welsh, and it is unlikely anyone will do so either.'

Thirty years later the situation had not improved much according to the novelist Islwyn Ffowc Elis who mentioned, while discussing themes in Welsh novels, 'compared to the literature of other countries, War has bypassed the Welsh novel nearly as completely as if Wales were a neutral country'. Tecwyn Lloyd,

whose pioneering study in 1969 of Welsh literature regarding the
First World War set the basis for much future research, had
remarked in 1966:

> With a few exceptions such as the work of Cynan, we did not have
> First World War literature in Wales. Plenty of writing about seeing the
> world and less morose experiences of war but nothing in the tradition of
> Aneirin or Cynddelw Brydydd Mawr, because the central social ethos of
> the conformist religion which aimed the lads towards the gun's muzzles
> was niceness, refraining from saying ugly words and mentioning stench
> and drinking and prostitution . . .

As late as 1984, two up-and-coming authors, Wiliam Owen Roberts
and Iwan Llwyd, stated that 'one of the saddest features of our
literary history in this century is the fact that vast territories of the
Welsh experience have not been mapped at all . . . how many times
have people pondered why only a handful of literary works were
produced as a result of the massacre of the Great War?'

How does Welsh literature, accused of not responding to the
creative challenge of the First World War, plead: guilty or not
guilty?

Certainly there was a popular response to the war. One need only
refer to poetry columns in local, denominational and literary
periodicals such as *Y Rhedegydd, Y Brython, Y Goleuad* or *Y
Geninen* which were more or less taken over by war-related poems.
These Welsh 'poetic experimentalists' can hardly be accused of
shirking their duty in producing tons of pro-war propaganda and
anti-German doggerel. Pacifism may have been part of the
Nonconformist creed, yet the column inches running into miles
devoted to war themes suggest a fair degree of popular support for
militarism. For those lucky enough to have been graced with
anything as sophisticated as a historical perspective, countless
references to Llywelyn, Glyndŵr and Arthur proved that the heroic
ideal, which had been a cornerstone of the Welsh bardic tradition,
had some life in it yet. For a sociological approach to the study of
literature, this verse provides a valuable source; for the critic in
search of more aesthetic delights it offers neither creative substance
nor intellectual depth.

One can hardly deny the sheer quantity of mass-produced prose
either, most of it being in a journalistic vein, regarding the war. Yet

of that produced during the war itself or in its immediate aftermath, only a few examples—such as Saunders Lewis's recollections regarding his period in the army—deserve critical attention. The pacifist preacher Tegla Davies produced a few short stories at the time, and the war was also central to various serial stories for women. William Glynfab Williams published a trilogy of comic novellas between 1918 and 1920 written in the Rhondda Valley dialect and relating the exploits of two Laurel-and-Hardy-type characters in the war. Between 1927 and 1939, three novels for children in which the war figured largely were also composed. Once again, substance and depth are in short supply and Gruffydd's complaint of 1930 is easily substantiated.

However, all was not lost. Although the situation regarding prose would not improve until the 1930s, various poets of national calibre did respond to the war at the time, the most prominent amongst them being Ellis Humphrey Evans (Hedd Wyn), R. Williams Parry, J. Dyfnallt Owen (Dyfnallt), Albert Evans-Jones (Cynan), T. E. Nicholas, T. Gwynn Jones and T. H. Parry-Williams.

Hedd Wyn (1887–1917) has long been regarded as the epitome of Wales and the First World War. A young, mostly self-educated poet from rural Welsh-speaking Merionethshire, he reluctantly took up arms in 1917 and was mortally wounded less than three hours into his first attack. A shepherd at that, with evocative Christian and pastoral imagery in tow, his posthumously published collection of verse was inevitably titled *Cerddi'r Bugail* (The Shepherd's Poems, 1918). Such a dignified symbol of creativity and vulnerability was automatically at odds with all the philistinism and militarism of war. Pathos was added to tragedy when just over a month after his death, at the National Eisteddfod held in Birkenhead, Hedd Wyn was awarded the Chair—a long-held ambition of his—for his *awdl*, 'Yr Arwr' (The Hero).

Alan Llwyd regards Hedd Wyn as 'the last great Romantic poet to compose in Welsh'. Although Hedd Wyn's death provided the Romantic movement, which had been riding high in Wales since the 1890s, with a suitably young martyr, the far from romantic war severely undermined Romanticism and validated modernism. The title and theme of Hedd Wyn's *awdl* alone suddenly sounded anachronistic; as Arthur Marwick has neatly pointed out elsewhere, following the war 'the land fit for heroes became the waste land'.

Hedd Wyn had some difficulty grappling with the Romantic response. Reading his war poems, one can see that it had a detrimental effect upon more pragmatically intended elegiac verse addressed to some of his contemporaries, local lads killed in action. This extract from a poem written in memory of Corporal Robert Hughes, Fronwynion, Trawsfynydd is a case in point:

> Bu farw a'r byd yn ei drafferth
> Yng nghanol y rhyfel mawr:
> Bu farw mor ifanc a phrydferth
> Â chwmwl yn nwylo'r wawr.

[He died, the world in a bother / In the midst of the great war; / He died as young and as pretty/ As a cloud in the hands of the dawn.]

The delicate understatement of the first line is swiftly ruined by the overused Romantic simile in the final line.

Although probably anathema to him on a personal level, Hedd Wyn's experience as a soldier in an English training camp did wonders for the poet. Dislocated in Litherland from his natural habitat, he was no longer prompted automatically into commemorative mode but developed a more thoughtful outlook on matters:

> Our wages are dreadfully poor here, considering that we are *agents* for 'Justice' and similarly big things.

His perspective was tinged with a touch of irony as he himself attained more creative autonomy; he took a more cynical attitude towards an abstract such as 'Justice' which he had treated with unquestioned reverence in previous poems—'Gwladgarwch' (Patriotism), for instance—where war had been portrayed in a Romantic light. 'Rhyfel' (War) is the most lasting testimony to this new independent phase in Hedd Wyn's experience:

> Gwae fi fy myw mewn oes mor ddreng,
> A Duw ar drai ar orwel pell;
> O'i ôl mae dyn, yn deyrn a gwreng,
> Yn codi ei awdurdod hell.
>
> Pan deimlodd fyned ymaith Dduw
> Cyfododd gledd i ladd ei frawd;

Mae sŵn yr ymladd ar ein clyw,
    A'i gysgod ar fythynnod tlawd.

Mae'r hen delynau genid gynt
    Ynghrog ar gangau'r helyg draw,
A gwaedd y bechgyn lond y gwynt,
    A'u gwaed yn gymysg efo'r glaw.

[Woe that I live in this dire age, / When God on far horizon flees, /
Yonder men high and lowly wage / Their little vile authorities. // On
seeing God had turned away, / A sword they raised to slay their own; /
We hear the tumult of the fray, / On humble homes its shadows frown; //
And there, the weeping willow trees / Bear the old harps that sang
amain, / The lads' wild anguish fills the breeze, / Their blood is mingled
with the rain.*]

Balanced and compact, the poem points to the dilemma facing the
Welsh Nonconformist civilization which had nurtured Hedd Wyn.
Written with a literal waste land in mind, it is an early example in
modern Welsh literature by one who had seen things first-hand of the
spiritual void increasingly characteristic of twentieth-century man.

R. Williams Parry (1884–1956) was another poet who was forced
to readdress the Romantic response. Since his celebrated *awdl* 'Yr
Haf' (The Summer)—'a tapestry luxuriously woven in rich Pre-
Raphaelite colours' as Bedwyr Lewis Jones succinctly described it—
had won the National Eisteddfod Chair in 1910, his name had
become synonymous with that season and the popular title, *Bardd yr
Haf* (The Summer Poet), was to plague him relentlessly for the rest of
his days. A self-admitted failure as a soldier, Williams Parry was
never drafted abroad due to his poor eyesight. The poems he
composed during his period in the army form the final section of *Yr
Haf a Cherddi Eraill* (The Summer and Other Poems, 1924) and
provide a sombre counterpoint to the melodious title poem; less than
a decade separates them, yet it is as if they belong to different worlds.

Williams Parry's response to the war was contained in two
forms: elegiac *englynion* and Shakespearean sonnets. The two
forms apparently offered him contrasting artistic outlets: the *englyn*
suggested a functional and reserved vehicle to express public
sympathy following the death of loved ones in battle; the sonnet

---

*Translated by Tecwyn Lloyd in 'Welsh literature of the First World War',
    Planet, 11 (May 1972), 21.

provided a means for more private contemplation on the impact of war. Yet Williams Parry was to remain restrained in his response in both *englynion* and sonnets—oddly enough, more so in the sonnets. 'Plygain' (Dawn) serves well as an example. 'This sonnet is a detailed and correct chronicle of a specific dawn in Essex', stated the poet in a note in his 1924 collection; he was stationed from June 1918 until the end of the war at Billericay. The lulled and passive world described in the poem is suddenly destroyed by the cock crowing seven times followed by *Taranau cyntaf Fflandrys tros y môr* (The first thunder of Flanders across the sea) which signalled the recommencement of conflict. Again in a footnote, Williams Parry displays a sense of irony which is not reflected in the sonnets themselves: 'He crowed eight times, unaware that the figure seven is more scriptural and poetical.' He did not venture to embody such an observation, symptomatic of the imperfect state of civilization, within his sonnet. His subject-matter may have become more contemporary and concrete, yet he still retained a conservative assumption as to what was truly 'poetical'.

Williams Parry performed an amazing juggling-act in his *englynion coffa*. One of the most well-known, 'Ar Gofadail' (On a Monument), can be seen inscribed on war memorials in Pen-y-groes and Bethesda:

> O Gofadail gofidiau tad a mam!
> Tydi mwy drwy'r oesau
> Ddysgi ffordd i ddwys goffáu
> Y rhwyg o golli'r hogiau.

[Oh! memorial to the anguish of fathers and mothers! / You alone throughout the ages / will teach us how to solemnly remember / The wrench of losing the lads.]

This is a lesson in diplomacy and dignity for it pays due regard to the fallen soldiers and respect to their parents. And yet it includes the minimum of poetic or personal compromise. The bleak implications for a deprived future are hinted at and, Williams Parry being an agnostic, he does not dare explain or justify the bereavement. Certainly no attempt is made to place the loss within a Christian context, an ironic feature of these *englynion*, as R. Gerallt Jones has commented, when one considers the strong Nonconformist character of the society which Williams Parry served in Gwynedd.

In his war poems it seems as if Williams Parry, having broken free from the constraints and conventions of the Romantic mode, has moved swiftly from the fanciful to the dismal. He was uncertain of his creative freedom, unwilling to test its limitations. Referring to the novel by T. Hughes Jones, *Amser i Ryfel* (A Time for War, 1944) in 1949, Kate Roberts remarked: 'As I see it, a Welshman can only create vital literature out of a war for his own independence. That's why I believe that T. Hughes Jones's *Amser i Ryfel* is not as good as his other stories.' Although highly debatable, her suggestion might have some relevance in Williams Parry's case. Not until 1936 when the proposed bombing range in the Llŷn Peninsula was set alight by three prominent Nationalists, an event which symbolized a pacifist 'war' for Wales, was Williams Parry prompted to revamp the sonnet form which he had previously treated with reverence and inject it with vitriolic satire. In the mean time he had moved patiently from a Romantic to a Georgian response before finally achieving his own brand of modernism in the 1930s.

To appreciate truly both Hedd Wyn and Williams Parry's achievements as war poets one needs to recognize the peculiar role of the Welsh poet within his community and culture. One needs to assess his predicament, aware of the social expectations put upon him. Another category of creative artist more obviously constrained was the preacher-poet, two of whom—Dyfnallt and Cynan—experienced the war as chaplains.

The preacher in Dyfnallt (1873–1956) certainly had the upper hand over the poet as most of the verse and diary extracts included in *Myfyrion a Chaneuon Maes y Tân* (Meditations and Songs of the Battlefield, 1917) prove. This brief volume, based upon Dyfnallt's experiences during his three-month stint in 1916 as chaplain in northern France, is historically significant for it is the first substantial creative record in Welsh to stem directly from the war. Although Dyfnallt alludes to Morgan Llwyd and although his prose style bears the imprint of his influence, Dyfnallt's work certainly does not consist of a twentieth-century reworking of that of the seventeenth-century Puritan and chaplain in Cromwell's New Model Army.

Dyfnallt's poems suggest the confusion and turmoil which characterized much of Welsh Nonconformity during the war years: its loss of independence and the compromising of its identity in its readiness to associate itself with the state and act as a recruitment agency. It seems Dyfnallt was convinced that the war was a just

affair, and ventured abroad with his belief in a Christian crusade
to rid the world of the German Anti-Christ tucked neatly in his
kit-bag. Although his faith was tested from time to time amidst
the atrocities of war, he took a so-called common-sense
approach to matters and saw no point in straying from the
Christian path.

   'Awr Arswyd' (The Hour of Terror) displays Dyfnallt's flair as
well as his limitations as a war poet. The poem is based on a true
experience and describes a soldier running into the YMCA tent, a
deserter seeking refuge from the battlefield:

>   Nid af yn ôl;
>   'Rwy'n dweud nid af yn ôl.
>   Pa waeth gen i am wg a rheg gŵr mawr,
>   Neu fwled bore yfory gyda'r wawr:
>   Nid wyf yn llwfr nac yn rhyfygus ffôl.

[I won't go back: / I tell you, I won't go back. / What do I care about the
scowl and curse of a mighty man, / Or a bullet tomorrow morning at
dawn: / I'm neither cowardly nor recklessly foolish.]

It includes the most graphic description available in Welsh war
poetry of a gas attack:

>   O dan y nwy:
>   O Dduw, o dan y nwy
>   Y ces y gip ar wyneb glasddu 'mrawd,
>   A'r gwaed yn rhuddo'i faluredig gnawd:
>   Nid fi yw'r gŵr 'aiff dros y clawdd byth mwy.

[Beneath the gas: / O God, beneath the gas / I saw a glimpse of my
brother's blue-black face, / The blood reddening his mutilated flesh: /
I'm not the man who'll go over the top ever again.]

Yet the poem comes to a safe conclusion: the tension is completely
defused for the desperate soldier is persuaded to pray:

>   A ffodd y nos:
>   Do, ciliodd gwg y nos
>   Oddi ar ei ael, a safodd yn ei hyd:
>   Do, safodd fel pe bai yn ben y byd;
>   Cyfarchodd, gwenodd, a throes tua'r ffos.

[And the night retreated: / Yes, the scowl of night retreated / From his brow, and he stood up: / Yes, he stood as if he were on top of the world; / A greeting, a smile, and he set off towards the trench.]

How convenient for the chaplain. One is tempted to ask whether he would have allowed the soldier to voice his subversive stand had he not miraculously seen the light before the end of the poem. Sadly, it reveals more about Dyfnallt's prejudiced view of the war than about the agitated state of mind of the soldier in question.

Cynan (1895–1970) is a more interesting poet altogether, and certainly the most important of all those who came to prominence by means of the war. A collection of his war poems, *Telyn y Nos* (The Harp of the Night, 1921), was successful in the 1920 National Eisteddfod but the poem that brought him immediate national recognition was 'Mab y Bwthyn' (Son of the Cottage), the ballad which secured him the Crown in Caernarfon in 1921. Hedd Wyn's 'Rhyfel', Williams Parry's 'Englynion Coffa Hedd Wyn' (Hedd Wyn's Memorial *Englynion*) and Cynan's 'Mab y Bwthyn' have long established themselves in the Welsh psyche as the three single most famous poems of the war, their popular appeal being similar to that of Rupert Brooke's 'The Soldier' and John McCrae's 'In Flanders Fields' to an English audience.

Cynan certainly had the common touch and a tendency to play to the gallery, characteristics which he employed later in life with dazzling success in his role as the archetypal Archdruid in the National Eisteddfod. However, academic critics have not, on the whole, been kind to Cynan, Bobi Jones, for instance, regarding him as 'happily vulgar . . . he belongs to the history of the *gorsedd* [of the bards] rather than the history of literature'. Yet there is no denying the enduring attraction of his poetry to the general reader. 'Anfon y Nico' (Sending the Goldfinch), for example, has become a victim of its own popularity. The more highly respected T. H. Parry-Williams, in critical circles at least, is usually acknowledged as having overhauled Welsh poetic diction in the unassuming *rhigymau* he composed during the 1920s; yet surely Cynan too deserves some credit for having released the diction from the strict and often suspect Classicism imposed by John Morris-Jones upon the poets. It might be difficult to regard Cynan as a radical, yet his use of North Walian colloquialisms in 'Anfon y Nico' was so unorthodox that the editor of *The Welsh Outlook* initially assigned it to his litter bin. The lyric, written from Macedonia by a homesick Cynan, showed that he could tug as dextrously on the heartstrings as any Victorian sentimentalist. He managed to manipulate and massage what is regarded as the most quintessentially Welsh of emotions, *hiraeth*, to startling effect: *Cân nes teimla hitha'r hirath / Sydd yn llosgi nghalon i* (Sing until she feels the longing / That is burning in my breast.*) Time and again in Cynan's poems, the narrator is overcome by longing. Specific persons and places are named—Wil and Megan, Llyn Traffwll, Talcymerau—which ensures that the poems retain credibility and focus; the same Housmanesque feature characterizes Williams Parry's war *englynion*. Cynan exploited *hiraeth* both ways: listening to a tedious financial report in a chapel meeting in the 1920s, he reminisces about a romantic interlude between him and Chloe, a shepherd girl, during the war in Salonica: *Gwybu fy nghalon hiraeth dir* (My heart recognized certain longing). A case of wanting his *hiraeth* and eating it perhaps?

All is not slush in Cynan's war poetry: his combination of just enough realism to convince his readers together with a sprinkling of emotion to engage their empathy ensured that they were not alienated by the experiences he described. There is no doubt as to his accessibility as a poet, but did he have to compromise so much?

'Mab y Bwthyn' contains emotion recollected without tranquillity. It opens with a sketch of Jazz Age London and before long the narrator—not to one's surprise—is pining for the lost Eden of his youth in Arcadian Llŷn; he recalls his childhood days, his Christian upbringing, and his sweetheart, Gwen Tŷ Nant. All this was destroyed by the war: the narrator joined the army and became a soldier and Gwen became a munitions worker in London. On hearing that Gwen has fallen foul of the evil city her former boyfriend becomes enraged and is so successful as a soldier that he is promoted to captain's rank. Having returned to Blighty, he sets himself up as a London businessman, exploiting the cheap labour of factory girls. However, he is spiritually unfulfilled and becomes determined to return to his little Welsh home. Realizing that he cannot do so without Gwen, the ballad ends in salvation with former partners reunited and paradise regained.

*Translated by Dafydd Owen in *Cynan* (Cardiff, 1979), 7–8.

Many features deserve acclaim: the fact that Cynan has blended a contemporary fable about modern war into a love story with immense human interest; the off-beat and satirical descriptions of army commanders, worthy of Sassoon. And as Hywel Teifi Edwards has pointed out, 'There is in it the ingredients of a spectacular rock opera and to say so is to acknowledge the strength of its lasting appeal'. But the compromised ending provided too easy an answer to the problem of that age and seemed to extinguish the social tensions highlighted in the rest of the poem. A less jubilant finale would have been more aesthetically satisfying, although needless to say the original ending provided much psychological comfort. Neither Cynan nor Dyfnallt dared conclude on a socially discordant note.

Of the poets so far discussed, only Hedd Wyn could technically be categorized as a soldier-poet. This again sets the Welsh literary experience of the war apart from the English experience. This should not necessarily be classified as a weakness: a discussion of the Welsh literature regarding the First World War is an egalitarian exercise which involves consideration of poetry written by conscientious objectors and pacifists. Three significant poets in this respect are T. E. Nicholas, T. Gwynn Jones, and T. H. Parry-Williams.

T. E. Nicholas (1878–1971) was, until 1918 at least, an Independent minister who defied accepted social mores or bourgeois respectability. His poetry, aimed unashamedly at the common man and drawing on the democratism inherent in the poetry of Walt Whitman coupled with a socialist reading of the scriptures, was an extension of his Marxist manifesto. During the war he was regarded as a dangerous political agitator and his sermons were attended by police officers. A blatant populist, he parodied familiar hymns as well as the campaigning *agitprop* verse of Victorians such as R. J. Derfel, Ieuan Gwynedd and Iorwerth Glan Aled to achieve his goal.

Cerddi Rhyddid (Freedom Poems, 1914) and *Dros Eich Gwlad* (For Your Country, 1920) contain various poems opposing the war. Because of all his ranting and raving and his constant references to 'brotherhood' and 'republicanism', his poems tend to strike a rhetorically shrill chord; not even his most ambitious project, the long poem 'Gweriniaeth a Rhyfel' (Republicanism and War), succeeded in this sense. Yet his unswervingly committed work certainly influenced two Christian poets of paramount importance in the history of twentieth-century Welsh poetry, namely Waldo Williams and D. Gwenallt Jones. Also, T. E. Nicholas's political unorthodoxy—despite the fact that it amounted to a severely uncritical Marxist orthodoxy in his poems—brings with it a breath of exotic air into the sometimes politically-stuffy atmosphere of twentieth-century Welsh literature.

Mae'r amser i ganu'n mynd heibio (It's time to give up writing poems) said an impatient T. E. Nicholas at the beginning of 1914, a rather self-contradictory statement for such a prolific poet. It does, however, reveal how Nicholas seems to have placed the utilitarian and practical aims of his poetry above all else during the war. In the case of T. Gwynn Jones (1871–1949), the opposite seems to have happened for he more or less abandoned his popular voice altogether. The journalist turned academic, whose 'Ymadawiad Arthur' (The Departure of Arthur, 1902) was considered a cornerstone of the Romantic movement at the turn of the century and a fanfare for the nationalist movement, distanced himself increasingly from public sentiment during the war and took a determinedly individualistic stance. Although initially critical of the Nietzschean materialistic tendencies that had typified German society and culture during the decades leading up to the war, he increasingly directed his criticism at Britain's slide towards German militarism as the war progressed.

His creative response to the war was dual. On the one hand he composed a number of concise pieces—short sharp shocks—in which he satirized unambivalently the current direction of Welsh political and social life. His attack was nearly as devastating as that of Caradoc Evans in *My People* (1915) and *Capel Sion* (1916) around the same time on the idealized Liberal Wales of the Lloyd George era, though with less malice and personal prejudice. At least one of his poems led to a head-on collision between him and the Victorian icon, O. M. Edwards; similarly, his friend, the journalist E. Morgan Humphreys, came into conflict with both John Morris-Jones and Revd John Williams, Brynsiencyn—the most prominent Methodist minister of his day and a leading figure on recruitment platforms—because of his criticism of Lloyd George. Whilst the Welsh Wizard held court at Downing Street, one sees evidence in all this friction of a Welsh consensus cracking and collapsing during the war.

T. Gwynn Jones also applied his talents during the war to poems on a wider and more ambitious scale, the most notable example being 'Madog'. The long poem continued T. Gwynn Jones's lifelong experimentation with *cynghanedd* and the twenty-four metres of the Welsh bardic tradition: every couplet in 'Madog' includes thirty syllables and consists of a reworking of the four-lined *englyn unodl union*. The poem is set in the twelfth century and depicts the feud between two brothers, Hywel and Dafydd ab Owain Gwynedd; it was obviously intended as an allegory of the First World War. The territorial rivalry between them, which eventually leads to Hywel's death, sickens their other brother, Madog, who cross-examines Mabon, a monk and a former tutor of his, with philosophical rigour:

'Dywed, O, dad' medd Madog, 'O, dad, a oes Duw yn y nefoedd?
    Onid aeth byd i'r annuw, O, dad, oni threngodd Duw?'

'Duw,' medd y llall, 'ni adawodd ei nef, na'i ofal amdanom,
    Duw a luniodd ein daear, Duw o'i thrueni a'i dwg;
Byrr yw ein dyddiau, fel barrug y ciliant rhag heulwen bore,
    Mil o flynyddoedd fel undydd sydd yn ei hanes Ef;
Diau, pe gwelem y diwedd, dychryn y dechrau a giliai,
    Dafn, er dyfned ei ofnau, yw dyn yn ei funud awr.'

['Tell me, O, father,' said Madog, 'O, father, is God in the heavens? / Has not the world gone to the godless, O, father, has not God died?' // 'God,' said the other, 'has not abandoned His heaven, nor His care for us, / God has fashioned our earth, God will bring it from misery; / Short are our days, like hoar-frost they flee from the sunlight of morning, / In His story like a single day are a thousand years; / If we saw the end, it is certain, the beginning's terror would vanish, / A drop, though so deep his fears, is man in his minute of time.'*]

The panoramic setting in 'Madog' places it a world apart from the limited journalistic scope of T. E. Nicholas's verse. Although Nicholas too as a republicanist would certainly have sympathized with sentiments such as: *Brodyr, er pob bâr ydym—tost na baem hefyd gytûn!* (Brothers, despite all wrath, are we—bitter if we lack

---

*Translated by Joseph Clancy in *Twentieth Century Welsh Poems* (Llandysul, 1982), 4–5.

concord!) his was a revolutionary call to arms against the ruling class, not a plea for humanity and pacifism.

'Madog' has rightly been regarded as a major achievement in T. Gwynn Jones's canon and is included in the same list as 'Ymadawiad Arthur', 'Broseliawnd', 'Anatiomaros', 'Argoed' and 'Cynddilig'. Yet it is difficult to avoid mixed feelings about it as a poem born of the First World War. The author himself admitted that the poem would most probably not be understood at the time. How should one regard its archaic syntax, baroque diction, philosophical depth, and unrelenting medievalism? As a constructive protest against the debasement and sloganization of language, the superficial level of public debate, the blinkered appeal of short-term temporal aims? Or does it suggest academic escapism, a case of playing the lyre whilst civilization burned? Certainly Madog's inability to find a sacred refuge at the end of the poem, his boat wrecked in a storm, provides the poem with a pessimistic finale and a dramatic antithesis to T. Gwynn Jones's previously positive Romanticism. Be that as it may, I find it difficult to classify 'Madog' alternatively as an early modernist poem. I am forced to make the paradoxical observation: had T. Gwynn Jones experienced the war as a combatant, might it not have released him creatively further still and led to a modernist classic, combining various registers and literary influences, in a manner reminiscent of David Jones in *In Parenthesis* (1937)?

The war poetry of T. H. Parry-Williams (1887–1975) offers a somewhat stronger case for modernism. A colleague of T. Gwynn Jones in the Welsh Department at Aberystwyth, their conscientious objection to the war was a source of much resentment in the small academic community. Parry-Williams was also a national winner, having won both the Chair and the Crown on two occasions, firstly in 1912 and again in 1915. His gloomy portrayal of Parisian life in 'Y Ddinas' (The City)—he had returned to Wales in 1914 following a period at the Sorbonne—was far more uncompromising than Cynan's portrayal of London life in 1921, so much so that one of the three adjudicators in the Crown competition in 1915 refused to commend it. Alienated and ostracized to some extent during the war, the tension between Romanticism and modernism was more apparent in Parry-Williams's work than in that of any of his contemporaries, as was his cerebral approach to such tension.

Having mastered the traditional techniques in flamboyant style in the national arena, his poems underwent a gradual metamorphosis during the war years. By 1919, his previously confident social outlook had given way to a more fractured and solitary, questioning and marginalized view of things. His Christian belief had also suffered a severe blow—or at least his view of institutionalized religion—and a new spiritual ambivalence came to characterize his work.

Although he had long established his authority as a Welsh-language poet, his credentials being impeccable, throughout the war he continued to compose alternately in Welsh and English, a fact that suggests a continuing quest on his part for a settled poetic identity. Versions of some poems appeared in both languages, 'To a Dog' (1917) and 'I Gi' (1919) being a useful case in point. The victimized Parry-Williams is perturbed when an Aberystwyth dog growls at him:

> Why should'st thou scorn me, when the scorn of men
> About me makes me proud of life? A man's
> Hate I can bear and glory in, but when
> A dog scorns me, a brother dog, I feel
> The pride I take in being scoffed of men
> Slackening its heartening throb. O why should'st thou
> —For thou art not man—show me thy teeth?

Although Dyfnallt Morgan in his study of Parry-Williams's early literary career favours the English rather than the Welsh version of this poem, I suspect that the use of dated and bookish syntax and the awkward amalgam of dictions indicate that Parry-Williams was not fully at ease. The poem closes with a plea for solidarity, the poet identifying with the lowly canine:

> Give me thy paw, old dog: for I have marked
> The clean life of thy brothers, and have felt
> Ashamed to be a man; and I have prayed
> Unto some Power Unknown, in this mad world,
> To plant in me the soul-seed of a dog.
>
> Come, street-dog, peace! and if thou wilt, I'll tell
> Thy brothers in the mountains of a friend
> In Aberystwyth streets, who dared to love,
> Like them, a lonely mortal, scorned of men.

It is here that I sense a moderate strain of Welsh modernism developing, typically accessible and wary not to alienate. As in 'I Gi' where a more relaxed colloquial tone is adopted, the situation is basically ironic, the approach introspective. The rather Victorian expanse and heavy subject-matter of the eisteddfodic *awdlau* and *pryddestau* are replaced by an almost cartoon-like image in a modest frame. The mature outcome of this development, on which Parry-Williams's war experiences had an influence perhaps not hitherto fully acknowledged, was the 1931 collection, playfully unassuming in title, *Cerddi* (Poems).

The 1930s also saw the first serious attempts to tackle the war in novel form, a decade vividly dramatized in Emyr Humphreys's *Salt of the Earth* (1985). Pacifism being in vogue and nationalism at last organized with the formation of the Welsh Nationalist Party in the previous decade, the conscientious objector who had previously been vilified and accused of betrayal during the war attained respectability. He was regarded as having acted as the guardian and true spirit of Nonconformity, the defender of the private conscience who had gallantly withstood the totalitarian-like demands of an increasingly centralized state. His independence and freedom of mind presented an ideal for an independent Wales and his defiant stand would be mirrored by the three Nationalists—all of whom had differing experiences of the First World War—who opposed the militarization of Llŷn in 1936. One could present a case for Gwilym Peris's *Y Llwybr Unig* (The Lonely Path, 1933) and, more so, Gwenallt's sardonically and politically titled *Plasau'r Brenin* (The King's Mansions, 1934), to be read as early documents in the literary catalogue of nationalist martyrdom.

Plasau'r Brenin relates the experiences of Myrddin Tomos, a character obviously based on Gwenallt himself who was imprisoned as a conscientious objector in Wormwood Scrubs and Dartmoor between 1917 and 1919. Gwenallt's conscientious objection whilst still in his teens reveals a lot about his commitment and strength of character. Whether or not a nascent sense of nationalism figured in his objection to the First World War is unclear, although it is certainly an issue in the novel. One cannot dismiss the influence of the militant T. E. Nicholas on the young Gwenallt. A conventional note is included at the outset of *Plasau'r Brenin*—'This is a small novel, and the characters are fictional'—yet the truth of the matter is that Gwenallt, like various other war authors, had difficulty distinguishing between fact and fiction. Saunders Lewis regarded the novel as a 'poet's autobiography' and it must be said that its author discovered his forte as a poet rather than a creative prose-writer, as the posthumously published *Ffwrneisiau* (Furnaces, 1982), a chronicle of his youth in the Pontardawe and Alltwen region, further confirms.

As a novelist *per se*, Kate Roberts (1891–1985) dealt far more successfully with the biographical material at her disposal in the final sections of *Traed Mewn Cyffion* (Feet in Chains, 1936). The novel portrays the trials and tribulations of a closely-knit Welsh slate-mining community in the Nantlle Valley from around 1880–1916. Although stoically attempting to keep their heads above the water, the characters are gradually swamped by deprivation, unemployment and depopulation. The war comes as the final straw, with an arrogant ease which they cannot hope to combat:

> Those people who were at home began to ask themselves and others what was the meaning of it all. They had seen bad times very often. They had endured wrongs and injustices in the quarries; the tyranny of masters and owners, the oppression of favouritism and corruption. They had seen their friends and sons killed alongside them at work, but they had never experienced their children being taken away from them to be killed in war . . . As for his own people, they had endured hardships all their lives, and as if that had not been enough, suddenly the war came like an invisible hand to crush them into the ground.*

With the death in action of his younger brother Twm, Owen Gruffydd succeeds the matriarch Jane Gruffydd as focus of the novel. It is left to this representative of a new generation—Kate Roberts's own recently educated generation—to review the past and discover a fresh vision for the future:

> And his eyes were opened to the possibility of doing something instead of simply enduring like a dumb animal. It was about time that somebody challenged this injustice and did something about it. Come to think of it, that was what was wrong with his people. They were courageous in their capacity to endure pain, but would do nothing to get rid of what caused that pain.*

The allegiance to stoicism is finally challenged.

*Translated by Idwal Walters and John Idris Jones, *Feet in Chains* (London, 1980), 143–5, 159.

Kate Roberts was never an overtly political writer in her strictly creative writings. Yet she often mentioned her experience of the war as a crucial stimulus to her career as a writer. For instance, when asked by Saunders Lewis in the late 1940s what had stirred her to write, she answered:

> ... the death of my youngest brother [David] in the 1914–18 war, failing to understand things and being forced to write lest I smother. (Politically, it drove me to the Welsh Nationalist Party.)*

Traed Mewn Cyffion has an essentially political message at its heart. It is a critique of late Victorian and Liberal Wales when the *gwerin*—with the advancement of education and enfranchisement—was supposed to be breaking free from its chains at last. As T. Gwynn Jones and Caradoc Evans had done during the war itself, the novel gives the lie to Lloyd George's masterplan. The all-too-familiar fate of Twm could hardly be regarded as a glowing example of the democratic ideal. As in the above quotation, *Traed Mewn Cyffion* succeeds as a creative classic with its political subtext placed in brackets. With deftness and subtlety and logic throughout, it provided a political rationale and justification for the Welsh Nationalist Party's existence.

Tegwch y Bore (Fair Weather in the Morning, 1967), originally serialized in *Y Faner* between 1957 and 1958, further reveals the influence of the First World War upon Kate Roberts. It deals with a more concentrated time span, 1913–1917, and, as Derec Llwyd Morgan has pointed out, is 'so, so close to her own [story], it is almost autobiography in parts'. This time, the main character is in a more comfortable female guise and the schoolteacher Ann Owen remains the focus of the novel throughout, an obvious vehicle for Kate Roberts's observations on the war. *Tegwch y Bore* is more overtly political than *Traed Mewn Cyffion* where the reader is left to draw his own conclusions as to its political implications. It is as though Kate Roberts, wary of being accused of propaganda, felt more confident to deal with political debate within a fictional work by the late 1950s. Ann visits her brother, Rolant, who is convalescing in a London hospital before returning to France.

---

*Translated by Joseph Clancy in *The World of Kate Roberts* (Philadelphia, 1991), xi.

Whilst discussing with the doctor her brother's unhappiness, the rift between Wales and England becomes obvious:

> 'Tut-tut, a good soldier doesn't think of danger, and all of them the same as him should think of their country and do their best for her. The quicker the war will come to an end.'
> 'Yes, but my brother isn't fighting for his country.'
> The doctor looked at her for the first time: he had previously been looking at his notes. He stopped a moment before speaking.
> 'For whom is he fighting?'
> 'Not for his country, Wales is his country.'
> The doctor looked at her now as if he could see a relic in a museum sitting on the chair. His eyes ran over her face as if he was searching it.
> 'I don't understand you.'
> 'No, an Englishman can't understand.'

It is surely the mature Kate Roberts talking here, inspired by the Welsh Nationalist Party's neutral stance during the Second World War. Although written from a completely different political standpoint, *Tegwch y Bore* brings to mind Vera Brittain's courageous *Testament of Youth* (1933), and in fact Kate Roberts expressed her admiration of Brittain's work in correspondence with the author.

So far Welsh novels had focused attention on the war from the home front, Gwilym Peris and Gwenallt dealing with the war from the perspective of the conscientious objector, Kate Roberts chronicling its effect upon domestic life and never venturing with her soldiers across the Channel and onto the battlefield. This depiction of the war, concentrating on 'the shadow of the war' 'cast upon our homes' to paraphrase Hedd Wyn, seemed to emphasize its lasting effect upon Welsh society whilst also suggesting Wales's distance from the event. Wales is seen as a victim with no direct part in any massacre. This underlines what Ned Thomas has described as 'the dissociation of a minority nation from the political aims of the State'. Yet authors could hardly promote an image of separateness or neutrality, however strong their nationalist aspirations: 280,000 Welshmen had served in the armed forces during the war, 40,000 of whom did not return alive. With the Second World War in full swing, it was still nigh on impossible to read a substantial Welsh novel recounting the experiences of a Welshman in the trenches. That suggests the psychological and cultural difficulties imposed by the actual topic. At last in 1944 the first Welsh novel devoted entirely to a discussion of the war and written by a veteran was eventually published.

Amser i Ryfel (A Time for War) by T. Hughes Jones (1895–1966) must have appeared oddly anachronistic in 1944. A result of a pact between two college friends in Aberystwyth following the war—a period again richly re-enacted by Emyr Humphreys in *The Best of Friends* (1978)—Gwenallt had honoured his part of the bargain and had described his wartime experiences in *Plasau'r Brenin* ten years previously. T. Hughes Jones obviously felt some unease regarding the venture and its final publication seemed like a reluctant admission of Wales's part in the 1914–1918 war at a time when the 1939–1945 war proved without doubt that talk of the war to end all wars had been a mere recruiting slogan.

Having waited so long, *Amser i Ryfel* must surely be regarded as an anticlimax. Certainly, military life is described with a historian's accuracy and the tension between the sexes is conveyed with sociological insight. Yet in the atomic 1940s, was this not yesterday's news? The most interesting aspect of the novel is the cultural clash between Welsh Nonconformity and English imperialism as dramatized in the following scene. It should be explained that the dialogue in the novel between English officers and Welsh soldiers occurs in English with the intervening narrative in Welsh, the author adopting an innovative bilingual approach which confirms the novel's realism:

> There were no problems regarding the name or number or regiment, neither was there a problem regarding the denomination of the majority,— 'Church of England' they answered, and that was it. When it was Manod's turn to give his details he was asked about his denomination.
>
> 'Calvinistic Methodist' he answered.
>
> 'What's that mob?' asked the sergeant.
>
> He started to explain, but before he got very far the sergeant turned to the clerk and said,
>
> 'Put him down as Wesleyan.'
>
> 'But I'm not a Wesleyan,' remarked Manod again. The sergeant looked at him, and in a voice full of emphasis he answered,
>
> 'You'll bloody well learn not to argue here. If the army says you're a bloody fool, you are one,' and that was the end of that. As he went out having received his card he heard the sergeant saying,
>
> 'Here's another of these Calvin buggers,' and he knew without having to turn round that it was Ifan trying to uphold the rights of Calvinistic Methodism.

One recalls Ann Owen's attempts to explain her nationhood to the English doctor in *Tegwch y Bore*.

Only in such scenes of conflict does *Amser i Ryfel* take off as a novel. As a work of fiction it must otherwise have appeared rather bleak and unadventurous, published as it was during the heyday of T. Rowland Hughes as a compulsive and entertaining storyteller. Again, this is not only a war writer's difficulty in amalgamating fact and fiction but a symptomatic unease with the novel form in Welsh. After Daniel Owen at the end of the nineteenth century had gallantly unshackled the novel from the constraints of Victorian piety and utilitarianism, future novelists had failed to exploit the freedom inherent in the *genre*. *Amser i Ryfel* would have been a far more absorbing novel, for instance, had it been written from the perspective of Ned Beynon—unorthodox, adulterous, worldly— rather than the predictable and decent Manod.

Paul Fussell in his monumental study, *The Great War and Modern Memory* (1975), has referred to the ironic fact that once censorship laws were abandoned in Britain in the 1960s and the literary means were at last available to suggest fully the atrocities of the war, it was then that the actual generation which had experienced that trauma was rapidly disappearing. Certainly since the 1960s in Wales there has been a revived interest in the war for whatever reason.

Various autobiographies have appeared, the two most remarkable being Ifan Gruffydd's *Gŵr o Baradwys* (A Man from Paradwys, 1963) and *Tân yn y Siambar* (Fire in the Chamber, 1966), and Lewis Valentine's *Dyddiadur Milwr* (The Diary of a Soldier, 1969–1972; republished 1988). The experience of Ifan Gruffydd (1896–1971) suggests the type of innocence that was contaminated by the military machine in 1914–1918. An unknowing volunteer from Anglesey, where recruiting proved a difficult task, he spent four years in the army. (One is reminded of Robert Graves's reference in *Goodbye to all That* to a certain corporal from Anglesey who was so heartbroken that he was granted an unconditional discharge and returned home to his wife and pigs.) His recollections are conveyed in a style which adheres to the oral tradition. The diary of Lewis Valentine (1893–1986) is in striking contrast: although from humble stock, he was a theological scholar at Bangor when, in 1916, he joined a specially-formed student unit of the RAMC to conduct non-combatant duties; the fate of this unit is recorded by R. R. Williams in *Breuddwyd Cymro mewn Dillad Benthyg* (The Dream of a Welshman in Borrowed Clothes, 1964) and Alan Llwyd and Elwyn Edwards in *Y Bardd a Gollwyd* (The Lost Poet, 1992). At least two other authors, Cynan and David Ellis, were members of the same company. Lewis Valentine's recollections contain far more introspection and analysis than those of Ifan Gruffydd. Characteristically, whereas Gruffydd was merely glad to return in one piece to his native Anglesey at the end of the war, Valentine came home a committed nationalist; in 1929 he stood as the Welsh Nationalist Party's very first parliamentary candidate and in 1936 he was imprisoned along with Saunders Lewis and D. J. Williams for his part in the burning of the Bombing School.

Various novels have also appeared since the 1960s. *Seirff yn Eden* (Serpents in Eden, 1963) again draws on autobiographical material as Gwilym R. Jones (1903–93) portrays a group of children in the Nantlle Valley growing up against the backdrop of the war. More recently, childhood experiences of war have been the stuff of *Mam a Fi* (Mam and Me, 1983) by Harri Williams (1913–83), and *Dyddiadur Nant-y-Wrach* (The Diary of Nant-y-Wrach, 1987) by Hilma Lloyd Edwards (1959–). Rhydwen Williams (1916–97), on the other hand, in *Y Siôl Wen* (The White Shawl, 1970), the second novel in a trilogy, documents the effects of the war upon one particular family in the coal-mining community of the Rhondda Valley. In so doing he managed to reclaim for Welsh literature an area of history more commonly contained within Anglo-Welsh fiction, the novels of Lewis Jones and Richard Llewellyn in particular. A far more cynical streak may be detected in his subsequent novel, *Gallt y Gofal* (Hill of Tribulation, 1979): the main character is a hopeless case, a dismal failure in war as in the rest of his life; one is reminded of him when reading Emyr Humphreys's later novel, *Jones* (1984). *Gallt y Gofal* can be grouped with *Cynffon o Wellt* (A Tail of Straw, 1960) by W. Leslie Richards (1916–89) and *Y Pabi Coch* (The Red Poppy, 1983) by T. Wilson Evans (1923–), for at last in all three novels one can chart the rise of the Welsh soldier of the Great War as anti-hero. That in itself is a sign of cultural sophistication and confidence in the treatment of the war.

Two novels remain: *Gwaed Gwirion* (Innocent Blood, 1965) and *Marged* (1974). They stand apart as the most extensive and creatively stimulating depictions of the Great War and its effects on Wales. It is unlikely that either novel could have been written before the 1960s: both are products of the new tolerance and secularity which typified that decade; they also owe a debt to *Un Nos Ola Leuad* (One Moonlit Night, 1961) by Caradog Prichard (1904–80), a novel with as far-reaching significance for Welsh fiction as *Ulysses* (1922) for English fiction. *Un Nos Ola Leuad* can be regarded as a partial reworking of *Traed Mewn Cyffion*, a study of life in a Welsh slate-quarrying community in the Ogwen Valley between 1915 and 1920. However, things are not seen through the eyes of a responsible adult but alternately from the warped perspective of an emotionally deprived child and a mentally unstable adult. People do not weather the storm with pride and dignity despite their dreary circumstances; instead they exert physical violence upon one other, rape and murder one another, commit suicide. Here is a sadistic territory more reminiscent of Caradoc Evans's paradoxically-named Manteg, a landscape where the literal madness which afflicts various characters is a mirror to the figurative madness afflicting the western world in a time of war. It is a travesty of *Traed Mewn Cyffion*, breaking dramatically with that novel's naturalistic form and disrupting its chronological orderliness. Elevated and formalized Welsh is replaced by an uncompromising mixture of puerile banter and local dialect. All in all, next to this dystopia *Traed Mewn Cyffion* presents a positively utopian vision.

Neither *Gwaed Gwirion* nor *Marged* display the extreme nature of Caradog Prichard's *Un Nos Ola Leuad*, but both were influenced in varying ways by it. Saunders Lewis suggested that *Un Nos Ola Leuad* had provided *Gwaed Gwirion* with a model of how to write a colloquial novel, and certainly Emyr Jones (1914–) was eager to ensure that his characters were represented in a diction and dialect which was typical of them and breathed authenticity. His sparsely-educated main character, Yr Hen Sarjant (The Old Sergeant)—a soul mate of Frank Richards in *Old Soldiers Never Die* (1933)— would have been more at home with Ifan Gruffydd than Lewis Valentine. The novel does not attempt to make any political statements beyond those regarding the futility of war, man's inhumanity to man, the pointlessness of nation fighting nation. The Old Sergeant is thrown into a cesspit from the outset and all he can do is wade on and try as best he can to keep his head above the water and below the parapet.

Gwaed Gwirion is a picaresque novel written from the standpoint of an unremarkable character representative of the millions who were sent like lambs to the slaughter. Despite the hectic pace as the narrator describes the persecution of war, things occasionally slow down and experiences are poignantly described:

> At the far end of the ditch, in a small dugout, we saw a young officer lying dead with his violin case in his hand and inside the violin there was a bundle of manuscripts. There were many pages of music written in ink—his own work, more than likely. It crossed my mind at the time— who was he? Perhaps, had he survived, he would have been one of the world's great composers today. Whoever he was he thought the world of his violin to have brought it with him, here to the front line. What was that violin worth? Hundreds?—thousands perhaps. It wasn't worth a thing to me. And what about the music?—another 'Unfinished', for neither did that one see the light of day. We will never know how much the war cost us in things like that.

Unmistakably Welsh in idiom and outlook, such scenes speak with universal humanity. It was no wonder that Saunders Lewis remarked when *Gwaed Gwirion* was first published, 'At last, at long last, the 1914–18 war has received its epic in Welsh'. This novel, written by a veteran of the Second World War, is the most successful Welsh novel wholly devoted to describing the Great War.

T. Glynne Davies (1926–88) in *Marged*, on the other hand, deals with the period between 1872 and the Great War. His panoramic novel could just as well have been called 'Llanrwst', so central is that town in the Conway Valley to the work. It is in this novel that the soldier as anti-hero at last comes into his own; this anti-heroism is partly due to *Un Nos Ola Leuad*. As in that novel, *Traed Mewn Cyffion* is once again a counterpoint, although the main chronological structure is far more in keeping with Kate Roberts's example. Yet what she might have regarded as *ciaridyms*—an alternate and less-dignified *gwerin*—as in *Un Nos Ola Leuad* are once again placed centre-stage.

The novice Robat-jon, much influenced by the worldly Royston Edwards, goes overboard completely: in France, he sleeps with a prostitute; at home, he succumbs to the charms of Ann from Sgot—the slum district of town—rather than the more dainty Megan (the same name as Cynan's dearly regarded cousin in

'Anfon y Nico', incidentally). Previous Welsh novels had merely hinted at such sexual looseness in a moralistic fashion. *Marged* is a liberal, cosmopolitan novel. Its treatment of patriotism, for example, is totally different from the more predictable responses in previous novels dealing with the war. For once, Welshness is regarded with cynicism and apathy. Robat-jon is here portrayed amidst the wilderness of the Somme when he comes across some fellow Welshmen:

> Robat-jon made his way towards them: the first group of Welshmen for him to come across in this foreign land and from North Wales at that. But as he stood and listened, after the first greetings and 'Where do you come from?', they too were merely soldiers talking in soldier's lingo, the taste and colour and smell of lyddite thick in the cannon-like bases of their windpipes.

So much for Cynan's *hiraeth*.

All in all, *Marged* is a savage and unstinting attack upon the forces which sent Robat-jon and his compatriots to war. T. Glynne Davies himself commented:

> The First World War was the most significant watershed I can remember in the whole history of Britain. People like Royston Edwards in the novel—people who had been brought up in the sound of Christianity—went out to France and saw their mates falling dead in droves around them, and then had to return to little Wales afterwards where they discovered that the whole basis of the society they had previously known was a myth or a fable. From then onwards the society which we know today developed—without foundations and without basic co-operative principles.

It extends into the twentieth century the survey of hypocrisy and corruption in the Welsh establishment which Daniel Owen had conducted with such brilliance with regard to the nineteenth century.

Had he survived, Robat-jon would not have returned to Wales: he would instead have established himself as a businessman in Liverpool. He could not imagine having to return to the tight folds of his former locale. *Marged* speaks for the thousands who either did not return alive or who could not envisage taking up where they had left off in Wales after the betrayal of war. The nationalist ideology offered them no alternative, coming too late in the day.

Yet funnily enough, although *Marged* provides an alternative view
of twentieth-century Wales to *Traed Mewn Cyffion*, some sort of
future for the country is ensured. At the end of the novel Ann is
carrying Robat-jon's child and it is his grandson—from Ann's
bastard son—who is referred to in an epilogue to the novel set in
1972 as Wales's brightest political hope. It might be relevant to
remember that Plaid Cymru made a political breakthrough in
1974—in the same year as *Marged* was published—and succeeded
in trebling its previous parliamentary representation. Half a
century later, Wales had survived the war—through a process of
hit-or-miss.

Marged can therefore be read in the wider perspective of Welsh
literature regarding the First World War in general. Although the
response at times has appeared spasmodic and reluctant, the actual
issues touched upon in many of those literary works suggest how
vital the war and its repercussions have been in shaping the history
of twentieth-century Wales. The war has produced a literature of
relevance.

FURTHER READING

W. Beynon Davies, *Thomas Gwynn Jones* (Cardiff, 1970).

Hywel Teifi Edwards, *The Eisteddfod* (Cardiff, 1990).

Donald Evans, *Rhydwen Williams* (Cardiff, 1991).

Bedwyr Lewis Jones, *R. Williams Parry* (Cardiff, 1972).

R. Gerallt Jones, *T. H. Parry-Williams* (Cardiff, 1978).

D. Tecwyn Lloyd, 'Welsh Literature and the First World War', *Planet*, 11
     (May 1972), 17–23.

Idem, 'Welsh Public Opinion and the First World War', *Planet*, 10
     (February/March 1972), 25–37.

Alan Llwyd, *Gwae Fi Fy Myw* (Llandybïe, 1981).

Alan Llwyd and Elwyn Edwards (eds), *Gwaedd y Bechgyn* (Llandybïe,
     1988).

Alun Llywelyn-Williams, 'The Poetry of Cynan', *Poetry Wales*, 9 No. 1
     (Summer 1973), 330–6.

Derec Llwyd Morgan, *Kate Roberts* (Cardiff, 1974).

Dyfnallt Morgan, *D. Gwenallt Jones* (Cardiff, 1972).

Idem, *Rhyw Hanner Ieuenctid* (Swansea, 1971).

James Nicholas, *Pan Oeddwn Grwt Diniwed yn y Wlad* (Llandysul, 1979).

John Rowlands, '*Marged* T. Glynne Davies', in J. E. Caerwyn Williams
     (ed.), *Ysgrifau Beirniadol*, 11 (Dinbych, 1979), 264–78.

Meic Stephens (ed.), *The Oxford Companion to the Literature of Wales* (Oxford, 1986).

Ned Thomas, 'The Chains around my Feet', *The Welsh Extremist* (London, 1971), 64–71.

Gerwyn Wiliams, *Y Rhwyg* (Llandysul, 1993).

Idem, *Tir Neb* (Caerdydd, 1996).

CHAPTER 3

POETRY BETWEEN THE WARS

T. ROBIN CHAPMAN

Although the poetry of the early years of the twentieth century varied in both quality and style, it was underpinned by a common perspective. Writers as diverse as Gwili, Elfed, the young T. Gwynn Jones and the even younger W. J. Gruffydd, for example, all active between 1890 and 1914, produced work which unselfconsciously shared the assumptions of its intended audience. For the Georgians, poetry was still regarded by poet and reader alike primarily as a craft. There was tacit agreement on what constituted a suitable poetic persona and acceptable subject-matter for verse. The perceived quality of a poet was determined as much by his ability to frame familiar ideas in an original way as by the originality of the ideas themselves. Eisteddfod culture, still unassailable in Welsh literary life, presupposed that any poet worth his salt could compose great verse on any given topic.

What followed the First World War can perhaps be broadly characterized as a shift to a more self-conscious, unreconciled attitude. The experience of the war itself, as Gerwyn Wiliams has shown, had a profound effect. Romanticism had relied on a conspiracy of innocence in which both poet and reader were complicit. This could scarcely be expected to survive intact. The break with the past was not a clean one; such breaks seldom are. The arch-Romantic Gwynn Jones, as will be seen, made a successful transition to a more direct mode of expression whereas younger moderns like Cynan and Iorwerth Peate continued to write lyric verse throughout their careers. The overriding poetic sensibility of the period was, however, individualistic, alienated and analytical. Throughout the 1920s and 1930s those poets whose work commanded most attention were academics increasingly divorced by reason of education, leisure and vocation from the preceding generation, writing for a public who enjoyed similar advantages. The immediate post-war years saw a growth in the

Welsh departments of the University of Wales. Late in 1918, W. J. Gruffydd was appointed professor of Celtic at Cardiff, replacing the antiquary Thomas Powel; a year later two chairs were established (in language and literature) at Aberystwyth, occupied by T. H. Parry-Williams and T. Gwynn Jones respectively; and in 1920 the new constituent college in Swansea attracted Saunders Lewis to his first post in Wales. Iorwerth Peate worked as an extramural lecturer between 1924 and 1927 before moving to the National Museum of Wales in Cardiff, and Williams Parry hovered ambiguously between the departments of Welsh and Extra-Mural Studies in Bangor throughout the 1920s and 1930s.

This new direction in poetry was, therefore, accompanied from the outset by developments in what can be justifiably termed 'professional' literary criticism. Gruffydd's quarterly, *Y Llenor* (The Writer), launched in 1922, was the semi-official journal of the University's Welsh departments, with a distribution network inside the colleges. As a platform for creative talent it was impressive: Saunders Lewis published his early poetry there, as did Gwenallt and Iorwerth Peate. Virtually the whole of Parry-Williams's *Ysgrifau* (Essays) and a good proportion of *Cerddi* (Poems) first found an audience on its pages during the 1920s and Cynan and Williams Parry were regular contributors over the following decade. *Y Llenor*'s lasting value, however, was as a focus for debate. Gruffydd embarked on a systematic re-evaluation of nineteenth-century literature, and Saunders Lewis sought to explain the European dimension of what he called 'the Welsh Aesthetic', exemplified in the work of the fourteenth- and fifteenth-century *cywyddwyr*. In their attempt to establish the canon, both men found themselves increasingly at odds over questions of religion, tradition and authority. Their dispute culminated in Lewis's 'Llythyr ynghylch Catholigiaeth' (Letter on Catholicism) and Gruffydd's 'Atebiad y Golygydd' (Editor's Reply) in the summer 1927 issue of *Y Llenor*. Lewis self-consciously sought to outrage liberal Nonconformist opinion by asserting that 'an awareness of sin', as found in medieval Catholic Wales but since lost, was a prerequisite of great literature. For his part, Gruffydd drew attention to Lewis's English upbringing and education, arguing that his opponent was constitutionally unable to appreciate the world from which the nineteenth-century aesthetic had sprung. It was a debate incapable of resolution. In open opposition to both Gruffydd's Nonconformist and Lewis's Catholic claims on contemporary literature, Alun Llywelyn-Williams's periodical *Tir Newydd* (New Ground, 1935–9) and Dafydd Jenkins and Aneirin ap Talfan in *Heddiw* (Today, 1936–42) argued the case for modernism and recognition of Wales's urban heritage.

The rise of academic criticism signalled a corresponding decline in the prestige of the Eisteddfod, hitherto popularly known as *coleg y genedl* (the nation's college). After 1918 no major poets continued to compete in eisteddfodau once they had ensured recognition; it was regarded as a means of gaining an audience for more mature verse. The eisteddfodic 'career' post was dead. The institution was dismissed in university circles at best as a school for apprentices, at worst as a populist irrelevance. Indeed, poets within the University made a conscious effort to distance themselves from its ethos. With the exception of Gwenallt, the only poets of any standing who continued to write under bardic names—Crwys, Cynan, Wil Ifan, for example—were producers of popular, adamantly unintellectual verse. When academics co-operated with the Eisteddfod authorities in the mid-1930s to revise the festival's constitution, they were moved more by a concern for the Eisteddfod's survival as a national institution for preserving the Welsh language than by a belief in its merit as a forum for literary excellence.

A further factor in determining a new poetic idiom was the growth in Wales of an interest in the New Psychology, what William James, one of its early advocates, had called 'psychology without a soul'. It marked a move away from the idea of the mind as the seat of the conscious expression of will, joy, sadness, hatred, love and so on, to an emphasis on the instinctive biological mind operating independently of the will. One of the curiosities of the poetry of the period is the apparent delight with which so many of its exponents portrayed man as prey to his whims and lusts.

All these changes are typified in the work of T. H. Parry-Williams (1887–1975), professor of Welsh at Aberystwyth between 1920 and 1952. He has been described by one critic as arriving on the Welsh literary scene like a large, black crow in the midst of nightingales. He came to prominence at the Wrexham Eisteddfod of 1912 by winning both the Crown and the Chair, but achieved notoriety when he repeated the feat three years later at Bangor. In 1912 his winning *awdl*, 'Y Mynydd' (The Mountain) and *pryddest*, 'Gerallt Gymro' (Giraldus Cambrensis), were conventional responses to stock Edwardian subjects. By 1915 he had shocked and impressed the adjudicators in equal measure with 'Y Ddinas' (The City), his own choice of *pryddest* subject in a year when the competition was left open. His portrait of the whores, thieves, suicides and empty lives of contemporary Paris caused one of the judges, Eifion Wyn, to dissent from the decision of his colleagues to award him the Crown. His discomfort was prompted as much by what the piece did not contain as what it did: 'I searched [his city] assiduously but saw no temple therein, nor faith nor love nor loveliness.' Eifion Wyn's assertion that 'Y Ddinas' had no redeeming features was quite literally true. Parry-Williams adopts the disinterested perspective of a documentarist. He records the futility of urban life with a commentary on its obvious horrors, but does not intervene to offer either condemnation or redemption. Despite their archness of expression, Eifion Wyn's reservations had a sound foundation in Nonconformist theology: admission of guilt as a prerequisite of grace. In rejecting the second, Parry-Williams necessarily rejected the first. In 'Y Ddinas' he created a world of the fallen without acknowledging the Fall.

After his *succès de scandale* of 1915, Parry-Williams did not compete again at the Eisteddfod and never published his prize-winning poems. The Eisteddfod had fulfilled the function of drawing attention to his name. 'Y Ddinas' only gives the vaguest intimation of the nature of his mature output. The idiom of his later work is far more personal, the form shorter and the style more direct. What the Bangor Eisteddfod did was to establish him as a poet of ideas, however uncongenial those ideas may have been to his more squeamish critics.

His first-published volume of work was *Ysgrifau* (Essays) in 1928. The *ysgrif* form, Parry-Williams's own innovation, requires some definition. It can briefly be said to be a piece of discursive prose, generally no more than two thousand words in length. It takes as its subject a single item, word, place or phenomenon and expands on the associations this evokes in the author. It can be light or serious in tone and almost invariably contains an autobiographical element. The confessional nature of these essays provides a valuable gloss on the poetry, and they deserve attention in their own right.

The craft of *Ysgrifau* lies in the meticulous care with which Parry-Williams gives the impression of a stream of consciousness. The essays are both an attempt to convey the workings of the mind in connected prose and a commentary on the process. In 'Oedfa'r Pnawn' (Afternoon Service), for instance, the shift between experience and analysis is rapid and astute. The author arrives at chapel for the afternoon service. He adds the digits on the number-plate of a passing car—157—and finds that they equal thirteen. He muses briefly on the bad omen that this might presage. Inside the chapel he is relieved to find that the twelve panes of glass in the window are divided into four rows of three, a more auspicious number. Looking through the panes he notes the phenomenon whereby faults in the glass distort the shape of the landscape outside. A fly climbs the wall and he remembers his amazement as a child that insects seem to defy gravity. A cock crows and brings thoughts of betrayal; he hears the gurgle of the river; the sky is blue: *awyr las*. He toys with the words, trying to fit them into a line of *cynghanedd*. His mind wanders to other lyrics. A farmer in the congregation reminds him of a man from Anglesey who spoke almost entirely in *clichés*, and he recalls some of his sayings. A crow flies by, or is it a rook? He recites to himself a rhyme about birds as harbingers of joy or sorrow. The sound of a car in the distance reminds him of a bike ride he once made. Drops of rain run together down the window-pane and he watches their course, trying to discern some pattern in it. His attention is drawn to scratches on the bench where he is sitting—his own initials carved into the wood. He regrets that he had not dated them. He thinks of the past and the terrors of the future, *os caf fyw*—'if I am spared'. The service ends with a prayer and memories of an older preacher. The flights of an overactive imagination over the course of an afternoon, condensed into a little more than one thousand words.

This same preoccupation with the corners of human experience suffuses the rest of the collection. 'Glaw' (Rain) and 'Gweld y Gwynt' (Seeing the Wind) explore the fascination of superstition. 'Boddi Cath' (Drowning a Cat) makes a case for the value of all experience, however unpalatable. 'Dieithrwch' (Strangeness) argues that the glory of the familiar can only be appreciated when that familiarity is temporarily lost. 'Yr Ias' (The Chill) articulates the sense of disorientation:

> Ni wnaeth yr ias imi chwerthin na chrio; yr oedd fel pe bai rhywbeth diarth wedi cyrraedd ym môn yr ymennydd o rywle, gan bwyso ar feddalwch yno a chlwyfo a drysu popeth yn y peirianwaith am ennyd.

Nid yw'n feddyliad nac eto'n deimlad, na breuddwyd na gweledigaeth na sioc na dim o'r fath, ond rhyw gosfa losg dreiddiol yn y rhan honno o'r pen.

[The chill did not cause me to laugh or cry; it was as if something foreign had arrived at the base of the brain from somewhere, pressing on a softness there and wounding and confounding everything in the machinery for a moment. It isn't a thought, nor yet a feeling, nor a dream or a vision or a shock or anything of the sort, but some burning, piercing itch in that part of the brain.]

Parry-Williams's description of the brain as machinery is part of a larger belief that all experience and feeling is theoretically explicable in scientific terms. The dilemma for him lies in deciding whether such investigation is always desirable. He is a reluctant reductionist. In 'Cydwybod' (Conscience), for example, he states that conscience is a faculty possessed by those who have—*ysywaeth* (more's the pity)—come to know themselves and have attempted an analysis of their own instincts and emotions. The idea of conscience as a learned disposition, without which people would on the whole be far happier, permeates prose and poetry alike. To possess conscience is to know guilt. In the same essay he writes that when he hears of the execution of a murderer he feels that the rope could be put around his own neck with equal justice. *Ysgrifau* is a satisfyingly uncomfortable volume.

Cerddi (Poems) was published in 1931 but contains work dating back to 1919, the year when, as a self-confessed pacifist and suspected atheist, Parry-Williams was passed over for the chair in Welsh Language at Aberystwyth. In protest he surrendered his lectureship and registered as an undergraduate in the School of Medicine. The college eventually relented and he was granted his professorship the following year. He was later to call 1919 his *annus mirabilis*, a year's voluntary exile from routine.

Like *Ysgrifau*, *Cerddi* draws its energy from the unresolved opposition of emotion and intellect, spirituality and worldliness, freedom and powerlessness. The contents fall broadly into three categories: sonnets, a sequence of travel poems written during a trip to South America in 1925, and what Parry-Williams, with typical self-mockery, termed *rhigymau*, rhyming couplets whose whimsical metre belies their stark subject-matter.

The sonnets themselves can be subdivided by date of composition. Those written in 1919 often address abstract notions: 'Gwahaniaeth' (Difference), 'Nef' (Heaven), 'Lliw' (Colour), 'Ofn' (Fear), 'Argyhoeddiad' (Conviction), 'Cydbwysedd' (Balance). The Shakespearean form is used to point up innate conflicts. A statement is made in the octet only to be contradicted or modified in the sestet. More often than not the argument ends in a paradox. 'Nef' is as good an example as any:

> Am fod yr anghyfiawnder arna' i'n bwys,
> Suddais yn drwm i'r gwaelod isaf oll,
> Ac yn nhywyllwch y distawrwydd dwys
> Arhosaf heddiw fel petawn ar goll . . .
> Ac eto nid oes gwenwyn yn fy ngwaed,
> Ond rhyw farweidd-dra melys: nid oes cri
> O'm genau'n galw am ddial fy sarhaed,
> Na her anobaith yn fy safiad i,
> Am fod mwynhad ymhell o gyrraedd llef
> Mewn uffern ddigon dofn i fod yn nef.

> [Because injustice was a weight upon me,
> I sank heavily to the lowest ever depth,
> And in the darkness of the solemn silence
> I remain today as if quite lost . . .
> And yet there is no poison in my blood,
> Just some sweet sluggishness: there is no cry
> From my mouth calling for my insult to be avenged,
> Nor the challenge of hopelessness in my stand,
> For there is enjoyment beyond the reach of lamentation
> In a hell deep enough to be a heaven.]

The later sonnets, composed mostly in 1931, are concerned not only with the broad questions posed in the early ones, but also the poet's native Snowdonia, although these, too, have their abstract themes. What distinguishes them from 'Nef' and the rest is their lack of nervous energy. The voice is more subdued, the tone more measured. 'Llyn y Gadair' is a hymn of praise to a lake which the casual visitor would hardly notice; 'Moelni' (Bareness) and 'Tynfa' (Tension) suggest an inexplicable link between character and environment and 'Tŷ'r Ysgol' (The Schoolhouse) explores the guilt which causes children to keep on the family home long after they have flown the nest, *rhag ofn i'r ddau sydd yn y gro / Synhwyro*

rywsut fod y drws ynghlo (for fear that the couple in their grave /
Will somehow sense that the door is locked).

To this 1931 group also belongs arguably Parry-Williams's best-
known sonnet, 'Dychwelyd' (Returning). The tone of the sestet in
particular is magisterial, the pacing immaculate—an example of the
nobility that detachment can attain if voiced with commitment:

> Ac am nad ydyw'n byw ar hyd y daith
>   O gri ein geni hyd ein holaf gŵyn
> Yn ddim ond crych dros dro neu gysgod craith
>   Ar lyfnder esmwyth y mudandod mwyn,
> Ni wnawn, wrth ffoi am byth o'n ffwdan ffôl,
> Ond llithro i'r llonyddwch mawr yn ôl.

> [And since our life throughout its course
>   From the cry of our birth until our last sigh
> Is nothing but a passing wrinkle or the shadow of a scar
>   On the smooth surface of the gentle hush,
> We, in fleeing for ever our foolish commotion,
> Do no more than slip back into that vast silence.]

The travel poems are themselves *rhigymau*, the diary jottings of a
man witnessing the unfamiliar and striking unexpected resonances
within himself. They are vignettes describing places and people: the
Azores, a nun aboard an ocean liner whose crucifix swings with the
motion of the waves, the Gulf of Mexico, a mad girl caressing a
white rat on the quayside in Rio, the vastness of the Pacific, a sea-
burial in the Channel. Some are written in the first person, some in
the second, and one, 'Yng Ngwlff Mecsico', is a unique example of
the poet talking about himself in the third person as *y llanc o Arfon*
(the lad from Arfon):

> Ni ddysgodd y truan eto mai hud
> Enwau a phellter yw 'gweld y byd'.

> [The poor thing hasn't learned yet that 'seeing the world'
> Is only the magic of names and distances.]

The *rhigymau* have the directness of epigrams, pointed affronts
to Romantic lyricists like John Morris-Jones and Elfed less than a
generation before. The former had sung that his love had eyes as

bright as two gemstones, the latter that death and sleep were brothers. Parry-Williams was more direct in 'Yr Esgyrn Hyn' (These Bones):

> Beth fyddi dithau, ferch, a myfi,
> Pan gilio'r cnawd o'r hyn ydym ni?
>
> Diffydd y nwyd pan fferro'r gwaed,
> Derfydd am siom a serch a sarhaed.
>
> Ni bydd na chyffwrdd na chanfod mwy:
> Pan fadro'r nerfau, ni theimlir clwy.
>
> Ac ni bydd breuddwyd na chyffro cân
> Mewn penglog lygadrwth a'i chraciau mân.
>
> Nid erys dim o'r hyn wyt i mi—
> Dim ond dy ddannedd gwynion di.
>
> [What will you and I be, my girl,
> When the flesh retreats from what we are?
>
> Passion will fade when blood congeals,
> Disappointment and love and offence will cease.
>
> There will be no more touching or discovery:
> When the nerves fester no wound will be felt.
>
> There will be no dream or thrill of song
> In a staring skull with its tiny cracks.
>
> Nothing will remain of what you were to me—
> Only your white teeth.]

Parry-Williams published two other volumes before the outbreak of the Second World War: *Olion* (Impressions, 1935) and *Synfyfyrion* (Reveries, 1937). Both comprise a mixture of essays and poetry. In one sense it would be true to say that neither shows any development on *Ysgrifau* and *Cerddi*, but this is misleading if not qualified. Because of the relatively late age at which he came to creative writing Parry-Williams had already found modes of thought and means of expression with which he felt comfortable at the outset of his literary career. His work thereafter consisted of variations on the same broad

themes of interior monologue and studiously casual observation.
There are, however, subtle shifts of emphasis. The tone of *Olion* is
more stately, less frantic, than that of *Ysgrifau* and *Cerddi*. It opens
with two quatrains on 'Hyfrydwch' (Delight):

> Mae gennyf dduw hollol i mi fy hun,
>   Ac nid ymyrrir â'i ragluniaeth ef.
> Mae ef a minnau'n gallu byw'n gytûn.
>   Cas gennym uffern: hyfryd gennym nef . . .
>
> A chan fod gennyf dduw i mi fy hun,
>   Caf ochel uffern a mwynhau fy nef.
>
> [I have a god completely to myself,
>   And his providence is not questioned.
> He and I can live in harmony.
>   We both hate hell: we both love heaven . . .
>
> And since I have a god all to myself
>   I shall avoid my hell and enjoy my heaven.]

The rest of the volume expands on manifestations of this self-
created god, this heaven of self-limitation, this delight in wilful
denial, the intellectual as happy vegetable. In 'I'm Hynafiaid' (To
My Forebears) the poet goes so far as to thank his ancestors for
endowing him with the capacity to shun speculation:

> Mi gefais gennych fodd i synio'n glir
> Mai mewn anwybod y mae nef yn wir.
>
> [I got from you the means to see clearly
> That heaven truly lies in ignorance.]

Indeed, a large part of the volume is dedicated to the idea of
individuality as inheritance. The poet takes what is given: looks,
intelligence, curiosity, his native heath, even the blood in his veins,
and makes them his own. The poems chart the process of
ownership and the responsibility that this entails.

Synfyfyrion is equally familiar territory: essays, *rhigymau* and
sonnets—although there is perhaps more of a concession to
nostalgia here than in previous works. As in *Cerddi*, the *rhigymau*

consist mainly of traveller's tales of the United States, but the
writer is less of an innocent abroad now, more a world-weary man
making a second (and last) visit to confirm his suspicion that, as he
grows older, novelty fades. Six lines suffice to describe his view of
the Pacific from Santa Monica, none of them about the ocean itself:

> Pan welais di gynt, nid adwaenwn neb
> A welsai dywod dy draethell wleb;
>
> Ond dyma fi'n gwybod i mi fy hun
> Dy weled o'r blaen,—ac 'r wyt ti'r un un,
>
> A minnau'n newid. . . . Ffarweliaf â'th li:
> Mae dwywaith yn ddigon i'th weled di.
>
> [When I saw you before, I knew no one
> Who had seen the sand on your wet shore;
>
> But now I know within myself
> That I have seen you before,—and you are still the same,
>
> And I have changed. . . . . Goodbye to your flow:
> Twice is enough to have seen you.]

The sonnets 'Crefft' (Craft) and 'Ymbil' (Entreaty) both ask for the
gift of escape from consciousness—*llonydd gan holl derfysgiadau'r
llawr* (relief from all the tumults of the earth), as Parry-Williams
terms it, recalling the 'voices of the earth' in 'Dychwelyd'. 'Y
Rhufeiniaid' (The Romans) discusses the folly of worldly ambition.
The volume is more reconciled to life's diversity.

Parry-Williams's verse had from the outset displayed a tongue-in-
cheek detachment. By 1937 the roguishness of *Cerddi* had been lost,
but not the freshness. Literature continued to perform for him the
often disagreeable but always necessary therapeutic function of
marrying thought and fancy. As he wrote in the essay 'Llenydda'
(Writing)—and the parenthesis here is crucial: *Heb fyfyrio rywsut—
o fodd neu anfodd—a'i ddehongli gyda dychymyg, nid oes gwir
lenydda* (Without somehow meditating—willingly or unwillingly—
and interpreting this with imagination, no true writing is possible).

Lloffion (Gleanings, 1942), among other things, is an attempt to
map out what might be called a theology of the imagination.
'Nefoedd' (Heaven) calls for a personal paradise for:

Yr estron brith na all hyd ben ei daith
Ymhonni'n Bagan nac yn Gristion chwaith.

[The confused stranger who cannot throughout his life
Claim to be a Pagan or a Christian either]

'Un a Dau' (One and Two) tackles the theme of duality of mind
and matter, claiming that no science has yet found a gap between
the *deunydd dwbl* (double stuff), of body and soul. The theme is re-
echoed in the *rhigwm* 'Y Tramp', where the poet talks of his own
body as a burden of flesh and bones, and in 'Awen' (The Muse),
where he posits the idea of surgery to discover the seat of artistic
inspiration. Were such a procedure possible, he concludes, the
desire to see would so *angerddoli* (impassion) the eyes of the
observer that:

Ond odid na chanfyddir nad yw hi
Yn ddim ond ffynnon fach o ddagrau'n lli.

[Doubtless one would find that it is only
A tiny fountain of flowing tears.]

The idea of the observer somehow affecting the outcome of his
observation parallels an artistic paradox, that of the inspiration of
literature lying beyond that which it describes. In 1919 Parry-
Williams, in what sounded at the time like a weak pastiche of John
Morris-Jones's 'Cwyn y Gwynt', had written that he wept *am fod
rhaid i'r duwdod wrth fy nagrau i* (because the godhead had need of
my tears). Nearly a quarter of a century later, in 'Ffynnon'
(Fountain), he elaborated on the idea:

Y dafnau duwdod nad oes iddynt hwy
  Na thristwch na llawenydd dynol-ryw,
Na dim ond rhin prydferthwch, sydd yn fwy
  Ei ras na gwae a gwynfyd bod a byw . . .
Dagrau sy'n creu holl gelfyddydwaith byd,
A dagrau sy'n dehongli'r creu i gyd.

[The drops of the godhead which are not part
  Of the sadness or joy of mankind,

But are solely the charm of beauty, which is greater
  In grace than the woe and rapture of our lives . . .
Tears create the whole art of the world
And tears interpret all acts of creation.]

Ugain o Gerddi (Twenty Poems, 1949) is again imbued with *lacrimae rerum*, or more accurately the Welsh *dagrau pethau*, a more's-the-pity resignation to life's vicissitudes. His conscience still pricks him—most famously in 'Hon' (literally 'This', i.e. Wales)— where membership of a marginal nation is a fate as inescapable as death. The claws of his native country 'torture' him with memories of *lleisiau a drychiolaethau* (voices and phantasms) from his past:

Duw a'm gwaredo, ni allaf ddianc rhag hon.

[May God spare me, I cannot escape from her.]

Death remains a preoccupation. It is referred to twice, in a borrowing from Ellis Wynne, as *Brenin Dychryniadau* (the King of Terrors). Death is a paradoxical figure, an object of fear which destroys the very apprehension it engenders:

Oherwydd ni wnaeth yr Angau hwn ddim byd
Ond cymryd yr ofn a'r einioes i ffwrdd yr un pryd.

A rhoi ar ddeall i ddeiliaid byd-a-ddaw
Mai Bywyd ac nid Angau yw Brenin Braw.

[Because this Death never did anything
But take fear and life away together,

And let residents of the world to come understand
That the King of Dread is Life not Death.]

'Ymwacâd' (Self-emptying) described the process of death as a final transcendental house-clearance, a putting away of *yr holl betheuach* (all the stuff), a baring of the inside of one's existence. It is *megis trasiedi* (like a tragedy), but lacks tragedy's heroism:

Ni bydd dim yn aros ar ôl wedi'r ymwacáu
Ond tydi dy hun—a'r nos amdanat yn cau.

[Nothing will remain behind after the emptying
Except yourself—and the night closing around you.]

One sees again the skull of thirty years before, but there is not even
a grinning rictus this time.

It is appropriate to close with all four lines of 'Bardd' (Poet), an
all-embracing tribute to the craft, and a fitting epitaph to the
double motivation of the man who wrote them:

> Canodd ei gerdd i gyfeiliant berw ei waed;
> Canodd hi, a safodd gwlad ar ei thraed.
>
> Canodd ei gân yn gyfalaw i derfysg Dyn;
> Canodd hi, ac nid yw ein llên yr un.
>
> [He sang his poetry to his blood's anxious accompaniment;
> He sang it, and a land attended.
>
> He sang his song in harmony with Man's agitation;
> He sang it, and our literature is changed.]

Parry-Williams's cousin, Robert Williams Parry (1884–1956),
has both enjoyed and suffered the reputation of being what Idris
Bell has called 'a pure poet'. His work is superficially the antithesis
of that of his more worldly relation. Like him, he came to prominence through the Eisteddfod, taking the Chair at Colwyn Bay in
1910 for an ode on 'Yr Haf' (The Summer) and, like him, too, he
subsequently rejected pseudo-medievalism in favour of a more
personal and accessible idiom. An early sonnet, 'Adref' (Home-
wards), published in his first collection, *Yr Haf a Cherddi Eraill*
(The Summer and Other Poems, 1924), encapsulates the change:

> Bu amser pan ddewisais rodio ar led,—
>   Gan roddi heibio'm genedigaeth fraint,—
> Trwy ddiflanedig ddydd marchogion Cred,
>   A thrwy'r distawrwydd lle bu'r twrnamaint. . . .
> Ond hiraeth doeth y galon adre a'm dug
>   Oddi ar ddisberod bererindod serch,
> I brofi o'r gwirionedd sy'n y grug,
>   Ac erwau crintach yr ychydig gerch.
> Digymar yw fy mro trwy'r cread crwn,
> Ac ni bu dwthwn fel y dwthwn hwn.

[There was a time when I chose to roam abroad,—
   Putting aside my birthright,—
Through the fleeting day of the knights of Christendom
   And through the silence where the tournament had been. . . .
But the heart's wise longing brought me home
   From the aimless pilgrimage of love
To taste the truth which is in the heather
   And the grudging acres thinly sown with oats.
My home is matchless throughout the whole wide world
And there is no day to compare with this.]

'Home' in the final couplet is only a partial translation of *bro*, meaning more precisely one's own home area or native patch; the word carries a sense of the intimate relationship between place and people. The concept of *bro* is an important element in understanding Williams Parry's idiosyncratic Romanticism, simultaneously brusque and lyrical, sardonic and naive, drawn to nature yet always aware of its horrors. In his second, darker volume *Cerddi'r Gaeaf* (Winter Poems, 1952), from which the poems discussed here are taken, he is by turns pantheistic, atheistic and agnostic, and his fascination as a poet lies in the apparent ease with which he balances these contradictions.

His own *bro* was Dyffryn Nantlle and subsequently Dyffryn Ogwen in Caernarfonshire, both overwhelmingly Welsh-speaking yet industrialized; scarred, as he put it, by *hagrwch Cynnydd* (the blight of Progress). For a man of his nervous temperament and almost legendary impracticality one can scarcely imagine a more antipathetic environment. The description he gives of himself and his wife in 'Sgyfarnog Trwy Sbienddrych' (A Hare though a Telescope) watching the creature feeding on the crest of a hill above the tumult of the town and fearing for its safety is an apt metaphor. Nature is always vulnerable. In 'Y Peilon' (The Pylon) another hare races zig-zag across the moor from under the white skeleton of a newly planted pylon, like some electrical charge itself, assuring the poet that its habitat is not yet lost; a tree-lined lane in Eifionydd charms him because it leads nowhere; 'Clychau'r Gog' (Bluebells) celebrates the short-lived miracle of May which 'arrives, then says farewell'; a blackbird perched 'so prettily' on a branch and the poet who admires it face a common fate: death awaits them both; silly geese refuse to heed the poet's warning that autumn means an untimely trip to market in the farmer's wife's basket. At times

Williams Parry displays an almost cosmic misanthropy. In the sonnet 'Rhyfeddodau'r Wawr' (Dawn's Wonders) the poet trespasses by chance into a paradise where cuckoo, wood-pigeon, hedgehog, rabbit and heron live unafraid on the doorstep of sleeping humanity. The sestet calls for the greatest wonder of all:

> Rhyfeddach fyth, O haul sy'r tu arall i'r garn,
>   Fai it aros lle'r wyt a chadw Dyn yn ei deiau,
> Nes dyfod trosolion y glaswellt a'u chwalu'n sarn
>   Rhag dyfod drachefn amserddoeth fwg ei simneiau;
> Ei wared o'i wae, a'r ddaear o'i wedd a'i sawyr,
> Cyn ail-harneisio dy feirch i siwrneiau'r awyr.

> [More wonderful still, O sun, who waits behind the mountain,
>   Would be for you to stay there and keep Man in his houses,
> Until the crowbars of the grass come and smash them to smithereens
>   So that the time-wise smoke of his chimneys rises no more;
> Free him from his woe, and the earth from his form and scent,
> Before harnessing again your steeds for their skybound journeys.]

There is often a sense in Williams Parry's work that man has over-reached himself. Man for him is the measure of all things, but 'Pagan' points out the implicit irony of humanism:

> Darfydded pob rhyw sôn
> Am anwadalwch dyn!
> Hyd byth fe ddewis dduwiau
> O'i waith a'i wedd ei hun,
> Ei ddinod wedd ei hun . . .

> Tragywydd ydyw dyn,
> Sefydlog yn ei fryd.
> Mae heddiw a doe i'r duwiau
> Ond erys dyn o hyd;
> A dyn sy'r un o hyd.

> [Let all talk cease
> Of the inconstancy of man!
> He always chooses gods
> Of his own handiwork and form,
> Of his own insignificant form . . .

> Man is eternal,
> Steadfast in his purpose.

> Gods have their today and their yesterday
> But man remains the same;
> And man is still the same.]

To ask what Williams Parry *does* believe is more problematic because he revels in paradox. In 'Gair o Brofiad' (A Word to the Wise), written in early 1939 but looking back as much on past follies as forward to impending war, he calls himself cowardly and courageous, sombre and high-hearted, a non-believer who nevertheless turns to his Creator in times of crisis:

> 'Rwy'n wych. 'rwy'n wael, 'rwy'n gymysg oll i gyd;
> Mewn nych, mewn nerth, mewn helbul ac mewn hedd
> 'Rwy'n fydol ac ysbrydol yr un pryd.
>
> [I am fine, I am feeble, I am all one dreadful mix;
> In frailty, in force, in panic and in peace
> I am worldly and unworldly both at once.]

For him the paradox resolves itself into a sweeping impatience with systematized belief of any kind. His spirituality, like his paganism, is a solitary pursuit. Williams Parry's god, created in his own image, reflects man not as an ideal but as a fickle, feckless creature.

He reserves his admiration for individuals: for A. E. Housman who sits apart from both *uniongred ac anghred ynfyd* (orthodox and asinine unbeliever); for the poet, minister, educationalist and *Hen Sosialydd* (Old Socialist) Silyn Roberts, *fflam ar gerdded* (a walking flame); W. J. Gruffydd whose poetry is *yn llawn o ryfel ac yn llyn o ras* (full of fury and a lake of grace). Certainly, admiration as well as political sympathy coloured his response to the trial and subsequent imprisonment of Saunders Lewis, D. J. Williams and Lewis Valentine for the arson attack on the bombing range at Penyberth, Llŷn, in 1936. The event was cataclysmic for him, a symbolic act of defiance. The sonnet 'Cymru 1937' invokes the muses in a plea for some evidence of human reaction:

> Dyneiddia drachefn y cnawd a wnaethpwyd yn ddur,
> Bedyddia'r di-hiraeth â'th ddagrau, a'r doeth ail-gristia;
> Rho awr o wallgofrwydd i'r llugoer tu ôl i'w fur,
> Gwna ddaeargrynfeydd dan gadarn goncrit Philistia

[Humanise again the flesh that has turned to steel,
   Baptize the unyearning with your tears, and re-christen the wise;
Give the lukewarm within his walls an hour of madness,
   Cause earthquakes under the solid concrete of Philistia.]

Williams Parry felt acutely not only the injustice of the punishment
meted out at the Old Bailey, but also University College Swansea's
decision to suspend Saunders Lewis from his lectureship even
before he was sentenced. Lewis becomes 'Y Gwrthodedig' (The
Rejected One—the word echoing the biblical 'despised and rejected
of men'):

Hoff wlad, os gelli hepgor dysg
Y dysgedicaf yn ein mysg,
Mae'n rhaid dy fod o bob rhyw wlad
Y fwyaf dedwydd ei hystâd.

[Dear land, if you can forego the learning
Of the most learned in our midst,
Then you must be of every land
In the most ever blessed state.]

The title is attributed again in 'J.S.L.', where it is intimated that
Lewis's genius and avowed Catholicism have set him apart. Like
some brightly-coloured bird fallen among common farmyard fowl
he finds himself *digymar*—translatable as both peerless and
friendless. Academe is indifferent:

Ninnau barhawn i yfed yn ddoeth, weithiau de
   Ac weithiau ddysg ym mhrynhawnol hedd ein stafelloedd;
Ac ar ein clyw clasurol ac ysbryd y lle
   Ni thrystia na phwmp y llan na haearnbyth celloedd.
Gan bwyll y bwytawn, o dafell i dafell betryal,
Yr academig dost. Mwynha dithau'r grual.

[As for us, we sip philosophically, sometimes tea,
   And sometimes scholarship in the afternoon peace of our rooms;
And on our hearing and on the spirit of the place
   Breaks no sound of either parish pump or the iron doors of cells.
Sagely we eat, slice after square slice,
   The academic toast. May you enjoy the gruel.]

His poetry is rarely so bitter; his fears and anger are more often turned in upon himself. At times, as in 'Canol Oed' (Middle Age), it verges on the solipsistic. As a child, he says, three terrors kept him awake at night: thoughts of lightning, earthquakes and the end of the world. The first he now understands, the second he can rationalize as improbable, but:

> A diwedd y byd, nid disyfyd y daw,
> Namyn gan bwyll, heb frys na braw.
> Cans araf yw'r bysedd gynt a fu'n gweu
> Miraglau'r synhwyrau, i lwyr ddileu.
>
> O! pan na bo'r galon na chynnes nac oer
> Y claeara'r haul, y clafycha'r lloer.
> A phan rydd yr hydref ei ias i'r mêr
> Y disgyn y dail yng nghoedwigoedd y sêr.
>
> [The end of the world does not come suddenly,
> But rather by stealth, without rush and panic,
> For slow are the fingers that once wove
> The miracle of the senses, to destroy them.
>
> When the heart is neither warm nor cold
> The sun grows tepid, the moon grows sick.
> And when autumn gives its chill to the marrow
> The leaves fall in the forests of the stars.]

It is ironic that a poet who wished for the compensatory heightened sight of the deaf and hearing of the blind, should slide into senility before his death.

Thomas Gwynn Jones (1871–1949) was already nearing middle age at the end of the Great War. His response to a changed world contrasts curiously with that of his fellow professor at Aberystwyth, T. H. Parry-Williams. Whereas Parry-Williams embraced the post-war scientific view of personality as a collection of conditioned biological impulses, Gwynn Jones's acceptance was less sanguine. In his protest against the brute fact of individual impotence he became by the mid-1920s a modern despite himself.

Jones's reputation had been established by the baroque eisteddfodic odes 'Ymadawiad Arthur' (The Departure of Arthur, 1902) and 'Gwlad y Bryniau' (The Land of Hills, 1909); but his early work was informed as much by the social idealism of Ruskin as by a Celtic twilight of mists and melancholy. For the first twenty years of his career the two coexisted uneasily. His large-scale compositions were long on evocative imagery and technical dexterity, but short on ideas; his verse on contemporary themes was more suited to his purpose as a polemicist, but tended to be arch and simplistic—a world of cut-out worker heroes and bloated capitalists. Occasionally, the two would clash. 'Y Nef a Fu' (The Heaven that Fled, 1901–3) typifies the stylistic dilemma. The opening verse promises a spiritual vision:

> Gwae fynd y golau a'r gwirionedd fry,
> A dyfod yma wyll a chelwydd du;
>   Pand ymbalfalu'r ydym ninnau'n awr
> Yn uffern heddiw am y Nef a Fu?

> [Alas that light and truth have gone,
> And in their place dusk and black deceit,
>   Leaving us to grope half-blind
> In the hell of today for the Heaven that fled.]

As the poem progresses, however, it emerges that this hell has specific social causes. Bosses exploit workers and are themselves corrupted by their own devices. The businessman is not a pauper living on the parish but a moral bankrupt living in a palace. Injustice is implicit in the system:

> Er sôn offeiriad da ac athro doeth
> O hyd am galon lân a meddwl coeth,
>   Swm popeth a glybuwyd ydyw hyn —
> Prif amcan bywyd, golud yw, a moeth.

> [Despite the constant words of priest and scholar
> About pure hearts and cultured minds,
>   The sum of all that has been said is this—
> Life's chief aims are luxury and wealth.]

Gwynn Jones was essentially a narrative poet and story his natural medium. The failures of his early polemical verse were due to shallow characterization and an overweening desire to tailor plots to conform to epigrammatic conclusions. With 'Madog' in 1917 he at last exploited the symbolic potential of traditional tales to make pertinent comments on a fallen world.

For Gwynn Jones, Madog, the legendary explorer, is motivated
by despair. His country is beset by civil war and, inspired by his
spiritual mentor, Mabon, with tales of an island of sanctuary across
the sea, he sets sail. A storm breaks:

> Rhonciodd y llong, a rhyw wancus egni'n ei sugno a'i llyncu,
> Trystiodd y tonnau trosti, bwlch ni ddangosai lle bu.

> [The ship heaved, a greedy energy sucked and swallowed her,
> The waves broke noisily over her, no breach showed where she
> had been.]

'Ymadawiad Arthur' had ended with Arthur's leaving for Avallon
and Bedivere's reconciliation to his loss. 'Madog' differs from the
earlier work in essence rather than in degree. Nothing is left: not even
a ripple on the water's surface marks the venture. Madog's attempt
to reach his own Avallon is too vainglorious to be poignant.

Gwynn Jones's major compositions throughout the 1920s
reiterated the same themes of restlessness and escape. In
'Broseliawnd' (Broceliaunde, 1922) Merlin conjures a magic forest
from his own desperate imagination. His predicament over whether
to lose himself within it becomes the existential debate of a would-
be suicide:

> Ba ddim o aberth boddi ymwybod
> A'i gymar, ing, yng nghwsg y mawr angof?
> Ai gwell yw gwybod trwy golli gobaith
> Na thagu anobaith ag anwybod?
> Pe na bai gof, oni pheidiai gofid?

> [What sacrifice is it to drown the consciousness
> And its partner, agony, in the sleep of forgetfulness?
> Is it better to know by losing hope
> Than to stifle hopelessness with unknowing?
> If there were no memory, would not worry cease?]

His decision to enter is inevitable. At the end his face is set,
emotionless. It is an act neither of bravery nor cowardice.

In 'Argoed' (1927) the suicide is real and collective. A Gaulish
tribe chooses to put itself to the sword rather than undergo the
humiliation of Roman rule.

Gwynn Jones's last major volume appeared in 1944, but comprises material composed between 1934 and 1935. *Y Dwymyn* (The Fever) is a chronicle of betrayal, sickness, violence, fear and despair, presenting a portrait of mankind 'in whom hope and doubt commingle'. The tone is set with the opening poem, 'Y Saig' (The Dish), addressed to the head of a dead fish lying on a bed of lettuce, 'and the rest of you eaten by other mouths'. The fish's own jaw is frozen in a smirk. Having lived its life avoiding the terrors of the sea its fate was to be caught by a mere worm:

> Ac onid digrif hynny?
> Diau. Chwardd.
>
> [And isn't that amusing?
> Doubtless. Laugh.]

Y Dwymyn's pessimism is tinged with decadence. In 'Y Ffenestr' (The Window) a pastoral scene—grazing cattle, scattered cottages set amid tended fields — distorts (or reverts) in the mind's eye into a wasteland red in tooth and claw; 'Ofn' (Fear) depicts contemporary man as 'an armed weakling', in thrall to a technology over which he has no control:

> I'w ddyfais a'i gyrfa y bydd ef was gorfod,
> hi a'i gyrr am na ŵyr ef ei gyrru
> na darostwng ei grym a'i medruster
> i bwyll na dyniolaeth na barn . . .
> Yn druan direol
> rhag uthrwch cynddeiriog ei weithred
> y ffy i'w ffeuau
> yn lloerig llawrudd.
>
> [To his own device he will be a slave,
> it will drive him for he knows not how to drive it
> nor how to subjugate its power and skill
> to sense and humanity and reason . . .
> Like an unruly wretch
> from the rabid awfulness of his action
> he will flee to his den
> a murderous lunatic.]

'Dynoliaeth' (Humanity) pursues the lunatic to his den. The citizens of an imperial power flee underground from an air attack to orgiastic death:

> Ac yno yn y braw a'r cynnwrf,
> wyneb yn wyneb ag angau yr enynnwyd
> yn un ias mewn mynwesau
> y nwyd rhwng deugnawd annedwydd,
> y wanc am uno cyn myned,
> brys y reddf am barhad,
> eiliad o gyd-ddialedd,
> gweithred anorfod gythrudd,
> cyd cas . . .

> [And there in the terror and tumult,
> face to face with death was engendered
> the same urge in every breast,
> the passion between two unhappy bodies,
> the desire to unite before departing,
> the urgent instinct for survival,
> a second of mutual vengeance,
> a response to irrepressible provocation,
> a hateful coupling . . .]

In the dystopia of *Y Dwymyn*, romantic love retreats into cynicism, the sick die unreconciled, exiles suffer their exile. Only in the penultimate poem, 'Y Ffin' (The Border), is the hysteria silenced. The poet arrives at 'the final limit, where life slows'. The rush and sound of the world recede. He is alone. We have followed Merlin into Broceliaunde, Madog through the unbroken surface of the ocean. The narrator stands 'on the brink of unknowing' and is afraid:

> Yna'r dolur a dawelodd . . .
> dyn, onid un ei dynged ef,
> un â phob creadur byw yn ei awr?
> minnau weithion, ai gwaeth i mi na hwythau,
> yn eu hawr, rhyw fodau aneirif,
> rhyw fydoedd dirifedi . . .?

> Trueni a hoen troeon einioes,
> mwy nid oeddynt namyn diddim,
> yn eu lle o ddyfodiad rhyw un lleddf hyder,
> yr hyder a roed i bob dim crëedig,

hwnnw a ddaw i bob peth yn ei ddydd,
i adar nef a phob creadur yn ei awr;
i ddyn, pan ymroddo ef,
o arafu ei anwadalwch a'i ryfyg,
wedi mynd o wres ei ferr dwymyn drosodd,
a'i ado ef yn ei waed oer,
yn ei dro yn druan,
o'i fwrw heb ddim ond cynhysgaeth ei oferedd;
ac erddo efô ddyfod y drugaredd fawr,
rhyfeddod y rhyfeddodau,
tawelwch y seibiant olaf . . .

[Then the pain abated . . .
man, isn't his fate the same,
as that of every living creature in its season?
I now, was it worse for me than them,
in their season, these countless beings,
these innumerable worlds . . .?

The pain and pleasure of life's adventure,
were no longer anything,
because of the arrival in their place of one solemn confidence,
the confidence given to all created things,
which comes to each one in its day,
to the birds of the air and each creature in its season;
to man when he surrenders himself,
when his fickleness and presumption cease,
when the heat of his short fever passes,
leaving him cold-blooded,
wretched in his turn,
cast out with nothing but the dowry of his vanity;
and for his sake comes the great mercy,
the wonder of wonders,
the quietness of the final rest . . .]

Head and heart send conflicting messages in Gwynn Jones's poetry. On a cerebral level he accepted the findings of science and could dismiss human consciousness as 'the uniting of grains of matter', but he drew no comfort from this analysis. To divest man of the uniqueness of his personality was to deprive him of his soul.

W. J. Gruffydd (1881–1954) shared Gwynn Jones's Romantic sensibility but fought shy of his out-and-out pessimism. He discovered what eisteddfod adjudicators used to term 'his true voice' late in life, with the publication of *Ynys yr Hud* (The Magic

Island) in 1923. His earlier volumes, *Telynegion* (Lyrics, with Silyn Roberts in 1900) and *Caneuon a Cherddi* (Songs and Poems, 1906), were clever Georgian pastiches, derivative, formulaic and cold: the work of a gifted mimic who knew how such poetry was meant to sound. He claimed in 1938, with characteristic hyperbole, that he had written nothing before the age of twenty-seven of which he was not 'heartily ashamed'. The style of *Ynys yr Hud* is coarser, the edges rougher, the tone more strident.

Primarily a critic, Gruffydd is one of the few poets of the period who felt it necessary to explain the inspiration behind his verse, the principal reason being that he was one of the few who affected to regard poetry as the product of inspiration. He saw the poet as a visionary, a man apart, living outside time and inherently moral because of the transforming capability of his vision. 'Nothing in the world lies outside the world of poetry,' he wrote in the Introduction to *Ynys yr Hud*, 'even though in itself it may be supposed prosaic, because there is nothing outside the poet's mind, and it is not the thing in itself that is poetic but the thing as the poet sees it.' When a poet proposes that his verse be read as a commentary on himself rather than on the subject-matter addressed, it is an interesting exercise to take him at his word. In fact, Gruffydd's introduction is a quasi-mystical justification for good old-fashioned, anti-puritanical populist tub-thumping. His 'vision' is Hardyesque, at its best an assertion that ordinary lives contain the stuff of tragedy, at its worst a declaration that they absolutely must. The extremes can be seen in two poems written within a year of one another. 'Y Pharisead' (The Pharisee, 1920) consists of a fatuous syllogism reiterated five times in as many quatrains. One example will suffice:

> Mae hwn yn gwario'i arian i wasanaethu'i Dduw,
> A dwys gynghori'r werin i'w dysgu sut i fyw;
> Dilychwin yw ei fywyd, a'i foes fel rhosyn gwyn,—
> Clywais nad oedd fy Arglwydd yn gweled fawr yn hyn.

> [This man spends his money in service of his God,
> And sternly counsels common folk on how to live their lives;
> His own life is without blemish, his virtue like a rose,—
> I have heard that my Lord sees little worth in this.]

The pharisee of the title is a pharisee. Not only does Gruffydd repeatedly hit us over the head with the observation, he does so with a jocose earnestness guaranteed to make the reader squirm. Like T. Gwynn Jones, when Gruffydd moves from the general to the particular, from polemic to narrative, he makes his point. 'Gwladys Rhys' (1921), unlike 'Y Pharisead', has a beginning, a middle and an end. The eponymous young woman tells her story; Gruffydd surrenders centre-stage:

> Pa beth oedd im i'w wneuthur, Gwladys Rhys,
> Merch hynaf y Parchedig Thomas Rhys,
> Gweinidog Horeb ar y Rhos? Pa beth
> Ond mynych flin ddyheu a diflas droi
> Fy llygaid draw ac yma dros y waun,
> A chodi'r bore i ddymuno nos,
> A throsi drwy'r nos hir, dan ddisgwyl bore?
> A'r gaeaf, O fy Nuw, wrth dynnu'r llen
> Dros y ffenestri bedwar yn y pnawn,
> A chlywed gwynt yn cwyno ym mrigau'r pîn,
> A gwrando ar ymddiddan nhad a mam.

> [What was there for me to do, Gwladys Rhys,
> Eldest daughter of the Reverend Thomas Rhys,
> Minister of Horeb ar y Rhos? What
> Except continually, wearily yearn and turn my bored
> Eyes back and forth across the moor,
> And wake in the morning to wish for night,
> And toss and turn through the long night, waiting for morning?
> And in the winter, Oh my God, pulling the curtain
> Across the window at four in the afternoon,
> Hearing the wind complaining in the branches of the pines,
> Listening to father and mother's conversation!]

Unlike the ventures of Gwynn Jones's verse, Gruffydd's disaffected characters retreat into themselves. Gwladus sees Someone come to the house, feels Something strange stir within her, draws the curtain for the last time and leaves home:

> Am hynny, deithiwr, yma 'rwyf yn gorwedd
> Wrth dalcen Capel Horeb,—Gwladys Rhys,
> Yn ddeg ar hugain oed, a 'nhad a 'mam
> Yn pasio heibio i'r Seiat ac i'r Cwrdd,
> Cyfarfod Gweddi, Dorcas, a phwyllgorau
> Cymdeithas Ddirwest Merched Gwynedd; yma
> Yn nyffryn angof, am nad oedd y chwa

A glywswn unwaith o'r gororau pell
Ond sŵn y gwynt yn cwyno yn y pîn.

[For that reason, traveller, here I lie
At the gable end of Horeb Chapel—Gwladys Rhys,
Thirty years old, and my mother and father
Pass by to the Fellowship and the Service,
Prayer Meeting, Dorcas and committees
Of the Gwynedd Women's Temperance Society; here
In the vale of forgetfulness, because the breath of air
I felt once from far away was only
The sound of the wind complaining in the pines.]

The poem works—*just*. It is a matter of voice. Out of her depression Gwladys contrives her own salvation. The Someone—a stock nineteenth-century conceit for a secret love—becomes for her a person so real that she follows him out into the snow to her death.

'Thomas Morgan yr Ironmonger' (1922) is another interior monologue delivered from the grave. Thomas leaves the rural paradise of his childhood 'as a fifteen-year-old lad, when lads were simple' to serve an apprenticeship in Caernarfon. He marries:

Rhoes imi galon lân ac aelwyd glyd,
A mynwes esmwyth i orffwyso 'mhen,
Ond ni ddywedais i fy rhin wrth neb,
Ond dal mewn gobaith am y dyddiau gwell
Pan gawn reteirio, a mynd eto'n ôl
I'r wlad . . .

[She gave me a pure heart and a cosy hearth,
And a smooth breast where I rested my head,
But I didn't tell my secret to anyone,
Living in hope of better days
When I could retire and go back again
To the country . . .]

For forty years his life is circumscribed by the shop, half an hour in the Red Cow with friends when work is over and occasional holidays in the Isle of Man:

Ni chefais ddysg, nac amser i drafferthu
Am anfarwoldeb, dim ond poeni weithiau
Wrth feddwl am ffarwelio gyda'r nos.

[I had no learning, nor time to bother
With immortality, I just worried sometimes
Thinking about saying goodbye at night.]

Kate Roberts, the short-story writer, has one of her characters say that 'we go through life without living it, because we are always expecting something better.' Implicit in the observation is the corollary that expectations sustain uneventful lives. Thomas's dream is never realized, of course. His only hope of immortality lies in being remembered by ageing cronies from the Red Cow passing the cemetery. The final line, *Bydd imi anfarwoldeb tra foch byw* (I shall be immortal while you live), indicates however that immortality itself is finite. In the case of Gwladys Rhys even that recognition is denied.

The poem of which Gruffydd himself was proudest appeared in *Caniadau* (1932), a collection of all the verse with which he said he was 'happy to have his name associated'. 'Y Tlawd Hwn' (This Poor Man, 1930) is the summation of what Gruffydd understood by poetic inspiration and response. The pauper of the title is the ironic name the poet gives to himself, his motivation couched in intentionally unspecific terms:

Am fod rhyw anesmwythyd yn y gwynt,
   A sŵn hen wylo yng nghuriadau'r glaw,
Ac eco'r lleddf adfydus odlau gynt
   Yn tiwnio drwy ei enaid yn ddi-daw,
A thrymru cefnfor pell ar noson lonydd
   Yn traethu rhin y cenedlaethau coll,
     A thrydar yr afonydd
   Yn deffro ing y dioddefiannau oll,—
Aeth hwn fel mudan i ryw rith dawelwch
   A chiliodd ei gymrodyr un ac un,
A'i adael yntau yn ei fawr ddirgelwch
   I wrando'r lleisiau dieithr wrtho'i hun.

[Because of some uneasiness in the wind,
   And the sound of ancient weeping in the beating of the rain,
And the echo of past doleful wretched rhymes
   Singing ceaselessly within his soul,
Because the heaving of a far-off sea on a still night
   Was telling secrets of lost generations,

> And the burble of rivers
> Was waking the agony of every suffering,—
> This man went like a mute to face some silent illusion
> And his colleagues, they retreated one by one,
> Leaving him to face the great mystery
> And listen to strange voices on his own.]

The ambiguity in 'Y Tlawd Hwn' is reminiscent of that in Gwynn Jones's 'Broseliawnd'. Gruffydd's visionary and Jones's Merlin seek refuge within their own imaginings. The creative urge in both is allied with a disposition to self-annihilation. Gruffydd's poet loses himself in the world of the Mabinogi, entranced by the sounds of the Birds of Rhiannon and lost in reverie.

Variations on the theme of retreat can be discerned in the work of a range of more popular poets. For I. D. Hooson there was vicarious escape into nature. His *Cerddi a Baledi* (Poems and Ballads, 1936) reads like Williams Parry's *Cerddi'r Gaeaf* with the latter's smouldering dread extinguished because Hooson is happy to ascribe human impulses to natural phenomena. His foxes, swallows and bluebells feel, think and act like holy innocents, prophets of a way of life to which men should aspire. A similar escapism, with theistic colouring, inspired Cynan: snowdrops are an earnest of the truth of the resurrection; 'something like the Face of God' is visible above the waves in a moonlit seascape. In his 1921 *pryddest* 'Mab y Bwthyn' (The Cottager's Son) the picture of shebeens, jazzbands and trenches is a foil the better to emphasize the simple beauty of rural values, a solid wall of corruption against which the hero can launch himself to redemption. Iorwerth Peate constructed an elaborate metaphysics of *hiraeth*, a longing for the irretrievably lost. Poetry became for him a means of fleeing the confines of the body to find his own soul. More prosaically, Crwys escaped the present by contemplating the dying embers in his own fire grate:

> Nid wy'n dlawd er maint fy nhlodi,
> Nid wy'n hŷn, nid wy'n dihoeni,
> Nid yw'n hwyr ac nid yw'n oeri
> Heno wrth y tân.

> [I am not poor for all my poverty,
> I am no older, I do not sicken,
> It is not late and does not grow cold
> Tonight by the fire.]

Enough has been said already, however, to suggest that mainstream poetry in the 1920s and 1930s was wilfully iconoclastic. All the major poets mentioned so far had a strong sense of what was seemly and took pains to question it: the cultural patriotism of O. M. Edwards gave way to a sharper political nationalism derived from Emrys ap Iwan; sexual orthodoxy was notoriously, if clumsily, assailed by young poets like Prosser Rhys and J. T. Jones; John Morris-Jones's prohibitions on the use of 'unpoetic' vocabulary (for instance, that the more euphonious *grudd* be used rather than *boch* for 'cheek') were flouted and anglicisms and dialect found their way into serious verse. Praise of God, love of Wales and the charm of beautiful girls—staples of the Georgian diet—were replaced by more complex responses. Arguably the only topic which survived intact from the pre-war period was a preoccupation with death, but never before had world-weariness been expressed with such vigour.

Even so, this iconoclasm had its limits and the poetry of the period inevitably created its own orthodoxy. Wales, having been denied its own aesthetic movement at the turn of the century, sought to rectify matters after the Great War. Poets increasingly adopted a donnish, disinterested air. It was certainly fashionable not to be politically or religiously *engagé*. Behind the self-confidence of men like Gruffydd and the rest, one senses always a detachment, a feeling that liberal humanism is less a creed than a stance by default.

In this context David Gwenallt Jones (1899–1968) can be viewed as either revolutionary or reactionary or both. He was an instinctive egalitarian Socialist, but sought to marry this instinct with Christian apologetics. 'Man has two masters,' he wrote in 1949. 'The Capitalist System on the one hand, and a God of Love on the other. Man is subjugated in slaving for his worldly master; he is elevated in serving his God. He is transformed.'

Gwenallt's own transformation was occasioned by aesthetic as well as spiritual concerns. He was born in Pontardawe, a child of the economic diaspora from the rural west to the mines and steelworks of the Swansea Valley at the turn of the century. After an early flirtation with Marx (he claimed to have sung the Red Flag as the rest of the family sang a hymn at his father's funeral), he recognized a spiritual void within himself and painstakingly constructed a personal theology, drawing on sources as diverse as

Pantycelyn, Dafydd ap Gwilym, Kierkegaard and Karl Barth. He labelled his belief system Christian Humanism, characterized by 'reason and understanding as well as grace'. It was a catch-all formula, too neat ever to be more than a compromise. During his adult life he played hide-and-seek with Quakerism, Catholicism and his parents' Nonconformism before embracing High Anglicanism. His verse reflects the zeal of the perpetual convert.

He served his Eisteddfod apprenticeship besotted with the language and imagery of Catholicism. 'Y Mynach' (The Monk, 1926) contains a long elegiac on the mysteries of the mass, and in 'Y Sant' (The Saint, 1928) ritualistic images tumble over one another. One is reminded of a second-language user littering his speech with idioms to convince others of his fluency.

In his more mature work the touch is lighter and the faith it expresses more sincere. Superficially, much in his first volume of verse, *Ysgubau'r Awen* (Sheaves of the Muse, 1939), comprising work written over the preceding six years, resembles that of his Anglo-Welsh contemporaries. Its setting is south Walian, industrial and dispossessed. The opening lines of 'Sir Forgannwg' (Glamorgan) could have come from the pen of Idris Davies or Huw Menai:

> Mor wag dy lowyr yn eu dillad gwaith
> A llwch y glo yn fwgwd ar eu pryd,
> Arian papur y gyfnewidfa faith,
> Allforion ym mhorthladdoedd gwanc y byd . . .

> [Your miners are so empty in their working clothes,
> The coal dust on their faces like a mask,
> Banknotes of the vast exchange,
> Exports through the ports of the world's greed . . .]

What sets Gwenallt apart is a quality rare in any of the poets of the period, in either language: a recognition of the need for and the existence of redemption. The poem ends:

> Y Sul a rydd amdanynt ddillad glân
> Ac yn eu hwyneb olau enaid byw,
> Ac yn y cysegr clywir yn eu cân
> Orfoledd gwerin bendefigaidd Duw;
> Tynnir y caets o waelod pwll i'r nef
> Â rhaffau dur Ei hen olwynion Ef.

[Sunday dresses them with clean clothes
And in their faces shines the light of living souls,
And in the sanctuary in their song is heard
The joy of the ordinary aristocrats of God;
The cage is pulled from the pit's depths to heaven
By the steel ropes of His ancient wheels.]

Not the happiest metaphor, perhaps, but one which conveys the balance between social realism and transcendence at the heart of his work. Gwenallt has been called 'the Eliot of Wales'; it is a telling comparison in the sense that a theistic cosmology and strong consciousness of tradition inform both men's commentary on contemporary issues. Like Eliot, too, Gwenallt distrusted Romanticism for divorcing passion from reason. What Parry-Williams, Gwyn Jones, Gruffydd and the rest had inherited from the Georgians was a presupposition that the interest in a poem was the persona of the individual. For Gwenallt individual *ennui* was self-indulgent, the poet merely the prophetic observer in what he elsewhere termed 'the blessed drama of God'. 'Y Gristnogaeth' (Christianity) condenses the epic of Good and Evil into eight frenetic quatrains, the first and last but one of which are given here:

A ddaeth Dy awr, O Dduw, Dy awr ofnadwy Di?
Ai cyflawnder yr amser yw yn ein hoes a'n heinioes ni?
Oes athrist yr Anghrist hy, awr yr her a'r trawster a'r tranc,
Awr y finegr a'r fynwent, oes dwym y ffagl a'r ystanc. . . .

Os mynni ein gwaed, o fyd, yf bob diferyn coch,
Rho'n cyrff yn ogor i'th feirch, rho'n cnawd yn soeg i'th foch,
Yr enaid a ddaw'n ôl o'r anwel, oddi wrth Grist â gwyrthiau gras;
Tynnwn y cread o'r tonnau, y byd o'i ddiddymdra bas.

[Has Your hour come, Oh God, Your awful hour?
Is our age and life the fulfilment of time?
The dreadful hour of the Antichrist, the hour of challenge,
    conceit and death,
The hour of vinegar and graveyard, the hot age of the brand
    and the stake . . .

If you demand our blood, oh world, drink every red drop,
Give our bodies as feed for your horses, our flesh as swill for
    your pigs,
The soul will return from heaven, sent by Christ with gifts of grace;

We shall save creation from the waves, the world from its
    debasement.]

'Ar Gyfeiliorn' (Astray) pursues the symmetry of opposition
between worldly corruption and divine intervention. The setting is
again the Valleys of the depression, where industrial decay serves as
a symbol for moral collapse and spiritual indifference:

Nid oes na diafol nac uffern dan loriau papur ein byd,
Diffoddwyd canhwyllau'r nefoedd a thagwyd yr angylion i gyd.

[There is no devil or hell under the paper floors of our world,
The candles of heaven are extinguished, the angels have all
    been choked.]

The final verse contains the familiar divine invocation and implies
something more:

Gosod, O Fair, Dy Seren yng nghanol tywyllwch nef,
A dangos â'th siart y llwybr yn ôl at Ei ewyllys Ef,
A disgyn rhwng y rhaffau dryslyd, a rho dy law ar y llyw,
A thywys ein llong wrthnysig i un o borthladdoedd Duw.

[Oh Mary, set Your Star in the dark heavens' midst.
And show with your chart the path back to His will,
Come down among the tangled ropes, and put your hand on
    the helm
And steer our stubborn ship into one of God's harbours.]

Gwenallt inhabits a world where words are made flesh.
Conventional imagery (drawn from both Catholic and Nonconformist traditions) is reworked and reinvigorated. Here Mary, the
Queen of Heaven and Star of the Sea, descends through confusion
to intervene in a faithless world; in the verses of 'Cymru', Wales
shelters her saints 'like chicks under the hen'; sin takes on the form
of a polecat and a serpent; Christ travels the earth 'in a caravan of
flesh'. The natural world is a reflection of divine purpose. God the
Prime Mover is not an abstraction: He creates. The language of 'Y
Duwdod' (The Godhead) may echo the Platonism of the Early
Church Fathers but the tone is closer to the simplicity of Francis of
Assisi:

Ffynnon pob bywyd a phob golau sy,
Symudydd disymud pob symud yw,
Crogodd yr heulwen yn Ei oriel fry
Yn ddarlun perffaith o wynfydedd Duw;
Plannodd y bydoedd yn ystrydoedd cain,
A pharciau rhyngddynt, ar lecynnau nef,
A'r lloer fel Eglwys Gadair rhwng y rhain,
Ar blan Ei bensaernïaeth brydferth Ef.

[Fountain of all life and all light that is,
He is the unmoving mover of all movement,
He hung the sun in his gallery above
As a perfect picture of the blessedness of God;
He planted out the worlds like elegant streets,
With parks between them, in heaven's realms,
And the moon like a Cathedral at their centre,
In accordance with the plan of His beautiful architecture.]

Gwenallt's spiritual austerity is always tempered and lightened by sensualism. On the one hand, the corruption of the world is palpable: images of dust, rust, rot and ash; civilization is 'soggy dough / Without the yeast of Christ to make it into bread'. At the same time, notably in 'Cnawd ac Ysbryd' (Flesh and Spirit), divine ordinance is cited for human pleasure:

Duw ni waharddodd inni garu'r byd,
A charu dyn a'i holl weithredoedd ef,
Eu caru â'r synhwyrau noeth i gyd,
Pob llun a lliw, pob llafar a phob llef:
Bydd cryndod yn ein gwaed pan welwn ôl
Ei fysedd crefftgar ar y cread crwn,
A berw, pan waeddwn mewn gorfoledd ffôl
Na fynnwn fywyd fel y bywyd hwn.
A phan adawo'r ysbryd wisg y cnawd
Yn blygion stiff ac oerllyd yn yr arch,
Odid na ddelo rywbryd ar ei rawd
I'w wisgo eilwaith fel dilledyn parch;
Dwyn ato'r corff, ei ffroen a'i drem a'i glyw,
I synwyruso gogoniannau Duw.
[God did not forbid us to love the world,
And to love man and all his works,
Love them with all the naked senses,
Every picture and colour, every word and cry;
There is a quaking in our blood when we see the trace

Of his deft fingers on creation . . .
And when the spirit leaves the garment of flesh
As stiff, cold folds within the grave,
No doubt it will return in time
To wear it as a dress of grace;
Bring back the body to it, its nose and eyes and ears,
To sensualize the glories of God.]

Gwenallt eventually found a meeting-place for worldly concern
and heavenly aspiration in the institution of the Church Universal,
y ddwy-un Eglwys (the two-in-one Church). His second collection,
Eples (Leaven, 1951), is discussed in the following chapter, but its
emphatic ecclesiasticism deserves mention here as the culmination
of a process begun in *Ysgubau*. Gwenallt variously states that the
Church Victorious above and the Church Militant below are the
same, an encampment on the slopes of the Mount of
Transfiguration, a company of martyrs sanctified by gas chambers,
courts and labour camps, the legacy of Christ the Carpenter:

Nid oes maen ar faen na phren ar bren
   O'r holl dai a gododd i gyd,
Ond fe erys adeiladwaith Ei eglwys gain,
A gododd gyda deuddeg o seiri coed a main,
   Tan ddiwedd y byd.

[No stone stands on stone nor plank on plank
   Of all the houses that He built,
But the structure of His fine Church remains,
   Which He raised with twelve masons in stone and wood,
   Till the end of time.]

Gwenallt had written in his 1935 poem, 'Cymru', that the very soil
of Wales was blessed with the dust of martyrs. In October of the
same year, in Alun Llywelyn-Williams's periodical, *Tir Newydd*,
Gwilym R. Jones (1903–93) acknowledged the dust but expressed
reservation about the blessing. The direct target of 'Cymru, 1935'
was the self-sufficient escapism of Gruffydd's 'Y Tlawd Hwn', but
his accusation had wider resonance:

Gwyn eu byd
dy brydyddion brwysg
a glybu ymbil pibau pêr

yn nhrybestod dy dymhestloedd,
canys eiddynt y chwedl nas dehongla cnawd . . .

Atgof a fydd dy hen ogoniant bellach—
dim ond atgof
yn ymdonni fel cysgod hunllef
dros fôr tywyll cwsg.

[Blessed are they,
your intoxicated poets
who heard the plea of pure pipes
in the commotion of your storms,
for theirs is the legend which flesh will not interpret . . .

Your ancient glory will now be a memory—
only a memory
rippling like the shadow of a nightmare
across a dark sea of sleep.]

The work of Cardiff-born Alun Llywelyn-Williams (1913–88) contains perhaps the fullest expression of a growing impatience with stylized Romanticism. He was to write in 1937, on the pages of Gruffydd's own *Llenor* no less, that poets of the previous generation were digging a hole in the sand to bury their heads. In the strictest sense of the word, he argued, contemporary Welsh poetry simply did not exist: there was no awareness of the imminent danger which the politics of the 1930s posed for European (and by extension, Welsh) civilization, culture, morality, religion and industry. Poetry had become 'a consecrated cell in which to pray to the Virgin Mary and the saints'.

As a poet Llywelyn-Williams's model was the aesthetic socialism of Auden, Spender, C. Day Lewis and Rex Warner, his motivation a concern that Wales's urban heritage be given due poetic consideration. Curiously, however, his repudiation of religiosity and the rural idyll led him to produce genuinely lyrical verse. *Cerddi* (Poems, 1942), his first published collection, contains work dating back to 1934. In some senses it harks back to themes touched upon a generation before. 'Cefn Cwm Bychan', for instance, a meditation on love and mortality, calls to mind both R. Williams Parry's 'Cysur Henaint' and Gruffydd's 'Trystan ac Esyllt':

Dywedir: derfydd y rhain oll. Ni wn—
odid nad erys o'r cyd-yfed hir,
y drachtio dwfn o'r pêr, hiraethus win,
o'r profi ar dy wefus hedd di-fraw,
ryw atgof egwan o'n munudau ni
i nofio'r awel, genedlaethau a ddaw.

[It is said: all these must pass. I know not—
surely there will remain of the long, shared sip,
of the deep draught of sweet, forgetful wine,
of the taste of careless peace upon your lips,
some feeble memory of our minutes
to float on the breeze in future generations.]

Even when the subject-matter is contemporary—the threat and actuality of war—the response is the timeless one of the lyricist. Turmoil in Europe is an intrusion into a more civilized way of life, a suspension of friendships, a blight on the growth of love. The agony of 'Rhyngom a Ffrainc' (Between Us and France) is that books have lain unread on their shelves and that three springtimes have blossomed 'whose secret will never be repeated'. Taken out of context, there is nothing in the sonnets 'Gan Fod yr Angau'n Ymyl' (Since Death is at Hand) or 'Pan Rodiwn Eto'n Rhydd' (When We Roam Freely Again), for example, to suggest that they are war poems at all. The occasion of the disruption may be specific, but its effects are seen *sub specie aeternitatis*. 'Cui Bono?' could have come from the pen of T. Gwynn Jones twenty years earlier:

Mwy dall na'r dall yw'r drem a welodd farw'r
ffydd a bylwyd gan ystrywiau'r byd,
troi'r gwir yn anwir, a'r mwyn air yn arw,
pob cred yn w'radwydd, a phob cerdd yn fud.
Pa fore'r Pasg 'ddwg eto'i ryfedd rin
I gynnau'r gwanwyn yn y llygaid blin?

[Blinder than blind is the gaze that saw the death
of a faith besmirched by the world's deceit,
the truth made false, and the fair word rough,
all belief disgrace, all songs dumb.
What Easter morning will bring again its mystery
to kindle the spring in weary eyes?]

A comparison of Llywelyn-Williams's 'Cui Bono' with, say, Gwynn Jones's 'Madog' or Parry-Williams's 1919 sonnets reveals the extent to which a tendency prevailed throughout the period to look upon crisis in this universal way. Robert Williams wrote in 1940 of 'Armageddon, which makes the world / And this life into one great question.' By the end of the 1930s the nature of the questions had changed, yet a lyrical predisposition to emphasize individual experience prevented the emergence of a truly social response. The poetic mainstream was either indifferent or incapable. It was in the end left to others—and too late. I shall close with Edgar H. Thomas, an Anglesey schoolmaster who would doubtless be surprised to find himself bracketed with Gruffydd, Williams Parry, Gwynn Jones and the rest. His 1944 sonnet, 'Gwleidyddion, 1919–39' (Politicians, 1919–39) expresses a shared helplessness acutely felt during the preceding two decades; it is easy to read it in hindsight as a commentary on lost poetic opportunities:

> A rhag mor fyr eich cof am rai a aeth
> Ym mherigl einioes gynt ar fôr a thir,
> Wele, ar sathr eu hil ddiniwed, daeth
> Gaea'r amseroedd yn y dyddiau ir;
> Bellach, wŷr stad y gwledydd, a fu'n nyddu'r
> Dynged a'n daliodd, o feddyliau gŵyr,
> A droech chwi raid yn gysur, a'n llonyddu
> Am angof doe, a'r edifeirwch hwyr,
> Am fod y plaeniau dur yn poeri'u tân
> Ar hen ac ifanc heddiw'n ddiwahân?

> [And since your memory is so short of those who went
> To risk their lives on sea and land
> Behold, on the footsteps of their innocent race, has come
> A time of winter to these green days;
> And now, rulers of the world's estate, who wove the
> Fate that held us, from your twisted minds,
> Will you make need a comfort, and mollify us
> Over yesterday's forgetfulness and late repentance,
> Because the steel planes spit their fire today
> On young and old without discrimination?]

FURTHER READING

Translations of a number of poems referred to can be found in D. M. and E. M. Lloyd (eds), *A Book of Wales* (London and Glasgow, 1953), and R. Gerallt Jones (ed.), *Poetry of Wales, 1930–1970* (Llandysul, 1974).

T. Robin Chapman, '"O Weledigaeth i Waeledigaeth"', *Taliesin* 87 (Hydref 1994), 36–52.

W. Beynon Davies, *Thomas Gwynn Jones* (Cardiff, 1970).

Bedwyr L. Jones, '"Yr Academig Dost"', *Taliesin* 76 (Mawrth 1992), 32–47.

Idem, *R. Williams Parry* (Cardiff, 1972).

D. Tecwyn Lloyd, 'Llenyddiaeth Cyni a Rhyfel' in J. E. Caerwyn Williams (ed.), *Ysgrifau Beirniadol* 4 (Dinbych, 1968), 153–87.

Dyfnallt Morgan, *D. Gwenallt Jones* (Cardiff, 1972).

T. J. Morgan, *W. J. Gruffydd* (Cardiff, 1970).

John Rowlands, 'Bardd y Gaeaf', *Taliesin* 50 (Nadolig 1984), 9–33.

Gerwyn Wiliams, 'Rhamantiaeth Realaidd Cynan', *Taliesin* 76 (Mawrth 1992), 105–12.

CHAPTER 4

POETRY 1939–1970

ROBERT RHYS

The year 1936 is perceived by many as marking a more significant watershed in the development of Welsh-language culture than the beginning of the Second World War. And 1936 in this context refers not to Spain nor to any other troubled European state, but rather to Penyberth in Llŷn, site of the bombing school where the Nationalist Party that had been founded in 1925 performed its most spectacular example of direct action. Several members were involved in setting the buildings alight in September 1936, but responsibility was assumed by three of the party's most prominent figures, Lewis Valentine, D. J. Williams and Saunders Lewis. After a Caernarfon jury had failed to reach a verdict the three were retried at the Old Bailey where they were sentenced to terms of imprisonment. As a result the University College of Swansea sacked its distinguished lecturer, Saunders Lewis, thus elevating him to martyr status. The 'Fire in Llŷn' and its political fallout changed utterly the tenor and dynamic of Welsh cultural life.

Tensions and divisions which became apparent in 1936 were deepened and exacerbated by differing attitudes to the war effort and by a bitter by-election for the University of Wales parliamentary seat in 1943, when W. J. Gruffydd, professor of Welsh at Cardiff and eminent poet, critic and editor, was persuaded to stand as an official Liberal candidate against the charismatic Lewis. After 1936, it is argued, significant Welsh-language poetry sheds its romantic fetish with death and *hiraeth* along with its fashionable cynicism, and becomes a vibrant, committed poetry written by people who inhabit, as Saunders Lewis said of Gwenallt in 1940, 'a cosmos, a world which has meaning, a world which has been given an aim and an objective'. Viewed from a formalist perspective we find that this new wine demanded new bottles, and that all the major poets were intent on forging a new poetic idiom free of the stultifying influence of Romantic and Georgian diction and imagery.

The cultural *zeitgeist* of the war years was captured on the pages of *Baner ac Amserau Cymru*, the weekly newspaper owned by the writer Kate Roberts and her husband Morris Williams, which carried a leading article by Saunders Lewis in every issue as well as reviews by Lewis and others and important new poetry. In reviewing Gwenallt's slim volume of verse, *Cnoi Cil* (Ruminating) in 1943 Lewis again attempted to define Gwenallt's importance as the harbinger of a new age:

> the days of the lonely poet who draws his material from his own emotional life are numbered. European civilization, the history and wealth of social life, the convictions and spiritual nourishment that Christianity has to offer men, those things which infuse the lives of men in Wales with meaning and fulness, the reader comes into contact with all these things in the opening poems of this book.

Lewis and Gwenallt, of course, shared the same sociopolitical convictions, and Gwenallt's poems give unambiguous support to the Welsh Nationalist Party's anti-industrial policies. In his view, an exploited and deluded proletariat can be healed and restored only by a Christian nationalism. In the sonnet 'Cwm Rhondda' the poet reflects in the octet on the industrial and social history of the valley; it is a history of capitalist exploitation and socialist betrayal. In the sestet the workers are addressed directly, and urged in visual imagery typical of Gwenallt's metaphorical technique to climb from the valley floor to the living hills, the physical ascension imagizing a spiritual one:

> Dringwch, a'r milgwn wrth eich sawdl, i'r bryn,
> I wlad y ffermydd a'r ffynhonnau dŵr,
> A gwelwch yno ein gwareiddiad gwyn
> A dyrnau Rhys ap Tewdwr a Glyndŵr;
> Ac ar ei gopa Gristionogaeth fyw
> Yn troi Cwm Rhondda'n ddarn o ddinas Duw.
>
> [Climb, greyhounds at your heels, to the hill,
> To the land of farms and water springs,
> And see there our blessed civilization
> And the fists of Rhys ap Tewdwr and Glyndŵr;

And on its summit a living Christianity
Transforming the Rhondda into a part of the City of God.]

Not everyone shared this vision, indeed *Cnoi Cil* was a controversial volume, savagely denounced by the young Marxist critic Tecwyn Lloyd for its reactionary content, but defended by Pennar Davies as expressing a welcome Christian realism. Gwenallt, whose first volume of note, *Ysgubau'r Awen* (The Sheaves of the Muse) had been published in 1939, went on to write some of his best-known and most widely appreciated poems during the 1940s; these were published in the opening section of his volume *Eples* (Leaven) in 1951.

In the opening lines of the first poem 'Y Meirwon' (The Dead) Gwenallt reflects that after reaching the age of fifty one is able to recognize clearly the people and places that have moulded one's life. There follows a sequence of poems, all physically located in the industrial south, which offer us the poet's reflective assessment of his own people and times. 'Y Dirwasgiad' (The Depression) is exceptional in that it does nothing but record the ironic fact that ecological renewal and social collapse coexist as consequences of economic conditions. The other poems in this group imply or proclaim an unambiguous Christian worldview. 'Colomennod' (Doves) opens with an image of the workers, released from their joyless, soul-destroying dayjobs being restored and humanized by their interest in racing pigeons:

COLOMENNOD

Bugeiliai'r gweithwyr eu colomennod gyda'r hwyr
Wedi slafdod y dydd, ar y Bryn,
Pob cwb â'i lwyfan yn nhop yr ardd
Yn gollwng ei gwmwl gwyn.

Fe'u gyrrid i Ogledd Cymru ac i Loegr
A'u gollwng o'r basgedi i'r ne',
Ond dychwelent o ganol y prydferthwch pell
At ein tlodi cymdogol yn y De.

Amgylchynent yn yr wybr y pileri mwg
Gan roi lliw ar y llwydni crwm;
Talpiau o degwch ynghanol y tawch;
Llun yr Ysbryd Glân uwch y Cwm.

Yr Ysbryd Glân yn sancteiddio'r mwg,
A throi gweithiwr yn berson byw,
Y gyfundrefn arian yn treiglo yn nhrefn gras
A'r Undebau yn rhan o deulu Duw.

[DOVES

The workers would shepherd their pigeons in the evening
After the toil of the day, on the hill.
Each coop with its platform at the top of the garden
Releasing its white cloud.

They would be sent to North Wales and to England
Released from their baskets to the heavens
But they'd return from the faraway beauty
To our neighbourly poverty in the South.

In the sky they would encircle the pillars of smoke
Adding colour to the bowed greyness:
Pieces of beauty in the midst of the haze,
Holy Spirit's image above the valley.

The Holy Spirit sanctifying the smoke,
Transforming worker into living person,
The financial system running in the order of grace,
And the Unions part of the household of God.]

The pigeons, like the greyhounds, pigs and gardens of other poems,
are humanizing agents; significantly, they are a link with the land,
with a rural, pre-industrial past. But in this poem the pigeon is also
a dove ('colomen' covers both), the symbol of the Holy Spirit, the
only regenerative agency that can transform and renew industrial
society.

Gwenallt has been referred to as a truly national poet because of
his empathy with both rural and industrial communities, and
because of the way, in Ned Thomas's words, that 'his religion and
his rebelliousness fit a Welsh pattern'. In another of the *Eples*
poems, 'Sir Forgannwg a Sir Gaerfyrddin' (Glamorganshire and
Carmarthenshire), Gwenallt's analysis of his own dualistic cultural
inheritance becomes a song of praise to Christianity as a creed that
can envelop and use all that is best in both traditions.

Sir Forgannwg a Sir Gaerfyrddin

Tomos Lewis o Dalyllychau,
A swn ei forthwyl yn yr efail fel clychau
Dros y pentref a'r fynachlog ac elyrch y llyn;
Tynnai ei emyn fel pedol o'r tân,
A'i churo ar einion yr Ysbryd Glân
A rhoi ynddi hoelion Calfaria Fryn.

Dôi yntau, Williams o Bantycelyn,
Yn Llansadwrn, at fy mhenelin,
I'm dysgu i byncio yn rhigolau ei gân;
Ond collwn y brefu am Ei wynepryd Ef
Ar ben bocs sebon ar sgwâr y dref
A dryllid Ei hyfrydlais gan belen y crân.

Ni allai'r ddiwydiannol werin
Grwydro drwy'r gweithfeydd fel pererin,
A'i phoced yn wag a'r baich ar ei gwar:
Codem nos Sadwrn dros gyfiawnder ein cri
A chanu nos Sul eich emynau chwi:
Mabon a Chaeo; Keir Hardie a Chrug-y-bar.

Y mae rhychwant y Groes yn llawer mwy
Na'u Piwritaniaeth a'u Sosialaeth hwy,
Ac y mae lle i ddwrn Karl Marcs yn Ei Eglwys Ef:
Cydfydd fferm a ffwrnais ar Ei ystad,
Dyneiddiaeth y pwll glo, duwioldeb y wlad:
Tawe a Thywi, Canaan a Chymru, daear a nef.

[Glamorganshire and Carmarthenshire

Tomos Lewis of Talyllychau,
The sound of his hammer in the smithy like bells
Ringing over village and abbey and the swans on the lake;
He'd pull his hymn like a shoe from the fire,
Beat it on the Holy Spirit's anvil,
And place in it the nails of Calvary Hill.

He would come, Williams of Pantycelyn,
In Llansadwrn, to be at my elbow,
To teach me to sing in the grooves of his song;
But I'd lose the panting after His countenance
On the soapbox in the town square,
And His pleasant voice would be shattered by the ball of
    the crane.

The industrial proletariat couldn't
Wander through the works like a pilgrim,
Empty in pocket and with burden on back:
Saturday night we'd proclaim a cry of justice,
And Sunday night sing your hymns.
Mabon and Caeo; Keir Hardie and Crugybar.

The span of the Cross is greater by far
Than their Puritanism and Socialism,
And there is room for Karl Marx's fist in His Church:
Farm and furnace can cohabit His estate,
Coalpit's humanism, countryside's godliness:
Tawe and Tywi, Canaan and Cymru, heaven and earth.]

This poem, like many of Gwenallt's, is likely to be the object of
vigorous reappraisal as interpretative communities who do not
share the poet's worldview subject his work to a more rigorous
analysis than has been the case so far. Although the present writer
shares the poet's worldview this poem seems to me likely to face the
deconstructionist charge that poets use rhetorical devices in order
to conceal tensions and inconsistencies. Gwenallt's ability to
persuade his readers of the validity of his cultural and religious
analysis is achieved by stunning use of imagery and allusion to the
hymns of Thomas Lewis and Williams Pantycelyn, common and
resonant cultural currency at the time but not so to later
generations. It could be argued that the stylistic devices, alliterative
antithesis and parallelism in particular, try to spellbind us into
accepting a simplistic and distorted picture of the respective
cultural features of Gwenallt's native county, Glamorganshire, and
the idealized rural Carmarthenshire of his forefathers and his
school holidays. (For Carmarthenshire, read the Towy Valley, not
the industrial valleys of Aman and Gwendraeth whose cultural and
political patterns had far more in common with the Tawe Valley.)
And yet it cannot be denied that the poem is a powerful and
evocative expression of the tensions Gwenallt felt bound to resolve
in the course of his intellectual and spiritual pilgrimage.

The Companion to Welsh Literature closes its entry on Gwenallt
by comparing him with Idris Davies as a poet who has expressed
the experience of living in an industrial society. This is a
representative but statistically misleading comment, since industrial
images and locations play a relatively minor role in his work (only

some 10 per cent of his poems can be labelled in any way 'industrial'), and a comment that reflects a desire on behalf of his readership for a more modern and industrial poetry. In his last two volumes, *Gwreiddiau* (Roots, 1959) and *Y Coed* (The Trees), published posthumously in 1969, the Christian convictions and Jeremaic commentaries are more prominent than ever, although it has been argued that the poet's figurative imagination and stylistic vigour are on the wane. This judgement may prove to be a premature one, since it seems to me that in the poems of the 1950s in particular Gwenallt is a mature, composed craftsman producing a series of magisterial pronouncements on man's estate.

The 1940s also saw the significant development of a poet whose prophetic voice was more reminiscent of Isaiah. The war years were traumatic ones for the Pembrokeshire poet, Waldo Williams; private grief, the death of his wife, Linda, in 1943, compounded the anguish of a committed pacifist who believed in the innate goodness of man and who saw his fellowmen in wartime as deluded pawns in a militaristic power game. Although he came to align himself with the Welsh Nationalist Party during these years, his views as a left-wing Christian socialist and Nonconformist were in marked contrast to those of Gwenallt and Saunders Lewis. For all his personal tribulations the war years were fruitful ones in his poetic progression. By 1946 his transformation from derivative lyricist and writer of light verse into a complex, challenging poet, author of the first genuinely 'difficult' poems of the century, was well advanced. His first war poem, 'Y Tŵr a'r Graig' (The Tower and the Rock) had been written in 1938 as a response to a motion put forward in the House of Lords calling for the introduction of conscription. In it he grounded his conventional socialist views on the brotherhood of man and the brutalizing power of the modern nation state in his own land of Pembrokeshire. Williams ('Waldo' always to the Welsh-speaking reader) had been born in Haverfordwest in 1904, but had not become a fluent Welsh-speaker until his schoolmaster father had taken his family across the Landskerline to Mynachlogddu in 1911. The family home then moved to Clunderwen, and it was from this vantage point that the poet was inspired by two objects visible on the skyline to the east. Roch Castle, filtered through the poet's imagination, became the tower, symbol of military might and state oppression. The rock is the Plumstone near Camrose, symbol of the eternal and transcendent values. 'Y Tŵr a'r Graig' is a long *cywydd*, unashamedly polemic and prophetic in tone, and in it the poet realized that he could imbue his native landscape with symbolic resonance in order to propagate his own brand of socialist metaphysics. It praises the virtues of *y werin* (the common people), condemns the destructive influence of a militaristic and imperialist state, and projects a transcendent vision of a future when the rock, and Waldo was well aware of the image's scriptural connotations, will have outlived the tower. The Landsker castles, of which Roch is one, were old symbols of past oppression; the poet now saw his beloved Pembrokeshire landscape being scarred by more contemporary ones, namely the military institutions at Brawdy and Castle Martin and Trecŵn. In his poetic imagination Pembrokeshire, land of St David and of idealized co-operative communities, becomes a battleground between the people and the coercive state machine, indeed between the cosmic forces of good and evil. Many of Waldo's important poems from 1939 onwards survey this battleground.

When the army commandeered thousands of acres of land in the Castle Martin area in 1939 Waldo's dismay at the prospect of land formerly used as winter pasture by the hillfarmers of Preseli becoming a practice ground for tanks was recorded in the *cywydd* 'Daw'r wennol yn ôl i'w nyth' (The swallow will return to its nest); the poem is an elegy to a shattered and depopulated community. Reworking a familiar *topos* within his native poetic tradition, that of the empty, abandoned hearth, he paints a black picture of social displacement:

> Tewi'r iaith ar y trothwy
> A miri'r plant, marw yw'r plwy.
>
> [The language falls silent on the doorstep,
> And the children's merriment. The parish is dead.]

But the apparent finality of this assessment is rejected by a poet who proclaims a vaticination which is the illogical and transcendent creation of his imagination:

> Gaeaf ni bydd tragyfyth,
> Daw'r wennol yn ôl i'w nyth.

[Winter will not be eternal,
The swallow will return to its nest]

The Irish poet A.E.'s definition of a prophet as one who judges the politics of time in the light of the politics of eternity is certainly true of Waldo Williams.

'Diwedd Bro' (End of a Neighbourhood) is another 1939 poem, and one of his darkest ones; not a beam of prophetic light is allowed to penetrate the gloom that descends upon the poet as he once again ponders the fate of the displaced and the conscripted. Much of the poem's power and poignancy is produced by the reworking of one of the Mabinogi tales located in Dyfed. In the original tale a shower of mist, *cawod niwl*, descended on Manawydan and his companions, leaving them in an unhabited desolation. The mist is used as an image to convey the state's ability to confuse and mislead its subjects. 'Ar Weun Cas' Mael' (On Puncheston Common) was written at a time of great personal stress in the spring of 1942. Waldo had appeared as a conscientious objector at a tribunal, and had been misled into believing that his dismissal as teacher at Puncheston School was imminent. In the poem the poet walks, a lonely, troubled soul on Puncheston Moor and is inspired by the signs of spring; the gorse bushes are in flower, and the skylark, always a potent symbol of hope in his poetry, sings above. Both are flourishing in adverse circumstances, inspiring him to do likewise. The poem goes on to suggest that the physical environment has the ability to shape men's values and actions, and there is something sad, pathetic even, in the poem's apostrophic appeal to natural objects to bring us back to a primitive nobility which a fallen humanity can never regain. The pacifist's frustration is evident again in the angry 1943 poem, 'Gŵyl Ddewi' (St David's Day). The saint's headland has been colonized by arms dump and aerodrome, and the Nonconformist *gwerin* in whom Waldo placed so much faith are caught up in the madness of war. The poet can do nothing but appeal to the 'power of David' to come as a tempest to sweep away all the tents of Mamon. In many of these poems the poetic stance adopted is a Romantic one which believes in the redemptive and transforming power of the poetic imagination. Although many readers will not find Waldo's analysis and arguments persuasive, his tortured efforts to reconcile a naive belief in the goodness of man with the grim realities of wartime resulted in a body of moving and important poems. The most important of all is probably 'Preseli' written in 1946 when Waldo was employed as a casual farmworker in the county of Huntingdon. It is an exile's poem, written as tribute and exhortation to the people of the Preseli hills in north Pembrokeshire. The political context is once again paramount. The War Office had announced its intention to use a large area in the Preseli Hills for military purposes, thus threatening everything Waldo held dear, and on this occasion his views were not minority ones. Various groups joined in protest, and the scheme was abandoned. In the poem the threat to Preseli is a threat to the values of brotherhood, to a civilized order that has evolved over a long period, a threat even to the poet's identity. This is expressed in a condensed, vigorous style which in rhythm and imagery is far removed from the popular lyrics that had first brought the poet to national attention. The final call to action became a battlecry for a later generation of Welsh-language activists. Here are the final two stanzas:

> Fy Nghymru, a bro brawdoliaeth, fy nghri, fy nghrefydd,
> Unig falm i fyd, ei chenhadaeth, ei her,
> Perl yr anfeidrol awr yn wystl gan amser,
> Gobaith yr yrfa faith ar y drofa fer.

> Hon oedd fy ffenestr, y cynaeafu a'r cneifio,
> Mi welais drefn yn fy mhalas draw.
> Mae rhu, mae rhaib drwy'r fforest ddiffenestr.
> Cadwn y mur rhag y bwystfil, cadwn y ffynnon rhag y baw.

> [My Wales, and land of brotherhood, my cry, my religion,
> The world's only balm, her mission, her challenge,
> Pearl of the infinite hour held hostage by time,
> Hope of the long course on the short turning.

> This was my window, the harvesting and the shearing.
> I saw order in my palace yonder.
> There is roar, there is rape through the windowless forest.
> Let us guard the wall against the beast, let us guard the well
>   against the mire.]

Waldo's development as a poet continued right up to the publication of his only volume of serious verse, *Dail Pren* (Leaves of the Tree) in 1956. During these years his poetry became increasingly allusive and challenging, a progression seen most markedly in two difficult autobiographical and metaphysical poems, 'Cwmwl Haf' (A Summer Cloud) and the extensively discussed 'Mewn Dau Gae' (In Two Fields). Both meditate upon the personal and cosmic significance of childhood experiences. Waldo said of the experience reflected upon in 'Mewn Dau Gae': 'It was in the gap between the two fields around forty years ago that I realized suddenly, vividly, in specific personal circumstances, that men were, first and foremost, brothers.' The content of this 'mystical' experience was entirely consistent with his family's religious and political stance, and the vision of the universal brotherhood of man projected in the poem's second half (critics divide the six stanzas equally between singular and plural, personal and collective, or memory and vision) manages to refer to the everyday co-operative patterns of Preseli farm-workers as well as awaiting in apocalyptic and millenarian tones the coming of the 'Brenin Alltud', the Exiled King. 'Mewn Dau Gae' is regarded by many critics as Waldo's greatest poem and one of the major Welsh poems of the century; rigorous close readings have been supplied by Bedwyr Lewis Jones, Gwyn Thomas and Dafydd Elis Thomas, but perhaps the most significant critical response to this poem, and to Waldo's poetry in general, has been Ned Thomas's attempt to locate the poet within the early Romantic strain which 'held together the hope of social transformation and poetry springing from the individual heart'.

The third important poet of the 1940s was Saunders Lewis; he published at least three poems which lay a claim to greatness during the decade; 'Y Dilyw 1939' (The Deluge 1939), first published in the slim collection, *Byd a Betws* (The World and the Church), in 1942 is a major poem, perceived ideological blemishes notwithstanding; 'Mair Fadlen' (Mary Magdalen) of 1944 has been nominated as the finest poem of the century by Bobi Jones; and his majestic elegy to the great Welsh historian Sir J. E. Lloyd, 'Marwnad Syr John Edward Lloyd' (1948) has been universally praised. Lewis's definition of great poetry in his 1947 essay 'The Essence of Welsh Poetry' sets out his objective as a poet, and can fairly be said to have been fulfilled in the poems mentioned: 'Poetry is great and classical when a high seriousness of function in society and profound philosophical content meet with a form that is unique and subtle and richly expressive.' Since his sociopolitical views are

often described as traditionalist and reactionary it is easy to
overlook the fact that Lewis was one of the main promoters of
modernism in Welsh poetic circles. (In the European context, of
course, right-wing politics and modernist poetics were no
strangers.) His revealing review of Keidrych Rhys's anthology
Modern Welsh Poetry in 1946 suggests that he felt more than a hint
of frustration that 'the enemy', as he then referred to the Anglo-
Welsh poets, were fulfilling his own agenda to a greater extent than
his Welsh-speaking colleagues. He blamed a poetic culture that
could not free itself from the shackles of Romanticism. 'The reason
why Welsh poetry is stuck in the old rhythms, and why so many
poets and critics cannot understand recent developments in rhythm
and figurative language, is that they still inhabit the early romantic
period.' During the 1920s Lewis had urged Welsh-language writers
to reject English influences and ground their aesthetics in the native
and European traditions. His own poetry conformed with these
aims without rejecting the possibilities offered by modernism. *Byd a
Betws* sees him working the traditional modes of the Welsh bards,
eulogy and satire, and the satire is often of a vituperative strain,
'succinct, savage and scurrilous' in Gwyn Thomas's words. The
satire is aimed towards the world, towards those aspects of Welsh
life and Western civilization which Lewis found repulsive. The
objects worthy of praise are God's creation, joyfully celebrated in a
number of poems, and God's church. Many of the poems also
contain an autobiographical subtext which makes them all the
more compelling. In 'Mabon' (1946) and 'Caer Arianrhod'
(Arianrhod's Fortress or The Milky Way, 1947) both written at a
time when Lewis was suffering from political burnout, we see
personal disillusion and frustration expressed in richly textured
poems which make resonant use of myth and imagery. 'Caer
Arianrhod', subtitled 'Owain's soliloquy before meeting the Abbot'
refers to a tale told of Owain Glyndŵr meeting the abbot of Valle
Crucis near Llangollen early one morning on Berwyn Mountain.
The abbot is said to have replied to Owain's words, 'You are up
early' by saying that it was Owain who had risen early, in fact a
hundred years before his time. And with those words Owain is said
to have disappeared.

CAER ARIANRHOD
(Ymson Owain cyn cyfarfod a'r Abad)

Gwelais y nos yn cau ei haden dros y waun,
Dros brin fythynnod brau, braenar, anfynych gŵys,
A daeth y sêr a chaer Arianrhod, firagl dwys,
I dasgu plu'r ffurfafen â'u mil llygaid paun.

Taenais aden fy mreuddwyd drosot ti, fy ngwlad;
Codaswn it—O, pes mynasit—gaer fai bêr;
Ond un a'r seren wib, deflir o blith y sêr
I staenio'r gwyll â'i gwawr a diffodd, yw fy stad.

[ARIANRHOD'S FORTRESS

I saw the night close its wing over the moorland,
Over a few brittle crofts, fallow, infrequent furrows,
And the stars came, and the Milky Way, sombre miracle,
To spatter the firmament's feathers with its thousand peacock eyes.

I spread the wing of my dream over you, my country;
I would have built you—Oh, had you but desired it-a fortress fair;
But to be like the shooting star, cast out from among the stars
To stain the gloom with its dawn and then to die out, that's my lot.]

Not all Welsh poets were pacifists or political Nationalists. Of those who saw action during the Second World War the most significant poet is Alun Llywelyn-Williams. Born and bred in Cardiff, Llywelyn-Williams studied Welsh under W. J. Gruffydd in his home city and after graduating edited a new literary magazine, *Tir Newydd* ('New Ground', a title that probably echoes Geoffrey Grigson's *New Voices*) in the latter part of the 1930s. His tentative, meditative reflections on the crises of the thirties, on his wartime experiences, on the drift of post-war life in general and on more domestic affairs strike a very different chord to the conviction poetry of many of his contemporaries, and his urban background and manner might lead us to expect a different, less traditional voice. This is only partially true; author of a masterly study of Welsh Romantic poetry at the turn of the century, Llywelyn-Williams's own idiom seems at times to owe too audible a debt to the poetry of Gruffydd, Gwyn Jones and Williams Parry. In his best poems, however, we are aware of a powerful poetic personality searching for, and celebrating, 'y golau yn y gwyll', (the light in the

gloom), the phrase which Llywelyn-Williams used as title of his
collected poems in 1979. The 1950s poem, 'Taith i Lety'r Eos' (A
Journey to Llety'r Eos), is one of his finest. It describes a journey
made in winter to the home of his sister and brother-in-law, Llety'r
Eos, literally 'the nightingale's hospice' in Llansannan in
Denbighshire. It is a wonderfully evocative description of a winter
night's car journey, but it is also an image of twentieth-century
man's troubled, nervous search for security and solace, and of
cultured society's ability, in the poet's opinion, to provide it,
rebuffing the 'oppressive silence' of a threatening environment.

TAITH I LETY'R EOS

Ni chân yr eos heno'n siwr mewn nos eiraog:
dirgelwch yw sut y mentrodd y cantor llwyd erioed,
ryw hafau anhygoel gynt, ar dro mor bell o'r coed
gwastadol, mor agos at nefoedd welw Hiraethog.

Wyth gan troedfedd fry, dechreua'r eira lynu, daw'r
nos yn olau; hyd y cloddiau gwyn sglefria lampau mawr
y car yn esmwyth, ond gwichia'r olwynion 'gochel!'
Arafwn, a throi'n garcus wrth y groesffordd uchel.

Rhythwn o'n daearen gyfeiriedig ar burdeb
bydysawd y ffriddoedd distaw; llithra'r llidiardau
caeedig heibio o un i un, a llinellau
llwyd beudy a bwthyn yn bwrw cwsg i'w ceudeb.

Tywyll didrydar yw'r llwyn gwarchodol ar ael y bryn;
ond trwy'r llidiard gwahoddus olaf, disgleiria'r lawnt
yn llain ddifrychni, ac ymffurfia'r tŷ y tu hwnt
yn gyfandir goddefgar o'r goresgyniad gwyn.

Pan saif y modur wrth y porth, pan agorir y drws,
teflir mudandod llethol yr eira yn ôl i'r nos
gan leisiau'r croeso, a chan barabl siriol y tân
a golau'r gwmnïaeth ar aelwyd hafoty'r gân.

[JOURNEY TO LLETY'R EOS

The nightingale will certainly not sing in this snowy night:
it's a mystery how the grey songster ever ventured,
incredible summers ago, so far from the trees of the lowland,
So near to Hiraethog's pallid heaven.

At eight hundred feet, the snow begins to stick,
the night is lit up; along the white hedges the car's big lamps
Skate easily, but the wheels squeal 'take care!'
We slow down, and turn gingerly at the high crossroads.

We stare out from our directed earth-mobile on the pure
universe of the quiet fields; the closed gates
slide by one by one, and the grey lines
of cowshed and cottage cast sleep into their hollow.

The sheltering bush on the brow of the hill is dark, without
    song;
but through the last welcoming gate, the lawn dazzles,
a spotless square, and the house takes shape beyond it,
out of the white conquest, a tolerant continent.

When the motor stops at the porch, when the door is opened,
the snow's oppressive silence is thrown back into the night
by the voices of greeting, by the cheerful chatter of the fire
and the light of companionship on the hearth of the
    summerhouse of song.]

   By the end of the 1940s two new voices had emerged who were to
become two of the most productive and controversial poets of the
latter part of the century. Although they were poetic contemporaries, Euros Bowen, born in 1904, was twenty-five years older
than Robert Maynard (Bobi) Jones. Despite being of poetic stock
Bowen only came to poetry in middle age; he had studied art before
following the not unpopular path among nationalists away from a
Nonconformist upbringing towards a more aesthetically pleasing
church, in his case the Church in Wales. He spent the years covered
in this chapter as rector of Llangywair and Llanuwchllyn parishes
near Bala. A committed nationalist and supporter of Saunders Lewis
during the war years, Bowen, along with the irrepressible valleys
scholar-poets J.Gwyn Griffiths and Pennar Davies, founded a new
literary magazine, *Y Fflam* (The Flame) in 1946, one of its aims
being to provide a forum and platform for those who felt that they
could no longer support W. J. Gruffydd's *Y Llenor* (The Writer).
Bowen's first faltering steps as a poet were taken on the pages of *Y
Fflam*, and before 1950 a new generation of poets had been given the
encouragement of publication. As well as Bobi Jones and a certain
R. S. Thomas who would make his mother tongue his poetic

medium, Rhydwen Williams, T. Glynne Davies and Gareth Alban Davies, all poets whose work deserves greater attention than this essay will be able to provide, saw their careers launched. Bowen dated his poetic genesis in the hard winter of 1947, when he realized that he could express his thought through the medium of images. The dating is instructive; a 1946 sonnet, 'Delw Duw' (God's Image) sees Bowen labouring under Gwenallt's influence. The transformation after 1947 to innovative leader of the *avant-garde* in Welsh poetic circles is indeed a dramatic one; Euros Bowen and Bobi Jones differ from Waldo Williams and, to a lesser extent, Gwenallt in that their discovery of a personal idiom which set them apart from the popular, indeed, canonized Romantic and Georgian poets of the north, was not a gradual voyage of discovery. And yet they still felt the need to rid themselves of the Romantic and Georgian shadows, both by defining the ground of their own poetics and by launching aggressive attacks on the poetic grandfathers of their generation, as Bobi Jones once referred to them.

Bowen underwent the familiar eisteddfodic rites of passage, winning the Crown at the National Eisteddfod in 1948 and 1950. It was in the writing of these long poems that he mastered the combination of *cynghanedd*, the alliteration and rhyming system usually confined to the traditional strict metres, with *vers libre*. His expansive use of a technique first used by E. Gwyndaf Evans and T. Gwynn Jones in the mid-1930s was to have a far-reaching influence on a younger generation of poets which included Alan Llwyd and Donald Evans. His 1950 Crown poem, 'Difodiant' (Annihilation) reflected a dark post-Hiroshima mood which permeated Welsh poetry in general at the time. The opening lines provide us with a typical example of Bowen's style:

> Mae marc gwaed ar y mwyar a'r cyll.
> Daw ar yr ysgaw bryder o'i hoedl,
> A hen yw'r griafolen eleni.
>
> [Blood marks the bramble and hazel,
> The elder is concerned for her life,
> And old is the rowan this year.]

The international unease of the late 1940s is suggested symbolically by natural objects. Euros Bowen is a symbolist poet, or as he would have us put it, a sacramentalist one. His role as a poet is to celebrate those visible elements in the world around him which have the power to symbolize an invisible world. He went to great pains to set himself apart from the mainstream of Welsh poetry. When establishing the major differences between his 'poetry of presentation' (*cerddi cyflwyniad*) and the 'poetry of communication' (*cerddi cyfathrach*) of the majority, he took as an example of communication poetry a stanza from one of R. Williams Parry's most popular lyrics ('Clychau'r Gog'). While other poets regarded metaphor and image as stylistic adornment without which the poem would still be intelligible, his own poems rejected the need for an intelligible, non-metaphorical core, and made metaphor the essence of their expression. He was then able to refute criticism of his poetry as being opaque and needlessly difficult by saying that traditional readers would have to adapt their reading strategies in order to respond to a new kind of poetry which possessed its own kind of clarity, the clarity of the interrelationship between images.

After his Eisteddfodic success Euros Bowen turned to the short poem, but forsook the sonnet and conventional lyric forms for a twenty-line unit which he called an *ugeined*. 'Yr Alarch' (The Swan) is one of his most widely appreciated poems:

YR ALARCH

> Gweld argoeli a dirgelwch
> yw celfyddyd encilfa heddiw,
> gweld lliw a chyhyredd, gweld llacharwyn
> ymwelydd nef rhwng moelydd ein hoes:
> Nawf ei unigrwydd yn nistawrwydd dŵr
> yn bererin yng nghynefin hesg,
> a'i ddull a ylch dywydd y llyn
> fel paladr main a wisgai nwyd
> anadl enaid â'i oleuni
> ar araflwm hynt yn oerfel Mawrth:
> Ei fwnwgl a âi'n wylfa yno,
> yn fraich hela ddifrycheulyd,
> sefydlogi, safiad ei lygaid,
> a phlymiai i bwll fflam ei big:
> A'r mynyddoedd yn drem anniddig,
> deil i slefrio, ymlithro hyd li:
> Â'n iasau ei adain, aros wedyn,
> ac ar drawiad egr e dyr o'r dŵr:

Yn araf yr âi, yna i'r awyr fry,
a thyn enaid o'i annwyd â thân ei adenydd.

[THE SWAN

The art of the retreat these days
Is to behold portent and mystery,
to behold colour and grace in motion, beholding
heaven's dazzling visitor between the bare hills of our times:
His aloneness swims in water's quiet
a pilgrim in a habitat of rushes
his style washing the lake's weather
like slender beam that would clothe
in its light the soul's breath
on its sluggish course in the cold of March:
His neck goes as a watching place there,
a hunting arm without spot,
settled his eyes stand,
and his beak's flame dives into pool:
the mountains an uneasy aspect,
he still slides, he glides along lake:
thrills through his wings, then a delay
and in a savage stroke he breaks from the water:
Slow did he go, then to the sky above,
Pulling the soul from its chill with the fire of its wings.]

Bowen's manifesto claim that he will have nothing to do with
bald statement is only partially true; the opening lines seem to be a
compromise in this respect, and there are other poems where he
seems to lose his symbolist nerve. As far as difficulty is concerned,
as this poem attests, it is rarely more than skin deep in Bowen's
poetry and it cannot be denied that it is sometimes caused by
technical clumsiness on his part. The more ambitious alliterative
correspondences are often forced and his apologia for his
sometimes bewildering syntax, namely that poetry has a syntax all
of its own, is unconvincing. Once a reader has adjusted to Bowen's
style there is much truth in Bobi Jones's description of him as a
poet who is so simple as to be transparent. The celebration of the
swan as symbol of transcendent, spirit-refreshing purity in troubled
times exemplifies a common theme in his poetry. Although there
sometimes seems to be a manufactured, programmed element in
Bowen's innovations, there is no doubt that he found for himself a
poetic voice in which he could proclaim his vision with stylistic

conviction in a number of important poems. His first volume, *Cerddi* (Poems), was published in 1957, a year after the death of the most canonized of all twentieth-century poets, R. Williams Parry, whose second volume, *Cerddi'r Gaeaf* (Songs of Winter), had not been published until 1952. Williams Parry was a lyric poet of consummate craftsmanship, but his influence on a younger generation can be viewed as a regressive one. The delayed publication of his most important poems in book form ensured a cult status and prolonged the hold that some Romantic and Georgian conventions had on Welsh poetry. This explains why Euros Bowen and Bobi Jones were so fiercely aggressive in staking out their own foreground. Another of the poems in *Cerddi*, 'Hyn sydd fawl' (This is praise), a joyful celebration of God's creation, is a deliberate reply to the closing line of one of Williams Parry's best-known poems, 'Marwolaeth nid yw'n marw. Hyn sydd wae.' (Death does not die. This is woe).

Bobi Jones was born to an English-speaking family in Cardiff and learnt Welsh as his second language under the inspirational guidance of Elvet Thomas at Cathays School. His first forays into print as poet and debunking critic soon earned him a reputation as an *enfant terrible* the like of whom had not been seen since the Saunders Lewis of the 1920s. Jones recognized at the outset of his career that, despite the progression made by Lewis and Gwenallt, the prevailing literary climate would be antipathetic to the more challenging, intellectual poetry which he hoped to write. In an interview in the 1970s he had this to say:

> The four grandfathers of our years were T. Gwynn Jones, W. J. Gruffydd, Williams Parry and Parry-Williams. I never idolized these as my generation was expected to . . . No one would doubt, of course, that good poetry can sometimes be simple. Possibly most people would side with that which is comprehensible. But as regards staying forever with the elementary, staying forever within the limits of nursery school experience, that isn't all that literature can do, it's not all of life either.

The opening poem of his first volume *Y Gân Gyntaf*, announces the poet's manifesto and proclaims his allegiance to the rejuvenated Welsh praise tradition:

Y GÂN GYNTAF

Angau, 'rwyt ti'n fy ofni i
Am fy mod yn ifanc
Am fod fy ngwaed yn telori wrth wthio 'ngwythiennau.
Cryni yn y fynwent, heb hyder
I ddangos i mi dy ddihengyd.

Angau, 'rwyt ti'n fy ofni i
Am fy mod yn fardd
Am fod gwewyr fy ngwaed yn deall
Dy dywarchen di: ni ddeui ataf,
Ac ymwesgi dan gysgod y gornel.

Angau, nac ofna!
Ni wnaf ddim i ti
Am dy fod di'n hardd ac yn fach,
Fel deigryn ar fin môr,
Môr Cymreig fy mawl na threia dreio.

[THE FIRST SONG

Death, you are afraid of me
Because I am young,
Because my blood trills as it drives my veins,
You tremble in the graveyard, with no confidence
To show me your escape.

Death, you are afraid of me
Because I am a poet
Because the anguish of my blood understands
Your earth; you dare not approach me,
You huddle in the corner shadow.

Death, be not afraid!
I won't harm you
Because you are pretty and small.
Like a tear on the sea's edge,
The Welsh sea of my praise that will not try to ebb.]

Bobi Jones's poetic voice is clearly enunciated in this poem; the cheerful rejection of the tyrant who had terrorized the Romantic grandfathers was underpinned in his experience by something more permanent than an inevitable reaction to an older generation when he was converted to Christianity during the 1950s and established in the faith, with the aid of Welsh and Dutch Calvinist traditions in subsequent years. He went on to publish four volumes of poetry during the 1960s and indeed at the time of writing his prolific poetic career has spanned almost half a century, but there has been no real rapprochement between Bobi Jones and the mainstream Welsh readership. This can be explained partly in terms of his unfashionable adherence to evangelical Christianity, but mainly it seems because of his uncompromising attitude to his craft, which shirks away from anything that could be called remotely popular. Praise and satire are as central to his work as to Lewis's, the former being expressed in a variety of ways, such as in a number of exuberant love poems to his wife, the latter for example in poems on the post-colonial condition. Technical virtuosity and a provocative playfulness are also constant elements in his work. This short poem gives us another opportunity to listen to the unique voice of a poet who felt bound to write, in Michael Roberts's words, 'praise in an age of irony'.

'Roedd Eira

'Roedd eira. Twmblodd yr wybren ar wahân.
Un funud 'roedd yn gyfan saff, ac yna—
Ŵyn, crwyn, ewyn, gwydrau, yn sgyrion mân
A'r hollawyr wedi'i datod, yn ddrylliau eira
Ymdorrodd . . . Dyna un o nodweddion y nef, debygwn.
O! na allai'r ddaear ei hun ymwahanu ar chwâl
Fel yna. Hen wyrth y nef ydyw gogrwn
Paradwys drwy dyllau'r gaeaf ar bechaduriaid sâl:
Mae'r byd yn rhy ddiogel. Ond gynnau, ym mis Mai,
Un funud 'roedd y byd yn stafell daclus,
Yn uned sad a chadarn na ellid llai
Na chysgu'n dalog ynddi; ac yna'n ddilys
Gwelais danchwa cras crych caled ddail
Ar frigau. Siociwyd y cae a'r allt hyd at eu sail.

[There was snow

There was snow. The sky tumbled apart.
One minute it was safe and whole, and then—
Lambs, skins, foam, glasses, all splinters
And all the sky undone, it broke up
In pieces of snow . . . That's a feature of heaven, I suppose.

Oh! that the world couldn't come apart like that. Heaven's old
    miracle is to
Riddle paradise through winter's holes on mean sinners:
The world is too safe. But just now, in the month of May,
One minute the world was a tidy room,
A strong and steady unit that one could not but
Sleep in with confidence; and then assuredly I saw
The raucous rippling rough explosion of leaves
On branches. The field and the wood were shocked to their
    roots.]

The important new work of the 1950s suggested that Welsh
poetry was moving in an unquestionably modernist direction. The
old guard, represented most forcibly by Gruffydd's faithful
disciple, Iorwerth C. Peate, could still provoke some bitter
skirmishes, but the achievements of Waldo Williams, Bobi Jones
and Euros Bowen, along with T. Glynne Davies, author of the
acclaimed and influential 1951 National Crown poem, 'Adfeilion'
(Ruins) and Kitchener Davies, who wrote the major confessional
poem 'Sŵn y Gwynt sy'n Chwythu' (The Sound of the Wind that's
Blowing) on his deathbed in 1952, a poem that is puritan in the
intensity of its self-questioning, and acclaimed by Gwenallt as one
of the great poems of the twentieth century, all pointed to a more
intellectually confident and stylistically innovative generation.
R. Gerallt Jones, an emerging poet during the 1950s, and coeditor,
with Bedwyr Lewis Jones, of yet another new magazine, *Yr
Arloeswr* (The Innovator) has argued that the achievements of the
1950s were wasted and rejected by a later generation who insisted
on resurrecting traditional thematic and stylistic conventions. It
does not lie within the scope of this chapter to consider this
complaint, but we need to refer to another group of 'traditional'
poets whose output and influence cannot be ignored.

These are *y beirdd gwlad*, the folk poets. As the term suggests,
they were not a new phenomenon, but it seems that their
significance has been appreciated to a greater extent during the
latter part of the century. Typically, a *bardd gwlad* would have had
no university education, he would live his life without moving from
his square mile, and very likely be a farmer or smallholder or
craftsman. He would compete in local and national eisteddfodau,
writing in the strict metres and usually in sonnet and rhyming
stanza form as well. His song would be concerned with the

changing seasons and the natural world, but more importantly he would fulfil the traditional social function of the Welsh poets as voices of their community, greeting a birth, celebrating a marriage or mourning a loss.

Of all the folk poets none are better known than the family circle known as 'Bois y Cilie' whose base was the farm of Cilie on the South Cardiganshire coast. The very fact that I refer to a group rather than an individual poet underlines their communal ethos and contribution. Several members of the family were accomplished poets; these included Isfoel and Alun Cilie (Alun Jones) who both published volumes of poetry after 1960. Another clan member, Simon B. Jones, a minister of religion who won a National Chair and Crown in the 1930s, was joint editor of the popular literary magazine *Y Genhinen* during the 1950s, when its poetry columns were devoted for the most part to the kind of writing now under discussion. Other poets were afforded honorary membership of the circle; T. Llew Jones, whose most important contribution to Welsh literature has been as a children's writer of genius, won consecutive National Chairs in 1958 and 1959 and became a champion of the poetic values of lucidity, simplicity and relevance, all virtues or vices upheld by the folk poet. He was to be one of the founding members of *Y Gymdeithas Gerdd Dafod*, the traditional poetry society formed as a response to a renaissance of interest in strict-metre poetry during the 1970s. Dic Jones, a farmer from Aberporth, was drawn into the Cilie circle and achieved unparalleled competitive success as a young poet in the 1950s, winning the Chair at the Urdd Eisteddfod five times in succession. He graduated as a national winner in 1966, when his winning *awdl* 'Cynhaeaf' (Harvest) had Thomas Parry comparing him with Dafydd ap Gwilym, the greatest of all Welsh poets.

By 1960 the battle lines seemed to have been fairly clearly drawn between an intellectual *avant-garde* who agreed with Bobi Jones's view that a healthy poetic culture could not allow itself to be paralysed by fear of alienating a conservative readership, and the still powerful traditional forces on the other hand who regarded every step taken in a modernist direction as a false one, and any inclination towards difficulty, allusion or self-referential poetry as pretentious nonsense. (It should be noted in passing that Saunders Lewis and Bobi Jones would differentiate between the *beirdd gwlad*, honourable practitioners of an ancient craft, and the reactionary

upholders of Georgian aesthetics.) During the 1960s, however, a
poet emerged who believed that accessible poetry could be written
without fear of intellectual compromise and without clinging to
poetic conventions that had been overworked to the point of
impotence. Gwyn Thomas was born in the slate-mining town of
Blaenau Ffestiniog in 1936 and grew up in a culture whose
congregational centres of chapel and cinema were both to leave
their mark upon his work.

Gwyn Thomas is just as innovative a poet as Bobi Jones and
Euros Bowen, but he went against the grain of twentieth-century
poetry in general by forging a deceptively simple and direct idiom
which he felt addressed the challenge of the new media. But
traditionalists have been just as bemused by his work, and have
failed to comprehend his aim or achievements. Conservative
readers have tended to praise his first three volumes, all published
in the 1960s, when his poetic idiom is an emerging one, to the
detriment of his later, more obviously innovative work which is
discussed in another chapter. A poem from his second volume, *Y
Weledigaeth Haearn* (The Iron Vision, 1965) emphasizes the
potency of words, albeit in a satirical context in a poem which goes
on to note the power of the advertising machine:

> Y mae grym mewn geiriau i gynhyrfu dynion
> O'u hailadrodd yn ddigonol
> A'u cydio wrth y pethau sy'n cyfrif.

> [There is a power in words to move men
> When they are repeated often enough
> And linked to the things that count.]

His aim as a poet has been to release the latent power of ordinary
words by placing them in contexts where the use of traditional
devices such as rhythm, rhyme and alliteration can defamiliarize
our response to them. This does not seem to be a particularly
original agenda until we appreciate the creative balance between
tradition and innovation in his work, both thematically and
stylistically. On the whole he has chosen not to follow Saunders
Lewis, Waldo Williams, Euros Bowen and Bobi Jones along the
road to a more difficult and allusive poetics; but in a sense he has
attempted something more ambitious, to restore to supposedly
outworn figures and devices something of their primitive vitality

without sacrificing the rich resonance that traditional figures such as *goleuni, haul, môr, nos* (light, sun, sea and night) have accumulated over the centuries. Traditional devices, therefore, are often used in an unconventional context, the use of rhyme within *vers libre* poems being the most obvious example. Subtle use of literary devices, often within a pattern of internal deviation, manages to vivify words which in another poet's hand would be irredeemable *clichés*. As well as *Y Weledigaeth Haearn*, the other volumes which he published in the 1960s were entitled *Chwerwder yn y Ffynhonnau* (Bitterness in the Wells) and *Ysgyrion Gwaed* (Blood Splinters), fair indicators of the vision of a poet whose youth had been scarred by the death of three members of his family, including his mother, and from whose early poems death is never far away, whether it be the sudden death of a friend, the assassination of Kennedy, or the mass killings of Passchendaele or Hiroshima. But although the sting of death is painfully apparent, it is tempered by a resurrective hope which is inspired by the Christian scriptures and by the regenerative order of things in the natural world.

Euros Bowen, Bobi Jones and Gwyn Thomas differ from the important poets of the first half of the century in the volume of their output. Their poems are counted in hundreds, not in tens. This can be explained partly as a reaction to the earlier poets' obsession with being *cynnil* (concise), that obsession in turn a reaction to the worthless profligacy of much nineteenth-century verse, but economic conditions were also an important factor. State patronage by means of the Welsh Arts Council's Literature Committee, established in 1967 under Meic Stephens's director-ship, created a supportive and encouraging environment. The cultural environment had also been charged by a new political current, and as in the years covered at the beginning of this chapter, Saunders Lewis was once again a central figure. His 1962 wireless talk, 'Tynged yr Iaith' (The Fate of the Language), ignited the aspirations of a new generation of Welsh-speakers, resulting in the formation of the Welsh Language Society whose non-violent protest campaigns changed dramatically the mood of Welsh public life, resulting indirectly also in the growth of a Welsh pop culture whose influence on poetry would become more apparent. Alan Llwyd's comprehensive survey of Welsh-language poetry of the 1960s makes it clear that the bardic culture of the decade was a diverse and thriving one, and there are several poets who have not received mention who wrote verse of quality. But reference should be made to the two young Meirionnydd poets who made their mark in 1969 and whose early work points to two of the most significant developments of later decades. Gerallt Lloyd Owen's controversial anti-investiture poems led many younger poets back to the strict metres and to overt political poetry. Nesta Wyn Jones's *Cannwyll yn Olau* (A Candle Alight) heralded the belated advent of significant poetry written by women, one of the most obvious differences between the period after 1970 and the decades, indeed the centuries, which preceded it.

Saunders Lewis, writing on 'Welsh Literature and Nationalism' in 1965, when the impact of his wireless talk was becoming increasingly apparent, reviewed the period covered in this chapter and made the following comments:

> I make what I believe to be a statement of fact: the majority of Welsh poets and writers. . . have since 1930 onwards been avowed members of the Welsh Nationalist Party . . . In the thirties, English poets and writers, from the public schools and from Oxford and Cambridge, were frenziedly trying to proletarianise themselves, joining the Communist Party and the Left Book Club, enlisting for war against Franco in Spain . . . In the same period, Welsh creative writing was profoundly moved by the development of the Nationalist Party. It was the period of Williams Parry's great sonnets. Then came the poetry of Gwenallt and Waldo Williams and of Euros Bowen and the generation of Bobi Jones. It is the crisis of Wales that has given that period of poetry its *angst*.

This assessment is sure to be amended and revised but its basic thrust seems undeniable, and its final sentence seems just as applicable to the poetry of the century's final decades. If the sociopolitical context accounts for the *angst*, it does not account fully for the excellence of much of the poetry, because, if I may be permitted one final Lewis quotation, this time from a 1944 book review, 'poetry of the highest quality is not made with ideas or expositions. Words! Explosive words, revelatory words, creative words, words with rhythms which shake, that is the stuff of excellent poetry.' And formalist criticism has insisted that if the words of poetry are to retain these qualities, they must be engaged in a constant battle against convention and *cliché*. A stylistic review of an anthology of representative poetry written between 1939 and

1970 would reveal such a pattern in the most significant poems. Put another way, the poets discussed at any length in this chapter were ones (not the only ones, I should add) who insisted on discovering their own idiom, their own poetic voice in which to evoke their personal and communal feelings and visions.

FURTHER READING

A. M. Allchin, *Praise Above All* (Cardiff, 1991).

Joseph P. Clancy, *Twentieth Century Welsh Poems* (Llandysul, 1982).

Ceri Davies, *Welsh Literature and the Classical Tradition* (Cardiff, 1995). (Chapter 5 discusses poems by Euros Bowen, Saunders Lewis and Waldo Williams.)

Gareth Alban Davies, 'The Multi-screen Cinema: poetry in Welsh 1950–1990' in Hans-Werner Ludwig and Lothar Fietz (eds), *Poetry in the British Isles: non-metropolitan perspectives* (Cardiff, 1995), 115–33.

Alan Llwyd, *Barddoniaeth y Chwedegau* (Cyhoeddiadau Barddas, 1986).

John Rowlands, 'Literature in Welsh' in Meic Stephens (ed.), *The Arts in Wales 1950–1975* (Cardiff, 1979).

Bruce Griffiths, *Saunders Lewis* (Cardiff, 1979).

Harri Pritchard Jones, *Saunders Lewis: a presentation of his work* (Springfield, Illinois, 1990).

Saunders Lewis, *Selected Poems*, translated from the Welsh by Joseph P. Clancy (Cardiff, 1993).

Gwyn Thomas, 'His Poetry', in A. Jones and G. Thomas (eds), *Presenting Saunders Lewis* (Cardiff, 1983).

Emyr Humphreys, 'Poetry, Prison and Propaganda', *Planet*, 43 (1978), 17–23.

James Nicholas, *Waldo Williams* (Cardiff, 1978).

Robert Rhys, *Chwilio am Nodau'r Gân* (Llandysul, 1992).

M. Wynn Thomas, 'From Walt to Waldo: Whitman's Welsh admirers', *Walt Whitman Quarterly Review*, vol .10, no. 2, Fall, 1992, 61–73.

Ned Thomas, 'The Waldo Dialectic', *Planet*, 58 (1986), 10–15.

Ned Thomas, 'Waldo Williams: In Two Fields' in Ludwig and Fietz, *Poetry of the British Isles*, 253–66.

Cyril Williams, 'Waldo Williams: A Celtic Mystic', in Gavin Flood (ed.), *Mapping Invisible Worlds, Cosmos 9* (Edinburgh, 1993), 127–38.

A. M. Allchin, 'The Poetry of Euros Bowen' in Cynthia and Saunders Davies (eds), *Euros Bowen, priest-poet/bardd-offeiriad* (Penarth, 1993).

Euros Bowen, 'From a poem to a poem', *Poetry Wales*, 11/3 (1975), 5–16.

Euros Bowen, *Poems* (Llandysul, 1974).

John Emyr, *Bobi Jones* (Cardiff, 1991).

Bobi Jones, 'Order, Purpose and Resurgence in Poetry', *Poetry Wales*, 11/1 (1975), 1–9.

Bobi Jones, *Selected Poems*, translated by Joseph P. Clancy, 1987.

Michael Symmons Roberts, 'Bobi Jones and Praise' *Verse*, 9/3, Winter 1992, 141–4.

Elan Closs Stephens, 'The Poetry of Gwyn Thomas', *Triskel Two*, 166–81.

Gwyn Thomas, *Living a Life: selected poems 1962–1982*, selected and introduced by Joseph P.Clancy with translations by Joseph P. Clancy and Gwyn Thomas (Amsterdam, 1982).

CHAPTER 5

CONTEMPORARY WELSH POETRY: 1969–1996

T. GERALD HUNTER

The quarter-century stretching from the end of the 1960s to the middle of the 1990s is arguably the most diverse and dynamic period in the history of Welsh-language poetry. It has witnessed a renaissance, or a series of renaissances, in the traditional strict-metre poetry. Much of the best contemporary poetry has been cast in the centuries-old moulds provided by the *englyn* (plural *englynion*), the *cywydd* (plural *cywyddau*), and the *awdl* (plural *awdlau*). It has also seen a range of experiments in form and diction which have been brought to bear upon subjects relating to the new spheres of life, technology and thought which Welsh-language culture has encountered and made its own at the end of the twentieth century. In this period poetry has gained new audiences both outside Welsh-speaking Wales, with an unprecedented number of translations into English, and within it, as poets have stepped onto the new technological platforms provided by Welsh-language radio and television stations. The recent years have also been characterized by the growth in popularity of `low-tech' performances, that is, of poets performing their work in front of live audiences. The past quarter-century has also seen women poets begin to come into their own in Wales after centuries of comparative silence. Much of the significant poetry of this period has come to light in the National Eisteddfod, the annual week-long festival organized around two prestigious competitions, for the Chair (awarded for an *awdl*, a long strict-metre poem) and for the Crown (for free-metre verse). However, a great amount of poetry has emerged through less official channels, as an unprecedented multiplicity of literary `counter-cultures' has appeared within Wales.

It is a period characterized by political poetry and by the politicizing of the poet. While no period in the recorded history of Welsh literature is without poetry addressed to what can be called political and social concerns, a strikingly significant amount of the poetry written between 1969 and 1996 can be described as overtly sociopolitical in one way or other. Among the most common topics are: the politics of Welsh nationalism, or to put it in another way, the politics of anti-English imperialism; a spectrum of international concerns; gender politics; the internal struggles raging within Wales over the ways in which Welsh culture should be preserved and represented.

Two very different factors can be cited to account for the politicization of Welsh poetry in this period. The first, less obvious factor is the critical tradition in Wales. Throughout the twentieth century, this tradition, perhaps best seen in the rulings made by Eisteddfod judges for the poetry competitions, but also manifest in the pages of literary books and journals, has privileged poems which deal concretely with concrete topics over more abstract, philosophical poems. This critical tradition was enthroned with the 1925 publication of Sir John Morris-Jones's highly influential handbook *Cerdd Dafod* ('Poetry' or 'The Craft of Poetry'), which declared *Nid â syniadau haniaethol y mae a wnelo barddoniaeth, ond â syniadau diriaethol* (It is not with abstract ideas which poetry deals, but rather with concrete ideas). This edict has been repeated regularly by judges and critics right up into the 1990s. While this critical bias does not mean necessarily that all highly acclaimed poems are political, it has helped to create an environment in which such poetry has an advantage, as the tendency is to favour poems with an extremely clear message or 'prose sense'.

The second and more obvious factor is the political atmosphere of the period. The early 1960s initiated a period of increasing political activity centered around the Welsh language. In the wake of Saunders Lewis's 1962 radio speech *Tynged yr Iaith* (The Fate of the Language), Cymdeithas yr Iaith Gymraeg was formed. 'The Welsh Language Society' initiated a long campaign of civil disobedience and political lobbying, one of the main currents in a flood-tide of protest which was to win the Welsh Language Act in 1967, and, eventually, Welsh radio and television stations. However, despite the successes of Cymdeithas yr Iaith and various campaigns on behalf of the Welsh language and culture, this period has been marked by events which have acted as forceful reminders to many of the status of Wales as a nation subsumed into (what remains of) the English empire: protracted rule by a Conservative government never given anything close to a majority vote by the

Welsh people; the investiture of the Prince of Wales in 1969; the failure of the referendum on a Welsh assembly in 1979. The events of 1969 and 1979 were, and still are, seen by a large minority of the Welsh people (and a much larger percentage of the Welsh-speaking minority) as a failure of Wales as a nation to defeat and transcend the passive, subservient mentality imposed upon them by years of English rule. Many poets have reacted to this failure, or perceived failure, by stepping into the role of visionary prophet and dreaming, writing or singing a new, imagined Wales into a literary existence.

Thus a fitting starting place for discussing this period in the history of Welsh poetry is the investiture of Charles, eldest son of Elizabeth II, as prince of Wales at Caernarfon Castle on 1 July 1969. As might be expected given the resilient popularity of the English royal family at the end of the twentieth century, this event was met with celebrations and excitement in England as well as in Wales. However it was also met with protests throughout the Principality. To many Welsh people the investiture was seen as an insult, a callous reminder of the colonizer-colonized, conqueror-conquered, ruler-ruled relationship between England and Wales. The best-known poetry arising from the investiture controversy was written by a young poet, Gerallt Lloyd Owen, who was 25 years old in 1969. He had published one volume of youthful verse in 1966, *Ugain Oed a'i Ganiadau* (Twenty Years Old and Its Songs), but it was a series of poems set against the background provided by the investiture which won him a name as a poet of national standing. These poems, many of which first appeared in various journals, were published as a volume in 1972 under the title *Cerddi'r Cywilydd* (Poems of the Shame). The 'shame' of the title is twofold: the fact that an Englishman had, once again, been crowned prince of Wales, and another fact more difficult to face: that so many Welsh people had welcomed and cheered the event, or, at least, had failed to take an active part in protest.

In 'I'r Farwolaeth' (To the Death), a poem which begins by sarcastically observing that *Rhown wên i'r mab brenhinol* (We give a smile to the royal son), he characterizes those Welsh people who welcomed the prince as a herd of lemmings, rushing joyfully and thoughtlessly to their own death:

> Awn heb yr hoen i barhau
> I'r nos na ŵyr ein heisiau,

> Awn i gyd yn fodlon gaeth
> Efo'r hil i Farwolaeth.
>
> [We will go without the vigour to continue
> To the night which does not miss us,
> We will all go happily enslaved
> With the race to Death.]

Similarly, in 'Fy Ngwlad' (My Country) he describes a spineless nation smiling for the prince, oblivious to the implications of the situation:

> Ein calon gan estron ŵr,
> Ein coron gan goncwerwr,
> A gwerin o ffafrgarwyr
> Llariaidd eu gwên lle'r oedd gwŷr.
>
> [A foreign man has our heart,
> a conqueror has our crown,
> And a favour-loving folk
> of gentle smile where there were men.]

Gerallt Lloyd Owen has by no means confined himself to political verse; he is also an accomplished writer of moving tributes to individuals, and in this respect has one foot in the realm of the *bardd gwlad*, the traditional 'country poet' who commemorates the life of the local community. Despite the fact that he has written a number of powerful elegies, Gerallt Lloyd Owen is best known for commemorating a death which occurred seven centuries ago, that of the last native prince of Wales, and for writing on (what he sees as) the twentieth-century reverberations caused by that death.

The political poems in *Cerddi'r Cywilydd* employ a striking, often violent, imagery aimed at inspiring radical nationalism. These poems are also characterized by something else which has become a hallmark of Gerallt Lloyd Owen, a mastery of *cynghanedd* (a complicated system of internal line ornamentation using rhyme and alliteration) and the traditional strict metres. The volume contains an *awdl, cywyddau, englynion*, and several free-metre poems endowed with *cynghanedd*. The ancient systems of *cynghanedd* and the twenty-four strict metres were formalized in the fourteenth and fifteenth centuries, hence it could be said that Gerallt Lloyd Owen's preferred medium of expression is one that looks to the medieval past (though one should not make the mistake of assuming that these metres have been 'revived'; they have been in continuous use since the end of the Middle Ages).

Moreover, the history in which these poems are grounded, like their imagery, is often distinctly medieval. Gerallt Lloyd Owen's medievalism is anything but a romantic attempt to flee the modern world and take refuge in a misty, romanticized past. Medieval forms and imagery are to him a vehicle for discussing the condition of modern Wales. His poetry is a testimony to the belief that the shape of the present is owed directly to the past, and that the past must thus be remembered and analysed if one is to address the problems of the present. He writes not of the archetypical hero of medieval legend, Arthur, who left his Camelot to sleep on the misty Isle of Avallon, but rather of Llywelyn ap Gruffudd, the last native prince of Wales killed by the English near Cilmeri in 1282, whose severed head was sent as a trophy to London. The character of Llywelyn haunts these poems, which often display an obsession with the physicality of the dead prince; he is metonymically evoked by reference to his blood, his head, his eyes and his breath.

For the 1982 National Eisteddfod, it was decided to commemorate the 700th anniversary of Llywelyn's death by setting 'Cilmeri' as the subject of the *awdl* for the Chair competition. It came as no surprise that this Chair was won by Gerallt Lloyd Owen, who had composed so many shorter poems on the same subject at the end of the 1960s. As the *awdl* 'Cilmeri', which constitutes a visionary return to the scene of Llywelyn's fall, develops and hones many of the themes and imagery found in *Cerddi'r Cywilydd*, and as Gerallt Lloyd Owen has repeatedly stated himself that his subjects and their relevance had not changed over the years, the following discussion will draw examples from *Cerddi'r Cywilydd* as well as from the 1982 *awdl*.

In addition to the obvious points already mentioned—the focus on the thirteenth-century Welsh prince and choosing to write in the old strict metres—a more subtle kind of medievalism pervades Gerallt Lloyd Owen's political poetry. This can best be described by suggesting that he adopts a poetic persona, a particular, marked voice which reflects the medieval Welsh poet in many ways. On the one hand, it is the social role of the early Celtic poet, his place in recording his people's history and in advising political figures, which makes this persona so appropriate and powerful. On the other hand, invoking this persona also brings forth a definite view of the nature of poetry and its relationship to the internal processes of cognition and memory.

The way in which this persona is employed can be described, if in a somewhat simplified fashion, by reference to two interweaving strands of poetics, both organized around the verb *gweld* (to see). First of all, the medieval Welsh poet—like the early Celtic bards mentioned by Classical writers—accompanied the warriors and reported on the events which transpired on the battle field. In a sense, the poet fulfilling this social role can be thought of as a kind of pre-modern, versifying war correspondent. This aspect of the early Welsh poet's societal role is well known among Welsh speakers, due primarily to the preservation and canonical status of the medieval poetry attributed to poets such as Aneirin and Taliesin. These poems are often structured around the word *gwelais* (I saw); the poet is the one who, first of all, sees, and, secondly, records what he sees.

The early Welsh poet was also thought to be able to 'see' in another very different way; the poets were also prophets who could 'see' things which other people did not. A great number of medieval prophetic poems have survived (and been canonized in the twentieth-century anthologies), most of which focus on *y mab darogan*, the prophesied saviour of the Welsh, described at different times as Arthur, Owain (either a legendary Owain, Owain Glyndŵr, or Owain Lawgoch), and Henry Tudor.

In Gerallt Lloyd Owen's medievalistic political poems these two kinds of seeing are portrayed as part of the same process; the act of witnessing the history of the nation is bound up with offering a vision as to the nation's future. This is reflected in 'Y Gŵr Sydd ar y Gorwel' (The Man Who is on the Horizon). The body of the poem, which draws on the *mab darogan* tradition, is usually taken to refer to Saunders Lewis, but can also be readily interpreted as a description of any political martyr. This is framed by a couplet, appearing near the beginning and again as the final lines of the poem, which asks the nation to share the poet's vision: *Ac am hynny, Gymru, gwêl / Y gŵr sydd ar y gorwel* (And because of that, Wales, see / the man who is on the horizon). In one of the shorter *Cerddi'r Cywilydd* poems, entitled 'Cilmeri' like the later *awdl*, Gerallt Lloyd Owen describes a visit to the site of Llywelyn's death, using a description of the physical locality as a reminder that Llywelyn's death is still relevant in modern Wales:

Fin nos, fan hyn
Lladdwyd Llywelyn.
Fyth nid anghofiaf hyn.

Y nant a welaf fan hyn
A welodd Llywelyn.
Camodd ar y cerrig hyn.

[At nightfall, here
Llywelyn was killed.
I will never forget this.

The brook which I see here
Llywelyn saw.
He stepped on these stones.]

The verb *gweld* and the act of seeing pervade the *awdl* 'Cilmeri'. The opening lines of the poem present a description of what the poet sees:

Yn fraw agos ar frigyn
Gwelaf leuad llygadwyn
Mor oer â'r marw ei hun

[Frighteningly close on a small branch
I see a white-eyed moon
As cold as the dead man himself]

This is an *englyn milwr*, the first in a series of five. These opening five stanzas describe the poet's vision and the subsequent act of empathizing with his subject (*teimlaf ei anaf hen*—'I feel his old wound'), an act predicated on the preceding act of seeing. Next comes another series of five *englynion* (of the four-line *englyn unodl union* variety). These stanzas, which serve to introduce reflections on the nature of memory, are also introduced by reference to sight:

Â chof sy'n hwy na chofio fe welaf
Eilwaith ddydd ei lorio
Ac ail-fyw ei glwyfau o
Â galar hŷn nag wylo.

[With a memory which is longer than remembering I see
Again the day of his fall

And relive his wounds
With a grief older than crying.]

Gwelaf—the verb *gweld* (to see), in the first person singular
present indicative—comes back again in the dramatic narrative
centre of the poem, which describes the decapitation of Llywelyn.
The first lines of three successive stanzas are structured around this
word:

Gwelaf fflach y dur o'r awyr euog

[I see the flash of the steel from the guilty sky]

Gwelaf ei ben trwy wagle'n treiglo

[I see his head rolling through empty space]

Gwelaf ei freuddwyd heb ei freuddwydio

[I see his un-dreamed dream]

Taken together these lines, like the stanzas to which they belong,
betray a development in the poet's vision, a moving away from the
act of reporting on events to reporting on that which has not yet
happened, that which is a vision or a dream (*breuddwyd*). This is
echoed at the *awdl*'s end; the final twelve lines, which constitute a
coherent semi-independent unit serving to summarize the entire
poem, begin with the words *hyn oll a welaf* (all this I see). Again, the
poet-persona uttering this poem is a seer, and that which he 'sees' is
twofold; he records the communal experience, reminding his people
of a shared past while also providing them with his own personal
vision of their present and future.

The words *cof* (memory), and *cofio* (to remember), occur
regularly throughout 'Cilmeri', one of the implications being that
the poem is a verbal monument intended to fight *angof* (forgetting).
In this poem *angof*, portrayed as a kind of dangerous, active
forgetting, is as much an enemy as the English are. With its
emphasis on remembering Llywelyn, this *awdl* can also be described
as a *marwnad*, an elegy for the dead leader. As such, it reflects
another aspect of the medieval poet's social role, his relationship
with his lord or patron. The relationship between poet and patron
was symbiotic, and in return for material support the poet was

expected to advise and praise his patron in life and mourn him in death. Gerallt Lloyd Owen begins the *cywydd* 'Fy Ngwlad' by addressing the dead Llywelyn as if he is, in some way, still prince of Wales, and hence still the patron of the poet.

> Wylit, wylit Lywelyn,
> Wylit waed pe gwelit hyn.
> Ein calon gan estron ŵr,
> Ein coron gan goncwerwr,

> [You would cry, you would cry, Llywelyn,
> You would cry blood if you could see this.
> A foreign man has our heart,
> A conqueror has our crown.]

This is a strange, almost surreal, reflection of the medieval poet's function. The poet is reporting on a kind of battle, developments which he perceives as a battle for the soul of the nation waged in the late twentieth century, but the patron to whom he reports is the dead Llywelyn, unable to witness the present degradation of his land. However, by the end of the poem a transformation has taken place, as the closing lines indicate:

> Fy ngwlad, fy ngwlad, cei fy nghledd
> Yn wridog dros d'anrhydedd.
> O, gallwn, gallwn golli
> Y gwaed hwn o'th blegid di.

> [My country, my country, you will have my sword
> blushing for your honour.
> O, I could, I could lose
> This blood for you.]

The poet has turned away from the dead leader to address the present-day nation. Another significant shift has accompanied this change of addressee, a shift from the hypothetical tears of blood which the dead prince would shed in the poet's vision to the very real blood of the living man: *gallwn golli y gwaed hwn o'th blegid di* (I could lose *this* blood for you). While the power of (what is imagined to have been) the public persona of the medieval Welsh bard is used to fuel the *cywydd*, during the course of this short poem the focus is shifted from the pre-modern feudal or tribal system wherein allegiance is centered on the person of one ruler (Llywelyn) to a modern nationalism in which allegiance is given to the entire land (Wales). However, the same pronoun—the second singular informal—is maintained throughout, something which, coupled with the unchanging mode of direct address and the constant focus on blood, maintains a consistency of expression throughout the poem.

Gerallt Lloyd Owen was a key figure in what has been called the strict-metre poetry 'Renaissance' of the 1970s. Perhaps the word 'renaissance' is not entirely appropriate, for it may be that what was perceived as a rebirth was merely the result of a change in perception, of the fact that strict-metre poetry was again reoccupying a high-profile national stage—best, but not exclusively, represented by the Eisteddfod—after years of a comparatively quiet life in the smaller scale, localized realm of *y beirdd gwlad*, the 'country poets'. While the exact nature of the 'renaissance' of the 1970s still needs to be defined by further research, it is true that most of the major figures involved— including Donald Evans, Dic Jones and Alan Llwyd as well as Gerallt Lloyd Owen—owe much to the *bardd gwlad* legacy.

The year 1976 proved to be a milestone in the modern history of strict-metre poetry. The *Cymdeithas Gerdd Dafod*, the 'Poetry Society' which has been instrumental in publicizing, nurturing and patronizing the *cynghanedd* tradition over the past twenty years, was formally established in the National Eisteddfod that year. Moreover, the Chair competition in the 1976 Eisteddfod made it clear that a generation of accomplished young poets writing in the strict metres had come to maturity. The title which was set for the competition, 'Gwanwyn' (Spring), seemed to speak to poets with close ties to the rural, agricultural tradition, and it inspired Donald Evans, Dic Jones, Alan Llwyd and Gerallt Lloyd Owen to compose masterful *awdlau*. The way in which the contest apparently tapped the wealth of the *bardd gwlad* tradition was noted by one of the competition's judges, James Nicholas:

> 25 compositions were received in the competition, and among them were a number of *awdlau* which exhibited a very mature skill. Moreover, it was no surprise that the level of the poetry on the whole was good; much of the best Eisteddfodic poetry of the century has stemmed from the close relationship between the poets and the soil. Many of the poets

demonstrated that they have extensive experience living close to nature, that they are familiar with observing the course of the seasons closely, and the best were seen to express the charm of spring in a sensitive and refined manner.

The *awdl* initially judged best was by Dic Jones, though he was later denied the Chair because of a technical breach of Eisteddfod rules. Dic Jones, a farmer from south-west Wales, learned the technical aspects of the traditional metres from Alun Jones, or Alun Cilie, a member of the famous Cilie family of poets. With his close personal connections to the Cilie circle, Dic Jones grew up in a literary environment which critics have often taken as best representing the *bardd gwlad* tradition in the twentieth century.

Although he still composes occasional verse in keeping with the true nature of that tradition, Dic Jones has stepped out of the local community of poets onto the national literary stage. He is a master of humorous verse, and he has adeptly turned the *cywydd* and the *englyn* (as well as freer ballad-esque metres) to comic and satiric ends. As this talent is frequently brought to bear upon issues of general concern and interest in Wales (ranging from rugby to politics), he has gained a considerable audience.

Perhaps more significantly, Dic Jones has taken the traditional material of the *bardd gwlad*—occasional, commemorative verse and meditations on various aspects of rural life—and worked it into some uniquely individual and powerful poetry. His *awdl* 'Gwanwyn' testifies to the way in which traditional themes and imagery can be used to strike a fresh and powerful chord. As might be expected, his 'Gwanwyn' is in part a meditation upon the cyclical character of nature and life, and the long poem is itself characterized by an internal cyclic dynamism. This is generated by placing short, self-contained lyrical sections alongside very different reflections on death and the crueller face of nature. The poem opens with an invocation to a personified May-Day, a representative of spring equated with Noah, the ur-husbandman:

> O anfon, Glamai, dy fwyn golomen
> Goruwch y dilyw i gyrchu deilen,
>
> [O send, May-Day, your gentle dove
> Over the flood to bring a leaf.]

The light introduction promises a pastoral hymn, and like so many
of the lyrical lines which follow it lulls the reader into a false sense
of security. This mood is soon shattered as the speaker, the farmer
who narrates his walk about the land, observing the signs of the
season, comes upon a disturbing scene:

> Ym môn y clais gwelais gyrff
> Ŵyn barugog eu breugyrff.
> Toll lawdrwm dant y llwydrew,
> Teganau trist gwynt y rhew.
>
> Dau hyll geudwll llygadwag
> I wyll nos yn syllu'n wag,
> A haid gythreuliaid y rhos
> Am eu hawr yn ymaros.
>
> [In the bottom of the ditch I saw the bodies
> of lambs, their fragile bodies covered with frost.
> The heavy-handed tax of the hoarfrost's bite,
> Sad play-things of the icy wind.
>
> Two ugly-socketed empty-eyed ones
> Staring emptily into the night's darkness,
> And a swarm of the moor's devils
> awaiting their time.]

The scavenging birds lurking on the perimeters of this scene and
contributing to its horror are sinister members of the same cast to
which the dove of the opening couplet belongs. Groups of birds
dominate this poem; their migrations and efforts to glean food
from the land reflect the season-bound activities of the farmer, and
their singing provides the choral background for the poet's
meditative solo voice.

Alan Llwyd, the poet eventually chaired in 1976, also employed
the image of the crow preying upon the new-born lamb:

> Mamog ar ffridd yn griddfan,—a'i thymp hi'n
>   rhithmau poen, wrth duchan
>   oen o'i bru, cyn dyfod brân
>   i dyllu'r llygad allan.
>
> [A sheep groaning in a mountain pasture,—her time
>   [marked by] pain's rhythms, groaning

a lamb from her womb, before the crow comes
to dig the eyes out.]

Like Dic Jones, Alan Llwyd is a master of the strict metres. He has
put the *englyn* to an incredible variety of uses, creating excellent
examples of the more customary kind of epigram and elegy while
also bringing this compact form to bear effectively upon a wide range
of current issues. The following example displays Alan Llwyd's
creative use of the tradition; it begins soundly within the register of
the epitaph—a register commonly occupied by the *englyn*—and then
twists violently away from this conventional opening:

WRTH GOFEB FILWROL ABERYSTWYTH

Er mawrhau'r meirw o hyd—ofer oedd
    Eu llofruddio'n waedlyd;
    Dan anfri daw, yn unfryd,
    Eu rhegfeydd drwy'r garreg fud.

[BESIDE THE ABERYSTWYTH MILITARY MEMORIAL

Despite the continual glorification of the dead—it was in vain
    to murder them bloodily;
    United, in disrespect,
    Their curses will come through the mute stone.]

Alan Llwyd is one of the most prolific contemporary poets,
having similarly distinguished himself in the realm of free-metre
poetry. In fact, Alan Llwyd has followed T. H. Parry-Williams by
twice winning both the Chair and the Crown in the National
Eisteddfod (a feat also accomplished more recently by Donald
Evans). His best free-metre poems are characterized by a distinct,
personal voice which is used either to convey an experience rooted
directly—often disarmingly so—in the autobiographical, or for
producing candidly personal commentary on the social problems
and concerns of the times. Perhaps the most striking example of his
autobiographical verse is 'Cerddi'r Cyfannu' (Poems of the Union),
a sequence of ten poems comprising a meditation on his wife's
pregnancy.

Alan Llwyd's social commentary and observations are most
eloquently expressed in a series of free-metre meditations published

in the 1980s under the pseudonym Meilir Emrys Owen, (eventually presented as a collection in the 1988 volume, *Yn y Dirfawr Wag* (In the Vast Emptiness). The use of the pseudonym—clearly intended to accompany a new poetic voice—may suggest an attempt by Alan Llwyd to distance himself from the more aggressive persona which dominates much of his other poetry and criticism. While the poetic voice of Meilir Emrys Owen in some respects reflects an attempt to achieve a liberating anonymity, it might also be described as an attempt to create a poetic persona which is one with the general populace. Meilir's voice is that of the quiet, almost unseen person living next door, an unobserved observer who records, in fly-on-the-wall fashion, the ills of contemporary life. The topics of these poems include suicide, murder, vandalism and mental illness, and, especially when taken together, they reveal an individual made increasingly uneasy by the general condition of modern society.

A sense of alienation pervades these poems. This is perhaps best seen in 'Cymro di-wlad' (A Country-less Welshman), a dark piece describing one individual's experience of being alienated from his (supposed) country. While the speaker can be taken readily as the metonymical representative for a whole sector of the population, the sense of loss is described as a very private one, conveyed in terms of a personal failure to realize nationhood. It begins with the memory of a past success in imagining, or 'singing', the nation into existence:

> Unwaith 'roedd gennyf genedl;
> 'roedd y dydd yn breuddwydio iaith,
> ac 'roedd cân yn gerdd cenedl.

> [Once I had a nation;
> the day dreamt a language,
> and the song was a nation's poem.]

The personal nature of this nationhood, emphasized in the first line by the first person possessive construction *'roedd gennyf* (I had), is then stated more explicitly. The nation lives—*ynof y ganed y genedl* (inside me the nation was born)—and dies—*ac ynof y bu farw'r genedl* (and inside me the nation died)—within the internal orbit of the individual. Just as the nation is internalized and located within the person, so the country is personified, albeit obliquely, and described in terms of a human corpse. Rather than being a sentimental elegy for a dead Wales, the poem exudes a bitter ambivalence: the death leaves the speaker face to face with unsavoury remains which inspire only disgust:

> Y genedl nad yw'n amgenach
> na chynrhon bach yn rhannu bedd;
> burgynod briw o genedl.
>
> [The nation which is nothing better
> than little maggots sharing a grave;
> the minced carcasses of a nation.]

The vacillation between 'the little maggots' sharing a single grave and the 'carcasses' provides a subtle attempt to encompass the hermeneutical process involved in ascribing national identity. In identifying one's self as a member of a nation, a person is caught up in a never-ending circle, moving constantly between the judgements of the collective group—the ways in which the corporate body of the 'nation' either accepts or rejects the person as a member of the same corporate body—and the personal act of ascription, a private, internal feeling of belonging to, or being alienated from, the same group. Nationality is created somewhere in the interaction between group activity and personal ascription, as is suggested by the way in which Alan Llwyd captures this complex process with his grave-yard imagery.

Alan Llwyd is also a critic, and he has been heavily involved with *Cymdeithas Gerdd Dafod*, which he helped to found in 1976. The first issue of *Barddas*, the Society's monthly magazine, appeared in the October of that same year, under the editorship of Gerallt Lloyd Owen and Alan Llwyd. While Gerallt Lloyd Owen left the position in 1983, Alan Llwyd has continued as editor, contributing regular articles and editorials which have cast him in the role of spokesman for the society.

The *Cymdeithas Gerdd Dafod* and its monthly *Barddas* quickly accrued the status of literary institutions, playing a major role in the public and political aspects of contemporary Welsh literary life, and also occasionally earning the enmity which such institutional status often inspires. In the same year (1976), there appeared the first volume in a poetry series dedicated to presenting the work of poets very different to those found in the pages of *Barddas*, *Cyfres y*

Beirdd Answyddogol (Unofficial Poets' Series) of Y Lolfa Press. Robat Gruffudd, the publisher of the series, authored the first volume, revealingly titled *Trên y Chwyldro* (The Train of the Revolution). As Gerwyn Wiliams has written:

> Literary historians of the future will consider 1976 to be a very significant year in the history of Welsh poetry in the last quarter of the twentieth century. In a conveniently tidy manner, in that year the Poetry Society was established and the first number of their monthly *Barddas* was published, and in the same year the first volume in the Unofficial Poets series of Y Lolfa [Press] was also published.

In this perceptive essay (entitled 'Darlunio'r Tirlawn Cyflawn', 'Drawing the Complete Landscape'), Gerwyn Wiliams contrasts the culturally conservative stance of the *Barddas* poets, and that of Alan Llwyd in particular, with the very different character of the 'unofficial poets'. Both groups were concerned with the same general sociopolitical challenge, namely securing the continuance of the language and culture of Wales, and both groups offered distinct visions as to the present and future condition(s) of the Welsh language, culture and literature, but the ways in which they approached these problems and issues were fundamentally different.

> Both 'schools' reacted to the same political crisis, but the reactions were fundamentally different. Culture was seen by the Unofficial series as a changing, metamorphic thing, while it was treated by the Poetry Society as a monolithic concept.

The different natures of these two opposed poetic establishments (for the Unofficial series, for all its anti-establishment rhetoric, must be considered as a kind of establishment in its own right) can be illustrated by a series of contrasting pairs of affinities. *Cymdeithas Gerdd Dafod* has represented – or has been taken to represent – the old strict metres, rural life, Christianity, traditional Welsh 'high' culture (*cerdd dant*, the Eisteddfod, etc.), tradition; *Cyfres y Beirdd Answyddogol*, on the other hand, has been associated with free verse, urban life, a radical questioning of faith, popular culture (rock music, video, etc.), innovation and newness.

Of course, these oppositions and boundaries are by no means hard and fast. As far as the formal characteristics of the poetry are concerned, while the 'Unofficial' series presents itself as being non-traditional, or even anti-traditional, the old strict metres occasionally appear in the pages of its volumes; *englynion* can be found in several volumes, including the very first one by Robat Gruffudd, the series' architect. *Dagrau Rhew* (Tears of Ice), Siôn Aled's 1979 contribution, contains a *cywydd* as well as several *englynion* (indeed, a later volume by Siôn Aled was published not by Y Lolfa but by Barddas Publications!). Ifor ap Glyn's witty 1991 contribution to the series, *Holl Garthion Pen Cymro Ynghyd* (All the Rubbish of a Welshman's Head [collected] Together) assumes a playfully ambivalent stance regarding the traditional forms, for it contains several *englynion* as well as a comic free-metre piece entitled 'Englynion', which begins:

> Mae englynion fatha sgampi,
> sneb cweit yn siwr be ydyn nhw,
>
> [Englynion are like scampi,
> no one's quite sure what they are.]

Much of the poetry in this series can be described as ephemeral verse, addressed directly to the events and establishment figures of the day, and not beyond. Such a comment is not entirely out of keeping with the way in which these volumes present themselves; the early ones are adorned with (what appear to be) hastily drawn cartoons and amateurish photographs, a packaging which coalesces with the subject-matter and simple diction of the poems to suggest that this verse is to be taken as a kind of metrical graffiti. Like graffiti, it is essentially ephemeral, but also like graffiti, when read in the sociopolitical context in which it was written it can be very effective.

However, as with the modern confessional lyrics found in Elin ap Hywel's *Pethau Brau* (Frail Things), the series has also served to introduce fresh and powerful new voices, and several of the poets who first published with Y Lolfa have gone on to play important roles in the development of Welsh poetry over the last two decades.

The 'Unofficial' poets' tend to ally themselves overtly with what can be termed—albeit inadequately—'popular culture'. This is perhaps best seen in the connection between the poets of the series and the Welsh-language rock/pop music scene. If anything, this alliance has grown stronger over the years, becoming explicit in the 1980s and 1990s with the publication of volumes by two of Wales's more important contemporary singer/song-writers, Steve Eaves and David R. Edwards. One should not make the mistake of treating these artists as part of a single homogeneous cultural movement; while they share many superficial affinities they are separated by just as many differences.

As is suggested by the title of Steve Eaves's 1986 volume *Jazz yn y Nos* (Jazz in the Night), his work often exhibits a quiet blending of cultures, bringing the Afro-American strains of Jazz and blues, as well as a disciplined echo of the Beat and Mersey poets, to bear upon the Welsh tradition. This crossing, however, is not presented as a brash challenge to the tradition, but rather occurs quietly and harmoniously. While David R. Edwards's songs and poems also draw upon diverse backgrounds, they belong to an entirely different milieu. Sometimes macaronically incorporating phrases from English and German, his poetry and lyrics often have the feel of a post-modern, and post-national(istic), pan-European schizo-phrenic tirade. As suggested by the name of Edward's musical group, Datblygu (to develop), his work frequently focuses on the developments of, and within, language and verbal art. He takes as his subject art in the process of creating itself, yet instead of assuming an air of quiet awe like that of W. B. Yeats's attempt 'to know the dancer from the dance', David R. Edwards submits the creative process to an ironic scrutiny. A recent poem, 'Creadigol' ('Creative'), published in the summer 1996 number of the journal *Tu Chwith*, describes creativity as 'the first neurosis' (*y niwrosis cynta*'). Assuming a mock-academic tone, Edwards informs us that artistic creativity was developed:

> pan gafodd pobl
> lond bol o'i gilydd
> a mynd ati
> i grafu graffiti
> ar welydd.

> [when people
> got sick of each other
> and went at it
> to scratch graffiti
> on walls.]

While he has never published in Y Lolfa's series, Geraint Jarman has influenced many of the 'Unofficial' poets as both poet and performer. In the 1970s Geraint Jarman brought a new professionalism to Welsh-language popular music, which he also imbued with new, foreign sounds—most notably that of reggae. While the majority of his verbal artistry has found expression in song lyrics, Jarman has published two volumes of poetry, *Eira Cariad* (Snow of Love, 1970), and *Cerddi Alfred St.* (1976). As the title of his second book, 'Alfred St. Poems', suggests, this verse is grounded in the city streets; Jarman's muse is a distinctly urban one. He lives in the city of Cardiff, and much of his poetry, like his music, reflects an urban existence, an aspect of Welsh life which had been virtually invisible in the literature prior to the early 1970s.

In one of a series of articles entitled 'Cymraeg y Pridd a'r Concrid' (Welsh of the Soil and the Concrete), Vaughan Hughes described Jarman as an artist who 'gets to grips seriously with the experience of being a Welshman in the last quarter of the twentieth century'. These articles were part of a protracted debate concerning the nature—and success—of Welsh urban literature and culture, a manifestation of the rural-urban tensions which were part of the constellation of conflicts outlined by Gerwyn Wiliams and discussed above. The debate in print, which ran throughout the late 1970s, was often punctuated by critics allied with *Cymdeithas Gerdd Dafod* devaluing the urban contributions to Welsh cultural life, claiming, as did Gwynn ap Gwilym (in *Y Faner*, 19 January 1979), that:

> It is in the country that the roots of our culture lie, and it is there that our language is most alive. Thus our contemporary life must be grounded solidly on the foundations which are in the country.

The major milestone in this urban culture *vs.* rural culture debate was the 1978 National Eisteddfod, held in Cardiff, where the set title for the Chair competition was 'Y Ddinas' (The City). There was no winner; no *awdl* was judged good enough to be chaired. However, any support this may have lent to the position of those who claimed that a Welsh muse could not be successfully planted in the city's concrete was undercut by the end of the Eisteddfod week, for Siôn Eirian won the Crown with a sequence of free-metre poems set against an urban backdrop. In addition to successfully uniting the Welsh language with urban images, Siôn Eirian has also brought English and Welsh together in macaronic lines, fashioning a metrical border country. One of his best-known poems is 'Agro' (derived from the English word 'aggression'), which takes its name from the slang used by football hooligans. It begins:

> Wrexham agro,
> gorthrwm,
> trwm iawn, very heavy
> our boots, our byd.

> [*Wrexham* agro,
> oppression,
> very heavy, *very heavy*
> *our boots, our* world.

Words appearing in English in the original are italicized in the translation.]

The bilingual play begins immediately: Wrexham is spelled in the English way, not as Welsh *Wrecsam*, and thus the reader is warned that this poem should be read with an eye and ear open to both languages. The second word of the poem, agro, is a slang word which could be used in either language—especially if we accept the world that Siôn Eirian's poetry presents, a world populated by Welsh-speaking urban youths. We thus have a choice as to how to read the first line of the poem. First of all, it can be read as English, taking Wrexham as modifying agro; this, then, is a poem about the agr(ession) of Wrexham, a uniquely Wrexham kind of agr(ession) or agr(evation). Or it can be interpreted using the rules of Welsh grammar, in which the genitive construction is formed by placing one noun (designating the possessor) after another (the thing which is possessed). This yields 'agro's Wrexham', a town and environment possessed by the violent and unnerving condition which the slang term indexes. In the course of the short poem, these tensions are transformed into tensions between the generations, between the old and the new Wales, described in strangely genealogical terms:

> gwadnau lleder cenedlaethau
> o ddiaconiaid a landlordiaid

yn magu'r genhedlaeth hon
o wadnau trymion y traed ifainc;

[the leather soles of generations
of deacons and landlords
raising this generation
of heavy soles of the young feet.]

The poem ends by suggesting that, if the violence is committed by the young generation, it occurs within, and because of, an environment created by the older one:

eich palmentydd concrid chi
yw cynfas ein cynddaredd ni,

smotiau gwaed
o groglith
gwareiddiad.

[your concrete pavements
are the canvas of our rage,
drops of blood
from the crucifixion
of civilization.]

The 1978 Cardiff Eisteddfod and the urban culture debate surrounding it were landmarks in modern Welsh literary history, but these events were soon overshadowed, for the following year brought the Referendum and a new challenge to Welsh identity. After years of campaigning, the British government organized a vote on the establishment of an assembly for Wales and Scotland in 1979. While substantial numbers in both countries voted in favour, they were not sufficient to secure this legislative step towards devolution. Obviously, this was a blow to Welsh nationalism and was widely interpreted as a failure of the people to unite in their political visions.

As might be expected, a whole body of poetry was generated which treated, mourned and addressed the 1979 Referendum results. Some of the most sensitive post-Referendum verse came with T. James Jones's *Cerddi Ianws / Janus Poems*, a bilingual collaboration produced for the 1979 Eisteddfod including English compositions by the Welsh-American poet Jon Dressel. T. James

Jones has said of these poems that 'Our joint worrying about the injustice which we the Welsh had done to ourselves on St David's Day 1979 [the day of the vote] moved us to compose them'. This worrying, despite being shared by two poets working together, is very much a personal affliction; the events are removed from the national arena of politics and propagandistic blustering. The danger, the stormy weather, Jones suggests, is actually located in a quieter place, inside the people:

> Mi a'i dywedaf eto:
> ynom y mae'r hin.

> [I will say it again:
> it is inside us that the bad weather lies.]

This quiet, internal climate is devastatingly unique. The magnitude of the loss is equated with another loss, that occurring roughly seven hundred years prior, the death of Llywelyn, last native ruler of Wales:

> Eto, ni bu dydd fel hwn
> ers saith gan mlynedd.
> Hon yw'r hin na welsom
> ni, y rhai byw, mo'i thebyg.

> [Still, there has been no day like this
> for seven hundred years.
> This is the bad weather that we, the living ones,
> have not seen the likes of before.]

The reference to the medieval prince is oblique, and unlike much of the more aggressively political poetry of the sixties, seventies, eighties and nineties, T. James Jones wraps his meditations around the minute events marking the quiet life of one individual during the fateful week in 1979:

> Bore heddiw, mi gefais gyda'r llaeth
> gorryn yn ymguddio rhwng y poteli.
> Ac ar dalcen dwyrain y tŷ, y mae'r cocŵn
> a fu'n glynu trwy alanastra'r gaeaf,
> yno byth.

[This morning, I found with the milk
a spider hiding among the bottles.
And on the east side of the house, the cocoon
which has weathered all the onslaughts of the winter
remains there.]

The ability to bring a 'real', political nation into being seemed to slip further away after 1979, but Welsh poets continued to write an imaginary Welsh nation into a literary existence, as, to some extent, they had done throughout the century. Perhaps the most unique post-1979 poetic vision of the nation, its history and its future, came in the form of Bobi Jones's 1986 epic, or anti-epic, 'Hunllef Arthur' (Arthur's Nightmare). Although its author—one of the more important poets of the generation which first gained recognition in the early 1960s—has described it as the culmination of nearly thirty years' worth of thought and obsession, one cannot help but attribute significance to the fact that 'Hunllef Arthur' appeared in the years immediately following the referendum.

In over 20,000 lines arranged in twenty-four different chapters or books, 'Hunllef Arthur' presents a totally unique reading of Welsh history laced with Calvinistic theology. However, as the entire fabric of the work emphasizes, it is neither a real Wales nor its history which is presented here, but rather an explicitly imagined, or more exactly, dreamed nation. Even more exactly, it is a nightmare nation which haunts this poem, for it is loss and failure which pervade Bobi Jones's metrical pseudo-history. The following meditation on defeat, located in the fourth book's reading of the Gododdin poetry and the early struggles with the Anglo-Saxons, is in many ways typical of the work:

> Methiant fu'r ymladd. Y mae'r byd yn lloer
> A'i hil yn llwch, golygfa heb na thŷ
> Na thwlc yn unman hyd-ddi. Marwnad yw
> Y wawr pan ddaw'i phelydrau dof i'w cyrff
> Mor glwc ei hamdo. Rhoesant einioes hil
> Er mwyn galarnad.

> [The fighting was a failure. The world is a moon
> And its race is dust, a scene with neither house
> Nor pig-sty anywhere in it. The dawn
> is an elegy when its tame rays come to touch their bodies,
> So sad its shroud. They exchanged the life of a race
> For a lamentation.]

Arthur is the vehicle for the vision; the archetypical Welsh hero, having failed to realize his dream of a nation in his lifetime, sleeps in a cave and dreams—'nightmares'—Welsh history. Throughout the first book, the words *breuddwyd* (dream), *hunllef* (nightmare), and *hanes* (history) wrestle with each other in a creative tangle from which the ensuing narratives and reflections spring forth. Towards the end of the second book, in which Arthur dreams—or has night-mares—about his old battles, he describes himself as a kind of primal, somnambulant saviour:

> Myfi'r cysgadur cyntaf, heb fedru darfod,
> Dysgaf drwy adnewyddiad cwsg pa fodd
> I led oroesi . . . (II, 512–15)

> [I, the first sleeper, not able to die,
> I will learn from the rejuvenation of sleep how
> to partially survive . . .]

The words *lled oroesi* are highly significant; these lines seem to suggest that the Welsh national spirit lives only in a sleep-walking, zombie-like state. There is also a suggestion as to the artist's role in preserving a fallen nation; it is through mimesis, artistic reflection removed from reality, as dreaming is removed from waking life, that the fallen nation can be realized anew. While 'Hunllef Arthur' is a difficult poem which has won only a very limited readership, it is surely one of the more interesting experiments in poetic expression of the period.

In addition to Bobi Jones, several other important poets of the pre-1969 years continued to be major voices in the 1970s and 1980s. Euros Bowen continued to write his special strain of dense, symbolist-imagist verse. And Gwyn Thomas, who started publishing in the early 1960s, went in new directions in the seventies and eighties, developing a lighter, more colloquial style. Grounding his verse in an idiom closer to the spoken language, Gwyn Thomas has engaged a much wider audience with the six volumes published in this period: *Enw'r Gair* (The Name of the Word, 1972); *Y Pethau Diwethaf a Phethau Eraill* (The Latest Things and Other Things, 1975); *Croesi Traeth*, (Crossing a Beach, 1978); *Symud y Lliwiau* (The Movement of the Colours, 1981); *Wmgawa* (1984); *Am Ryw Hyd* (For Some While, 1986).

'Cymylau Gwynion' (White Clouds), from the 1978 volume *Croesi Traeth*, displays Gwyn Thomas's talent for mixing esoteric references with a simple, memorable versification. This *ballade*, which takes its cue from the late medieval French poet François Villon's line *Mais ou sont les neiges d'antan?* (But where is the snow of the time gone by?), is a variation on the classical *ubi sunt* theme. However, this dose of referentiality is distilled into a simple refrain which has the gnomic quality of an age-old folk song:

> Cymylau gwynion yn y gwynt,
> Hen gyfoedion dyddiau gynt.
>
> [White clouds in the wind,
> The old companions of former days.]

The title poem of the same volume, 'Croesi Traeth', describes the poet's meditations on time and life as he watches his young children run across a beach. Much of Gwyn Thomas's poetry is essentially autobiographical, and many of its more memorable moments are ones in which he examines the encounters between growing children and the world around them. In this, Gwyn Thomas has strong affinities with other poets writing in the seventies, eighties and nineties, most notably Menna Elfyn and the earlier Einir Jones. All of these poets use the child's vision to skate close to those ultimately incomprehensible questions—death, the nature of time, the essence of sensory perception.

Children's encounters with language have provided Gwyn Thomas with very productive material. As is suggested by the title of *Enw'r Gair* (The Name of the Word), his later poetry examines the ways in which we use language to understand the world, foregrounding the joys and frustrations involved in the linguistic interpretive processes. In 'Henffych Datws' (from *Croesi Traeth*), Thomas uses children's speech as the starting-point for a playful series of linguistic crossings and translations, interpretations and misinterpretations. The productive interaction between an infant's speech and adult meditation is initiated by the child's greeting *helo garatjan* (hello carrot), a mispronunciation of *carotsen*, a dialect word for 'carrot'. This is then used by the adult voice to refer to the conductor Herbert von Karajan. Thus a mispronunciation (that is, a linguistically 'incorrect' or non-standard pronunciation) of a dialect word (another kind of non-standard word), which happens to be borrowed into Welsh from English, is taken to invoke a foreign name.

Menna Elfyn has also turned the wisely naive worldview of the child into a powerful poetic vehicle, as seen in the title poem of the volume *Mynd Lawr i'r Nefoedd* (Going Down to Heaven, 1986), in which she describes a confrontation between her socially conditioned adult fear of death and her child's transformation of a graveyard into a playground:

> A thi sydd yn iawn:
> yn llunio dy nefoedd ar y ddaear,
> yn glanhau'n rhagrith â'th rialtwch,
> gan chwerthin â'th draed
> dros ddwyster
> ein tipyn beddau.

> [And it is you who is right:
> forming your heaven on the earth,
> cleansing our hypocrisy with your merriment,
> laughing with your feet
> over the seriousness
> of our insignificant graves.]

Menna Elfyn has brought her subtle diction and engaging tone to bear upon a range of different subjects taken from the diverse spheres of the autobiographical and the public-political. Her post-1979 poem 'Neges (ar awr wan)'—'Message (in a weak moment)', from the 1982 collection *Tro'r Haul Arno* (Turn the Sun On), offers one of the more striking views of post-Referendum Wales, describing national calamity with the immediacy and intimacy of that darkest kind of personal despair, the suicide wish.

> Gadewch in ddiflannu
> o gramen daear
> gydag urddas pobol

> [Let us disappear
> from earth's crust
> with the dignity of people.]

The plural pronoun of the collective group dominates this poem—it is overtly a message to the nation—yet it comes across like a very personal, quiet confessional whisper expressing a desire to:

> . . . llafarganu'n swynol;
> sugno'r nos,
> nes cysgu
> ar fronnau'n hiaith.
> [. . . charmingly chant;
> suck from the night,
> until [we] sleep
> on the breasts of our language.]

Menna Elfyn has developed her own unique strain of personal political lyric, perhaps best exemplified by a series of poems found in her most recent volume, *Cell Angel* (Cell Angel, 1996). In these poems she uses the experiences of a jailed political activist to synthesize a powerful constellation of meditations which touch upon the diverse spheres of the spiritual, the artistic and the political.

Menna Elfyn is perhaps Wales's best-known feminist poet. She has done much to bring women onto the centre literary stage in Wales, and she has edited two volumes of poetry by women to date: *Hel Dail Gwyrdd* (Gathering Green Leaves, 1985) and *O'r Iawn Ryw* (Of the Right Sort [or Sex], 1991). These aspects of her work are often inspired by foreign writings, be it French feminist theory, or the poetry of the American poets Anne Sexton and Sylvia Plath.

Many contemporary Welsh poets display a definite affinity for twentieth-century American verse. The Welsh poetic tradition has always been conservatively self-referential, as exhibited by the medievalism discussed at the beginning of this chapter. However, despite an understandable and common reluctance to leave the rich fields of the 'native' tradition, the development of Welsh poetry in the twentieth century has been punctuated by certain productive borrowings from other traditions. Notable examples are the influence of the English and German Romantics upon Welsh poetry at the turn of the century and Euros Bowen's extensive use of Classical material. However, from the 1960s on, Welsh echoes of American poetry have grown increasingly louder. The more obvious strains include those of Sexton and Plath (e.g., Menna Elfyn and a recent writer in the 'Unofficial' series, Elin Llwyd Morgan), as well as a spectrum of 'pop' rhythms of the 1960s ranging from Allen Ginsberg to Bob Dylan (e.g., Steve Eaves, Iwan Llwyd, Twm Morys). Dewi Stephen Jones, who introduced fresh and sophisticated tones into Welsh poetry with his recent volume

Hen Ddawns (Old Dance), has paid tribute to Anne Stevenson. And strains of William Carlos Williams and Wallace Stevens can be heard in the poetry of Bryan Martin Davies and Einir Jones.

The earlier work of Einir Jones often employed the child's point of view to profitable ends, and in this respect it is akin to much of the verse of Gwyn Thomas and Menna Elfyn discussed above. However, she has more recently developed a very different and more refined voice, while retaining the characteristic short line and economy of expression. This is perhaps best seen in her sequence 'Pelydrau' (Rays), which won the Crown in the 1991 Eisteddfod. The poems in the sequence are arranged according to a colour scheme. These poems tend to consist of a single compact image which the poet explores 'visually', only partially unpacking it for the reader. They are hushed meditations, occasionally rising to a more intense pitch, as with the poem 'Brân' (Crow), which is set under the rubric *du*, 'black'. This short poem falls into two different parts. The longer first part, opening with a tightly woven series of rhymes and alliterative pairs of words, is a meditation on a visual image akin in many ways to Wallace Stevens's 'Thirteen Ways of Looking at a Blackbird'.

BRÂN

Gloywblu, glasddu, herciog
yn casglu,

crynhoi cynhron,
pigo gronynnau'r cynhaeaf
ymhlith y conion gwenith

cyn agor adenydd rhacsiog
a chodi'n grawc du
o'r caeau aur.

Tywyllwch rhydd
yn hofran yn ei ffurf hen,
hedfan a throelli'n bwyllog
uwch y llwyn o goed.

Gwatwar a greddf
yn ei phig.

Gadewch iddi
fod.

[A CROW

Bright-feathered, blue-black, hopping
collecting,

gathering maggots,
picking the grains of the harvest
among the stalks of wheat

before spreading ragged wings
and rising up, a black croak
from the golden fields.

Free darkness
hovering in its ancient form,
flying and spinning deliberately
above the copse of trees.

Mockery and instinct
in its beak.

Let it
be.]

A new tone is struck in the final lines of the poem, as some interpretation—rare in the sequence on the whole, hence gaining added significance in this case—is added. The speaker, until now confining herself to the recording of visual stimuli, observes—or imagines—that the crow holds 'mockery and instinct' in its beak, and this revelation leads to a sardonic warning, 'let it be' (or 'let her be', as *brân* is grammatically feminine). The coupling of observations on the natural world and wisdom offered as a warning echoes the gnomic stanzas so common in medieval Welsh poetry. However, unlike some of the contemporary strict-metre poets who have employed this gnomic voice in a manner more in keeping with its medieval origins, the gnomic voice heard here is distinctly modern, tempering the unquestionable wisdom of the ages with a note of sarcasm.

In its commanding use of visual imagery and its rigorous working of the free-metre line into a disciplined, economical medium, the later work of Einir Jones has an affinity with the poetry of Bryan Martin Davies, one of the most accomplished free-metre poets of the past three decades. Bryan Martin Davies has

developed a fresh idiom, a language which manages to be stately
and sophisticated without being removed from the vitality of
spoken Welsh. He has sometimes been referred to as a Gwenallt of
the 1970s, chronicling the industrial, and post-industrial, life of the
south Wales coal fields in tightly woven verse. 'Glöwr' (A Miner),
from the 1970 collection *Darluniau ar Gynfas a Cherddi Eraill*
(Pictures on Canvas and Other Poems), begins with the disturbing
line: *Ni fynnwn dy gofio heddiw* (We do not wish to remember you
today). Another dark monument to the miner's life, 'Llwch' (Dust),
begins:

> Ti, sy'n tolio d'anadl
> ar y tyle hyn,
> sy'n tynnu dy hun
> gerfydd d'edau o wynt
> ar y rhiw . . .
>
> [You, who conserve your breath
> on this hill,
> who pull yourself
> by your strings of wind
> on the slope . . .]

This poem is contained in the 1976 volume, *Deuoliaethau*
(Dualities), an assembly of poems which readily reminds the critic
that to describe Bryan Martin Davies only as a metrical chronicler
of the hardships of life is to miss many of the subtler aspects of his
verse. The 'dualities' of the title can be taken to refer to many
aspects of modern Welsh life, including bilingualism and the
coexistence of two languages as well as the experience of being part
of a 'nation' which has no formally recognized nationality attached
to it. Note that the title is plural. This plurality, or multiplicity, of
dualities can also be taken as referring to the poetics of Bryan
Martin Davies, the quiet way in which his work explores the
double-sided, or multi-sided, nature of cognitive acts such as
perception, recognition and remembering.

   The centre-piece of this volume is the powerful sequence 'Y
Clawdd'. *Clawdd* literally means 'ditch' or 'barrier', but the *Clawdd*
of the title is Offa's Dyke, the earthen rampart built by an eighth-
century king of Mercia to keep the Welsh in Wales and out of what
was then becoming England. Despite the locating of these poems in

the geographical borderland, the heavy foot-falls of politics and history have left few obvious tracks on Bryan Martin Davies's poetic *clawdd*; his dyke is a more subtle, internal barrier. While suggesting that the most difficult borders to cross are the ones inside ourselves, Davies simultaneously examines the criss-crossing processes of recognition which connect sensory—particularly visual—stimuli to memory and feeling. These notes are struck immediately in the first lines of the sequence:

> Ynom mae y Clawdd a phob ymwybod,
> y tir hwn a godwyd
> rhyngom a'r gwastadedd blin,
> y pridd pêr a'r cerrig Cymreig
> sy'n ceulo'n gaer yng nghelloedd cof,
> ac sy'n crynu fel grym yng ngwthiadau'r gwaed.
> Ar ei lechwedd ac ar ei geuedd
> fe ddeilia'r deri a'r ynn
> fel penderfyniadau gwyrdd
> yn naear ein dihewyd . . .

> [It is inside us that the dyke and every knowing lies,
> this land which was raised
> between us and the angry low-lands,
> the sweet soil and the Welsh stones
> which coagulate into a fortress in the cells of memory,
> and which shake like strength in the blood's pulsing.
> On its slope and in its ditch
> the oaks and the ash-trees bear leaves
> like green decisions
> in the earth of our aspiration . . .]

Taken together, the poems of 'Y Clawdd' reflect upon a disquieting contrast, a contrast embodied in the image of the trees growing on Offa's Dyke, that representative of the geographical and psychological boundaries of the nation. The trees, described in several different seasonal guises, testify quietly to nature's cyclic renewal, a process which highlights the fact that the nation's life is not cyclical, that it may in fact be progressing linearly towards an end, a final death.

'Y Clawdd' may be instructively compared with Iwan Llwyd's sequence 'Gwreichion' (Sparks), which, though a very different group of poems, also combines reflections on 'natural' life with a consideration of the life of the nation. One of the more exciting developments in Welsh poetry over the past fifteen years has been the evolution of Iwan Llwyd's work. His first collection, *Sonedau Bore Sadwrn* (Saturday Morning Sonnets), was published in Y Lolfa's 'Unofficial' series in 1983. This volume displays two distinct traits: a bold political realism presented in stark, often ironic, free verse on the one hand, and a rich reflective lyricism on the other. Iwan Llwyd developed and honed these qualities throughout the 1980s, a development illustrated by the poetry from this period published in two later volumes, *Dan Anesthetig* (Under Anaesthetic, 1988) and *Dan Fy Ngwynt* (Under My Breath, 1992). As the decade progressed, an increasing interest in *cynghanedd* and the traditional strict metres brought more discipline to his free-metre poetry. He has also more recently published *cywyddau*.

Iwan Llwyd won the Crown in the 1990 National Eisteddfod with his sequence 'Gweichion'. These poems—thirteen in number—represent the best of his work from the period 1979–89; many of them are, in fact, pieces he wrote earlier in the decade but did not previously publish. The thirteen poems in the sequence are bound up in multiple, interlacing frameworks. First of all, each one of them can be taken as exploring different aspects of the vital and artistic 'sparks' referred to in the title. The first poem, or prologue, like the poet's pseudonym, Tjuringa, presents the work as a tribute to the writer Bruce Chatwin, who died in 1989. The poems draw heavily upon Chatwin's book about the native Australians, *The Song Lines*, and strands of Aboriginal mythology are also used to bind these thirteen poems together. Of central importance is Chatwin's recounting of the creation myths:

> Aboriginal Creation myths tell of the legendary totemic beings who had wandered over the continent in the Dreamtime, singing out the name of everything that crossed their paths—birds, animals, plants, rocks, waterholes—and so singing the world into existence.

The word *tjuringa*, with which Iwan Llwyd signed the sequence, is itself bound up in this creation mythology; it is a sacred object carved so as to represent the aetiological wanderings of the primal beings. 'Gweichion' offers Iwan Llwyd's vision of Wales past, present and future, and it openly echoes the Aboriginal creation myth in that it is the poet's attempt to *sing* a new nation into being. This ties into yet another structural frame used to organize the poems, a temporal frame of reference the important junctures of which are significant dates in recent political history. A prologue and an epilogue frame the body of the work, which consists of eleven poems arranged to form a temporal progression. Each of these is assigned a date: the first one is March 1979 and the last is New Year 1989. 'Gwreichion' is thus a poetic chronicling of the stormy decade which began with the Referendum of 1979. This chronicling takes the form of a series of lyrical tableaux, each of which is part of a triptych, a frozen scene telling part of a narrative.

The narrative, or one of the narratives, which can be pieced together from the eleven tableaux snap-shots involves a mother—in fact it is told in her voice—and her son, Rhys. We learn that her child was conceived in troubled times, that she considered aborting the baby, but that he was born and, as he grew, brought new meaning to her life. This child is the decade following the Referendum, and the first poem in the narrative series is appropriately titled 'Angladd' (Funeral). On the most obvious level, it describes the burial of a farmer on the island of Anglesey:

> Bûm mewn angladd ddoe:
>
> mewn mynwent wyntog ym Môn a glaw 'Werddon
> yn cipio gweddïau o enau'r gweinidog
>
> [I was in a funeral yesterday:
>
> in a windy graveyard in Anglesey with Ireland's rain
> snatching the prayers from the mouth of the minister.]

The minister's words are not heard by the speaker. They leave no impact or impression, and hence the religious service has no meaning. We are reminded that the old Wales, like the old farmer, is dead, and that its institutions do not have the meaning they once had. Yet despite this bleak scene, a child was conceived in the same graveyard:

> Yno fe'th genhedlwyd
> yn ochenaid rhwng y blodau a'r bedd,
> ac ym mhen naw mis
> dy eni'n gryf yn yr oed oedd arnat,
> a chenais dy enw, Rhys . . .

[There you were conceived
as a sigh between the flowers and the grave,
and at the end of nine months
you were born with strength in the age which was upon you,
and I sang your name, Rhys . . .]

The conception takes place *rhwng y blodau . . . a'r bedd*—between an attempt to mark, remember, or pay tribute to something (flowers placed on a grave) and that thing itself (the grave). The creation of new life is confirmed by verbal creation; the child's name is *sung* to the world.

The mother's singing *to* her child constitutes a significant part of 'Gwreichion'. Singing a lullaby represents the transference of language in a highly marked form (song; verbal art) from parent to child, and it is in the act of passing language from one generation to another that the main concerns of the poems are crystallized: vocalization as an act of creation; the ability to speak as a symbol of cultural continuity and survival. The fourth scene in the triptych is presented as the mother's song to her child; it is titled 'Mehefin 1982 Hwiangerdd' (June 1982 Lullaby). As is seen in the first stanza, her song instructs the child, drawing attention to the fact that his life is set against the background of social death:

Clyw ymson hen ŵr yn suo'r haf i gysgu
a rhythmau'r môr yn marwnadu'r mud
gymunedau a foddwyd gan y llanw estron:
clyw eu hanadliad olaf yn siglo dy grud.

[Hear an old man's monologue humming the summer to sleep
and the sea's rhythms singing an elegy for the mute
communities drowned by the foreign tide:
hear their last breath rocking your cradle.]

This poem differs from the bulk of the sequence in that it assumes the formal characteristics associated with lullabies: a semi-regular line length and a simple, *abcb* rhyme scheme. It has the appearance of a 'song', and as such represents the woman's successful attempt to communicate on a heightened level, expressing her reactions to the times in a meaningful form.

The 'Gwreichion' poems speak directly to the importance of artistic expression and the ways in which such expression can be silenced. The prologue, which is an elegy for Bruce Chatwin, also mourns the loss of artistic articulation. In describing the last days of Chatwin, who died in the grips of a debilitating disease, Iwan Llwyd voices the fears of a writer facing silence:

> Ni fedrai gyfansoddi ar sgrîn a'i fysedd clonciog
> yn hercian o sill i sill, o saib i saib
> yn heneiddio'n anniddig:
>
> yr oedd dydd pryd y gwelai glai'r dyfodol
> yn ei ddwylo llaith i'w fowldio a'i fwydo,
> ei danio a'i dylino ar ddelw rhyw ddinas ddihalog
>
> [He could not compose on a screen with his awkward fingers
> jerking from syllable to syllable, from pause to pause
> irritably ageing:
>
> there was a day when he saw the clay of the future
> in his damp hands being moulded and softened,
> fired and formed in the shape of some immaculate city.]

Despite this dark opening which borders on being an elegy for artistic expression, the following series of poems describes a successful succession of attempts to give voice, to create with words. 'Gwreichion' is an optimistic celebration of survival and creation placed in a pessimistic package. The epilogue, like the prologue, is a kind of elegy. Yet this final song, which echoes the lullaby as it reawakens its rhyme-scheme, ends on a very different note; its last stanza triumphantly pronounces that an act of creation has preceded death:

> ond cyn llifo'n un â'r elfennau
> cleisiodd y glasddydd â bloedd,
> ag enfys rhwng y dyfroedd a darfod
> datganodd dy genhedlu ar goedd.
>
> [but before flowing as one with the elements
> the early morning dawned with a shout,
> with a rainbow suspended between the waters and death
> he/she proclaimed your procreation publicly.]

'Gwreichion' unifies and harmonizes different strands of the modern Welsh poetic tradition. Although Alan Llwyd, one of the judges of the 1990 Crown competition, poured lavish praise upon the sequence, he also said that it might be called *tywyll*. Literally meaning 'dark', the adjective *tywyll* is used to describe poetry which is opaque or difficult to understand. It has played an important, if negative, role in the history of twentieth-century poetry criticism, being used from time to time to condemn or marginalize poems thought to be too philosophical, complex or abstract. Euros Bowen, one of the most original and productive poets of the later half of the century, was branded as *tywyll* in the early 1960s, and the stigma stuck to him throughout his life. The condemnation of a poet or poem as being *tywyll* is one aspect of the critical tradition referred to above, namely the favouring of poetry with an easily understood meaning over more complex compositions. 'Gwreichion' is driven by an easily grasped narrative, and it clearly refers to the political climate of the post-1979 decade. Yet it is also a complex, multilayered examination of the process of creation and the relationship between this process and the ways in which identity, both individual and national, is constructed.

Iwan Llwyd is also an accomplished composer of *cywyddau* and *englynion*, and he has played a part in what critics have come to call the strict-metre 'renaissance' of the 1990s. Although it may be more accurate to avoid this label and view this literary movement as a natural extension of the 1970s 'renaissance' (although the term may not be entirely appropriate in that context either, as has been discussed above), there are in Wales today a large number of young poets currently writing in the strict metres. In 1990, the same year that Iwan Llwyd won the Crown, Myrddin ap Dafydd, one of the more prolific members of this young generation of *cynganeddwyr*, won the Chair with his *awdl* 'Gwythiennau' (published in the 1991 collection *Cadw Gŵyl*, 'Keeping a Feast'). This poem is a celebration of life, and combines a marvelling at the miracle of childbirth with an optimism regarding the life and future of Wales:

> Mae yn ein bro don ifanc yn codi
> A hon yw ton y dilyniant inni,
> Hen ddawn yn newydd ynni—a dyfroedd
> Ein hen deuluoedd yn dal i loywi.
>
> [In our land there is a new wave rising
> And this, for us, is the wave of continuance,
> An old gift [becomes] a new energy—and the waters
> of our old families are still shimmering.]

A similarly optimistic tone dominated the *awdl* of Meirion MacIntyre Huws, which won the Chair in 1993. This poem, which constitutes a lively description of the new life awakening in the semi-urban environment of the town of Caernarfon, reads like a transformation of Siôn Eirian's dark urban poetry into an up-beat, strict-metre creation:

> Â mynwent y palmentydd—yn gwawrio
> i guriad to newydd,
> neon sy'n tanio'n hawydd;
> bore gwyn ar derfyn dydd.

> [With the graveyard of the pavements—dawning
> to the beat of a new generation,
> it is neon which ignites our desire;
> a bright morning at the day's end.]

In the realm of strict-metre poetry, this 'new wave' is perhaps best exemplified by the two volumes of *Cywyddau Cyhoeddus* (published in 1994 and 1996). The title literally means 'Public *Cywyddau*', and reflects the fact that these poets are committed to taking their work directly to their audiences, performing their poetry in a variety of venues, ranging from pubs to schools. It should be noted, however, that performing poetry is not the exclusive preserve of the strict-metre poets; in fact, the public performances of the 'cywyddwyr cyhoeddus' can be seen as part of a larger movement which was spear-headed in the 1980s by several free-metre poets, including Menna Elfyn, Steve Eaves and Gerwyn Wiliams. And, indeed, traditions such as that of the Eisteddfod have ensured that poetry has always had a public-performance face in Wales.

The uses to which this generation applies the *cywydd* are incredibly varied, as a survey of the 171 poems contained in these two volumes will confirm. There are numerous examples of traditional occasional verse, elegizing the dead and com-memorating other significant events in the life of the local community. These poets also commemorate events of national, and international, significance, with the result that the titles of many of these *cywyddau* read like the newspaper headlines of the 1990s (for example, Emyr Davies's 'Bosnia' and Huw Meirion Edwards's 'Trychineb y *Sea Empress*' (The Sea Empress Disaster)).

Although the *cywydd* is technically a 'strict' form, all of the metrical constraints are confined to the couplet structure; any number of couplets can be added together, so that these modern *cywyddau* – unlike their medieval ancestors which tended to be very long by comparison—can vary in size from twelve lines to nearly one hundred. Emyr Lewis has turned the long *cywydd* into an excellent vehicle for self-consciously post-modern, comical narrative. An example is 'Malu' (Nonsense), which describes a humorous drunken encounter between a conservative, traditionalist poet (explicitly associated with *Barddas*) and:

> Dyrnaid o ôl-fodernwyr
> a bôrs yr ôl-farcsiaeth bur
> a thwr o ôl-strwythuriaid
> ar led yn yfed mewn haid
>
> [A handful of post-modernists
> and bores of the pure post-Marxism
> and a group of post-structuralists
> spread out drinking in a swarm.]

At the end of this metrical narrative, after dozens of lines of exaggerated insults have been thrown back and forth between the two politically opposed literary factions, the bartender intervenes and asks the narrator to pass judgement and settle the debate. He refuses—*na, nid wyf am feirniadu* (no, I will *not* judge)—and makes this refusal final, for the poem finishes with what Dafydd Johnston has called a sophisticated post-modern joke, the disappearance of the author:

> Hyd fy oes fy nhynged fu
> dweud fy lein a diflannu.
> A 'rwyf yn mynd i brofi
> hynny'n awr . . .
>
> [Throughout my life my fate has been
> to say my line and disappear.
> And I am going to prove
> that now . . .]

The humour is heightened by the fact that, like a coward running to escape a bar-room brawl, the narrator does not even quite complete saying 'his line'; the final line of the final couplet is incomplete, having neither the appropriate number of syllables, nor the complete *cynghanedd*, nor the end rhyme required by the *cywydd* form.

This self-conscious post-modernism is placed in direct dialogue with the pre-modern tradition. In another poem, entitled 'Gofyn byrger' (Requesting a burger), Emyr Lewis lampoons the medieval genre of the *cywydd gofyn*, or 'request cywydd', by melding it with a narrative located in a drive-through MacDonald's. Between the lines of the comic narrative slip observations on the confrontation between traditional Welsh culture (the speaker identifies himself *hen fardd truan*, 'a pitiful old poet') and the Americanized, international consumer society which the fast food restaurant represents. However, any serious commentary is thoroughly overshadowed by the prevailing playful tone. In fact, when this poem was first published (in the 1996 Summer issue of the journal *Tu Chwith*), Emyr Lewis prefaced it with a note calling it a 'cyber*cywydd*', undermining his own role as author and inviting other poets to add on to it freely.

The work of Twm Morys, another contemporary *cywyddwr*, is similarly shrouded in a great deal of play. He prefaced his first volume of poetry, *Ofn fy Het* (Fear of my Hat, 1995), with a spurious academic introduction by the fictitious professor Neil Sagam, the name itself being a pan-Celtic linguistic joke using the Irish phrase *níl a fhios agam*, meaning 'I don't know'. This should not obscure the fact that Twm Morys has produced some very sensitive and serious poetry. He is particularly adept at writing extremely short, reflective *cywyddau* which artfully describe one scene or a single train of thought and end with a twist, a sudden realization, or a surprising turn. The following *cywydd*, 'Mam am y bwrdd â mi' (Mother at the table with me), is an excellent example:

> Roedd Mam am y bwrdd â mi,
> â'i dwy law'n dal i weini.
> Byth yn sôn am y llonydd,
> a grisiau mawr distaw'r dydd,
> heb y plant, heb Tada'n tŷ,
> yn sachaid o besychu,
> ond yn cydio'n y cadach,
> fel ar hyd ei bywyd bach,
> â'i holl nerth yn golchi a llnau
> a smwddio, hyd nes maddau . . .

Llyncais lond ceg o regi:
roedd Mam am y bwrdd â mi.

[Mother was at the table with me,
her two hands still serving.
Never talking about the calm,
and the big silent steps of the day,
without the children, without Grandfather in the house,
a sack-full of coughing,
but rather taking hold of the cloth,
as she had done throughout her little life,
and, with all her might, washing and cleaning
and ironing, until forgiving . . .

I swallowed a mouth-full of swearing:
mother was at the table with me.]

A lot takes place in the twelve lines of this poem; the narrator observes his mother (and by extension, the plight of any woman in a traditional family situation), growing increasingly angry at her condition so that, by the end, he is moved to curse. A tension is maintained throughout, as the narrator-poet's violent emotional reaction is contrasted with the way in which his mother silently suffers. The final couplet closes the poem with an ironic, multiple twist. The poet wants to swear, to give voice to his anger and thereby let his mother know that he empathizes with her, but that swearing is silenced by the same thing which caused it in the first place, the family tradition and manners; he cannot swear in front of his mother. He must 'swallow' the cursing, the verbal expression of outrage. This, to use Wordsworth's phrase, is the 'emotion re-collected in tranquility' which later emerges as a more organized verbal expression, the *cywydd* itself. This poem is also a narrative about its own genesis; it is a meta-poetical examination of the connection between experience, emotion and verbal art.

Recent critics have observed that the sonnet appears to be dying in Wales. This is no tragedy; it was in many ways a form alien to the Welsh poetic tradition which really only gained a foothold in the twentieth century because of the efforts of two poets, R. Williams Parry and T. H. Parry-Williams. However, it might be that the short *cywydd*, especially in the hands of the more able contemporary poets like Twm Morys, is coming to occupy the place left vacant by the end of the Williams Parry and Parry-Williams sonnet tradition (and that allied form, the Parry-Williams *rhigwm*, or short 'rhyme'). The short *cywydd* is being transformed into something akin to the better sonnets and 'rhymes' of the century, a compact vehicle ideal for conveying contemplative vignettes. (It should be noted, however, that poets such as Alan Llwyd, Gwyneth Lewis and Grahame Davies continue to produce striking sonnets.)

As has already been suggested, speaking of a *cynghanedd* 'renaissance' of the 1990s as separate from the 'renaissance' of the 1970s can be misleading, for there is a great deal of continuity and interaction between and among the different generations of poets. The younger *cynganeddwyr* have been inspired, encouraged and taught by the figures of the 1970s 'renaissance', most notably Dic Jones and Gerallt Lloyd Owen. Gerallt Lloyd Owen has been particularly influential, hosting and judging the popular radio show 'Talwrn y Beirdd' (The Poets' Cockpit), which has recently been transformed into a successful television show. 'Talwrn y Beirdd' has given a new and lively shape to the medieval *ymryson* or poetic competition, and it is in itself an incredible pheno-menon attesting to the continued prominence of poetry in Welsh-speaking Wales.

In addition to providing strict-metre poetry with a popular, entertaining face, these competitions generate a good deal of fine poetry. And, as poets compete on teams, they have encouraged more direct co-operation in the process of composition, so that the future anthologies of Welsh verse will surely contain a substantial number of co-authored poems. The following *englyn*, by Twm Morys and Iwan Llwyd, was written for a competition held at the 1993 Llanelwedd Eisteddfod. Two background facts are necessary to understand this stanza: first of all, Llanelwedd is very close to Cilmeri, the site of Llywelyn's fall. And, secondly, in 1993, as in many years, it rained a good deal during the Eisteddfod week. This powerful epigram celebrates the national spirit, moving elliptically from the comparably insignificant struggle of the Eisteddfod-goers who brave the rain, to the survival of the Welsh nation in the face of centuries of defeat.

> Glaw mawr sydd yng Nghilmeri—glaw yn llafn,
>   Glāw yn llawn picelli,
>   Glaw yn arf yn ein gŵyl ni,
>   Glaw a laddai arglwyddi.

[There is a great rain in Cilmeri—a sharp rain
A rain full of spears,
A rain as a weapon in our festival,
A rain which could kill lords.]

In several ways this chapter ends where it began, with a new
generation of poets turning to the traditional strict metres, and with
an acute awareness of the past used to temper a vision for the
present and the future. However, this element of continuity should
not be taken as uniformity. It must be remembered that the con-
tinuation of tradition is but one aspect of an age which has
witnessed a multiplicity of voices, schools, and experiments,
making the quarter-century extending from the end of the 1960s to
the middle of the 1990s one of the most exciting and dynamic
periods in the history of Welsh poetry.

FURTHER READING

Joseph P. Clancy, *Twentieth Century Welsh Poems* (Llandysul, 1982).
Gareth Alban Davies, 'The Multi-screen Cinema: poetry in Welsh
    1950–1990', in Hans-Werner Ludwig and Lothar Fietz (eds), *Poetry in
    the British Isles: non-metropolitan perspectives* (Cardiff, 1995), 115–33.
Dafydd Johnston (ed.), *Modern Poetry in Translation*, New Series no. 7
    (Spring, 1995).
Dafydd Glyn Jones, 'Some Recent Trends in Welsh literature', in J. E.
    Caerwyn Williams (ed.), *Literature in Celtic Countries*, Taliesin
    Congress Lectures, lecture 8 (Cardiff, 1971), 177–207.
John Rowlands, 'Literature in Welsh', in Meic Stephens (ed.), *The Arts in
    Wales 1950–75* (Cardiff, 1979), 167–206.

CHAPTER 6

THE NOVEL

JOHN ROWLANDS

There is nothing peculiar about the slow and stunted growth of the novel in the Welsh language, for it is a *genre* which has not flourished in minority literatures, where the short story has usually been the preferred prose form. The novelty of the novel cut across the grain of the long tradition of idealistic writing in Welsh, with its backbone of praise poetry stretching as far back as the sixth century, so we perhaps lacked the necessary realist mode. The eighteenth-century Methodist Revival has also to take part of the blame, and particularly its nineteenth-century pietistic aftermath. As Saunders Lewis put it: 'A puritan thumb had smudged the sensuousness out of the language.'

But it would be wrong to suggest that we were somehow temperamentally averse to the kind of imaginative portrayal of human relationships offered by the new form. Too much has been made of the so-called 'essence' of Welsh literature, and its variegated nature has been too often underplayed. The fantastic (in more than one sense) story-telling technique of the medieval tales of the Mabinogion contrasts vividly with the more sombre and formal poetry, but even within that there is abundant playfulness and risk-taking as illustrated by such diverse poets as Dafydd ap Gwilym and Guto'r Glyn. Even in the post-William Morgan period, all is not gloom, for Ellis Wynne's *Gweledigaetheu y Bardd Cwsc* (Visions of the Sleeping Bard) verges on the carnivalistic and outrageous.

I am not of course suggesting that the vestiges of the Welsh novel can be found in the medieval romances or in the Swiftean satirical visions of Ellis Wynne. The late emergence of the Welsh-language novel is a truism which cannot be explained away. In a country priding itself on the widespread literacy among its *gwerin* or peasantry, and on the volume of its publications during the last century, the failure to take the novel seriously (it was in fact called a *ffug-chwedl*, 'a false tale' or 'fictitious story') may have been due to a large degree to the lack of an educated middle class. The 'Blue Books' controversy of 1847 had also made people nervous of any literature which could be construed as not morally edifying and uplifting.

We must however avoid the pervading *clichés* of Welsh literary history and bury the myth that Daniel Owen (1836–95) was the first Welsh novelist. E. G. Millward has done a great deal to place him in the context of a not inconsiderable body of novel writing in Welsh. More research needs to be done in the periodicals of the nineteenth century to unearth the works of Daniel Owen's predecessors, whether they be translations, historical romances, temperance novels or moralistic tales. Whilst this would redress the balance, it would do nothing to diminish the towering presence of Daniel Owen, whose persistent striving for 'the truth, the whole truth, and nothing but the truth' ironically forced him to acknowledge that man's rife hypocrisy subverted this endeavour. Owen has variously been criticized for his lack of architectonic design, his stylistic infelicities and his over-zealous Calvinism, but in the more liberal critical climate of today his subtext seems more subversive than was once realized. He is ripe for reappraisal, for the tensions in his work—between town and country, pub and chapel, industry and agriculture, English and Welsh, conservative and liberal—form fault lines which disturb any perceived equilibrium. By dint of his canniness he wooed his audience into accepting the realism of the novel in the guise (in his first major novel, *Rhys Lewis*) of the autobiography of a religious minister, but this autobiography was a very private one, which was never supposed to see the light of day, so it had an almost parodying relationship to the 'official' autobiographies of the day.

Yes, Daniel Owen is the incontestable father of the Welsh novel, and yet he hardly fathered any sibling novelists. Critics and literary historians bow their heads in shame and embarrassment when talking, not only of the paucity of novels at the turn of the century, but also of their *naïveté*. Glyn Ashton admitted that 'we are dealing with second-rate literature when discussing the modern Welsh novel'. Some are quite content to see this lack as more than compensated for by the vigorous revival in poetry associated with names such as John Morris-Jones, T. Gwynn Jones, W. J. Gruffydd and R. Williams Parry, but whilst not denying the vigour of that revival, the weakness of the novel is to be regretted for wider cultural reasons as well as for narrower literary ones. A steady stream of good, readable novels would have played a part in making the Welsh language attractive to a wider audience. In reacting to the challenge of modernism, it could have explored a sensibility which was out of reach of poetry. It is one of the tragedies of Welsh literature that it did not assert itself at this period as the major literary form. It is, however, a consolation that it was catapulted into the post-modern era by the innovative young writers of the 1980s and 1990s, and its development was con-certinaed as if to make up for lost time, as we can see later.

Needless to say, notwithstanding the lack of literary merit, there is in the novels of the end of the last century and the first quarter of the present one some material of interest to researchers—in the field of the representation of children, for example, or of women, and such studies would undoubtedly provide amusement as well as sociological enlightenment. Some of the titles give an indication of the concerns of some of these novelists—for example, *O'r Pwlpud . . . i'r crogbren, Ffug-chwedl Ddirwestol* (From the Pulpit . . . to the gallows, A Temperance Novel, 1905) by William J. Griffiths, and *Eluned Naunton, neu ddiota ym mhlith y merched* (Eluned Naunton, or drinking amongst the women, 1910) by E. William Davies. There is a sprinkling of historical novels—or perhaps costume romances would be a more apt description—such as *Ednyfed Fychan* (1903) by T. J. Jones Lewis, *Cyflafan y Castell* (The Massacre of the Castle, 1909) by Evan R. Evans and *Ifor Owain* (1911) by Henry Elwyn Thomas. The depiction of period is ponderous and the style turgid. The typical faults of novels set in contemporary Wales are their melodrama and *naïveté*, as in *Arwriaeth John Anthony* (The Heroism of John Anthony, 1909) by Evan Rowlands (also known as Ap Llechwedd).

More modest efforts, such as the sweetly innocent novels of R. D. Rowlands (Anthropos) or the unpretentious works of W. Llewelyn Williams, provide easier and less embarrassing reading, possibly because both on occasion wrote about and for children. The former's *Y Pentre Gwyn* (The White Village, 1909) is based on his childhood experiences at his native Ty'n-y-Cefn near Corwen, and his *Tŷ Capel y Cwm* (The Manse at Cwm, 1905) and *Merch y Telynor* (The Harpist's Daughter, 1909) are written in a similarly unaffected vein. W. Llewelyn Williams, a historian and journalist who later became a barrister and a Member of Parliament for

Carmarthen, published his *Gwilym a Benni Bach* (Gwilym and
Little Benny) in 1894—a charming tale about two children, and
followed it with *Gŵr y Dolau* (The Master of Dolau) in 1899, whose
characterization is fairly vivid, despite a weak and untidy plot.

Dafydd Jenkins has observed that 'the Welsh novel did not begin
to come of age until it had gone through a period of childhood and
youth—that is, a period delineating children and adolescents'. In
this kind of unambitious writing there is a straightforwardness and
humility often lacking in novels for an adult audience, and the
authors seem to be freed from the encumbrances of a complicated
plot and a high-flown style. The prime example which springs to
mind is Winnie Parry's *Sioned* (1906), with its use of an easy,
colloquial style, and its ability to delve into a young girl's emotional
growth. The same author's *Y Ddau Hogyn Rheiny* (Those Two
Boys, 1928) does not display the same level of sensitivity. The fact
that the Welsh women's publishers, Honno, recently reissued
Sioned suggests that it expressed a feminine sensibility long before
the days of *écriture féminine*.

It is noticeable that more women novelists came to the fore
during the first quarter of this century, although as R. M. Jones
remarked, the force of their presence is stronger than their number.
Not by any flight of the imagination could they be classed radical
feminists, but their femininity makes itself felt, even if that is a
product of gender conditioning. Moelona, a teacher from
Rhydlewis, and a fervent patriot, published over thirty books for
children and adults, the most popular being the novel, *Teulu Bach
Nantoer* (The Little Family of Nantoer, 1913). Her overtly
pedagogic stance jars on present-day readers, but her concern for
women's rights in such novels as *Cwrs y Lli* (The Current's Flow,
1927) is commendable, if rather naïvely expressed. Gwyneth
Vaughan first published her four novels as serials in *Y Cymro* and
Y Brython, and at least two of them achieved popularity in book
form. *O Gorlannau y Defaid* (From the Sheep Folds, 1905) tells the
story of the 1859 religious revival, and *Plant y Gorthrwm* (The
Children of Oppression, 1908) is based on the 1868 general election.
Her inclination to instruct her readers on religious and political
matters mars her work, and yet there is an authenticity about her
portrayal of country life and customs.

T. Gwynn Jones was the most prolific writer of his generation,
and unquestionably the major poet of the literary revival, but it is

not always remembered that he wrote a considerable amount of prose, much of it remaining uncollected in newspapers and periodicals. Four of his novels were published in book form. *Gwedi Brad a Gofid* (After Betrayal and Sorrow, 1898) has a stirring plot, culminating in a double wedding following a double funeral. *Gorchest Gwilym Bevan* (Gwilym Bevan's Exploit, 1900) manipulates a quarrymen's strike to provide added excitement to the plot, but the characterization is stereotypical, and as Raymond Williams has suggested, making industrial life a 'setting' for a novel does not create an industrial novel: 'In the true industrial novel . . . industrial work, and its characteristic places and communities, are not just a new background: . . . they are seen as formative.' T. Gwynn Jones's two other novels, *John Homer* and *Lona,* were both published in book form in 1923, but they are as different as chalk from cheese. *John Homer* is a rumbustious satire on the obsessive country poet whose pseudo-Homerian ambitions make him compete in eisteddfod after eisteddfod purely for the sake of making a name for himself. Unfortunately, the humour lacks subtlety, and is more farcical than witty. *Lona,* on the other hand, has a completely serious tone of voice, but is too sentimentally romantic to rise above the ordinary run of popular fiction.

How is it that a brilliant poet such as T. Gwynn Jones failed to rise above the average level in his novels? Part of the answer lies in the overwhelming hold (one could almost say the stranglehold) of the poetic tradition on him. His poetic diction is medieval, and many of his long dramatic poems take their themes from the Celtic twilight. There are indications, even in his poetry, that he was being pulled in two opposite directions—towards realism on the one hand, and Romanticism—to which he succumbed—on the other. He failed to pick up the thread of realism which had become all but invisible in the tradition. Either by choice or temperament, he failed to wear the mantle of Daniel Owen.

Of course the renaissance in our poetry at the beginning of this century was a neo-Romanticism, not blithely copied from the English or the Europeans, but made muscular by its homage to the past, and electrified by a burning concern for the contemporary. Its dying fall was heard well into the inter-war years, and it prevented the rise of an uncompromising modernism. I am not one of those stalwarts who decry any incursion of foreign cultural influences on Welsh literature, as if the fact that they are usually mediated through English makes them inherently poisonous. Welsh literature eventually had to endure the paroxysms of modernism, and writers had to struggle to express them in a language which might crack under the strain. Some poets—such as T. H. Parry-Williams— succeeded admirably in expressing the spirit of modernism without alienating a suspicious audience. Not surprisingly, the novelists did not fare so well.

E. Tegla Davies's *Gŵr Pen y Bryn* (The Master of Pen y Bryn, 1923) was the first of a breed of 'new' novels to appear in the inter-war years, and—somewhat contradictorily—the most old-fashioned. Tegla was a Wesleyan minister from Llandegla who made his name early as a children's writer. The fact that he did not belong to the class of poet-preacher may account for the fluidity of his prose. As Pennar Davies has said: 'he had no pretensions to any mastery over verse forms and his limpid prose nowhere shows any sign of poetic afflatus'. His whimsical boy's own story, *Hunangofiant Tomi* (Tommy's Autobiography, 1912), has a refreshing colloquial style, and some irreverent touches. Around half a dozen of his children's stories—including some unusual fantasies—have achieved the status of minor classics.

Gŵr Pen y Bryn is a study of the spiritual awakening of a weak character who has lived a life of pretence in a parochial and introverted agricultural community in mid Wales. The story is told against the background of the Tithe War of the 1880s, but the historical aspect is not really taken seriously; it merely provides a backdrop. John Williams, the self-regarding eponymous anti-hero, joins the ranks of the tenant farmers—all of whom are of course Liberals and Nonconformists—who refuse to pay tithe to the coffers of a conservative and Anglican Church. But in contrast to the other protesters, he acts not from conviction but from a deep-seated wish to be worshipped as a martyr, to compensate for his feeling of inadequacy in the face of the onset of middle age. He is patently riddled with hypocrisy, but is gnawed inwardly by a sense of inefficacy. Gradually he slithers deeper and deeper into a pit of his own making, and has recourse to bootlicking in order to conceal his real self. His is not a conversion on the road to Damascus, but a slow and piecemeal process, helped by superficially simple and undramatic events and experiences—such as his empathy with Rofar, his dog, which is a secret sheep-killer unbeknown to the farmers of the vicinity, and the dignified and confiding death of his simple-minded former farmhand, Mathew Tomos. His envious and devious 'friend', Dafydd Huws the carpenter, threatens his downfall, because of his insider knowledge, but this is not the last straw which leads to his public confession. He undergoes a Christian conversion which gives him courage to divulge his failings to a congregation of people who revered him for his apparent self-denial. Dafydd Huws also undergoes a kind of conversion, and the two are reconciled. The novel ends somewhat predictably with John Williams's tranquil death.

This novel succeeded in dividing the critics into two opposing camps. Some, like D. Tecwyn Lloyd, made extravagant claims for it, injudiciously comparing it with the works of Dostoevsky, Cervantes and Kafka. Saunders Lewis, on the other hand, acknowledged the ambitiousness of its theme, but condemned it unreservedly in these now well-known words:

> The one serious attempt at a full-sized psychological novel is *Gŵr Pen y Bryn,* by E. Tegla Davies. Unhappily the work is planned on the pattern of a sermon, with an introduction and three heads, and what should have been a rigorous study in the development of a weak nature turns in the end to piety and edification. The mildew of evangelicalism taints Tegla Davies' work . . .

There is some truth in the accusation of sermonizing. The first edition of the novel was divided into four sections, the introductory one indicating that the soul of John Williams was asleep, and the three subsequent ones showing it awakening at the bidding of the voice of the country, his own inner voice, and the voice of God. The conversion itself is rendered unconvincing by the long-winded use of a kind of theological mumbo-jumbo. And the final give-away of the novel is the fact that Tegla is unable to do anything with his John Williams once he is 'saved', apart from letting him drift in peace into the next world where he can presumably wallow in his perfected state.

This novel is not as bad as the above description might suggest, but it is flawed, and testifies to the fact that the novel cannot grapple with the transcendental. Tegla succeeds, however, in conveying the atmosphere of the countryside, and in depicting unselfconscious country folk, and he has a penchant for biting satire. It may be that his career as a serious novelist was cut short by Saunders Lewis's scathing criticism, but his short satirical novel, *Gyda'r Glannau* (Along the Shore, 1941) showed him to be an unsubtle satirist and an immature novelist. His subsequent concentration on producing volumes of popular essays or *belles-lettres* may have been the right one.

Saunders Lewis obviously bristled at the simplistic pietism of late Welsh Nonconformity, and caused not a few raised eyebrows with his 'Letter on Catholicism' in the literary journal, *Y Llenor* (The Writer) in 1927. As if to trounce those writers prone to piety and edification he stated categorically: 'The loss of sin is a loss to literature . . . And to the Christian mind, sin is man's special attribute, the most human trait in existence, and therefore indispensable in poetry and literature.' He confessed an admiration for writers such as André Gide who gave sin its due place in their work.

Three years later he caused a furore when his concise novel, *Monica*, was published. Its candid depiction of erotic love was considered lacking in taste in strait-laced Nonconformist circles. Yet this was no Welsh *Lady Chatterley's Lover*, and there were no equivalents of four-letter words to cause anyone to squirm, nor explicit scenes of steamy sex to curdle the blood of the prudish. There is no denying the novel's serious intent. It is set in dreary suburbia, in a rootless *petit-bourgeois* environment in English-speaking Wales, in a lacklustre cultural void. The eponymous heroine, ironically taking her name from St Augustine's mother, is driven by an obsessive lust to 'steal' her sister's *fiancé*, and their subsequent marriage is solely based on carnal desire. She is psychologically unprepared for motherhood, and when she becomes pregnant, she regards the baby in her womb as the harbinger of death, and the sound of her husband making the wooden cradle sounds to her ear like that of a carpenter making a coffin. Her subconscious death-wish turns her into a slattern who almost wallows in the squalor of her filthy bed. Because of her unnatural behaviour her husband is driven into the arms of a prostitute, and contracts a sexually transmitted disease, presumably syphilis. When she inadvertently finds out his secret, it dawns on her that she herself is nothing better than a prostitute whose marital life has been nothing more than a lascivious craving for physical domination of her husband. The novel hurtles headlong towards its fateful end, with no attempt to redeem Monica.

Uncharacteristically for a Welsh novel, there is hardly any mention of religion in *Monica*, the whole atmosphere is bleak and opaque, and Monica's vulgar tittering does nothing to relieve it. The book was criticized, not only for its sleazy subject-matter, but also for being 'un-Welsh'. One reviewer complained that the story could just as easily have been written about English or German characters, and could have been set in Harrogate or Wiesbaden. Tegla took the opportunity to take his revenge on his former critic by comparing the novel to a dung-heap, which could legitimately be examined scientifically in the laboratory, but Saunders's offence was to spread the muck in the full public gaze.

There was complete consternation that a committed Christian such as Saunders Lewis (although it would be two years before he would be formally admitted into the Catholic Church) could create an amoral character such as Monica, and the bewilderment was compounded by his dedication of the novel 'to the memory of Williams Pantycelyn, the only pioneer of this kind of writing'. This was an oblique reference to Pantycelyn's *Ductor Nuptiarum*, an innovative eighteenth-century marriage guidance manual in dialogue form which treated sexual love in a surprisingly explicit manner.

It is only in recent years that *Monica* has been properly appreciated. In the context of Saunders Lewis' *oeuvre* as a whole it can be seen as an implied treatment of his favourite theme *agape v. eros*, with *eros* in this instance associated with an urban rootlessness. Far from being an obscene work, it is now regarded as highly moral in its condemnation of sensuousness as an end in itself. Yet the author himself detested the simplistic interpretation of it as a morality tale. He had not set out to condemn Monica utterly, for he sympathized wholeheartedly with her psychological predicament. Nevertheless there is hardly a glimmer of this in his portrayal of her. She is very much the *femme fatale*, and some feminist critics have remarked on the way her husband, although an equal accomplice in their lustful partnership, is seen as somewhat of a victim of her wantonness.

The novel was at one time criticized for the gaucheness of its style and the unnaturalness of its dialogue, but R. M. Jones is probably right in championing Saunders Lewis's cold and objective distancing from his characters and action. He claims that the apparent formality of the style emanates from the author's

treatment of language as a 'thing'. Delyth Beasley has drawn a
convincing parallel between *Monica* and Mauriac's *Thérèse
Desqueyroux*, and P. Mansell Jones compared it with *Madame
Bovary*. R. M. Jones claims that it excels Flaubert's classic in its
superior intellectual energy, and adds: 'I am not certain that there is
any Welsh novel which surpasses it.'

Many would dispute such a claim by saying that Saunders
Lewis's second novel, *Merch Gwern Hywel* (The Daughter of
Gwern Hywel, 1964) shows more elegance and poise, and that by
treating a historical theme it displays more easily its author's
strengths. He was never completely at ease with contemporary
subjects, although there is no disputing the compelling contemporary relevance of most of his work. *Merch Gwern Hywel* was
formally called 'a historical romance' by its author, and it deals
with the love affair between the daughter of a fairly well-to-do
farming family and an ordinary Methodist preacher from *y werin*
or the peasantry. In the days of arranged marriages, this was a
romantic affair which was very much frowned upon by the girl's
mother. However there is much more at stake in this short novel
than personal relationships. It is set in the early years of the last
century, immediately after the Calvinist Methodists finally broke
away from the Anglican Church to form a separate denomination,
and it treats the 'inner politics' of the new denomination. The
writing—especially the almost exclusive use of dialogue—exhibits a
great deal of panache, with Saunders Lewis adroitly displaying his
complete mastery of the niceties of Nonconformist theology,
without in any way cloying the reader's appetite.

The novel deals with a theme very close to Saunders Lewis's heart,
namely how is the process of history to be renewed without cutting it
off from its life-giving roots and traditions. Saunders was, of course,
very much a traditionalist and a conservative (with a small 'c'), but it
is sometimes forgotten that he also—paradoxically—had a radical
turn of mind, and in dealing imaginatively with the development of
Welsh Nonconformity in his second novel he grapples with the
problem of reconciling tradition and innovation. The protagonists
embody in their relationship the fine balance between the two. As
one of the characters says: '. . . the path of truth is the narrow path of
the razor's edge. That is the path of tradition'. This vision from one
so often dubbed a reactionary came as a revelation to those who
failed to acknowledge the complexity of Saunders Lewis's attitude

towards the past. And in contrast to his first novel, romantic love is now regarded with equanimity.

Some have suggested that *Monica* was a deliberate attempt to jolt younger novelists into taking up new and more *risqué* themes, to dispel the image of a dull *cliché*-ridden literary scene. Very few writers took up the challenge. Welsh novels appeared in dribs and drabs during the next decade, and only two or three writers seemed to be taking the form seriously. Nevertheless there appeared a few innovative—if tentative—attempts to develop the *genre*.

The poet Gwenallt's *Plasau'r Brenin* (The King's Mansions, 1934) was based on the author's imprisonment in Wormwood Scrubs and Dartmoor as a result of his stand as a conscientious objector during the First World War. We are introduced to three very different conscientious objectors in the novel: one is a Welsh Nationalist who refuses to partake in a war between major powers, another is a Communist who sees the war as an imperialist one, and the third is a born-again Christian who is a pure pacifist. The mundane and monotonous life of a prisoner is chronicled in detail, and there is an authentic attempt to convey the turbulent mind of a person in solitary confinement, with liberal use of a technique bordering on stream-of-consciousness. *Plasau'r Brenin* was a brave attempt to answer W. J. Gruffydd's complaint that no Welsh novelist was bold enough to tackle the effect of the First World War on Wales, but a novel about a conscientious objector can hardly be described as a 'war novel', and as Dafydd Jenkins has remarked, Gwenallt's story deals with a character who was not changed by his experiences. The characters seem to embody abstractions and fail to create the illusion of real people in real predicaments. The whole novel is too much of a chronicle.

That is the accusation brought against Gwenallt's posthumously published novel *Ffwrneisiau* (Furnaces, 1982) as well. The author would probably have redrafted the novel had he lived, and its editor, J. E. Caerwyn Williams hesitated in calling the work a novel, preferring instead to give it the subtitle, *Cronicl Blynyddoedd Mebyd* (The Chronicle of the Years of Youth). Despite the fictitious names and setting, the book is obviously based on the author's reminiscences, and is an attempt to recreate the world of his youth in Cwm Tawe or the Swansea Valley. It has all the hallmarks of a well-researched project, with the skeleton of the research all too apparent. As in the earlier novel, the characters

seem representatives of various types, and fail to mature into
unique individuals. It is regrettable that Gwenallt did not write a
straight autobiography to supplement his chapter in J. E.
Meredith's anthology of essays, *Credaf* (I Believe, 1943).
Ffwrneisiau will be read as a fictional substitute. In the absence of a
fully-fledged industrial novel in Welsh, it fills a gap. It has many
memorable scenes depicting the industrial landscape, and shows
that the Welsh language has the potential to tackle an industrial
theme, although Gwenallt himself lacked the imagination to
metamorphose his raw materials into a mature work of fiction.
Despite the work's inherent flaws, it should be read for the light
it throws on Gwenallt's background, and the fictionalized retelling
of his own father's death in a stream of molten metal is very
moving.

Plasau'r Brenin was the result of a pact struck between Gwenallt
and T. Hughes Jones that each would write a novel arising out of
the experiences of the First World War. T. Hughes Jones did not
fulfil his part of the bargain until 1944, when he published *Amser i
Ryfel* (A Time for War). Unlike Gwenallt, he was a combatant in
the war, and therefore able to write about it from first-hand
experience. His main character, Manod, undergoes a series of
harrowing experiences, but they do not seem to impinge on his
inner being as one would expect, so the novel leaves one with the
impression once again of reading *reportage* rather than felt
experience sieved through a writer's imagination.

We had to wait until 1968 before seeing a really powerful novel
about the Great War. It was then that Emyr Jones published his
Gwaed Gwirion (Innocent Blood), a closely woven story of an old
soldier told in a first-person dialect narrative. There is no attempt
at overdramatization here, and no trace of sentimentality, but the
apparent artlessness of the novel conceals its finely tuned artistry.
The delayed reaction of this novel is symptomatic of the retarded
nature of Welsh fiction, but it presaged a burgeoning of more
courageous writing in the decades which followed.

Retracing our steps back to the 1930s, we find the emergence of
some fine writing by women novelists. Elena Puw Morgan, despite
her lack of an academic education, first came into prominence as a
children's writer, and gained confidence by competing anony-
mously at eisteddfodau. She published three novels for adults.
Nansi Lovell (1933) is an old gipsy's story written in the form of a

long letter addressed to her grand-daughter, and it shows that its author was well-versed in Romany customs, and the use of Romany terms adds some exotic colour. *Y Wisg Sidan* (The Silken Dress, 1939) is a longer and more ambitious novel written in a traditional mould. It is set in Cardiganshire in the latter part of the last century, in a harsh rural environment. It traces the development of its protagonist, Mali, who becomes infatuated with a young man of superior rank. She becomes pregnant with his child, and despite his reprehensible behaviour towards her, she idolizes him from afar. The portrait of Mali is meticulously drawn, and there is a strong story line (somewhat marred by too many coincidences), but the villains have been painted too black, and the whole atmosphere is unrelentingly austere. The silken dress of the title is a leitmotif throughout the novel, and its burning at the end achieves a symbolic significance. *Y Wisg Sidan* was successfully adapted as a television serial in 1995.

Elena Puw Morgan's last novel was *Y Graith* (The Scar) which won the Prose Medal at the National Eisteddfod in 1938, and appeared in print in 1943. Again we have a female protagonist, Dori, who endures a great deal of suffering, from the day she leaves school after her dream of following a teaching career is shattered, through her years as a maid in Liverpool, to her lonely life as a farmer's wife. Her mother's unrelieved animosity towards her as a child culminates in her being lashed with a belt, the buckle leaving a lifelong scar near her eye. The author creates a world of unremitting cruelty, as if to counterbalance the soft-centred romanticism of many portrayals of Welsh rural life.

There is no doubt that Elena Puw Morgan's work was undervalued during her lifetime, and it is to be regretted that she gave up creative writing when she was 39 years of age, mainly for domestic reasons. R. M. Jones commented wryly that 'her career is one of the strongest Welsh arguments in favour of feminism'.

She was also unfortunate to be writing in the shadow of the so-called 'queen of Welsh literature', Kate Roberts, with whom she was often compared unfavourably. Kate Roberts had come to be regarded as the foremost prose-writer of the period on the strength of her short stories, and had also published a children's novel, *Deian a Loli* (Deian and Loli), in 1927, followed by its sequel, *Laura Jones,* in 1930, which traces the development of the Loli of the former novel through the years of adolescence.

Her first novel for adults, *Traed Mewn Cyffion* (Feet in Chains, 1936), was adjudged joint winner in the novel competition at the Neath National Eisteddfod in 1934 with Grace Wynne Griffith's *Creigiau Milgwyn* (The Rocks of Milgwyn, 1935), a charming but rather lightweight novel. Another rather old-fashioned novel intended for the same competition, but not entered, was Moelona's *Ffynnonloyw* (s.d.), a complete antithesis to the work of her more controversial Rhydlewis contemporary, Caradoc Evans.

The competition called for a novel dealing with three generations, and Kate Roberts's novel suffers from trying to cover such a large canvas in around 200 pages. It is an impressionistic work where the characters' experiences take precedence over plot. It takes as its backdrop the bleak landscape of the upland quarrying area around Kate Roberts's native area of Rhosgadfan in the hinterland of Caernarfon, somewhat reminiscent of *Wuthering Heights*. The characters live a life of unremitting toil in order to survive the harsh economic reality of the period. There is hardly any room for relaxation, let alone indulgent pleasure, and yet the characters survive and seem to pride themselves on their stoical acceptance of their fate. This is not by any means a cheerful book, and its all-pervading gloom, as well as its parochial introversion, does not endear it to many people, yet its understated frustration has a kind of hidden power which eloquently conveys the proud apolitical stance of its characters.

Kate Roberts came from a humble background and in some of her work she seems to be paying a tribute to the society in which she was brought up, as if in complete contrast to Joyce's determination to fly by the triple net of nationality, language and religion. But it is also possible to sense in her work a modernist *angst* at living in a world whose ideological foundations were trembling. This aspect became much more pronounced as a result of the personal anguish she experienced because of her husband's death from alcoholic poisoning. She had married Morris T. Williams, a younger man than herself, in her late thirties, and they lived in Cardiff and Tonypandy for some years before moving to Denbigh, where they became proprietors of Gwasg Gee, the publishers of the weekly newspaper, *Baner ac Amserau Cymru*. After his death, the burden of running the business fell on her shoulders. His illness and ensuing death caused a hiatus in her career as a writer, and she published no books between 1937 and 1949.

The work of Kate Roberts's so-called Denbigh period is at first sight strikingly different from that of her Rhosgadfan period, and this is particularly true of three of the four novels. *Stryd y Glep* (Gossip Row, 1949) is in diary form, written by Ffebi Beca who is bedridden because of paralysis of the spine. It is deeply introspective and explores Ffebi's innermost thoughts about the futility of life and the impossibility of communicating with other people. The setting is a terrace house in a small parochial town where there are no earth-shattering events, only thoughts tumbling one after the other through a turbulent mind, and the small talk of gossiping relatives and neighbours.

One critic has suggested that her next novel, *Y Byw Sy'n Cysgu* (The Living Sleep, 1956), 'is perhaps the most unpopular', as if implying that all her books are not for popular consumption. This is particularly true of the novels, not only because of the lack of crafted plots, but also because of the unattractiveness of their main characters. Lora Ffennig in *Y Byw Sy'n Cysgu* comes over initially as a frosty and rather frigid person, obsessively house-proud, and her husband's desertion of her for a younger and more vivacious woman seems understandable. The novel does not explore their relationship, however, but begins with Lora's realization that her husband has gone. It then proceeds to uncover layer after layer of her psyche as if it had hitherto been asleep. The strains of her relationships with her children, her lodgers, her mother-in-law and sister-in-law, and her husband's employer might seem mundane and inconsequential at first sight, but her unearthing of her feelings in her diary show her to be a sensitive woman who has been constrained—either by nature or conditioning—to keep a tight rein on her emotions.

It is in *Tywyll Heno* (Dark Tonight, 1962) that the theme of the 'suffering queen' (as R. M. Jones has referred to it) is treated most profoundly. Bet Jones is a minister's wife who suffers a mental breakdown as a consequence of her loss of religious faith. She is an artistic woman caught between two generations, constrained by her cultural and religious environment, and by her role as a minister's wife, yet unable to participate in the so-called moral liberation of the late 1950s and early 1960s. Her experiences seem to be the embodiment of what the philosopher J. R. Jones called *yr argyfwng gwacter ystyr* which may be loosely translated as 'the crisis of meaninglessness'.

In *Tegwch y Bore* (The Beauty of the Morning, 1967) Kate Roberts abandons the psychological agonies of mid-century Wales and deals with the more concrete torments of the years between 1913 and 1917. This period was the fount of her own creativity, for she admitted that it was the death of her youngest brother in the Great War that prompted her to write. The main character of this novel, Ann Owen, also loses her brother Bobi in the war. Like her creator, she is a young graduate who embarks on a teaching career in south Wales, and struggles to compensate for the loss of Bobi by her rather prosaic relationship with Richard, who returns wounded from the medical corps. Her jealousy towards Richard because his life has been spared perhaps conceals thwarted incestuous feelings towards Bobi. Despite its superficial similarity to *Traed Mewn Cyffion,* this late novel differs from it in its hard-won final optimism.

R. M. Jones praises Kate Roberts for her feminine stoical acceptance of life's tribulations, but feminist critics such as Delyth George have perceived in her work an undercurrent of unease which seems to challenge the assumptions of a patriarchal society. This is never explicit, however, and Derec Llwyd Morgan's hyperbolic comparison of her with Germaine Greer must be taken with a grain of salt. Hers is an embryonic feminism, kept in check by the rigid conventions of a restrictive culture. She took the stance of a non-political writer, and bristled at the notion of *engagement.* Equally adamant was her disavowal of sexuality as a valid theme in her work. Despite her apparent fastidiousness, however, her work has a deep subconscious layer which would repay examination by a psychoanalytic critic.

Many of the novels which appeared in the 1940s were short and experimental, and did not form part of a substantial corpus of fiction by their authors. John Gwilym Jones's *Y Dewis* (The Choice) won the National Eisteddfod Prose Medal in 1939 and appeared in print in 1942. Despite its brevity it shows its author's remarkable psychological insight into the adolescent minds of his two main characters, Caleb and Nesta. This was followed in 1946 by a ground-breaking collection of short stories, *Y Goeden Eirin* (The Plum Tree), with its Freudian depiction of the subconscious mind. As is well-known, John Gwilym Jones devoted most of his energies to writing plays, and wrote only one other novel, *Tri Diwrnod ac Angladd* (Three Days and a Funeral, 1979). This is a *tour-de-force,* with its tightly woven plot, its penetrating analysis of a television newscaster's contorted mind, and its finely honed style.

Gwilym R. Jones's *Y Purdan* (Purgatory) appeared in 1942, and here again there is an attempt to unravel the unconscious mind of its main character. Two subsequent novels by the same author (who is incidentally better known as a poet), *Gweddw'r Dafarn* (The Publican's Widow, 1943) and *Seirff yn Eden* (Serpents in Eden, 1963) do not quite live up to the first novel's promise. Geraint Dyfnallt Owen is another novelist who began in an innovative and somewhat surrealistic vein with his rather eccentric book, *Aeddan Hopcyn* (1942). He then turned to historical romance with such works as *Cefn Ydfa* (1948), *Nest* (1949), *Dyddiau'r Gofid* (The Days of Affliction, 1950), and *Twm Siôn Cati, Yswain* (1969). His last novel was a political farce, *Cwymp y Blaid Wreiddiol* (The Fall of the Original Party, 1981).

Brief mention should be made here of Kate Bosse-Griffiths, who was born in Wittenberg in Germany, and had a distinguished academic career in Germany, England and Wales. She has written a number of books in Welsh, including a collection of short stories and two novels. The first novel, *Anesmwyth Hoen* (Restless Energy, 1941), was fairly unusual at the time in that it was partly set in London and Munich. It and the later novel, *Mae'r Galon Wrth y Llyw* (The Heart is at the Helm, 1957), were fairly daring in the Welsh context because of their frank discussion of sexual matters, and the feminist streak is far more explicit than in the work of Kate Roberts.

Many of the above writers made only brief forays into the realm of fiction, and some of their works are short and uneven in quality. However, with the publication of T. Rowland Hughes's first novel, *O Law i Law* (From Hand to Hand, 1943), it became immediately apparent that a very talented novelist had entered the field. Ironically, he turned his hand to novel-writing after the onset of a crippling illness, as Daniel Owen had tried to cheat fate by writing novels during a very different illness, so that his life could be prolonged at least in his own imagination. T. Rowland Hughes came from the quarrying village of Llanberis in north Wales, and stepped quickly up the academic ladder at Bangor and Oxford before becoming a lecturer at Coleg Harlech, and eventually joining the BBC's Welsh Service as producer. He made a name for himself as a poet by winning the National Eisteddfod Chair twice. His five novels, published annually from 1943 to 1947, were written in defiance of the encroachment of multiple sclerosis, as a way of combating the ensuing depression. This explains the fact that they are in some measure an escape from his condition. They are based to a large extent on reminiscences of his childhood in Llanberis.

As a storyteller, T. Rowland Hughes is second to none apart from Daniel Owen, and he is the most popular Welsh-language novelist of the twentieth century. He is good at delineating a variety of characters, and is excellent at writing dialogue in robust Welsh. He also succeeds in interweaving humour and sadness, and there is in his work none of the often unrelieved gloom of Kate Roberts's work. His *début* novel, *O Law i Law*, despite its apparent loose structure, cleverly—but seemingly unselfconsciously—construes a close-knit village community. Because of its anecdotal nature it gives the reader the impression of sifting through an album of old photographs, and convinces with its stamp of truth.

The second novel, *William Jones* (1944), achieved a certain notoriety by its protagonist's use of the phrase '*Cadw dy blydi chips!*' ('Keep your bloody chips!') to his slovenly wife. This is the comedy of the little man who rebels against his wife's treatment of him as a simpleton. Slapstick and farce are put to good use, and when William Jones leaves his native slate-quarrying district to join his sister and brother-in-law in the south Wales coalfield, we are treated to some comical misunderstandings between the speakers of north- and south-Walian dialects. There is no hope of work in the depressed coalmines for William Jones, but he succeeds in making a career for himself as an actor in radio plays broadcast from Cardiff. Despite the fact that the period is that of the Depression, this is a light-hearted novel on the whole, but the mood darkens towards the end, and William Jones develops into something of a hero who takes the place of his brother-in-law at the head of the table.

For his third novel, *Yr Ogof* (The Cave, 1945), T. Rowland Hughes turned to the New Testament story of Joseph of Arimathea for his subject-matter. He is not perhaps as much at home with this material as when writing about the quarrymen of north Wales, and his treatment of Joseph's conversion face to face with Christ is not altogether convincing, but this novel is a readable—and at times powerful—evocation of life in the time of Jesus.

Chwalfa (Dispersal, 1946) is generally regarded as T. Rowland Hughes's greatest novel. It is based on the quarrymen's strike at

Bethesda in north Wales at the turn of the century, and its drastic effect on the fictional family of Edward Ifans. The dispersal of this close-knit family is tragically conveyed, and is seen as a microcosm of the dispersal of the whole community. The growing number of strike-breakers—or *bradwyr* (literally 'traitors')—signals the gradual weakening of the workers' resolve, and they are eventually forced to succumb. The author in effect eulogizes their stand, despite its failure. As Raymond Williams said of this 'memorable example' of this type of industrial novel:

> The old simple nucleus, in which there are organically extending links between family, village, place and class . . . is at once affirmed and seen in dispersal. The very form of the affirmation . . . is then in effect an elegy: what is affirmed is also lost.

T. Rowland Hughes's last novel was *Y Cychwyn* (The Beginning, 1947), and it was supposed to be the first in a trilogy about the development of a Nonconformist minister. There is in it a reworking of some of the material used in earlier novels, but it promised to deal with the impact of modernism on Welsh religion in the second and third parts. The project never went beyond the first page of the second part, and the author was dead by 1949.

Five very readable novels in as many years, under extremely difficult physical and psychological conditions, was an achievement indeed. However the first flush of critical acclaim has been somewhat tempered over the years. T. Rowland Hughes seems too kind towards his favoured characters, and has a tendency to oversimplify the situations he describes. His novels lack both intellectual and psychological depth. Although he touches on political and religious themes, he does not succeed in properly grappling with them. He is much more approachable than Kate Roberts, but she is a much more profound writer.

The 1950s marked a watershed in the history of the Welsh-language novel. With each succeeding decade, more and more novels were published, and there was much more variety in style and subject-matter. The popular base of children's and young people's novels, plus *genre* fiction—romances, detective novels and adventure stories, became more and more widespread, especially after the foundation of the Welsh Books Council in 1961. There is no place in a concise survey such as this even to mention the many dedicated and talented people involved in this extremely vital activity, but their contribution is acknowledged.

The distinct change of mood is first seen in the work of Islwyn Ffowc Elis, a farmer's son from Dyffryn Ceiriog who studied at Bangor and served as a minister in mid Wales and Anglesey before joining BBC radio as a producer. For a period he even managed to be a full-time freelance writer in Welsh—a feat no one imagined possible in those days, although it is taken for granted in the era of the Welsh television channel, S4C. His first novel, *Cysgod y Cryman* (The Shadow of the Sickle, 1953), heralds a new confidence. Here there is no morose looking back at the bad old days of hard toil to make ends meet, be it on a farm or in a quarry. There is no dwelling upon the ravages of the Second World War, despite the presence of Karl, a German ex-prisoner of war. Although the setting is a rural one, this mid-Wales area of well-to-do farmers is a far cry from the humble smallholdings of Kate Roberts's Rhosgadfan. Harri Vaughan, the central character, is the heir of Lleifior, a flourishing farm which has been in the Vaughan family for generations, and where family traditions are venerated. However, during his period at university Harri comes under the influence of the Communist Party, and under the thrall of Gwylan, one of its leading lights, to whose sexual advances he is quite susceptible. This leads to conflicts at home—with the gentlemanly values of his father on the one hand, and with his rather doting and gullible girlfriend, Lisabeth, on the other. Despite the eventual rift which develops between him and Gwylan, he becomes a devoted Marxist, and with his family's characteristic mettle, he is ironically determined to quash all the *bourgeois* values they stand for. By the end of the novel he has left university, disowned his family, taken up a job as a manual worker and gone to live in a council house with the ordinary, uneducated daughter of a council worker.

This novel has a fast-moving plot, and more than one subplot has been dextrously interwoven with it. The story has a film-like quality, with events following each other with vivid ease. The style is sophisticated, and has an *élan* about it which contrasts with the more earthy and workaday prose of Kate Roberts and T. Rowland Hughes. Another appealing feature is the treatment of the rebelliousness of youth against the values of the older generation. And these young people enjoy healthy sexual appetites which are not made to seem sordid as in *Monica.*

In ordinary parlance, this novel was a roaring success. Of course it was its author's first novel, and its many virtues seem in retrospect to be balanced by quite a few flaws. The theme is an ambitious one, and all its implications are not developed to their inevitable conclusion. Some of the lesser characters are presented in monochrome—Karl the German is too saintly, Paul Rushmere the Englishman is a condescending prig. Delyth George has been rightly critical of the chauvinist manner in which the female characters have been portrayed. Yet, for all these faults, *Cysgod y Cryman* remains a milestone, and gave the younger generation an exhilarating feeling that the Welsh novel had at last come of age. It opened possibilities for new novelists to explore new ideas.

Following the success of his first novel, Islwyn Ffowc Elis ventured further in his next novel, *Ffenestri Tua'r Gwyll* (Windows Towards the Dusk, 1955), and took as his theme the sexual frustration of a middle-aged widow who had been prevented by her late businessman husband from developing her talent as a concert pianist. As compensation for lack of artistic expression she collects around her a coterie of artists in the small seaside university town of Caerwenlli (an ill-disguised version of Aberystwyth). Many of her friends are establishment figures, and venerable members of the town's academic and literary circles, but she also gives patronage to a gay painter, and she herself becomes infatuated with a young, shy, freckled poet who creates a furore by his swingeing attacks on the professor of Welsh's latest collection of poems. Driven by her obsession with this gauche creature, she tries to trick him into re-enacting with her the last fateful night of passion she spent with her husband at their summer house, and this leads to her eventual hysterical breakdown. This novel was slated by the critics, not so much because of its *risqué* theme, but because the characters and their milieu seemed strange and pretentious, let alone un-Welsh. This was unfortunate, for the novel is a serious attempt to grapple with significant themes, both psychological and artistic. Its multilayered nature is impossible to convey in a *resumé* such as the above.

Islwyn Ffowc Elis unfortunately buckled under the criticism, and ran for refuge back to the story of his first novel, whose sequel, *Yn Ôl i Leifior* (Back to Lleifior), he published in 1956. This is a delightful book, but it is too obvious an attempt to tie up the loose ends left at the end of *Cysgod y Cryman*. The next novel, *Wythnos*

yng Nghymru Fydd (A Week in the Wales of the Future, 1957) is an
arresting propagandist tract, giving the reader a choice between
two possible futures for Wales, a utopian independent Wales or a
dystopian Wales which is nothing more than a dark, anglicized,
culturally moribund western England. Then came *Blas y Cynfyd*
(The Taste of Antiquity, 1958), which dispels the myth of rural
Wales as an idyllic paradise. *Tabyrddau'r Babongo* (The Drums of
Babongo, 1961) is set in Africa, and comically satirizes imperialistic
attitudes. Islwyn Ffowc Elis's next three novels, *Y Blaned Dirion*
(The Gentle Planet, 1968), *Y Gromlech yn yr Haidd* (The Cromlech
in the Barley, 1970), and *Eira Mawr* (Snowbound, 1971) are short
and lightweight. He is one of those writers who feels that it is vital
to aim for as wide a public as possible if one is writing in a minority
language, and that abstruse writing only alienates an already
limited audience. In his best work he has proved that it is possible
to reconcile the serious and the entertaining.

Islwyn Ffowc Elis opened the doors wide for a number of
followers—young, and mainly female—to walk through with
confidence, although it has to be said that his ability to tell a
captivating story in an elegant style was too hard an act for most to
follow. At the 1957 National Eisteddfod the 21-year-old Catrin
Lloyd Rowlands won the prize for her novel *Ar Chwâl* (A Scattered
Life, 1958). Eigra Lewis (now Roberts) went one step further in
1959 when she won a similar prize for her novel *Brynhyfryd* (1959)
when still nineteen. At the Llanelli Eisteddfod of 1962, the 24-year-
old Jane Edwards won the prize for her *Dechrau Gofidiau* (The
Onset of Sorrows, 1962). It seemed as if the cult of youth had
reached Wales, and that we had more than one Françoise Sagan.
Not surprisingly, these young novelists wrote about youth, and
subjects such as illicit sex and illegitimate children were being
cautiously broached. A certain amount of kicking against the
puritanical traces of their elders could be felt in their work, as well
as a desire to be in the swim of the swinging 1960s.

It was natural for the work of this new generation to be warmly
welcomed, and it has to be said that Jane Edwards reacted
positively to the encouragement she gained from critics such as
Kate Roberts as well the economic support which came her way
from the Welsh Arts Council in the form of bursaries and prizes.
She has continued to be prolific up to the present day, and her work
has reflected to a certain extent the changes in her own life and

circumstances. Her second novel, *Byd o Gysgodion* (A World of Shadows, 1964), provides an eminently readable story about the conflicting emotions of youth and a restless dissatisfaction with a seemingly aimless existence. With *Bara Seguryd* (The Bread of Idleness, 1969) there is a more ambitious—but less successful—attempt to convey the *ennui* of three young wives belonging to a *nouveau riche* middle class. In *Epil Cam* (Cham's Offspring, 1972) and *Dros Fryniau Bro Afallon* (Over the Hills of Avallon, 1976) the covert political dimension adds substance, but Jane Edwards's characters never engage themselves earnestly with serious concerns. They skate over the surface of things, and their creator has been praised for her observant delineation of the vacuity of modern middle-class life. In her novella *Miriam* (1977), however, she turns her gaze to an adolescent girl's reaction to the loss of her mother, and her father's subsequent remarriage, and this book has a pleasant authenticity about it which has made it popular as a school text-book.

Jane Edwards has published three other novels to date. *Cadno Rhos-y-ffin* (The Fox of Rhos-y-ffin, 1984) introduces us to a motley crowd of rather pretentious and superficial characters, most of whom are the flotsam and jetsam of the 1960s who find it difficult to cope with encroaching middle-age, and indulge in affairs of one sort or another, without finding emotional fulfilment. To them, and surprisingly, to the representatives of the younger generation as well, life is simply a *charade*, acted out, in the main, in comfortable surroundings. *Y Bwthyn Cu* (The Cherished Cottage, 1987) is an abortive attempt by a middle-aged woman to resurrect the experiences of the 1960s. *Pant yn y Gwely* (A Hollow in the Bed, 1993) returns to the world of a young girl on the brink of womanhood in a working-class environment in north Wales. This, with *Miriam* and the author's collections of short stories about growing up, strikes a note of genuineness, in contrast to the affectation of the novels about middle-class life.

Eigra Lewis Roberts is interested mainly in portraying the extraordinariness behind the ordinary facade of terrace houses in villages and small towns, and she has more of a feel for working-class communities than most of her generation. Her second book, *Tŷ ar y Graig* (A House on the Rock, 1966), deals with a daughter's return home after a rebellious absence of five years, and concentrates on her feelings of alienation. *Digon i'r Diwrnod*

(Sufficient Unto the Day, 1974) is a much more complex study of the interweaving lives of a number of characters of varied ages. The use of dialogue in idiomatic Welsh gives the writing a powerful authenticity. Eigra's next novel, *Mis o Fehefin* (A June Month, 1980) portrays the life of an ordinary street during one particular June month. The life of the inhabitants normally trundles on unspectacularly, but during this particular month a certain rumbling disturbs their peace. This microcosm of a world is quite a sombre one, with each character having his private cross to bear, but it is a claustrophobic community as well, with a great deal of gossip, jealousy, and a little love. The novel was adapted as a television serial by its author, and became an immediate success. In contrast to a soap-opera such as *Coronation Street,* this serial about another street places almost all the emphasis on characterization rather than plot. Eigra Lewis Roberts wrote another television serial as a sequel to the initial one and this time translated the script into a novel rather than *vice versa.* This novel was called *Ha' Bach* (Indian Summer, 1985), and it makes extensive use of the authentic dialogue for which its author is renowned. Writing for television has provided a new and viable outlet for this author's talent, but in fairness to her she has not turned her back on the written word. She continues to publish prolifically, and has been particularly successful with the short story form.

It was during the 1960s that T. Wilson Evans published his first novels and asserted his individual voice. As a native of Flintshire and a former collier he was well-placed to introduce new subject-matter to the Welsh novel. His *Rhwng Cyfnos a Gwawr* (Between Dusk and Dawn, 1964) robustly portrays contemporary family tensions against the backdrop of a childhood in a coal-mining village in north-east Wales, and was deemed by Saunders Lewis to be 'a promise of greatness'. The same critic was less enthusiastic about *Nos yn yr Enaid* (Night in the Soul, 1965), but this analysis of a tormented minister's soul has some anarchically powerful descriptions of youthful love. *Trais y Caldu Mawr* (The Violence of Caldu Mawr, 1966) deals with a coalminers' strike, and is particularly concerned with the inner torment of their leader who feels betrayed by them. There followed three novels in a more experimental vein with much use of internal monologue and flashback techniques: *Iwan Tudur* (1969), *Melinau'r Meddwl* (The Mind's Mills, 1975), and *Cilfach Lamorna* (Lamorna Cove, 1977).

T. Wilson Evans was more successful, however, when he returned to the coalfield in *Y Pabi Coch* (The Red Poppy) which won the National Eisteddfod Prose Medal in 1983.

A more cerebral type of novel—or at least a type of novel which aimed at tackling burning issues—emerged in the 1960s. R. Gerallt Jones, a young English graduate, and coeditor of the *engagé* journal *Yr Arloeswr* (The Pioneer) ambitiously embarked on a trilogy in this vein. His first novel, *Y Foel Fawr* (The Great Bare Hill, 1960) traces the development of a young and idealistic Welshman who has been an activist in South Africa, but on his return to Wales after a period of imprisonment, he becomes disillusioned with the materialistic and politically apathetic society he finds there. In the sequel to this novel, *Nadolig Gwyn* (White Christmas, 1962), we are given an insider picture of academic politics at one of the colleges of the University of Wales, and the revolutionary Welshman is tempted to become a member of the Welsh establishment and to succumb to the politics of the possible. These novels were planned as the first two parts of a trilogy, but the project was abandoned, and R. Gerallt Jones tackled very different subjects in his subsequent novels. *Triptych,* winner of the National Eisteddfod Prose Medal in 1977, is a tense account of a leading rugby player's reaction to the knowledge that he is dying of cancer. As an agnostic and a cultural philistine, he has lived a very physical existence, devoting his energies to rugby, socializing and sex, and finds it extremely hard to come to terms with his impending death. Gerallt won the Prose Medal again in 1979 for his short novel *Cafflogion*, which describes the dark predicament of a co-operative community in the Llŷn Peninsula. His most recent novel, *Gwyntyll y Corwynt* (The Whirlwind's Fan, 1978), is in the nature of a political thriller, about a group of Irish terrorists and the kidnapping of a Welsh MP.

Bobi Jones is known mainly as a poet, theorist and critic, but he has written a large corpus of creative prose, including three novels. *Nid yw Dŵr yn Plygu* (Water Does Not Bend, 1958) tells the story of a young medical student at Grandfield who falls in love with the disabled sister of his best friend who lives in Llanlecwydd. There is consternation when the inhabitants of Llanlecwydd are told that their village is to be flooded to provide water for the English town of Grandfield. (The proposed flooding of Tryweryn was a burning issue at the time.) The plot takes some dramatic turns, but the author's main interest is not in providing a naturalistic story, but rather to examine the characters' motivation and to scrutinize the nature of romantic nationalism. *Bod yn Wraig* (Being a Wife, 1960) could superficially be seen as a variation on the eternal triangle, but again the author is more concerned with the underlying allegorical meaning of his narrative than with the surface of the story itself. Unfortunately both these novels are failed experiments, as the author has not solved the problem of integrating his theme and plot. A much more substantial novel appeared recently, with the intriguing title *Epistol Serch a Selsig* (Love's Epistle and Sausages, 1997). It deals with the desire of three generations of a London Welsh family for a return to the promised land of their roots. Written from an unashamedly nationalistic and Christian perspective, it will be seen by some to have too much of a missionary zeal, and yet it could hardly be described as simplistic; it is powerfully written, and provides much food for thought.

Another highly cerebral writer was Pennar Davies, an academic who became principal of a theological college in Swansea, but who nevertheless wrote in a provocatively irreverent manner. His mother tongue was English, yet he cultivated a polished literary style in Welsh, his second language. He was a member of the Cadwgan Circle, a coterie of *avant-garde* intellectuals who met at the Rhondda home of J. Gwyn Griffiths and his German wife, Kate Bosse-Griffiths, during the Second World War. His richly allusive poems, short stories and novels are not for the lazy reader, but he shuns any notion of simplistic accessibility, and claims that 'the Welsh language is of Europe and of the world'. His first major prose work was *Cudd fy Meiau* (Hide my Sins, 1957), a confessional diary which is remarkable for its honesty. Then came the 'apocalyptic' novel, *Anadl o'r Uchelder* (A Breath from upon High, 1958), a satirical extravaganza set in the future which is a caustic indictment of an American-style evangelical movement. There followed a loosely defined sequel called *Mabinogi Mwys* (An Enigmatic Infancy, 1979) which describes the birth and upbringing of a character hardly touched upon in the first novel. This is Arthur Morgan, whose infancy is described in a strangely alluring manner, faintly echoing the medieval tales of the Mabinogi on the one hand, and paralleling the story of Jesus's birth and childhood in the gospels on the other. The aptly named Arthur has the makings of a national saviour, and yet the nation itself is obstinately resistant.

The third novel in this trilogy, *Gwas y Gwaredwr* (The Saviour's Servant, 1991), is a modern *De Imitatione Christi*, showing Arthur Morgan's endeavour to follow in the steps of Jesus of Nazareth, not in an attempt to become a latter-day Messiah, but in a sincere devotional manner. Pennar Davies took a break from writing his trilogy to compose a *jeu d'esprit* entitled *Meibion Darogan* (Sons of Prophesy, 1968), a *roman à clef* depicting the world of the Cadwgan Circle in the early 1940s, albeit in a stylized manner befitting the pretentiousness of that group. Because of their dense style and thought-provoking themes, Pennar Davies's novels will repay close study.

Rhydwen Williams was another member of the Cadwgan Circle, although very different in temperament and literary bent from Pennar Davies. His poetry is full of verve and is exhilaratingly direct and unobscure, and his novels are robust and extremely approachable. They include *Breuddwyd Rhonabwy Jones* (Rhonabwy Jones's Dream, 1972), a playful 'beast fable' where Wales is ruled by birds and animals; *Apolo* (1975), an acerbic look at the clay-footed gods of the television world; and *Gallt y Gofal* (The Hill of Cares, 1979), a psychological study of Job Corniog in his unremitting battle against fate. *Adar y Gwanwyn* (The Birds of Spring, 1972) was a kind of riposte to Pennar Davies's *Meibion Darogan,* and an alternative portrait of the Cadwgan Circle, in a more realistic vein. It is, however, as a champion of the mining community of the Rhondda that Rhydwen Williams is best known, and his best-loved novels are the ones forming the trilogy *Cwm Hiraeth* (The Valley of Longing, 1969–1973). These are largely autobiographical, and offer a panoramic sweep of life in the Rhondda over three generations, spanning the period from the beginning of the century to the Second World War. Although somewhat marred by the eulogistic tone which the author adopts, they help to fill a little of the void of the Welsh-language industrial novel. Another important contribution is *Amser i Wylo* (A Time to Weep, 1986), an account of the Senghennydd pit disaster of 1913 when 439 mineworkers were killed—the most tragic mining catastrophe to happen in these islands. Rhydwen Williams published one novel in English—*The Angry Vineyard* (1975)—which relates the story of Dic Penderyn, the hero of the Merthyr Riots who was hanged in 1831. Another very different historical novel in Welsh appeared in 1988, *Liwsi Regina,* the passionate story

of the romance between Lucy Walter of Roch Castle in
Pembrokeshire and Prince Charles, who later became Charles II.
The author takes a great deal of poetic licence, and succeeds in
writing a very readable historical romance.

We now have to retrace our steps back to the beginning of the
1960s, to a novel which stands apart from all pervading literary
fashions, so as to give the impression of timelessness. It is *Un Nos
Ola Leuad* (One Moonlit Night, 1961), Caradog Prichard's only
real novel. The author was parliamentary correspondent for *The
Daily Telegraph,* that most conservative of papers, but despite
being based in London, his childhood memories of life in the slate-
quarrying village of Bethesda in Caernarfonshire during the early
years of this century haunted his imagination and drove him to
write an obsessional novel about the return of a convicted
murderer, after a long period of detention in a mental institution, to
his home village, to confront his motley reminiscences. During his
last fateful walk through the village, disjointed images cascade
through his mind, and we gradually perceive the web and woof of
his doleful being. These tumble haphazardly along the pages, giving
a kaleidoscopic effect, but mainly in different shades of black.
Things are seen through a glass darkly—sexual deviation, murder,
suicide, mental derangement, poverty, religious mumbo-jumbo, all
mixed up with joy, ecstasy, humour, play and the elation of sexual
awakening. There is no linear story, only a zig-zag swinging
between different points in time, from the present of the grown-up
man to the generally murky past of the fatherless boy, fixated on
his lunatic mother. The style changes its hue from childish patter to
a highly stylized psalm-like prose. This non-realistic discourse with
its minimalist story line succeeds in conveying the complex
psychology of the nameless Oedipal main character with an
unobtrusive precision. It is psychologically profound without any
overt mention of psychology, and succeeds as well in enmeshing the
psychological with the sociological, for it is not after all timeless,
but has a habitation and a name, in the primitive cultural
uncertainty of a deprived slate-quarrying village in north Wales, in
the shadow of the Great Strike at Penrhyn, in the throes of the 1904
religious revival, and ravaged from afar by the First World War.
This polyphonic novel was successfully made into a film by Endaf
Emlyn and given an English theatrical production by Helena Kaut-
Howson. Its power was felt in the 1960s, but it then seemed an

isolated work, and no one was directly influenced by it. By today it might be seen as the proto-postmodernist novel, much admired by the *avant-garde* writers of the 1990s.

Mention should now be made of two or three other isolated novels which stand out as remarkable examples of their *genre*. Emyr Humphreys is of course a major Welsh novelist writing mainly in English, although he has written plays, television scripts and poems in Welsh. His only novel in Welsh is *Y Tri Llais* (The Three Voices, 1958) which won the Hawthornden Prize in its English version, *A Toy Epic* (1958). As the English title implies, it treats an epic theme in miniature. The three voices of the Welsh title are those of three boys from different backgrounds growing up in Flintshire in the period preceding the Second World War. They represent differing aspects of Wales in microcosm, and there is a subtle interplay between their social milieu and their unique psychological make-up. The tension between the fluidity of their individual personalities and the conditioning influences of their backgrounds results in an open-ended conclusion as they embark on adult life in the wide world.

T. Glynne Davies is remembered mainly as a poet, but he also published two novels, the first of which, *Haf Creulon* (Cruel Summer, 1960), was rather slight, but added a new dimension to the Welsh novel in its depiction of factory life. His second novel, *Marged* (1974), was anything but slight, and was boasted to be one of the longest in the language. It attempts to 'say everything' about *Sgot*, the 'slum' area of its author's native Llanrwst in the period between 1872 and 1916. Despite showing the strain of over-diligent research, and a sprawling plot, this novel has numerous passages of powerful writing in the realist tradition.

Another poet, Dafydd Rowlands, rejected that tradition in his only novel to date, *Mae Theomemphus yn Hen* (Theomemphus is Old, 1977), and described it as a 'novel/poem', as if to reinforce the suggestion made in the title of his popular volume of *belles-lettres*, *Ysgrifau yr Hanner Bardd* (The Essays of the Half Poet, 1972), that he was treading the razor's edge between poetry and prose. The novel pendulates between a straightforward storytelling narrative and an italicized stream-of-consciousness exploration of the subconscious mind of its main character. It tells of his journey to Ireland in search of his hated father's past, and a better comprehension of his own convoluted present.

A writer of the same generation, Harri Pritchard Jones has
succeeded in opening the frontiers of Welsh prose quite
considerably, not so much in technical experimentation as in
theme. Born in Dudley of Welsh-speaking parents, he was brought
up on Anglesey and studied medicine at Trinity College, Dublin.
He has had an almost life-long love affair with Ireland, and became
a Catholic during his ten-year period there. His training as a
psychiatrist has also influenced his writing. His short stories have
been widely praised, and have been translated into English and
other European languages, but he has also published three novels.
Dychwelyd (Return, 1972) is set in Dublin, and vividly conveys the
bustling life of a group of burgeoning young intellectuals interwoven with that of Larri, who belongs to a different generation and
background. *Ysglyfaeth* (Prey, 1987) was based on a successful
television film, and is the story of a liaison between a half-
Welshman and a fervent Irish girl against the background of the
bloody politics of Northern Ireland. The novel combines a swift-
moving story with acute psychological insight. Harri Pritchard
Jones's latest novel, *Bod yn Rhydd* (To Be Free, 1992), breaks new
ground in its attempt to relate in Welsh the experiences of a black
prisoner from Cardiff's docklands in the 1960s, together with those
of his white wife who works in a hospital for the mentally
handicapped.

I hope that I have been able to show the growing vitality of the
Welsh novel during the 1960s and 1970s—the wish to experiment
and to tackle new themes, and I must confess a prejudice towards
the tendencies to free the novel from the shackles of a restrictive
tradition. Nevertheless I have to admit that the historical novel and
the historical romance seemed at times to vie for ascendancy with
the contemporary novel during the sixties and seventies. Of course
it could be argued that all novels are historical in essence, but the
corollary could equally be argued—that all historical novels are
contemporary. Without entering into critical controversy, it has to
be stated that some of the best prose-writers of the twentieth
century devoted themselves to writing about the past. It could be
argued that this was a symptom of a desire for a seemingly stable
base in a historical period when the Welsh language and its culture
formed a firm foundation. It could be interpreted as a kind of
escapism from the cultural and spiritual quicksands of the present.
However, there is a great deal of it, and I am afraid I shall have to

disappoint such commentators as the historian John Gwynfor
Jones who complained in 1982 about the paucity of critical studies
of the Welsh historical novel. The subject needs an article to itself,
and I can only touch on it briefly here.

A few historical novels have already been mentioned, and one
could add a sprinkling of others from the first half of the century.
The most notable, perhaps, is *Orinda* by the historian R. T. Jenkins
(1943), an urbane account of the royalist Richard Aubrey's eviction
from his post as Fellow of Jesus College, Oxford during the Puritan
period, and his rehabilitation in Wales by the poet Katherine
Phillips, 'the matchless Orinda'. This novel has been elevated by the
critics to the status of a minor classic, but its author wrote only one
other short novel, *Ffynhonnau Elim* (The Springs of Elim, 1945),
published under the pseudonym Idris Thomas. Another
professional historian who attempted to fictionalize history was W.
Ambrose Bebb, with his *Y Baradwys Bell* (The Distant Paradise,
1941), a fictional diary set in Wales in 1841, and *Dial y Tir* (The
Vengeance of the Land, 1946), which deals with Welsh emigration
to America in the last century, but his skill as a writer is not
commensurate with his vision.

It was with Rhiannon Davies Jones's work that the historical
novel gathered momentum, however. Her novels are many-faceted
and wide-ranging. The first was the intimate fictional diary of the
late-eighteenth-century and early-nineteenth-century hymn writer
and mystic, Ann Griffiths, entitled *Fy Hen Lyfr Cownt* (My Old
Accounts Book, 1960). The diary form is used again in a short
novel set in a thirteenth-century nunnery, *Lleian Llan Llŷr* (The
Nun of Llan Llŷr, 1965). In *Llys Aberffraw* (The Court of
Aberffraw, 1977) we are taken back to the age of the medieval
prince, Owain Gwynedd, and the story is related by Angharad, the
illegitimate daughter of one of the prince's daughters. In *Eryr
Pengwern* (The Eagle of Pengwern, 1981) the scene is set in the
seventh-century Powys of the Heledd saga. The next novel,
Dyddiadur Mari Gwyn (Mari Gwyn's Diary, 1985), deals with the
life of the Elizabethan Catholic recusant, Robert Gwyn. There
followed a trilogy of novels on a grand scale—*Cribau Eryri* (The
Ridges of Snowdonia, 1987), *Barrug y Bore* (Morning Frost, 1989)
and *Adar Drycin* (Storm Birds, 1993). These are set in the Age of
the Princes—Llywelyn the Great, his son Dafydd, and Llywelyn the
Last, covering the years 1234 to 1282. All Rhiannon Davies Jones's

novels are imbued with her concern for Wales and the Welsh language, and she unashamedly uses history to convey her impassioned nationalist point of view.

Marion Eames is another prolific and accomplished writer who has ranged far and wide, and has not limited herself exclusively to historical novels. *Y Stafell Ddirgel* (The Secret Room, 1969) deals with the persecution of Rowland Ellis and a group of Merionethshire Quakers during the seventeenth century, and its sequel, *Y Rhandir Mwyn* (Fair Wilderness, 1972), follows their emigration to Pennsylvania, and their attempt to create a New Jerusalem there. *I Hela Cnau* (To Gather Nuts, 1978) is a lively depiction of the emigration of people from north Wales to the expanding town of Birkenhead towards the end of the last century. Marion Eames ventured to medieval Wales in her next novel, *Y Gaeaf Sydd Unig* (Solitary Winter, 1982), published on the 700th anniversary of the death of Llywelyn the Last, and dealing with Mabli, the daughter of the castellan of Bere Castle, whose fateful life is intertwined with that of Llywelyn and Eleanor de Montfort. It is a well-told tragic story of unrequited love. In her next novels, Marion Eames turned to modern themes. After a children's novel, *Sionyn a Siarli* (Johnnie and Charlie, 1978), she published *Seren Gaeth* (Captive Star, 1985), a novel about the ill-fated marriage of a spiritually inclined Welsh music student in London with a chauvinistic atheist academic. This novel was stimulated by some of the remarks made by Freud's colleague and biographer, Ernest Jones, about his short life with the composer Morfydd Llwyn Owen: 'Her faith and devotion so admirable when related to her country and her people were also unfortunately attached to very simple-minded religious beliefs . . . My notion of adjustment in such matters consists in persuading the other person to approach my view of them, and that is what gradually and painlessly happened.' In her most recent novel, *Y Ferch Dawel* (The Quiet Girl, 1992), Marion Eames treats the theme of incest with great sensitivity.

I will do nothing more than mention briefly the best of the other historical novels published in Welsh during the past quarter century or so. Ifor Wyn Williams deals with the turbulent life of the medieval prince, Gruffudd ap Cynan, in his *Gwres o'r Gorllewin* (Heat from the West, 1971). John Griffith Williams delves into the neurosis of the Owain Glyndŵr period in his novel, *Betws Hirfaen*

(1978), which is set in Eifionydd towards the end of the fourteenth century. R. Cyril Hughes mined the rich reserves of Elizabethan Wales in his trilogy about Catrin of Berain, whose power and legendary beauty and four marriages made her an enigmatic figure. The three novels, *Catrin o Ferain* (1975), *Dinas Ddihenydd* (City of Destruction, 1976) and *Castell Cyfaddawd* (Castle of Compromise, 1984), chronicle Catrin's first three marriages, and it is expected that a fourth novel dealing with her final marriage will follow. In his prize-winning novel, *Eira Gwyn yn Salmon* (White Snow in Salmon, 1974), Dafydd Ifans traces the spiritual development of a Puritan convert who writes letters from Cambridge to his family in Wales. Nansi Selwood portrays the life of Breconshire gentry against the backdrop of the Civil War and the Cromwellian ascendancy in her two novels, *Brychan Dir* (The Land of Brychan, 1987) and *Y Rhod yn Troi* (The Turning of the Wheel, 1993). Elwyn L. Jones wrote about the seventeenth-century Nonconformist minister, Stephen Hughes, in *Y Winllan Wen* (The Pure Vineyard, 1987), and also wrote a trilogy about the eighteenth-century Trefeca 'family' of Methodists—*Cyfrinach Hannah* (Hannah's Secret, 1985), *Seren! . . . O, Seren!* (Star! . . . Oh, Star! 1988) and *Y Gadwyn Aur* (The Golden Chain, 1989). Emyr Jones writes about John Evans from Waun-fawr who travelled up the Missouri river in search of 'Welsh Indians' during the eighteenth century in his *Grym y Lli* (The Force of the Current, 1969). Harri Williams ventured further afield in his *Y Ddaeargryn Fawr* (The Great Earthquake, 1978), the fictitious autobiography of Kierkegaard, and *Deunydd Dwbl* (A Dual Nature, 1982), based on the life of Dostoevsky.

The above catalogue is of necessity selective, and fails to convey the diversity of style and approach. It is true to say, however, that the recent Welsh historical novel is fairly conventional in its technique. Some of the authors merely chronicle the events of the past, adding a little fictional colour. Others see in the past a mirror of the present, or at least eternal human themes in microcosm. There is hardly any attempt to grapple with history as a process. With one exception—*Y Pla* (Pestilence, 1987) by Wiliam Owen Roberts. This novel about the Black Death of the fourteenth century was first greeted with bewilderment because it turned all the conventions of the historical romance on their head. There is here no romance in the accepted sense, no princely stereotypes, no glamorous heroines. Instead we are introduced to a motley crowd of characters, some of whom are serfs with names like Chwilen Bwm (Beetle the Cockchafer) or Hwch Ddu (Black Sow), whose existence in the primitive feudal community in the demesne estate of Dolbenmaen in Eifionydd is grimy and obscene. With its putrid descriptions of a leper copulating with a goat, a priest mutilating his phallus with a sickle, and miscellaneous other revolting acts, this is not calculated to woo the fastidious reader. Yet intertwined with the story of the serfs of Eifionydd (who are like 'flies on a bullock's arse') is a thrusting picaresque tale about Ibn al Khatib, a student from the Madrasa academy in Cairo, whose mission it is to go to the 'dark continent' of Europe to avenge an old family wrong by killing the king of France, and Ibn eventually arrives by accident in Eifionydd, and is greeted as 'the Dark One'.

Impossible as it is to do justice to this panoramic novel (which has been variously compared by German reviewers to the work of Boccaccio, Chaucer, Shakespeare and Voltaire, and by *The Times* reviewer to that of Umberto Eco), it has to be explained briefly here that it does not purport either to 'recreate history' or to find in the past some immutable human characteristics. It is in fact a Marxist critique which explores the hiatus in history brought about by the Black Plague, which is shown here to have cracked the fabric of history by creating favourable conditions for the opportunism of capitalism. It could be argued that the juxtaposing of American tanks and helicopters and a member of the CIA with the renaissant medieval community at the end makes the point too allegorically obvious, and this episode was wisely cut from the English and German versions. However, the vitality of the novel is in no way diminished, and Wiliam Owen Roberts's next epic novel, this time set ostensibly amongst eighteenth-century London Welshmen, yet plunging back and forth in time and space, is eagerly awaited.

Wiliam Owen Roberts is one of a breed of new Welsh novelists whose work is not only imaginatively vivid but also intellectually challenging. After much fumbling, the Welsh novel is at last definitely showing signs of maturity. Of course, there are plenty of writers who still regard it as mainly a form of entertainment, and I have no complaint at the wide base of potboilers, detective stories, romantic novels and the like which help to keep the literate public occupied, but I have to apologize to many proficient writers for not mentioning their names in this survey simply because there are too many of them. The fact is that a mediocre novelist writing during the first half of this century is more likely to feature in the history of the Welsh novel than a much more accomplished novelist writing today. That is a measure of the progress achieved. It might strike some as surprising that this is the case, considering the obvious competition from the Welsh television channel, S4C, both for writers and for an audience. There is no doubt that television has devoured some talents which could have enriched our prose, but Wiliam Owen Roberts is the supreme example of someone who writes prolifically for television and so is enabled to buy time to write ambitious and serious novels.

I shall concentrate in the rest of this article on those writers who have extended the scope of the novel, either thematically or technically—or both. Meg Elis, a political activist on more than one front, a feminist, and a forthright reviewer and broadcaster, has published a novel about the activities of the Welsh Language Society, *I'r Gad* (Into Battle, 1975), and another one based on the anti-nuclear protests of women at Greenham Common, *Pan Ddaw'r Gaeaf* (When Winter Comes, 1985). Both novels catch the flavour of the language and anti-nuclear movements, and succeed also in transcending the propaganda element, but they are short works, and one hopes that Meg Elis will devote more time to a more ambitious project in the future.

Aled Islwyn is a more committed artist, and has published seven novels and one collection of short stories to date. He began, in *Lleuwen* (1977), by exploring the anguished relationship between a female and male student, and showed his intuitive understanding of the female psyche—a trait also apparent in *Ceri* (1979), his second novel, and in subsequent works. *Sarah Arall* (Another Sarah, 1982) is a study of a modern-day Sarah Jacob, the famous 'fasting girl' of the last century. The new Sara is a middle-class girl from Cardiff, surfeited with food and sex, who escapes from the pressures of city life to the apparent tranquility of west Wales in the hope of conquering her anorexia. The rhythms of nature evocatively counterpoint her feelings, but the novel ends in a bloody revenge against her rapacious lover. Next came *Cadw'r Chwedlau'n Fyw* (Keeping the Legends Alive, 1984), which spans the decade between the two 'treacheries' of the 1969 Investiture and the Devolution Referendum of 1979, but concentrates on the personal within the ideological framework, and traces Lois's affairs with her three boyfriends, Gethin, Gerallt, and Gareth against the wrinkled

backdrop of the 1970s. There is a touch of surrealism about
Pedolau Dros y Crud (Horseshoes over the Cradle, 1986), with its
sympathetic—yet unsentimental—study of a young unemployed
homosexual. Aled Islwyn's next novel, *Os Marw Hon . . .* (If She is
Dead, 1990), is his least realistic, and blocks of narrative are
juxtaposed to create a kind of literary *collage*, evoking a rich
texture of meaning. There is much of the poet about Aled Islwyn,
and his meaning is often transmitted through imagery. His latest
novel, *Llosgi Gwern* (The Burning of Gwern, 1996) is set in rural
Gwynedd, but the life of its characters is a far cry from that of Kate
Roberts's Rhosgadfan, as they flaunt their *nouveau* Welshness, with
the traditional farm transformed into an arm of the international
leisure industry. The overall theme is rather obscure, but there are
intimations of dark sexuality and multilayered psychological
significance, as if we were seeing things through a glass darkly.

Another very accomplished novelist, but of a very different hue,
is Alun Jones, who has published five substantial novels despite his
everyday commitments as a bookseller. He won the Daniel Owen
Memorial Prize with his first novel, *Ac Yna Clywodd Sŵn y Môr*
(And Then He Heard the Sound of the Sea, 1979), which is
ostensibly a detective story, but whose conventional technical
dexterity belies its acute sociological insight. There is no doubt that
Alun Jones is a master craftsman, who drafts his plots meticulously, as shown particularly in his second novel, *Pan Ddaw'r
Machlud* (When Sunset Comes, 1981), a compelling story about a
Baader-Meinhof-type group of international terrorists who lay
siege to a house in north Wales and keep the family hostage. This is
no glib gangster novel, however, for it is a penetrating study of
human nature in its strange and terrible frailty. *Oed Rhyw Addewid*
(The Age of Some Promise, 1983) is a bitter comment on the
ruinous effect of the pathetic Welsh obsession with educational
advancement and the wish to 'get on in the world'. We are shown
how a beleaguered community in north Wales is drained of its
talented youth, to the detriment of one particular family, and how
the desired fruits of success turn out to be grapes of wrath. The next
novel, *Plentyn y Bwtias* (The Child of the Bluebells, 1989), dallies
with the supernatural, and relates how Sioned, employed as a maid
in a mansion near Corwen, is being possessed by the spirit of a
maid who worked there thirty years earlier. For sceptical readers,
the strong story line does not compensate for the fanciful subject-

matter. Alun Jones's latest novel, *Simdde yn y Gwyll* (Chimney in the Gloom, 1992), again breaks new ground for its author in that it deals with a passionate incestuous relationship, sensitively and unpretentiously described within the framework of an intricate plot, against the backdrop of the preparations for the Gulf War of the early 1990s. As always, the style is sinewy, the plot elaborate (perhaps too much so), and the characters portrayed in a spare, no-nonsense manner. Alun Jones shuns all *avant-garde* experimentation, and yet his own work has been adventurous in its choice of new and off-beat subjects.

Few novelists have been as dedicated as Aled Islwyn and Alun Jones, but during the last fifteen to twenty years there have been a few innovative novels which should be mentioned. Siôn Eirian's *Bob yn y Ddinas* (Bob in the City, 1979), despite its brevity, is—rather surprisingly—one of the few Welsh novels to be set in Cardiff, or in any city. It is obliquely a kind of rewriting of Daniel Owen's *Rhys Lewis* in a modern setting, with Bob taking the name of Rhys's brother, the anti-religious rebel of the former novel. The mind of Siôn Eirian's Bob is a void filled with fuzzy images of boozy pubs and erotic undergrowths. Hefin Wyn's *Bodio* (Hitch-hiking, 1979) is also set in Cardiff, and is full of disparate images of laborious copulation, chapel kneeling and Welsh Language Society battle cries.

A writer who has not hitherto received his due is Dafydd Huws, *alias* Goronwy Jones, *alias* Charles Huws. His method is too unliterary, haphazard, and dead-pan to be taken seriously by our sombre men of letters. In his *Dyddiadur Dyn Dwad* (The Diary of an *Emigré*, 1978) he lampoons the new Welsh *bourgeoisie* of Cardiff and hilariously presents an alternative underclass of waggish boozers. By *Un Peth 'Di Priodi Peth Arall 'Di Byw* (It's One Thing to Marry, Another to Live, 1990), the main character is older, if not wiser, and tries to cope with the tribulations of married life. This is a playful novel which seems to poke fun at the *genre* itself at times, with its *doubles entendres* and word games, as if literature was a kind of linguistic masturbation, with the language playing with itself in a randy mood. Although he has less stylistic bravura, Twm Miall could be described as Dafydd Huws's blood brother, in his novels *Cyw Haul* (Sun Colt, 1988) and *Cyw Dôl* (Colt in a Dole Queue, 1990). Gareth Miles, better-known for his plays and writings for television and film, displays a similar cocky irreverence towards the icons of the establishment. His loose-knit novel, *Treffin* (1979) relates the exploits of a crowd of young Welshmen in a border town who combine a riotous life-style with political activism. *Trefaelog* (1989) is a more serious attempt to interpret the course of Welsh nationalism from the heady optimism of the 1960s to the reactionary 1980s. It is an undisguised critique—from a socialist writer—of Saunders Lewis's brand of nationalism.

One perceives in a number of recent Welsh novels an irreverent trampling over literary conventions. There are examples of metafiction and self-referential narratives, and a cheeky use of *collage, pastiche* and *bricolage.* The post-modernist novel has arrived with a vengeance, and not a few critics are displeased. We have already seen that Wiliam Owen Roberts displayed not a little impudence in his *Y Pla,* but despite its virtuosic techniques it is a novel underpinned by a political commitment. His earlier *Bingo!* (1985) had a more fatalistic theme. Its subtle gliding from film to prose narrative and back again into a film script is highly inventive and disturbing.

Angharad Tomos might seem an unlikely figure to mention at this juncture, for she has been compared with Kate Roberts, and would probably cringe at the idea of being coupled with the *avant-garde.* Nevertheless, one of her works has been described as 'anti-literature literature' by M. Wynn Thomas, and there is a sense in which she is waging a battle with words, as if she wants to flay them of their decorous literariness. Neither is she content to play with them with post-modernist abandon. In her first 'novel', *Yma o Hyd* (Still Here, 1985), she brushes aside any pretence at writing fiction. She sets out to convince the reader that this is the real diary of the imprisoned Blodeuwedd surreptitiously scrawled on prison toilet paper. It is an ill-disguised piece of autobiography based on its author's periods of imprisonment as a militant language activist. Call it propaganda if you will, but Blodeuwedd's ruthless self-mockery and sense of irony ill-becomes a soap-box orator. There is here no glib vision of an utopian future, and even nationalist icons such as Saunders and Waldo are railed against. A stint in an English prison can seem like a merciful escape from that larger and more formidable prison which is Wales. Even Dafydd Iwan's words taken as a title are double-edged in their significance, and convey, not their triumphant surface meaning, but the horrendous feeling of being trapped in a *cul-de-sac.* For Angharad Tomos, not only is the personal political, but the political is also excruciatingly personal.

Her apparent anti-literary stance conceals a subtle artfulness more reminiscent of recent Latin-American fiction than of the more solidly realist traditional novel. *Si Hei Lwli* (Berceuse, 1991) is a contrapuntal evocation of youth and old age, ostensibly written as a record of a car journey which the 25-year-old Eleni (the name itself suggesting the all-pervading present) undertakes to take her old aunt Bigw ('ninety-something') to visit the grave of her sister, who is Eleni's grandmother. The car journey, an expedition in space, is of course a metaphor for life, an expedition in time. The title itself has a topsy-turvy feel to it in that this is not a baby's cradlesong, but rather a lullaby to an antediluvian old lady in her second infancy. Life's omnipresent throb is conveyed by the car's pulsating engine, and the use of the first person narrative and the present tense gives an urgency to this helter-skelter journey towards death. This framework, however, is strained to breaking point by the use of shifting points of view and confounding time shifts. The immediacy of the journey is dashed by the knowledge that it has already come to an end before the novel begins. Bigw is already dead and buried. This black ice depiction of old age and death reaches Beckettian depths at times, and yet the gloom is relieved by a hard-won stoicism expressed by the metaphor of the ship at the end of the novel—a metaphor whose aptness is questionable.

Angharad Tomos's third novel, *Titrwm* (1994), is a kind of prose poem, whose first-person narrator is appropriately called Awen (Muse), a fairly common personal name in Welsh. Awen is a deaf and dumb young woman who has nevertheless learnt to read, and has become obsessed with books. The Titrwm of the title is the unborn child in her womb, the only 'person' in the world to whom she can relate properly. To complicate matters further, this foetus is the result of Awen being raped by an Englishman. This novel is poetically highly charged, and is relentless in its portrayal of an outsider's world, a life locked in silence, yet teeming with words and images. It could perhaps be read as a parable for the unbearable leprosy of solitude which any outsider has to suffer— whether a political outsider, a member of a minority, or a person deprived of his or her physical faculties. Its underlying theme, however, is that human beings live within a web of words, that their lives are intertwined tales, and that they read each other. This is therefore a highly self-conscious novel, and a very literary piece of fiction.

Robin Llywelyn has no qualms about quitting the realist mode. When his novels are mentioned, the name of Tolkien is often bandied about, as well as the medieval tales of the Mabinogion, and the eighteenth-century prose classic, *Gweledigaetheu y Bardd Cwsc* (The Visions of the Sleeping Bard). He is a playful teller of tales, set in imprecise periods and vague territories. The reader is hardly likely to encounter flesh-and-blood characters such as the next-door neighbours in his works. They are rather a chequered crowd of strangely named creatures such as Anwes Bach y Galon (Little Fondler of the Heart), Dei Dwyn Wya (Dei the Egg Stealer), y Du Traheus (The Arrogant Black One) or Llygad Bwyd (An Eye for Food). Incidentally, most of these names have been pinched from a fourteenth-century court document. Others have been deftly coined from Irish, Breton and French—for example, Stoti Fragw comes from the Breton *Stot e vragoù*, which means something such as 'to piss in his trousers'; Bas le Tart is derived from the Irish phrase meaning 'to die of thirst' (an appropriate name for a publican); Ws Wij is a rough attempt to convey the French *Ou suis-je?* (Where am I?) in Welsh, and has ironic connotations for a minister of transport. To excavate the underlying meaning of all personal and place-names in Robin Llywelyn's two novels would be a laborious task indeed, and it has to be admitted that both books are highly readable and comprehensible without unlocking all the subtle meanings.

Nevertheless, alarm bells were rung when *Seren Wen ar Gefndir Gwyn* (A White Star on a White Background, 1992) was first published, because many readers could not come to terms with its use of surrealism and fantasy. An audience familiar with Welsh medieval prose should have no qualms. But this novel is set in an indefinite future, and its trek across exotic uncharted lands, as well as its presentation of bizarre and caricature-like characters, unnerved conservative readers. Others were enchanted by these selfsame features.

The novel takes the form of a series of 'testimonies' jotted down by three characters in turn on their equivalent of a notebook computer. The discs are eventually kept amongst the archives of the fascist city of Entwürdigung, and come to the hands of a clerk called Zählappell, who slips them into his own computer and soporifically dozes off as the story unfolds on his screen. The story itself relates the picaresque adventures of Gwern Esgus in his escape from the clutches of the sinister secret agents of the Kafkaesque city of Entwürdigung. He teams up with two comrades, and after a long journey across unhospitable lands, they eventually arrive at their native country, Tir Bach (Tiny Land), and are sent on a difficult mission to form a league of friendly countries to withstand the encroachment of the fascist state, Gwlad Alltud (The Land of Exile). The exploits of the trio in these different countries (which could be construed as versions of France, Brittany, Ireland and India) are laced with humour and parody. The countries of the newly formed league go to war against Gwlad Alltud, and echoes of the Gulf War are clearly discernible. Interwoven with this main story is a tender love story, with hints of infidelity, betrayal and misunderstanding. Gwern dreams of his wife and son who are kept captive in the castle of Entwürdigung, and he succeeds in freeing his son Calonnog (Courageous) from that labyrinthine castle. He is eventually captured, however, shot in the back and decapitated. There are allusions to the death of Llywelyn Ein Llyw Olaf (Llywelyn the Last), and the story continues with the promise that his son will eventually be a 'son of prophecy' who will make sure that the banner of the title—'A White Star on a White Background'—will eventually fly over the castle of Entwürdigung.

Robin Llywelyn claims to be no more than an entertainer, but he is an extremely civilized and erudite one. What is more, he has a serious theme, which is a variation—and possibly an ironic comment—on Waldo's *Daw dydd y bydd mawr y rhai bychain, / Daw dydd ni bydd mwy y rhai mawr* (A day will dawn when the small will be large, / A day will dawn when the large will not be any more). The heraldic white star on a white background is surely a symbol of peace and surrender, and yet its position on the castle of Entwürdigung at the end of the novel questions this assumption. Are we to infer from the ominous knock on the door in the final sentence that power corrupts even the most innocent?

Robin Llywelyn's next novel, *O'r Harbwr Gwag i'r Cefnfor Gwyn* (From Empty Harbour to White Ocean, 1994), is less of 'a baggy monster' (in Katie Gramich's description) than its predecessor. It is architecturally sounder and better controlled. Again we witness a pilgrimage, that of Gregor Marini across the sea to a foreign city,

and then to Y Gogledd Dir (The Northern Land) and Y Gwynfyd
(Elysium), where he falls in love with Iwerydd, and also finds a
traditional and superior way of life which is besieged by hostile and
devastating forces. He and his lover decide to leave Y Gwynfyd to
embark on a new life in the New World. They encounter obstacles
on the way, and are separated, until they are finally reunited in
New York.

Although not on any map, the landscapes and cityscapes of this
novel have been painstakingly described. At some stages one is
reminded of Bosnia, and the theme of ethnic cleansing comes to the
fore. The novel has a distinct Eastern European flavour to it, and
despite its robust Welshness, it is definitely on a European
wavelength as well. Here Welsh is a worldwide language, to be
heard on the tongues of people in the most obscure corners of the
world. It epitomizes every language and culture which is in decline.
A further point is made about language here: that the
unadulterated spoken word takes precedence over every other
linguistic intercourse. This links up with the privileging of the oral
tradition in Welsh literature. As Y Du Traheus says, 'The best
record is that of memory'. In Y Gogledd Dir words proliferate in
the breeze, like birds against the red sun. Multifarious legends
abound in a multiplicity of voices. This rebuts the post-structuralist
theory that uttered speech has been wrongly privileged in our
culture because of its immediacy and its illusion of truth. Robin
Llywelyn's novel seems to revel in the diversity of the oral tradition.
On the other hand, it is of neccessity an artful creation, and its
author's lordship over written language is abundantly evident. He
is able to change the texture of the style to suit the context with
enviable ease. The tone can be profoundly serious at one moment,
and playfully post-modern the next. Robin Llywelyn is much more
than a promising young writer: he is already a magical storyteller
and an accomplished stylist.

Traditional moulds have been cracked by a number of other
writers in the past few years. Robat Gruffudd's *Y Llosgi* (The
Burning, 1986) is a far better novel than its lurid cover might
suggest. As we read, the novel is being simultaneously typed on a
word processor at a futuristic Welsh Books Council, and is a clever
satire—from the horse's mouth, as it were—on the illusive
Welshness of government-subsidized bodies which merely project a
glitzy PR image of Wales. There is a European and world context

to all this, and a psychological dimension has been intertwined with the political intrigue. A second novel appeared recently, entitled *Crac Cymraeg* (Welsh Crack, 1997), less experimental in nature, but continuing the relentless dissection of the darker side of public life. At times it reads like a thriller, but there is no mistaking the serious intent of its conspiracy theory of the role of British politics in Welsh life, and the easy collaboration of the Welsh establishment. Geraint Vaughan Jones writes in a rather different vein in his *Yn y Gwaed* (In the Blood, 1990), which is a powerful indictment of an in-bred culture in its death-throes. Its depiction of incest is both realistically repulsive and metaphorically apt. Manon Rhys's *Cysgodion* (Shadows, 1993) is a selfconscious study of a contemporary female novelist's attempt to grapple with the relationship between Auguste Rodin and Gwen John on the one hand, and with her own heady love affairs on the other. Ostensibly written from a liberal feminist point of view, this novel raises questions about the grey area between erotica and pornography, but is too compromising in its stance to please the more radical reader. Her second novel, *Tridiau, ac Angladd Cocrotshen* (Three Days and a Cockroach's Funeral, 1996) is less ambitious, but succeeds in conveying the adolescent café culture of the 1960s in a north Wales coastal resort. Androw Bennett had no qualms about describing his first book, *Dirmyg Cyfforddus* (Comfortable Contempt, 1994), as a pornographic novel. Furthermore, it portrays an uncompromisingly sexist male chauvinist whose affairs are uncomplicated by love, and many of whose partners share the same unambiguous enjoyment of physical pleasure. Needless to say, this is not a particularly subtle novel, but neither is it as offensive as some commentators have suggested. The final twist of the plot, in which the borderline between reality and hallucination is hazy, adds a gloss which questions the novel's apparent stance.

Perhaps the most intriguing newcomer on the literary scene, however, is Mihangel Morgan, who has published two volumes of poetry and four collections of short stories, which reflect a formidable repertoire of writerly techniques. His first novel, *Dirgel Ddyn* (Secret Heart, 1993), is a compellingly readable story, whose apparent realism is subverted by the incongruous and the apparently fortuitous. One is tempted to describe this work as post-modern, post-religious and post-sexual despite the fear of being relegated to pseud's corner. It is post-modern in its questioning of the realist mode. Is the character Ann Griffiths a reincarnation of the early-nineteenth-century hymn writer, or a figment of the author's imagination? The question of verisimilitude is constantly challenged, and the reader is sometimes annoyed at having his leg pulled. The novel is definitely post-religious in its irreverent use of a Methodist icon as a fictional plaything, and her role as a grotesque Welsh Margaret Thatcher. In all this the novel reverts to the aesthetics of camp. Despite the fact that this is not a gay novel as such, the fact that Mihangel Morgan has openly declared his sexual preferences, and has written elsewhere about gay characters, helps one to detect a gay sensibility at work here. And the novel is post-sexual in that it seems to yawn at the permissive society of the mid-twentieth century, taking it all as read, dispensing with its 'big deal' ecstatic approach, and replacing it with hilarious laughter. In one scene, the main character is 'raped' by the dragon-like Ann Griffiths, but the fact that he is dwarfly endowed turns the whole episode into a farce. This is a novel which changes its hue constantly: it can be entertainingly funny and darkly forbidding in turns. The characters are in the main eccentric, marginalized creatures, living on the rough edges of society, and they are never what they seem. Untypically, the scene is set in a city, and there is no awareness of an organic society. This is the underbelly of modern life, rarely encountered in Welsh-language fiction. Yet despite the drabness which the novel conveys, there is no modernist *angst* here, for it has been superseded by a post-modern playfulness.

I hope this survey of the twentieth-century novel in Welsh gathered impetus as we entered the final quarter of the century, for it is that period which has seen a real renaissance in Welsh fiction. Despite a feeling of pessimism on the linguistic and political fronts, literature has unexpectedly prospered. It is now more adventurous than it has been thoughout the century, with writers springing up from a wider variety of backgrounds, and adopting a multitude of viewpoints. The horizons have been widened, and old inhibitions laid aside. The old parochialism of *y filltir sgwâr* (the square mile) is a thing of the past. We are in and of Europe and the world. True, there is no consensus of certainty as we face the next millenium, and one would not expect literature to provide that kind of certainty. The important thing is that there is a willingness to explore and ask questions, and above all to create new and complex worlds in the imagination.

FURTHER READING

Criticism
John Rowlands and Glyn Jones, *Profiles* (Llandysul, 1980).

Volumes in the 'Writers of Wales' series (eds Meic Stephens and R. Brinley
  Jones, Cardiff, University of Wales Press):

E. Tegla Davies (Pennar Davies)
T. Rowland Hughes (John Rowlands)
Emyr Humphreys (Ioan Williams)
Bobi Jones (John Emyr)
John Gwilym Jones (William R. Lewis)
T. Gwynn Jones (W. Beynon Davies)
Saunders Lewis (Bruce Griffiths)
Kate Roberts (D. Llwyd Morgan)

J. Maxwell Jones, *Islwyn Ffowc Elis: Exponent of 'perthyn' and Brightest
  Star of the Welsh literary Renaissance* (Philadelphia, 1970).

Translations of Welsh novels into English
E. Tegla Davies (tr. Nina Watkins), *The Master of Pen y Bryn* (Llandybïe,
  1975).
Marion Eames (tr. by the author), *The Golden Road* (Llandysul, 1990).
Idem (tr. Margaret Phillips), *The Secret Room* (Swansea, 1975).
Idem (tr. Elin Garlick), *Fair Wilderness* (Swansea, 1976).
T. Rowland Hughes (tr. Richard Ruck), *From Hand to Hand* (London,
  1950).
Idem (tr. Richard Ruck), *William Jones* (Aberystwyth, 1953).
Idem (tr. Richard Ruck), *Out of their Night* (Aberystwyth, 1954).
Idem (tr. Richard Ruck), *The Story of Joseph of Arimathea* (Aberystwyth,
  1961).
Idem (tr. Richard Ruck), *The Beginning* (Llandysul, 1969).
Saunders Lewis (tr. Joseph P. Clancy), 'The Daughter of Gwern Hywel' in
  The Plays of Saunders Lewis, Vol. IV (Llandybïe, 1986).
Idem (tr. Meic Stephens), *Monica* (Bridgend, 1997).
Robin Llywelyn (tr. by the author), *From Empty Harbour to White Ocean*
  (Cardiff, 1996).
Caradog Prichard (tr. Menna Gallie), *Full Moon* (London, 1973); (tr.
  Philip Mitchell), *One Moonlit Night* (Edinburgh, 1995).
Kate Roberts (tr. Idwal Walters and John Idris Jones), *Feet in Chains*
  (Cardiff, 1977; London, 1980).
Idem (tr. Wyn Griffith), *The Living Sleep* (Cardiff, 1976; London, 1981).
Idem (tr. Joseph P. Clancy), 'Gossip Row' and 'Dark Tonight' in *The
  World of Kate Roberts* (Philadelphia, 1991).
Wiliam Owen Roberts (tr. Elisabeth Roberts), *Pestilence* (London, 1991).

CHAPTER 7

THE SHORT STORY

MEGAN TOMOS

'The short story proper, that is a deliberately fashioned work of art and not just a straightforward tale, belongs to modern times.' (R. J. J. Ratcliff)

'The short story like the novel, is a modern art form; that is to say it represents our own attitude to life.' (Frank O'Connor)

In many ways it can be said that it was in the early decades of the twentieth century that 'the short story . . . as *a deliberately fashioned work of art*' appeared in the Welsh language. But its beginnings can be traced back to over half a century earlier, when deliberately fashioned narratives had appeared regularly in the two Welsh periodicals for women, *Y Gymraes* and *Y Frythones*, except for a period between 1900 and 1913 when the editors of *Y Gymraes* were concerned about the ill effects of fiction on their female readers. It was Ieuan Gwynedd, the editor of the first Welsh periodical for women, *Y Gymraes*, who used its pages to inculcate the new paradigms of female behaviour. This was following the condemnation of Welsh women on account of their lax sexual behaviour in the *Report of the Commissioners of Inquiry into the State of Education in Wales* of 1847 ('Y Llyfrau Gleision' (The Blue Books), as they were referred to in Welsh). These stories on the theme of the virtuous woman who reaps the fruits of her sacrifices by adhering to the high moral standards of Nonconformist religion were aimed at women who would go into service in large cities. In many ways, it is not until the last ten years or so of the twentieth century that we see Welsh women beginning to cast aside the fetters of the model of the virtuous woman or the devoted wife foisted upon them by well-meaning editors such as Ieuan Gwynedd and Cranogwen (*Y Frythones*).

During the Victorian Age, the Welsh reading public increased substantially. The Industrial Revolution had created large Welsh-speaking communities which supported numerous new periodicals. It is also important to remember that Nonconformity had promoted literacy. As shown in chapter one, there was also a tendency towards the end of the nineteenth century to idealize the common people, *y werin*, regarding them as the upholders of Welsh culture. One of the chief promoters of this concept was O. M. Edwards who nurtured *y werin* through his popular periodical *Cymru* (Wales).

Between 1891 and 1927, *Cymru* published a variety of stories. Some of these were miniature novels which spanned the whole lifetime of their characters. But there also appeared another type of story or tale which represented the kind of story told around the fireplace. There is a particular homely atmosphere to these stories and a warm sense of belonging to a close-knit community. They often centred on a colourful personality, a *cymeriad*, or an extraordinary event. Stories written in this vein are those of Winnie Parry and T. Gwynn Jones, and they are in the same tradition as that of *Straeon y Pentan* (Stories of the Hearth) by Daniel Owen, although his stories also aimed at conveying a moral message.

It was this kind of tale, in fact, that the National Eisteddfod short-story competition had in mind. In 1910, the Colwyn Bay Eisteddfod asked for a story depicting Welsh life and which included original characters who lived in Denbighshire in the nineteenth century. A year later at the Carmarthen Eisteddfod, the task was to write a short story in one of the dialects of Wales. In 1912, the Eisteddfod asked for six stories describing Welsh life on the pattern of *Straeon y Pentan* Daniel Owen.

Although the wording of these competitions does not correspond to a modern definition of a short story—a deliberately fashioned work of art—it does reflect an important shift which made the emergence of the modern short story possible. The requirement for a moral message in a story had disappeared, but equally important is the fact that writing could be based on everyday life. Alongside this shift in content a flexibility of language was also gained, especially so in the stories of Winnie Parry and T. Gwynn Jones. In his book, *The Modern Short Story* (1941), H. E. Bates referred to a similar development in the history of the English short story:

> This breaking down of illogical moral prejudice against subject—murder was always for some reason a splendid and legitimate subject,

plain natural physical love a blue horror—is therefore as important as any development in form. Because of it, expression has been made freer, more direct, and an increase in flexibility is probably the most consistent development during the last hundred years.

O. M. Edwards promoted this flexibility and realized it was vital for the survival of the language. In this quotation, taken from the February 1914 issue of *Cymru*, we see the importance he placed on *y werin* and their use of language:

> It is the '*werin*' which thinks, talks, and if literature does not accept the words and the style of the 'werin' the language of the literature of Wales will be antiquated and classical and then unnatural and useless for the purposes of everyday life . . . If the language of literature does not come from the mouthpiece of the '*werin*', if dialect is frowned upon the style will lose its naturalness and charm.

T. Gwynn Jones based his stories on his intimate knowledge of the life of *y werin* in his native Vale of Clwyd. In fact although the style of his stories is akin to that of a local storyteller, the incidents are more similar to those of a modern short story—ordinary incidents of everyday life. He did not try to extract the significance out of an apparently trivial incident or mode of behaviour in the way Kate Roberts did later. His stories, unlike the rambling tales which were often found in *Cymru*, do, however, have some sense of form and immediacy. His opening sentences make immediate contact with the reader and do not have a long preamble as was often the case:

> 'Naci nid dyn oedd o.'
> 'Neli maent yn fy ngalw.'
>
> ['No it was not a man.'
> 'Neli is what they call me.']

This freer, more direct mode of expression paved the way for a more artistic approach to the subject such as we see in the works of D. J. Williams, whose early stories stem from the same kind of society and are a development of the same tradition of story-telling. But D. J. Williams was well aware of the subtle difference between that tradition and the writing of a modern short story. As he said in a radio interview with Saunders Lewis:

Storytelling aims at entertaining. It depends largely on the quality and mood of the company present at the time. But the literary short story calls for a more intensive reflection on life.

Frank O'Connor in his excellent study of the short story, *The Lonely Voice* also emphasizes the difference:

> Almost from its beginnings the short story, like the novel abandoned the devices of public art in which the storyteller assumed the mass assent of an audience. . . It began, and it continues to function, as a private art intended to satisfy the standards of the individual, solitary, critical reader.

It was in *Cymru* that the early stories of the three most important figures in the development of the short story appeared, Richard Hughes Williams—the pioneer—and Kate Roberts and D. J. Williams—the two great Welsh exponents of the modern short story. In the stories of Richard Hughes Williams we sense an awareness of a modern form of writing. He became known when he won the short-story competition at the 1914 Bangor National Eisteddfod (which was actually held in 1915). The competition asked for three short stories based on Welsh life. These three stories, 'Noswylio' (At the End of the Day), 'Y Colledig' (Lost Soul) and 'Yr Hogyn Drwg' (Bad Boy) were published in 1916 in a collection entitled *Tair Stori Fer* (Three Short Stories).

Like his Anglo-Welsh counterpart, Caradoc Evans, whose controversial *My People* also appeared in 1915, he sets his stories against the Nonconformist background and we sense a similar criticism of the hypocrisy of the leaders of their communities. But while this is conveyed by Richard Hughes Williams's sympathy for the misfits or underdogs of his society, in Caradoc Evans's stories we have a derisive satirical portrayal of Nonconformist leaders.

Richard Hughes Williams was born in 1887. He left school at an early age and became a quarryman, but after a few months he left the quarry to improve his education at Ysgol Jones Bach before leaving for England to make a living as a writer. He returned to Caernarfon but was not happy working as a journalist, although he was very fortunate in the literary company he kept there— E. Morgan Humphreys, Picton Davies and T. Gwynn Jones to name but a few. He was unable to settle down anywhere as a journalist, and when the First World War broke out he would have been happy to enlist but due to ill health had to be content with working at the arms factory in Pen-bre. This no doubt led to a further deterioration in his health, and in 1919 he died of tuberculosis at Tregaron hospital. It is quite remarkable that a young man with no educational opportunities should become so impassioned by the short story and should have made it his lifelong ambition to be a writer. This is what E. Morgan Humphreys had to say about him:

> Dick Tryfan talked about his stories incessantly, not because he was boastful but because to him they were the most interesting things on earth . . . he was a man conducting one experiment after another continuously searching for the best way of conveying what he had to say.

Like most of the early Welsh story-writers he based his stories on the community within which he grew up, but he adopted a more personal and individualistic approach towards his work since he was consciously using a story to express something about life: he had realized that the best way of saying something about life was to describe life itself.

All his stories spring from the few months he spent working in the quarry. His characters are often social misfits or outcasts. 'Y Sgolor' (The Scholar), 'Y Sowldiwr' (The Soldier) and 'Y Prydydd Llwyd' (The Melancholic Poet) are stories about characters who, because they are slightly different, do not fit in to the social network. Others like 'Robin Bwt', 'Harri Pry' (Sly Harry) and 'Robin Deg o'r Gloch' (Ten o'clock Robin) are about rather more colourful characters, whilst 'Y Colledig', 'Noswylio' and 'Mynd Adref' (Homeward Bound) are about the severely oppressed. They are the 'submerged population group' to which Frank O'Connor refers in *The Lonely Voice*. He argues that the modern short story can be seen 'in an attitude of mind that is attracted by submerged population groups, whatever they be at a given time,—tramps, artists, lonely idealists, dreamers. The novel can still adhere to the classical concept of civilized society . . . but the short story by its very nature is remote from the community, romantic, individualistic and intransigent.'

In Richard Hughes Williams's stories we sense this terrible loneliness as he describes his characters' futile efforts to escape from their tragic circumstances, be it poverty, the mockery of their fellow workers, or the arrogance of their so-called superiors. Throughout this unveiling of an underlying loneliness there is a directness of style which is quite different from anything written before him. This can be seen in his suggestive description of the rats in 'Yr Hogyn Drwg':

> He took a bit of cheese from Dick's lunch box, and placed it on a slab of rock in a prominent place so that no rat could fail to see it. For Dick's sake he was determined to kill them all.
>
> One rat after another came out from the dark, and stood within inches of the bait. Harri watched them intently, and he could not imagine why their bodies shivered while their eyes glowed so fiercely. But a man cannot understand a rat. He must kill each one. His chisel fell on one rat after another, and the fiery eyes died out quickly. So effective was the chisel that no squeak came out to warn the living that it was nothing but a new deadly trap.

Or the concise suggestive opening sentence of 'Y Pagan' (The Pagan):

> Ei enw priodol oedd Robert Huws, ond ni chlywais neb erioed ond y gweinidog a'r stiward yn ei alw felly.

> [His proper name was Robert Huws, although I never heard anyone except the minister and the steward call him that.]

This simple sentence has immediately told us a great deal, not only about the main character of the story but also about the society in which he lives. To develop character he makes extensive use of dialogue. In fact, in the above-mentioned story more than three quarters is nothing but dialogue. As John Rowlands says in his introduction to the recently published edition of Richard Hughes Williams's collection of short stories: 'It is the realism of Richard Hughes Williams which strikes us first, and he pushed Welsh fiction writing more than is often realised in the direction of simple plain unadorned descriptions.'

At the time that Richard Hughes Williams was writing these stories Kate Roberts did not have much patience with his talk about the marvels of the short story as a literary form. However, it was she, more than any one else, who later realized the extent of his contribution to the development of the short story as a literary form in Welsh. At this time she had been completely enthralled by 'Clawdd Terfyn' (The Boundary Hedge), an ornate story by Dewi Williams which appeared in *Y Beirniad* (The Critic) in 1911. She, like her fellow students studying Welsh at Bangor University College, marvelled at this 'masterpiece'. It has to be remembered that these were students who had been thoroughly grounded in the study of Welsh poetry, and the only two classical prose works they had to study were *Gweledigaetheu'r Bardd Cwsc* and *Drych y Prif Oesoedd* of the eighteenth century. They were thus thrilled to find a piece of current Welsh prose which showed artistic skill in developing similes and metaphors equal to that found in the poetic tradition. Myrddin Lloyd conveys the general attitude towards prose-writing in the early decades of this century in his chapter in *Y Traddodiad Rhyddiaith yn yr Ugeinfed Ganrif*: 'Poetry was a work of art but prose served a practical utilitarian function.'

Although we might find the humour of R. Dewi Williams's stories rather forced in its excessive dependence on puns, 'Clawdd Terfyn' did contribute indirectly to the development of the short story and of prose-writing in Welsh. With its publication, prose began to gain a new status. Dewi Williams took the popular fireside tale and dressed it up in its Sunday best, so that it pleased not only *y werin* nurtured by Owen M. Edwards but also more educated writers and scholars.

Despite Kate Roberts's initial admiration of Dewi Williams's style, when her stories began to be published in 1922 (first of all in *Cymru* and later in *Y Llenor*) we find that they display a greater similarity to those of Richard Hughes Williams. The work of both is based on the life of a quarrying community, but the similarity goes deeper than this. There is a great sense of disillusionment in their work, and also a similarity in their directness of style. They had both read English short stories and translations of the great European masters of the short story, Chekhov and Maupassant, and this is reflected in their approach to both subject and style.

Y Llenor, when it reappeared in 1922, was to be the periodical in which writers who had benefited from the newly established educational system could have their works published. There were forces at work with the disillusionment which emerged in the aftermath of the First World War and a certain rebellion against chapel religion. These forces were channelling creative activity into new directions and Kate Roberts's stories were a product of this development.

Kate Roberts always held that it was the death of her brother, David, in Malta in 1917 which spurred her to write. This personal tragedy opened her eyes to the general injustice of life and, in particular, the injustice in the life of the community within which she had been brought up. She objectified this sense of disillusionment by creating a series of stories in which the main characters (mainly women) struggle to preserve their dignity in a never-ending battle against adverse circumstances, most often poverty and sometimes death. They are courageous women, although many critics, like Owen in her novel *Traed Mewn Cyffion* (Feet In Chains), have pointed out that theirs is a passive type of courage. They are brave in their ability to endure, but never succeed in changing their circumstances.

The publication of Kate Roberts's first volume of short stories in 1924 created a considerable impact. Although as Saunders Lewis said at the time, very little prestige was gained by writing stories:

> In Wales if anyone wishes to be regarded as an important writer he must publish either poetry or scholar's critical writings such as this one. It is difficult to find anyone who will regard a play as a piece of literature, and as to the short story it gets no more mention than a few lines in a newspaper.

In her first two volumes, *O Gors y Bryniau* (From the Highland marsh of Cors y Bryniau, 1924) and *Rhigolau Bywyd* (Life's Ruts, 1929), the stories have been carefully designed to reveal a moment of truth, which is almost always a moment of disillusionment. In 'Y Wraig Weddw' (The Widow) all hopes of remarrying and becoming part of the mainstream of life are nipped in the bud when a neighbour points out to Dora Lloyd, the young widow, that her secret admirer did not even put a gravestone on his first wife's grave. In 'Y Golled' (The Loss) the whole story is designed to express Ann's disappointment when her husband shows that he is more concerned about having missed the argument between Wmffras and Lloyd in Sunday school than recapturing the romance of their courting days. These highly sensitive women are portrayed as the dominant figures, but they are still the victims of a patriarchal society where outside the domestic sphere the male will

always have ultimate control. This view is most strongly and openly
expressed in 'Pryfocio' (Provoking), where Catrin realizes that even
in death she would not be able to escape that spiteful grin of her
malicious husband. In these two volumes men are always portrayed
as weak characters and at times insensitive, selfish, and even
malicious, hence leading to desperation such as Dora Lloyd's
outburst in 'Y Wraig Weddw' where she throws the grass over her
calf and says: 'You're no better than a man. You prefer your place
to the person who owns the place.'

Her next volume of stories, *Ffair Gaeaf* (Winter Fair), was
published in 1937 and in it we see hints of a much mellower woman.
Men are the main characters of a number of the stories, and she
also ventures to portray life outside the community of her
upbringing. 'Buddugoliaeth Alaw Jim' (The Victory of Alaw Jim) is
set in the coal-mining valleys of south Wales and, although we see
here the effects of poverty creating the same old tension between
husband and wife, the truth of the story is the fact that Morgan can
bring himself to rise above his circumstances and is able to carry on
in the glow of the memory of his former courting days. Dafydd in
'Y Condemniedig' (The Condemned) is able to face up to his
terminal illness and even see it as an opportunity to rekindle the
warmth of his earlier relationship with his wife which had
disappeared in the struggle to make ends meet and bring up the
children. As Derec Llwyd Morgan puts it in *Kate Roberts* in the
Writers of Wales series:

> Poverty deadens physical response, it also roughens the finer edges of
> marriage, leaving only habit . . . Man and Woman are not fulfilled, life
> does not reach the beauty of its potential, because it is anchored in
> austerity.

But all in all there is a much more positive attitude towards marital
relationships, and the characters are able to come to terms with
their circumstances. In this volume the characters fully realize the
restrictions placed upon their lives and the focus is on the magical
moment, however brief, when they are able to escape from their
struggle.

It is the intensity and precision of Kate Roberts's early writing
which leaves a lasting impression, even when at times her general
attitude towards men and life leaves a bad taste in the mouth. Emyr

Humphreys has described her approach to her raw material as scientific. As he says, objective scientific writing could lead to mere reportage or documentary, but this does not happen since the alchemy of her imagination has worked upon that raw material. She writes in pictures which are so vivid and sensitive that a whole world comes into being. Her style is that of a cameraman focusing on the relevant suggestive detail. Her short stories are like lace. What goes unsaid is just as important as what is uttered, thus focusing attention and creating emotional intensity. A classic example of this would be the final paragraphs of 'Y Taliad Olaf' (Final Payment):

> The whole scene, with its silence and its sense of awe, took on the aspect of a sacrament. At the back, the shopkeeper in his fine white linen apron bent over his books. Ffanni Rolant let her eyes travel over the long shadows on the shelves, the white counter with its grooves and knots, the black scales and iron weights, the black tea canisters with 1, 2, 3 and 4 painted in yellow and the bars of soap. Next week, she would be in a shop with a red counter, brass scales, and the shopkeeper wearing a grey overall.
>
> No-one spoke, except to say 'Good evening'. One woman turned again to stare at Ffanni Rolant because she wore a cape instead of a shawl. When Ffanni's turn came, the shopkeeper made no comment on the fact that she was paying the full amount of the bill. He seemed to understand. He gave ten shillings discount, which alarmed her somewhat, as she expected half a crown. It had never occurred to her on her way down that she had spent over two thousand pounds in that shop since she was married. She bought a few things and paid for them.
>
> 'I don't suppose I shall be coming down here again,' she said. He nodded to show that he understood, and she walked out of the shop, fumbling for the latch, and then closing the door carefully behind her, she looked in through the grey window and saw the shopkeeper bending down over someone else's book.

These first three volumes, *O Gors y Bryniau, Rhigolau Bywyd* and *Ffair Gaeaf*, represent the Arfon period in Kate Roberts's literary career, where on the face of things she is principally concerned with the economic struggle against poverty in her native quarrying community. In her later works she begins to deal more directly with her own personal experiences. R. M. Jones has argued that the early development of the short story also falls into two corresponding periods:

> Before 1936, the main concern of our short story writers was the
> disintegration of society. After that they focused more on the
> disintegration of the individual.

But as early as 1927 W. J. Gruffydd was concerned about the
development of the short story. Kate Roberts was also aware of the
danger of Welsh writers becoming excessively influenced by English
short stories, although she argued that they could use the English
short story as a form but should not adopt the view of life expressed
in those stories. W. J. Gruffydd, however, was in favour of
reverting back to 'Clawdd Terfyn'.

> This story was the climax of the development of a story which was
> peculiar to us Welshmen. Almost every other Welsh story imitates the
> short stories of other countries but no-one blames them for doing so—
> all the literary culture of the former non-conformist Wales was distilled
> into 'Clawdd Terfyn'.

It was D. J. Williams more than any other Welsh short-story
writer who was able to extend the tradition of fireside storytelling
to serve a more literary purpose. As mentioned earlier, his first
stories appeared in *Cymru* and they were very similar to many
others published in that popular periodical, rather long-winded
narratives lacking in both form and sensitivity. In a radio interview
with Saunders Lewis, later published in *Crefft y Stori Fer*, he
completely disowned these early stories. However, there is one
story amongst these which heralds the satirical note which we find
in his later work. In 'Y Beindar' (The Binder) he describes the
impact of the war effort bureaucracy on the old Welsh way of life as
the *beindar* rolls into a small community to reap the harvest of the
war efforts of that community. But this was definitely not the note
which D. J. Williams struck in his first published volume, which
was a collection of *ysgrifau*, literary essays, portraying characters in
his native community. *Hen Wynebau* (Old Faces), published in
1934, was really his first autobiographical volume, followed in 1953
by *Hen Dŷ Ffarm* which has been translated by his old friend,
Waldo Williams, as *The Old Farmhouse*. *Hen Dŷ Ffarm* is more of a
biography of a community than a personal autobiography. In it he
describes this community and expresses how indebted he is to his
upbringing within it:

The society most blessed in its equality of which I was ever a member was the society in the district of my boyhood where everyone knew each other and knew everything worth knowing about each other, through generations; with the minister and schoolmaster (people from outside us, as it happened) as masters over us and servants to us at the same time, and the home and the chapel and the school, in that order, as the three safe pillars supporting our life.

This was his 'square mile', as he called it, an expression which he coined but which is now used generally when referring to an area to which one has a particular allegiance. In fact, it came to embody a way of looking at Welsh life which gave rise to Adfer, a political movement in the 1960s and 1970s which regarded the safeguarding of the economic and cultural life of the 'square mile' or *bro* (local community) as a possible political solution to the problems of Welsh-speaking Wales.

The stories found in *Storïau'r Tir Glas* (Stories of the Green Land), published in 1936, are based on incidents or characters from his square mile, Rhydcymerau. We learn from his radio interview with Saunders Lewis that during the years between the appearance of his stories in *Cymru* and the publication of *Storïau'r Tir Glas* he had made a detailed study of the modern short story as an art form and analysed hundreds of examples closely. Indeed, in some of his stories we can detect the underlying influence of English short-story writers like A. E. Coppard, H. E. Bates and D. H. Lawrence. The result of his detailed study of the form becomes quite clear when we compare the stories found in *Storïau'r Tir Glas* with those published in *Cymru*. These later stories, while superficially relating common incidents in country life, are designed to suggest the small ironies of existence. 'Blewyn o Dybaco' (A Bit of Tobacco) and 'Blwyddyn Lwyddiannus' (A Good Year) are the best examples of his writing at this stage. They are stories about common incidents in agricultural life but told by a writer interested in the ambivalence of human nature. The author sees his characters, their strengths and weaknesses, and can accept them all, revelling in the warmth of the close-knit community to which they belong. They strike the same note as that of the long poetic tradition seen in the work of the *bardd gwlad* or the community poet. They are a form of eulogy to a Welsh way of life as represented by one particular community.

When we take a close look at 'Blwyddyn Lwyddiannus' which in many ways is similar to 'Y Wraig Weddw' by Kate Roberts, we find the modern short-story writer and the traditional storyteller in complete harmony. The framework of the story is social, as is clearly seen from its final paragraph. Within this framework Rachel's fierce battle with her basic instincts is seen, and this is cleverly intertwined with her economic struggle to get the best price for her calf in order to pay the rent. Rachel's arousal at the coming of spring is suggestively conveyed:

> The magic of spring was in the air. Rachel saw the young buds opening out on every hand, in the currant and gooseberry bushes, and in the mass of red roses near the back of the cottage. She looked at them all, the miracle of sudden awakening, as though she had never seen it before, unconsciously relating it to the circumstances of her own life.

This is followed by the introduction to the male protagonist in this story, Teimoth, the cattle dealer:

> And the speaker came on and rested his elbows in a leisurely way on the top bar of the garden gate. It was obvious he knew that standing there he was master of the only entry to the garden, it came to a question of siege. He knew, too, that many gold sovereigns and half-sovereigns lay snugly in the gussets of his long brown purse at the bottom of his trousers pocket. A real old dawn-fox was Teimoth . . .

This is a highly suggestive story which sensitively portrays sexual feelings and tensions but where everything turns out well in the end:

> Yes, the story is quite true. That year is remembered even today as the most prosperous in the history of the locality.

But when we turn to *Storïau'r Tir Coch* (Stories of the Red Land, 1941), stories like 'Yr Eunuch' (The Eunuch) and 'Pwll Yr Onnen' (Ash Pool), although they depict a very similar agricultural community, reveal a rather perverted attitude towards the same basic instincts. There is already a hint in *Storïau'r Tir Glas* in stories like 'Yr Hers' (The Hearse) of the rot which was setting into his old community. But *Storïau'r Tir Coch* reveal a deep concern about the degeneration of a community, and we no longer have the earlier sense of wellbeing which belonged to this close-knit society.

This harsher note increases until we have in the five stories in *Storïau'r Tir Du* (Stories of the Black Land, 1949), as the adjective *du* suggests, almost total despair. Here he has moved away from his native community and creates stories which are satirical pictures of contemporary Wales, where the characters fall into two neat camps according to their political and religious convictions. On the one hand, we have the saved few who share D.J.'s strong nationalistic pacifist viewpoint and, on the other, we have the warmongers, the retired captain, etc. We have a rather idealized portrayal of the saved few while the offenders are derided cruelly. But one story, 'Colbo Jones yn Ymuno â'r Fyddin' (Colbo Jones Joins Up) does not fall into this category. It is a story told in the first person by a JP who was somehow deeply influenced by his fervent Welsh nationalist pacifist teacher, Colbo Jones. One afternoon after a disastrous lesson, where he loses all self control and starts thrashing the children, Colbo Jones in his disillusionment abandons all his previous principles and joins up. As Dafydd Jenkins neatly puts it in his book on D. J Williams in the Writers of Wales series:

> . . . the story is quite as much that of the J.P. who tells it as that of the schoolmaster about whom it is told. D.J. has got inside the J.P.'s improbable skin and seen that the skin was not wholly impervious.

Another story, 'Ceinwen', is an allegory about the pitiful state of Wales told by giving an account of a woman's life. Again the narrative framework is complex, the story being related by Ceinwen's best friend so that it can operate on several levels at the same time.

In fact, in these last two volumes, it is the skilful design of his stories which is most remarkable. He was obviously a story writer who took his craft extremely seriously, and it is no wonder that he disagreed so adamantly with Saunders Lewis in that radio interview when Lewis tried to label him neatly as a traditional storyteller. However, one would have to agree that it is in the more traditional style of 'Blewyn o Dybaco' and 'Blwyddyn Lwyddiannus' that we feel that the author is most at ease and able to draw fully upon his powers as a writer.

In *Storïau'r Tir Coch* and *Storïau'r Tir Du* we find that D. J. Williams was more openly concerned with the disintegration and deterioration of rural communities than the small ironies of life. The feeling we have is that he needed a wider canvas of a novel or a play to do justice to this subject. It may be that this was the reason why he gave up the short story in favour of autobiographical writing.

Hen Dŷ Ffarm covers only six years of D. J. Williams's life but it covers sixty years in the history of Penrhiw, the old farmhouse. With the publication of his autobiography we find that most of the stories of the first volume are based on actual occurrences in his early life in Rhydcymerau. When he moves away from writing stories about his early childhood, a harsher more severe note comes into his writing. This is also true of his second volume of autobiography, *Yn Chwech ar Hugain Oed*, where we learn that it was after having left his square mile that he realized and valued the uniqueness of his upbringing. In this volume we have the viewpoints which are the underlying themes of his later stories fully expounded.

Dafydd Jenkins maintains that there are two distinct types of short story in Welsh. This can be seen clearly, he says, when we compare stories written by Richard Hughes Williams or Kate Roberts with those by D. J. Williams or Islwyn Williams. Although the stories of Kate Roberts and Richard Hughes Williams are set in Welsh-speaking communities they are written according to the modern European tradition, while D. J. Williams and Islwyn Williams are telling tales of the old Welsh tradition in a new way. The contrast becomes most striking when we compare stories describing Welsh-speaking communities written by Islwyn Williams with those by Kate Roberts. Islwyn Williams wrote in the character of a Swansea Valley working man, but Kate Roberts's stories could never have been told by a quarryman's wife. It is quite evident from stories like 'Pryfocio' that the women in the quarrying village of Kate Roberts's upbringing formed a domain of their own and that within that domain they had a degree of independence, especially if we compare their situation with that of a farmer's wife. Tony Conran has expanded upon this in his article 'The Lack of a Feminine Voice':

> . . . she came from a working class society in which for the first time the men and women were quite separate in their work. The men went to the quarries, the women stayed in the villages. A woman could realise herself as a female 'I' sharing values not simply with the dominant males, but also with the female community in which she plays an independent part.

It would be interesting to know how these women responded to the stories written about them by Kate Roberts. I suspect that they would have much preferred her to have written stories which affirmed the idealistic picture of the quarryman as a devout cultured hard working man as portrayed by T. Rowland Hughes, with the wife playing a supportive role keeping an immaculate home for him. After all, Kate Roberts's main characters tend to be lonely women who choose to set themselves apart from their community because of their highly sensitive nature and their high self-esteem. They bear the same characteristics as those of their creator, and these characteristics seep through even in *Te yn y Grug* (Tea in the Heather, 1959) where Kate Roberts writes in the person of a very young girl.

In her early stories she appears to observe her characters with an objective clinical eye. Although D. J. Williams in his early stories portrays his characters from the outside, nevertheless a sense of belonging and an affinity with his characters is produced by the oral rhythms of storytelling. The same sympathetic approach was adopted by others who wrote in that tradition of oral storytelling. Not surprisingly, there is also a great deal of humour in these writers' work, for example *Storïau'r Henllys Fawr* (The Stories of Henllys Fawr, 1938) by W. J. Griffith, *Straeon y Gilfach Ddu* (The Stories of Gilfach Ddu, 1931) by J. J. Williams, and J. O. Williams's *Straeon Wil a Straeon Eraill* (Wil's Stories and Other Stories, 1950). Since Islwyn Williams's stories, *Storïau a Phortreadau* (Stories and Portraits, 1954) and *Cap Wil Tomos* (Wil Tomos's Cap, 1964), were first written for the radio, it is inevitable that they display the rhythms of an oral storyteller since he would be very aware of his audience. However, irrespective of the kind of story these early writers wrote, we do sense in them the life of various Welsh-speaking communities at a specific period.

We may not sense the atmosphere of a specific area in the stories written by R. G. Berry which also appeared in *Y Llenor* before they were collected in his only volume of short stories, *Y Llawr Dyrnu* (1930), but they also deal with an underlying social tension. His stories outwardly depict the loneliness of the eccentric, be that the Oxford don in 'Wyn M.A. (Oxon)', or the circus traveller in 'Buchedd Ned Smeilar' (The Life of Smiling Ned) but the social canvas on which he chooses to portray them is the rural life of a Welsh-speaking community during the first two decades of this

century. Stories like 'Yr Ymgiprys' (The Battle) and 'Y Ddau
Frithyll' (The Two Trouts) at the same time make a satirical
comment on contemporary religious life in rural Wales.

In *Storïau'r Tir Coch* we saw the meeting point of the two trends
which R. M. Jones discerned in the development of twentieth-
century literature—the trend up to 1936 was to deal with the
disintegration of the community and after 1936 with the
disintegration of the individual. Stories like 'Pwll yr Onnen', 'Yr
Eunuch' and 'Cysgod Trӧedigaeth' (Conversion's Shadow) deal
with the disintegration of the rural community while 'Y Cwpwrdd
Tridarn' (The Court Cupboard) and 'Goneril a Regan' (Goneril
and Regan) deal with the consequences of this by portraying the
disorientation of the individual as old values and conventions
disappear.

It was John Gwilym Jones who made the disintegration of the
individual one of the main themes of all his works. This is the
underlying theme of his remarkable volume of short stories, *Y
Goeden Eirin* (The Plum Tree) which appeared in 1946. On first
reading, the stories in this volume do not appear to relate a story in
the traditional sense since, in many ways, they are closer to the
genre of the *ysgrif* or literary essay. Less than a decade earlier T. H.
Parry-Williams in his introduction to the first collection of Welsh
short stories, *Ystorïau Heddiw* (1938), could make a clear
distinction between the Welsh short story and the *ysgrif* which were
two popular forms at the time. After admitting that the two forms
are closely related he goes on to say that:

> it could almost be said that what we often have in the 'ysgrif' (when the
> 'ysgrif' is something more substantial than a pointless piece of refined
> writing) is the appropriate mood for the action of a short story: that is
> one possible distinction between them.

The assumption made is that the *ysgrif* is more subjective while the
short story is a form where the writer finds a story to project his
personal vision. Ironically, it was John Gwilym Jones, more than
any other Welsh critic, who maintained that all literature in the
main, regardless of the writer's chosen literary form, should be a
metaphor to convey the author's response to the experience of
living in this world. It was with this aim in mind that he set out to
write his first stories. However, they turned out to be poor

imitations of Kate Roberts's stories. In a radio interview with Saunders Lewis he emphasized that he still felt that for him the best short story was the more objective one:

> I tried my best, but my stories were only poor loose imitations of Kate Roberts's stories. It became quite evident to me that I had neither the skill nor the necessary empathy with the quarrymen of my area to do justice to them in their brave struggle against poverty. Therefore I had to be satisfied with the method which was more becoming to me and more accommodating to my nature. Note that I did say be satisfied with, because I believe that forming a story out of objective external incidents is superior to analysing thoughts, just as tragedy is superior to comedy.

The method he employed was that of the 'stream of consciousness' and as he admits he was heavily influenced by English, American, and French writers such as Virginia Woolf, Hemingway, Sarogan, Sherwood Anderson and Proust. He had read Joyce, but at the time of writing *Y Goeden Eirin* he had yet to read *Ulysses*. He obviously felt that he was heavily dependent on these models, since he states that transforming the atmosphere of these stories to be Welsh was not very difficult since he was a Welshman and very aware of his Welshness.

I have expanded upon John Gwilym Jones's approach since in his work we again see the meeting point of earlier and later trends in the development of the short story. His characters, like those of R. G. Berry, and unlike the characters of the majority of the earlier short-story writers referred to up to this point (except perhaps Goneril and Regan in *Storïau'r Tir Coch*), do not belong to a specific community or a 'square mile' as D. J. Williams would put it. They belong instead to a specific class, a class which as yet had not been made the popular subject of short stories and novels. Earlier fiction had tended to concentrate on *y werin* or the working class, but John Gwilym's characters are ministers, artists or even literary critics. Saunders Lewis referred to them as the *nouveau riche* of the educational system. However, although they do not belong to a specific area they are the product of the old Welsh Nonconformist tradition, and John Gwilym Jones often portrays the tension they experience between their allegiance to the traditional way of life of their upbringing and their wish to free themselves of its fetters and enjoy the greater freedom that the new higher education has brought them. He aimed at conveying the inner dichotomy and struggle which he felt they experienced. It is he, as John Rowlands has pointed out, who has represented the Welsh psyche most convincingly.

The starting-point of all his writing is the fundamental loneliness of our existence, which is evident in *Y Goeden Eirin* in his portrayal of the gulf between the outer conduct and the inner life of his characters. This is most clearly seen in the first story, 'Y Briodas' (The Wedding), where outwardly we are moving through the service of a marriage ceremony while the writer is in fact recounting the innermost thoughts and emotions experienced by the six main characters standing in the front. This is a theme which recurs in his later plays, *Yr Adduned* (The Vow) and, *Ac Eto nid Myfi* (Yet, Not Myself). It is also the theme of the third story 'Y Garnedd Uchaf' (The Highest Peak). But in that story there is also a more sardonic view of life since the characters are deliberately exploiting each other. In 'Cerrig y Rhyd' (Stepping Stones) and 'Y Cymun' (The Communion) the characters find a way of resolving their inner tension either through literature or by a mystical experience of the world of nature. In 'Y Cymun' the prospective minister finds his inner strength not by acknowledging his dependence on the Lord but by yielding to the sensuous experience of feeling at one with nature, while Absalom in 'Cerrig y Rhyd' finds an aesthetic deliverance from his emotional turmoil.

The subject of John Gwilym Jones's stories naturally calls for the use of the 'stream of consciousness' technique. The external actions in the stories are of little importance, except maybe the title story where the narrator's fall from the plum tree has a decisive influence on the rest of his life, but this is told in retrospect in order to convey the point of the story, namely that we are all in the same boat and that the differences between us are caused by minor accidents. We have no control over our lives as he states in the final paragraph of 'Y Goeden Eirin':

> And we are back to the plum tree. The tree is as inevitable as one's birth or death. As Doomsday John Huws Pant would say, and perhaps he is right. The tree is still there between the outside lavatory and the wall, older, what remains of it, having gathered more green lichen and moss. Once upon a time Wil and I and I and Wil climbed it. I sat on a branch which had withered like Nain's right arm and fell and broke my leg. I had to stay in the house for weeks with nothing better to do than

read. Wil became friends with Lias and Harri bach the Garage, and used to come home every night talking about magneto and dynamo and clutch and changing gears and Bleriot and Jerry M. I don't care a damn about magneto and dynamo and Wil never reads unless he has to.

The external actions are convenient pegs upon which he can hang his stories, and because of this can appear at times to be rather forced. John Gwilym Jones was to abandon the short story as a literary form, and he later concentrated on writing plays where the inner conflict is projected into the various characters so that we can hear and see the conflict directly for ourselves.

It cannot be said that any of his immediate successors emulated his highly selfconscious style of writing. However, when Kate Roberts's novella, *Stryd y Glep* (Gossip Row), was published in 1949, after a long silence in her career as a writer, we find that the subject of her struggle is no longer the fight against poverty but against the self. In this volume she also employs the same method as John Gwilym Jones, although she does not delve quite as deeply into the Freudian pit. Her concern about inner motives is played out in her second novel, *Y Byw Sy'n Cysgu* (The Living Sleep) which is quite different from the first, *Traed Mewn Cyffion*, where characters from her native community are depicted in their bitter struggle against poverty and war.

Te yn y Grug (1959) was Kate Roberts's first volume of short stories after a long period of silence. According to her, this proved to be the easiest book to write, perhaps because Begw, the main character, is such a perfect projection of the intelligent, sensitive young Kate Roberts, into whose life we have an insight in her autobiography, *Y Lôn Wen* (The White Lane), published in 1960. It is in *Te yn y Grug* that we see the height of the influence of a contemporary short-story writer, Katherine Mansfield, who also wrote stories about childhood where the narrator is continuously moving through the chattering minds of young girls. External actions and descriptions are still important in *Te yn y Grug*, but Kate Roberts has exchanged her rigidly objective style for a more fluid way of writing, moving in and out of her main character's thoughts. This was partly necessary to create the impression of a child's personality, but it obviously was more in line with her style of writing at a time when she was depicting the inner struggles of her characters. In *Hyn o Fyd* (This Dismal World, 1964), there is very little difference between stories like 'Yr Atgyfodiad' (The Resurrection) and an *ysgrif*. But it is when we compare another story in this volume, 'Cathod mewn Ocsiwn' (Cats at an Auction), with an earlier one, 'Chwiorydd' (Sisters), on a similar theme that the difference in approach between the early Kate Roberts and the late Kate Roberts can be seen most clearly. In 'Chwiorydd' Sara is the blood sister of Meri and it is Sara's heroic struggle to safeguard Meri's great reputation for cleanliness which is the focus of the story. In the early story the social background is all important, and the fact that Meri is able to say to her neighbour at the end of the story, 'At least I saw to it that Meri died as she had lived—she was clean', is both an ideal and an ironic ending to the story. But in 'Cathod mewn Ocsiwn', Elen is no relation of the late Mrs Hughes, whose house where the auction of her things is to take place has fallen into a similar state of filth and decay. During the course of the story Elen develops into the spiritual sister of Mrs Hughes and makes the same decision as Sara made in the earlier story, namely that she would safeguard her reputation. But the different mood and approach of these two stories which belong to two distinct periods can be seen clearly when we compare significant descriptions from each of them. Both are descriptions of the dead woman; one is realistic and the other surrealistic:

> The memory of it stayed with Sara for many years. The dull light of the lamp. The filthy room. The floor covering ragged and ruffled. The wallpaper yellow with age, and with traces of water having run down it, in jagged streaks. A piece of it hanging in one place. A piece of the ceiling white, hanging by the thinness of a thread, and moving with the slight motion of the air. The ceiling was dark and gloomy, except immediately above the lamp. Underneath this point, the bedclothes and Meri's nightdress were white as driven snow, and Meri herself almost the colour of them. So long as she did not look around the room, the clean clothes gave pleasure to Sara. But in spite of herself, she had to look round and see what she would rather have forgotten. And then she knew there was only a patch of cleanliness in the midst of dust and disorder, like the white light of the lamp on the ceiling, bright in the surrounding gloom. In the centre of it all Meri lay smiling, for death had already given back beauty to her features.

In 'Cathod Mewn Ocsiwn' Elen loses interest in the auction and lets her thoughts run freely:

On the floor, just near her there was an old worn carpet folded anyhow. She stared at the folds and soon they began to take shape as a face, nose, mouth, forehead and ears. They turned into a corpse lying in a grave, putty coloured, indifferent to all criticism, the body of a woman disconnected from all that was being sold in her house today, separated from her friends. For a long time she kept looking at the face, expecting the features to change, something of a smile to appear because she had thought kindly of her. But there was no sign of it.

In the first story we have the clinical objective style of expressing emotion, while the later story uses a more surreal approach. Elen is helpless and unable to undo the harm done to Mrs Hughes's reputation, but a revelation during the course of the story brings relief and will lead to an action on her part which will safeguard her things from being exposed to indifferent friends. The action and development in the earlier story is external, while the development and significance of the second is psychological. This is once more expressed in a surreal picture:

Elen went into the sitting room . . . there was nothing left but the carpet folded in the middle of the floor. She looked again for the face she had seen in it and gradually it came back. There was Mrs Hughes' face looking at the empty room, as unconcerned as before but this time as if she had gained a victory over everybody, her mouth was firmly closed. Elen moved across to the window and looked again at the carpet. The afternoon sun shone through the window upon the floor. Someday, she thought, the room could be made to look cheerful again. She looked again at the carpet: the face had changed, the mouth was smiling.

In *Prynu Dol* (Buying a Doll, 1969), the stories 'Dewis Bywyd' (Choosing a Life*)*, 'Yr Enaid Clwyfus' (The Sensitive Soul) and 'Dyddiadur Siopwr' (A Shopkeeper's Diary) are in the form of soliloquies by the main character. It is true that there are some stories like 'Y Daith Olaf' (The Last Journey) and 'Dwy Gwningen' (Two Rabbits) which are more objective, but because of their lack of design they do not have the same intensity as Kate Roberts's earlier stories on similar themes. *Gobaith a Storïau Eraill* (Hope and Other Stories, 1972), *Yr Wylan Deg* (The Lovely Seagull, 1976) and *Haul a Drycin a Straeon Eraill* (Fortune and Misfortune and Other Stories, 1981) are also in the same monologue style as *Prynu Dol,* and the background of the majority of her stories in this second period in her literary career is the anglicized town of Denbigh where she had lived since 1935. But her main characters are still very aware of their roots in a Welsh rural community and are very critical of the more affluent urban way of life. This criticism often takes the form of irrational outbursts, where the main character attacks the patois Welsh spoken by the younger generation and recites a long string of rich idioms from her native dialect.

The main characters of the stories which appeared in *Storïau'r Deffro* (Stories of the New Awakening, 1959, ed. Islwyn Ffowc Elis), a second anthology of Welsh short stories, are also strongly rooted in a Welsh-speaking community. This is not the case when we move on to the later anthologies. In the 1960s and 1970s a regular series of Welsh short stories was published, the first of which was *Storïau'r Dydd* (Stories of Our Times, 1968, ed. Gwilym Rees Hughes and Islwyn Jones), followed by an annual volume by the same editors from 1970–4, then this series was followed by another, *Storïau Awr Hamdden* (Leisure Time Stories, edited by Urien Wiliam from 1974–9). The full title of the first volume in the second series was *Storïau Awr Hamdden gan Kate Roberts ac eraill* (Leisure Time Stories by Kate Roberts and others) as an acknowledgment of Kate Roberts's status as the chief short-story writer in Welsh. (It is also interesting to note that in these various anthologies there appeared as many stories by women as by men while in a corresponding anthology of contemporary poems, for example *Cerddi '71* (ed. James Nicholas), only four poems out of a total of sixty-five were by women.) In addition there was the series of Welsh translations of foreign short stories published by Gwasg Gomer. All this activity demonstrates the popularity of the short story at a time when the Welsh novel was going through a lean period.

Most of the stories written by women were strongly influenced by Kate Roberts's work. It could be said that under the influence of her later stories there had developed a stereotype Welsh short story for the female writer. The main character would almost inevitably be a female looking from behind a window at life passing her by, either because of unrequited love, bereavement or the restrictions of the traditional female role in a patriarchal bourgeois society. It is true that writers like Eigra Lewis Roberts developed their own voice eventually, but they are strongly influenced by Kate Roberts. Although Eigra Lewis Roberts's writing displays a similar classical literary style and a rich dialect, somehow we do not find in her

work the kind of fundamental vision of life which electrified Kate
Roberts's work. Another female writer who also displays her
influence is Jane Edwards. This is seen at its strongest in *Tyfu*
(Growing up), a volume of short stories about a young girl growing
up, where she uses a similar technique of focusing on the significant
moment. She also displays the same directness of speech and
cynical attitude towards life. It is interesting to note that Jane
Edwards and Eigra Lewis Roberts both had connections with the
slate-quarrying industry.

Stories written by men in these collections of short stories reveal
a greater diversity of subject and approach ranging from science
fiction to slapstick comedy. For such contributors as Alun T. Lewis
and Roger Boore the short story was their main literary form, while
for the others it was very much their secondary form. For example,
Glyn Ashton wrote a number of humorous novels, Dafydd
Rowlands and R. Bryn Williams are known first and foremost as
poets, Selyf Roberts and Geraint W. Parry are best known for their
novels, and W. S. Jones's main contribution has been to the theatre.
But these stories written by men displayed a gift for telling a story
at a time when this was lacking in those written by women.

The stories written in the more traditional style of storytelling
were also written by men and were skilfully constructed. A volume
of short stories by Tom Parri Jones, *Teisennau Berffro* (Berffro
Welsh Cakes*)* was published in 1958, and in 1979 W. S. Jones
published a volume of his stories, *Dyn y Mynci* (The Man with the
Monkey). In the 1970s and 1980s Harri Parri's comic stories, which
are in the same tradition, have proved to be extremely popular. The
characters of these humorous stories are strongly rooted in Welsh-
speaking rural Wales, and extensive use is made of the resources of
the local dialect. This is especially true in the case of W. S. Jones's
humour which is something of an acquired taste amongst Welsh
readers.

Harri Pritchard Jones at first wrote short stories which did reflect
Kate Roberts's strong influence. It is in the style and mood of his
stories that we see the greatest resemblance to her work, since his
characters are often taken from outside Wales, from rural Ireland
and also from the more complex life of cities. But it is in the stories
of another writer, Pennar Davies, that we come across characters
who are international in the sense that they do not belong to any
particular community or even country. In his volume of short

stories, *Caregl Nwyf* (The Chalice of Passion, 1966), he writes
about characters who are artists and dreamers and, like John
Gwilym Jones before him, Pennar Davies portrays them juggling
with ideas and working through their emotional or philosophical
crises. Bobi Jones, who has published five volumes of short stories
in all, also writes in the same vein. Pennar Davies and Bobi Jones
made everything and everywhere the subject of the Welsh short
story.

During the 1980s the novel re-emerged and surpassed the short
story in popularity, with young writers like Alun Jones, Aled
Islwyn and Wiliam Roberts setting new trends. But just as the
novelists of the late 1970s and 1980s brought back a strong story
line into the modern Welsh novel after a long colourless period of
psychological novels, so in the 1990s the short story appears to be
gaining a new lease of life. In the summer of 1994 six volumes of
short stories were published, *Ar y Cyrion* (On the Outskirts) by
Harri Pritchard Jones, *Unigolion Unigeddau* (Solitary People and
Places) by Aled Islwyn, *Chwalu'r Nyth* (Winding up a Home) by
Gwilym Meredydd Jones, *Te Gyda'r Frenhines* (Tea with the
Queen) by Mihangel Morgan, *Stripio* (Stripping) by Meleri Wyn
James, and *Unwaith Eto* (Once More) by Marged Pritchard. It was
Aled Islwyn's volume of short stories which won the 1994 Book of
the Year Award.

Young writers like Martin Davis, Meleri Wyn James and
Mihangel Morgan are developing the Welsh short story in new
directions. Their work has a strong story line and reflects an
interest in the short story as a form. One can almost say about
Meleri Wyn James that she has restored the O'Henry ending to the
short story, although her volume of stories, *Stripio*, perhaps
depends excessively on this technique. Kate Roberts also used this
technique excessively in her early stories, but unlike Kate Roberts's
characters we cannot say that those of Meleri Wyn James are
specifically Welsh. Her characters belong to the present age and
their problems are universal.

On the other hand, a Welsh learner or mongrel (as he has
referred to himself) like Martin Davis has chosen to depict the
importance of belonging from the point of view of the outsider as
well as the native born Welshman in an interesting volume of short
stories entitled *Llosgi'r Bont* (Burning down the Bridge). Here we
have one of the first attempts at depicting the tensions experienced

by immigrants in rural Wales. In this complex but rich portrayal of contemporary rural life there is a fresh approach as the Welsh reader sees himself through the eyes of his new neighbours.

But undoubtedly the young writer who has experimented more than anyone with the form is Mihangel Morgan. In him we have a powerful storyteller who is interested in the design of his stories. This is clearly seen in *Saith Pechod Marwol* (Seven Deadly Sins, 1993) where the characters are very much the victims of the Thatcherite era with its emphasis on the individual and material wealth. The careful design of the stories and indeed the tone of some of them do remind us of John Gwilym Jones's *Y Goeden Eirin*. There is also a certain selfconsciousness about his writing which is reminiscent of John Gwilym Jones. This is seen most clearly in *Te Gyda'r Frenhines* (Tea with the Queen, 1994), which calls into question cultural assumptions and undermines accepted notions of literary decorum. Both authors regard writing as a game, and there is a strong element of playing with style, text and form in their stories.

We have come a long way from the early days in the history of the short story when a story was told as a means of reforming young women. But the effects of the thinking of that period are still felt in our writing and it is only now that female Welsh writers are casting aside the constrictions of the ideal of the virtuous woman or devout mother placed upon them a century earlier. Female roles and social conditioning are explored in volumes of short stories written by Manon Rhys, *Cwtsho* (Snuggling, 1988) and *Genod Neis* (Nice Girls, 1993) by Eleri Llewelyn Morris. The Welsh short story has made a major contribution in the assertion of women's value. Unlike their non-Welsh-speaking female compatriots, who gained no such recognition as indispensable contributors to the genre, Welsh female writers have been central in the development of the short story. The reason for this may be that they have been more or less excluded from the macho tradition of the strict-metre poetry and therefore given total freedom to develop the short story. Kate Roberts has been the dominant force in the development of the modern short story, either directly through her own stories or critical writings or indirectly through her influence on others. Although some feminists have recently been rather critical of her stoical acceptance of the patriarchal order of society, she has expressed an independence of the female mind, which ironically, since her own characters fall prey to the patriarchal order, has made the female condition central in twentieth-century Welsh story writing.

FURTHER READING

Translations

Kate Roberts

A Summer Day and Other Stories (Penmark Press, 1946), translations of twelve early stories.
Te yn y Grug—Tea in the Heather, by Wyn Griffith (Rhuthun, 1968).
Y Byw Sy'n Cysgu—The Living Sleep, by Wyn Griffith (Cardiff, 1976).
Traed Mewn Cyffion—Feet in Chains, by Idwal Walters and John Idris Jones (Cardiff, 1978).
The World of Kate Roberts (Philadelphia, 1991)—Translations by Joseph P. Clancy of sections from Kate Roberts's autobiography, *Y Lôn Wên* (1960)—'Pictures' and 'The Last Pictures', 'Stories' (1925–37), *Stryd y Glep* (1949)—'Gossip Row', *Te yn y Grug* (1959)—'Tea in the Heather', *Tywyll Heno* (1962)—'Dark Tonight', 'Stories' (1964–81).
Two Old Men and Other Stories, a Gwasg Gregynog publication in celebration of Kate Roberts's ninetieth birthday was published in 1981.

D. J. Williams

Hen Dŷ Ffarm (1953)—*The Old Farmhouse*, by Waldo Williams (London, 1961).

Stories

'Bob, yr hen gel glas' (from *Hen Wynebau*, 1934), trans. as 'Bob, the old grey nag' by Wil Ifan in *Dock Leaves*, III, 8 (1952).
'Blwyddyn Lwyddiannus' (from *Storïau'r Tir Glas*, 1936), trans. by Wyn Griffith as 'A Good Year' in *Welsh Short Stories, An Anthology* (London, 1937), and in Gwyn Jones and Islwyn Ffowc Elis (eds), *Twenty-Five Welsh Short Stories* (London, 1971), and a considerably revised version as 'A Successful Year' appears in *The Penguin Book of Welsh Short Stories* (Harmondsworth, 1976).
'Y Cwpwrdd Tridarn'—(from *Storïau'r Tir Coch*, 1939) trans. as 'The Court Cupboard' in *Wales*, V (1945), also appears in *Welsh Short Stories* (London, 1958.)

'Pwll yr Onnen' (from *Storïau'r Tir Coch*, 1939), trans. by Dafydd Jenkins in *Welsh Short Stories* (Harmondsworth, 1936).

Translations of other stories

'Sion William' by Richard Hughes Williams, trans. under same title by Ll. Wyn Griffith in *Welsh Short Stories, An Anthology* (London, 1937). It also appears in *Short Stories from Wales* (Exeter, 1978).

'Y Briodas'—'The Wedding' from *Y Goeden Eirin* (1946) by John Gwilym Jones, trans. by Islwyn Ffowc Elis in *Twenty-Five Welsh Short Stories* (London, 1971).

'The Miracle' by Harri Pritchard Jones, trans. in *Twenty-Five Welsh Short Stories* (London, 1971).

'Deprivation' by Eigra Lewis Roberts, trans. by Enid R. Morgan, in *Twenty-Five Welsh Short Stories* (London, 1971).

'An Overdose of Sun' by Eigra Lewis Roberts, trans. by the author in *The Penguin Book of Welsh Short Stories* (Harmondsworth, 1976).

'Morfydd's Celebration' by Harri Pritchard Jones, trans. by Harri Webb in *The Penguin Book of Welsh Short Stories* (Harmondsworth, 1976).

'Blind Date' by Jane Edwards, trans. by Derec Llwyd Morgan in *The Penguin Book of Welsh Short Stories* (Harmondsworth, 1976).

Main books on the development of the Welsh short story

T. H. Parry-Williams (ed.), *Ystorïau Heddiw* (Aberystwyth, 1938).

Islwyn Ffowc Elis (ed.), *Storïau'r Deffro* (Dinbych, 1959).

Islwyn Jones a Gwilym Rees Hughes (eds), *Storïau'r Dydd* (Llandysul, 1968).

Dafydd Jenkins, *Y Stori Fer Gymraeg* (Llandybïe, 1966).

Derec Llwyd Morgan, 'Y Stori Fer' in Geraint Bowen (ed.), *Y Traddodiad Rhyddiaith yn yr Ugeinfed Ganrif* (Llandysul, 1976).

John Jenkins (ed.), *Y Stori Fer: Seren Wib Llenyddiaeth* (Abertawe, 1979).

Storïau Richard Hughes Williams, rhagarweiniad gan John Rowlands (Caerdydd, 1994).

Writings in English about the three main contributors to the development of the short story

Kate Roberts

Introduction by Storm Jameson to *A Summer Day and Other Stories* (Penmark Press, 1946).

Review of the above by H. E. Bates in the *Welsh Review*, V (1946).

Pennar Davies, 'The Short Stories of Kate Roberts', *Triskel One* (Llandybïe, 1971).

R. Gerallt Jones, 'An Introduction to the Work of Kate Roberts', *Anglo-Welsh Review*, ix/24 (1959).

Derec Llwyd Morgan, 'Dr Kate Roberts', *Planet*, ii (1970).

Derec Llwyd Morgan, *Kate Roberts* (Cardiff, 1974), also a revised version published at the centenary of her birth, 1991.

Ned Thomas, 'The Chains around my Feet' in *The Welsh Extremist* (London, 1971).

D. J. Williams

Gwynfor Evans, 'Tribute to D. J. Williams', *Anglo-Welsh Review*, xix (1970).

Dafydd Jenkins, *D. J. Williams* (Cardiff, 1973).

Saunders Lewis, 'A Tribute to D. J. Williams', *Anglo-Welsh Review*, xix (1970).

Ned Thomas, 'D.J.', *The Welsh Extremist* (London, 1971).

John Gwilym Jones

William R. Lewis, *John Gwilym Jones* (Cardiff, 1994).

John Rowlands, 'The Humane Existentialist', in *Welsh Books and Writers* (Autumn, 1980).

CHAPTER 8

A CENTURY OF WELSH DRAMA

ELAN CLOSS STEPHENS

'Cultures', wrote a social anthropologist, James Clifford, recently, 'do not hold still for their portraits. Attempts to make them do so always involve simplification and exclusion.' This short portrait of a century of Welsh-language drama bears the same health warning. Despite this, or perhaps because of this, it is fascinating to impose one's own sense of order and perspective on a field which offers differing philosophical discourses and stylistic theatre languages.

In trying to gain an overall portrait, artists sometimes mount a collage of smaller snapshots. If we were to follow a similar course, we would choose particular years or events when a dominant theatre language became established. One such year, 1913, sees the production of *Beddau'r Proffwydi* (The Graves of Prophets) by W. J. Gruffydd at the Theatre Royal, Cardiff. This extraordinarily melodramatic and powerful piece underlines the final establishment of naturalism as the dominant theatrical language in Wales, a language which was to remain powerful for almost forty years. The year 1948 and the production of Saunders Lewis's *Blodeuwedd* demonstrates the search for a symbolic, poetical discourse which will expand the possibilities of theatre language and challenge some of the evolutionary and deterministic standpoints of naturalism. It relates stylistically and philosophically to a similar English desire for a poetical theatre language and a sense of ceremony in life as manifested in the work of artists such as T. S. Eliot and Christopher Fry. The National Eisteddfod, at Aberafan in 1966, commissioned a play by Gwenlyn Parry, *Saer Doliau* (The Doll Mender), which challenged what Professor Ioan Williams has called 'the straitened stage' of the *drama de thèse* and substituted a drama where the set became an image of the action. In this play, in contrast to Saunders Lewis's theatre, the philosophical stance is unprescribed and ambivalent. Finally, with *Bargen* (1979) and Brith Gof's *Branwen* (1981) we see the establishment of the group as author and the growth of the devised play. In the case of *Bargen* (The Bargain), the devised play becomes a piece of *agit-prop*, whereas *Branwen* seeks to form physical images which resound underneath the threshold of the conscious mind. Both groups, however, subscribe to a common view that the single author is dead and that co-operative writing and directing seems the most productive way towards a new theatre language. Four snapshots, four voices over a full century; an oversimplification perhaps, but milestones also which focus the essential debates within Welsh theatre from 1890 to 1990.

The period leading up to the production of *Beddau'r Proffwydi*, on 12 March 1913 sees the painful establishment of a Welsh tradition of play-acting in the face of considerable opposition from the chapels, both Methodist and Independents. The Methodist 'Sasiwn' (Convocation) had been particularly virulent in denouncing play-acting in the same tone, and often within the same sentence, as gambling and other libertine and reckless pursuits, destined to lead the family to ruin and the soul to perdition. The old tradition of *anterliwtiau* (interludes) on fair days died with its greatest exponent Thomas Edwards (1738–1810), 'Twm o'r Nant', in 1810. Even before then, he is quoted in his autobiography as having given over such pastimes 'because of a guilty conscience and because I met and loved a woman who tended towards religion'. His description of throwing his fool's cap into the river near Conway in a moment of religious affirmation smacks of the true dramatic writer. Nevertheless, there is no doubt that the sweeping tide of Methodism was to drown theatre in Wales until the end of the century.

When the green shoots of revitalization occur, theatre emerges from at least three different impulses. The first lies within the chapels themselves. Just as the medieval Church was to find the dramatic presentation of the birth of Jesus an aid to a deeper appreciation of the Mass by an uneducated populace, so the chapels found that simple dramatic debates on abstinence were a useful educational tool. Although such material can hardly be counted theatre, it shows the existence of dramatic dialogue (albeit stilted!) within an apparently hostile environment. Years later, Wil and Huw, two characters in *Ac Eto Nid Myfi* (Yet, Not Myself, 1976) by John Gwilym Jones, slip into such dialogue, testifying to the continued use of dramatic dialogues by the temperance movement well into the twentieth century. The second impulse towards theatre comes from the growing acceptance and popularity of the novel and the desire to adapt some of the works of the most famous Welsh novelist of the period, Daniel Owen (1836–95), for the stage. Elsbeth Evans in her book *Y Ddrama yng Nghymru* (Drama in Wales, 1947) mentions the work of the Amateur Company from Trefriw near Llanrwst who toured extensively in 1888 with their adaptation of Daniel Owen's *Rhys Lewis*. Ap Glaslyn comments that 'their fame spread throughout Wales and their popularity served to clear many a chapel's debts and to help many other good causes'. In an age when chapels became larger and grander, putting in new pipe organs and galleries, the new drama ironically helped to pay the chapel's running debt, and we find drama once again within the portals of its arch-enemy—a reminder against any oversimplification of this complex period. One should also beware of dismissing companies like that of Trefriw and others, such as the Llanberis company, as amateur and therefore local manifestations. Myrddin ap Dafydd, in a hitherto unpublished thesis on Welsh drama, has recorded the stupendous activity of these companies. Their tours often encompassed long journeys throughout north Wales and into the south and their income, when shared, was almost half the quarryman's average wage for that week. Much of this activity is catalogued in detail in the volume *Hanes y Ddrama yng Nghymru* (A History of the Drama in Wales, 1948) by O. Llew Owain, who worked as a journalist on the two important north Wales newspapers, *Y Genedl* and *Yr Herald Cymraeg* during some of this period of dramatic activity.

Perhaps the most important point that needs to be made about the adaptations of *Rhys Lewis* belongs neither to the high level of activity of the companies nor to their involvement with the chapel. It is that *Rhys Lewis* was a naturalistic novel, commenting morally, socially and psychologically on a certain class of Welsh men and women. Thus, this dramatic adaptation was to start a new theatre language in Wales—the reasonable, discursive voice of naturalism. When theatre died with Twm o'r Nant, the death also occurred of a more flamboyant and direct theatrical style: his rhyming couplets, his alliteration and *cynghanedd*, his ballads and odes and parodies, his fool's cap and occasional phallus and his stereotyped characters linking him back to the misers of Molière and the *commedia dell'arte*. When the new drama struggled in its first birth cries in

1888, the voice of moral and social struggle was to be domesticated within a realistic set and an approximation of normal speech.

There was one other voice present during this formative period in the life of the Welsh theatre, that of the proponents of a Shakespearean drama. This is a period when men had discussed quite seriously whether Twm o'r Nant deserved the title 'Y Shakespeare Cymreig' (The Welsh Shakespeare) and had come to the decision that Twm's 'native woodnotes' were even wilder and more undisciplined than Shakespeare's. During the second half of the century, when the desire for Home Rule had been a plank of the Liberal vote in Wales as it had been in Ireland under Parnell, there was always a desire to produce literature which would reflect a seriousness and high moral aim worthy of a developing national region. The Miltonic epic poems of the nineteenth century show this desire clearly. Under the influence of social critics and moralists such as Lewis Edwards who edited the journal *Y Traethodydd*, there was a similar attempt to elevate the tone of the drama. Lewis Edwards published articles on the German playwrights—an interesting subject since Goethe and Schiller too subscribed to the idea of a moral tone and a high style for drama, and he also published translations of Shakespeare's *Julius Caesar*.

From 1884 the National Eisteddfod offered a prize annually for a play. The subjects—usually a given subject each year—were mainly historical and heroic. Even before then in 1879, the playwright Beriah Gwynfe Evans (1848–1927) had won in the South Wales Eisteddfod in Cardiff with his play *Gwrthryfel Glyndwr* (The Revolt of Glyndwr). In true Welsh bardic fashion, he had also won with the same play in the Llanberis Chaired Eisteddfod in a competition for 'Welsh playwriting in the style of Shakespeare'! Other plays followed on its heels, Beriah Evans's *Llewelyn* and *Caradog* and T. Gwynn Jones's *Dafydd ap Gruffydd* (1894). The style, the subject-matter, the treatment in these plays owe more to Shakespeare's patriotic *Henry V* than to his more tragic explorations, and although the matter is declaimed in iambic pentameters, the versifying lacks the subtlety and variety of rhythm that characterize Shakespearean blank verse. Unfortunately, the literary quality of much of this offering is encapsulated in the entry on Beriah Gwynfe Evans in *The Companion to Welsh Literature*. The whole of Evans's dramatic output is summarized trenchantly thus: 'He also wrote a number of plays on historical subjects, not one of which has any particular merit'!

This style—and its attendant ambitiousness—persists up to 1915 which sees the publication of Pedr Hir's *Owain Glyndwr*. Elsbeth Evans refers to this as the first bilingual play but its use of English is confined to Mortimer's romantic sub-theme and explores the perennial jokes of linguistic confusion and deliberate misleading. Had its English blank verse explored another culture's deafness to Wales's aspiration, one might call it truly bilingual. As it is, the use of English within the play is relegated to an amusing diversion. *Owain Glyndwr*'s rhythms are less mechanical and more varied than those of Beriah Gwynfe Evans; nevertheless, the whole, whilst attempting a richly heroic mode, remains thin, hollow and a little bombastic.

Given this context, one can see more clearly the significance of W. J. Gruffydd's *Beddau'r Proffwydi*. W. J. Gruffydd (1881–1954), Oxford educated, already well-known as a poet, later to become professor of Welsh at Cardiff and influential editor of the journal *Y Llenor*, entered his play in a competition for play-writing in Welsh and English sponsored by Lord Howard de Walden. (Lord Howard de Walden, Thomas Evelyn Scott-Ellis, was a noted patron of the arts, both the struggling English Opera and the new Welsh Drama. His contribution is not dissimilar to Miss Annie Horniman's for the Abbey Theatre—being possessed of a great desire to sponsor change.) This first important competition sponsored by de Walden may have given *Beddau'r Proffwydi* its initial prominence but the play subsequently won popularity wherever it was played. It was, of course, a direct descendant of the naturalistic and domestic adaptations of *Rhys Lewis*. Its setting, the farm kitchen of Sgellog Fawr, was to be duplicated in several hundred similar plays in the period from 1914 to 1945. It is the farm kitchen of a moderately prosperous farmer—no cottager but somebody of reasonable means who has his place in society. According to Aristotle's axiom, this is the home of someone who has enough standing to make it possible for him to fall. *Beddau'r Proffwydi* therefore presents us with the authentic voice of a body of people in Wales who led their society: articulate people, chapel people, small employers who are conscious of their own standing; important and sometimes self-important. Their counterparts are found in the naturalistic plays of Ibsen and belong to an emergent articulate and aspirational lower middle class.

Emrys in *Beddau'r Proffwydi* is the college educated son; his parents have sacrificed to send him to college and expect him to lead and change his society. Several critics, Dafydd Glyn Jones amongst them, have linked the aspirational, undefined optimism of such plays to the Welsh Liberal political struggle in which W. J. Gruffydd played a prominent part. One can understand the emphasis in a country without independent political structures on education as a means to produce social change. As Elin Williams, the mother in *Beddau'r Proffwydi*, says:

> Who scrimped every penny to send him to College when his father did nothing but grumble? Who went to chapel every Sunday looking shabby and down at heel so that he could live there as he deserved? Who believed that he would work miracles there and who believes that he will be a prophet and an evangelist in his own Wales yet? Who but his mother?

The aspirations of family and nation weigh heavily on this son and will weigh even more burdensomely on other sons in the work of John Gwilym Jones, who will explore this theme in more tortuous detail later on in the century.

In portraying the family of Sgellog Fawr, W. J. Gruffydd also tries to develop a dramatic language which mirrors naturalistic speech. It is a little too heavily overweighed with idiomatic excess—the first scene, which is more stylistically selfconscious, has two or three strong idiomatic expressions in any minor speech. Despite this, the play's linguistic success lies in taking the accent of Gwynedd and mirroring its patterns without departing too far from an underlying literary norm. It is a sincere attempt to put on stage a language whose only public appearances were in the pulpit or on the political platform. Gruffydd is not alone in this attempt at linguistic naturalism. One interesting contemporary is D. T. Davies, who in his play *Ephraim Harris* (1914) tries to mirror the Welsh speech of Glamorgan. He confines himself, like Gruffydd, to the flavour of an idiom or a particular pronunciation. In particular, he uses the notable Glamorgan sound change of 'a' as in 'cat' to a pronounced 'e' as in 'get'—a sound change that still occurs in part of north Powys today. On the other hand, his speech does not mirror truly the hesitation and vagaries of actual speech. What we have in these plays, therefore, are speeches which are literary and fully structured, mitigated by the rhythm and flavour of naturalistic speech.

Having praised this attempt at natural rhythms, one is also aware that these plays have their feet planted in the melodramatic nineteenth-century theatre which underlies even Ibsen. Writers such as Edward Bulwer-Lytton with *Money* (1840) or T. W. Robertson with *Caste* (1867) struggle hard to say something serious within a melodramatic form. W. J. Gruffydd belongs to a similar period which was trying hard to slough off the older forms but had not quite succeeded. Emrys returns from America having made his fortune, heaven knows how, kicks out the bailiff who is about to sell the farm and declares that his mother and father are saved and that they will enjoy 'breakfast in bed' for ever—obviously the highest point of indulgence for the Gwynedd working class. Thus, stylistically, the Welsh-language plays of the period are a curious mixture of the struggle for serious natural expression linked to a highly dramatic, 'eleventh hour' convention of melodramatic coincidence. We may view *Beddau'r Proffwydi*, therefore, as representative of a body of plays, conceived within a naturalistic setting, struggling for naturalistic expression and exploring the anxieties of an aspirational class against the underlying pull of melodrama.

A whole group of plays in this period, including D. T. Davies's *Ephraim Harris* (1914) and the later *Pobl yr Ymylon* (People on the Periphery) of 1927 by Idwal Jones (1895–1937), point forward to another fundamental preoccupation which is even more important. Whereas an Anglo-Welsh playwright such as J. O. Francis was able in his plays, *Cross Currents* (1923) and *Change* (1913), to talk about the emergent Independent Labour Party (Keir Hardie had after all been elected in 1900) and the growth of nationalism leading to the establishment of Plaid Cymru in 1925, the predominant theme of Welsh-language drama in this period is the problem of hypocrisy within the chapel-going community. When Emrys in *Beddau'r Proffwydi* is wrongly charged with stealing pheasant, his main source of hurt is that there were church elders who sided with the squire to revoke his full membership of the Church. Within this body of Welsh plays, the *seiat* (the Fellowship meeting) looms large. It is within the *seiat* that people pray *o'r frest* (from the breast/without a paper); it is within the *seiat* that full membership is discussed. In D. T. Davies's play, *Ephraim Harris*, Dinah has been excluded because she has married someone 'from the world' (i.e. not a Church member). When she reapplies after a revelatory experience, the elders tell her to wait a month. In *Beddau'r Proffwydi*, Emrys's membership is revoked by elders who are linked by trade to the squire, thus calling into question their whole moral stance:

> VAUGHAN: The Squire called with me today, stayed for hours as he does each week—you know that we are the best of friends—and he told me that he had decided to nip in the bud two things which are rife in this village: the first was poaching, and more importantly the wild new ideas that agitators and wrong-headed people are spreading in the community. That is his duty to God and man, as he sees it . . .
> *(Emrys enters and stands by the door, unseen.)*
> . . . Now Dafydd Dafis, where does the Plas (the Manor) buy all its groceries?
> DAFYDD DAFIS: With me. They buy almost everything in my shop.
> VAUGHAN: And who makes suits for the Plas, William Prichard?
> WILLIAM PRICHARD: We do, at the London House. We know exactly how much padding to put in the shoulders for him and for his father before him.

Thus is Emrys's case before the *seiat* defeated.

Linked to this revelation of the hypocrisy of the *seiat*, there emerges another strong theme within Welsh drama. The young seer, usually a disadvantaged girl who belongs to the lower classes, sees things more clearly than her privileged contemporaries. Thus in *Beddau'r Proffwydi* Ann, the maid, is the only one who believes in Emrys and redeems him. In *Ephraim Harris*, this theme is taken further when Dinah recounts her own revelatory experience of the mountain-top—an experience reminiscent of Christ's own mountain revelations:

> Last Thursday afternoon, I was sitting up on the hill with the village nestling tidily beneath me. I had seen it all a thousand times before, but I had some new vision of it at that time. There were the homes of men and women I had known all my life, and from all directions, by road, over the fields, over the hills and vales, I saw the old and the young, the strong and the weak, all gravitating towards this one place in the shadow of the mountain, the old chapel nestling within its graveyard of white stones. And I understood, that whatever the hypocrisy and the pettiness, there was still some wonderful element which drew people towards each other . . . and there I remained by myself on the hill, all alone, and the night starting to close in on the whole valley. I don't

remember what happened next—the next thing I knew was that I was offering myself back in the Seiat.

In *Pobl yr Ymylon*, we go a step further; the minister has a crisis of nerves before a preaching appointment. He meets a hustler and con-man, Malachi, who has always wanted to preach; inevitably, they change places. Malachi's sermon sweeps his audience because it comes from the heart of his experience. Is it a worse sermon for being preached by a tramp? At the end of the play, Malachi is confronted by one of the elders:

> DANIEL: But what was your aim? What on earth did you want? Did you want money?
> MALACHI: Do you think I would preach if I wanted to make money? What was my aim? I watched you from the pulpit tonight, Mr Evans, and there was a tear in your eye because of my sermon, the sermon of the tramp whom you are keen to send from your door by now. And you ask what was my aim?
> DANIEL: Well, are you going to tell me then . . .?
> MALACHI: I have spent my life in workhouses and caravans and prisons—with harlots and sinners, and respectable people closed their doors when I came to town . . . But tonight, with the chapel full and the people listening to me, each face turned towards me, caught by the emotion, and I preached, I preached . . . O Heavens! Tomos Simon, do your worst. I preached that sermon . . . and you felt its power.

A little earlier, he challenges a character named (significantly?) Lewis Edwards, directly:

> Is that sermon any the worse for coming from me, Mr Edwards? Are you any the worse for having heard it?

In the midst of this success, his erstwhile wife and daughter recognize him and challenge his own hypocrisy. We finish the play with different strata of knowledge and different perspectives on hypocrisy.

It seems to me that there are two layers present in these plays: (i) the indictment of hypocrisy within the small-minded grocery-class of church attenders; (ii) linked intimately to it is the revelatory/ mystical experience of the disadvantaged. I have already mentioned Dinah's in *Ephraim Harris*. Within this second group,

Anglo-Welsh playwrights such as J. O. Francis, present us with Dici Bach Dwl whose 'simple' mind understands the Sermon on the Mount better than those in 'Big Seat Salem'. Whatever Caradoc Evans may have said—and there is evidence enough within these plays to support some of his fear of the Methodist Ayatollah—the plays of Wales did explore steadfastly the combination of power and morality within Welsh Methodism. It is the struggle of a Methodist Revival which may at times have confused church-going with Christianity and which may have renounced the spirit for the letter. It is a theme which engages Welsh playwrights up to the Second World War. Daniel Owen, the novelist, remains for many people a literary champion in the battle against social and religious hypocrisy; it is time, perhaps, that people paid tribute to W. J. Gruffydd, D. T. Davies, Idwal Jones and other playwrights for taking this battle literally into the vestry.

In this necessarily constrained overview of Welsh drama, I have used particular plays as methodological tools whereby we can explore a dominant or emergent theatrical voice. The danger in such an approach is that these plays hover individually without their bustling context. Let me therefore emphasize that this period is one of pronounced theatrical activity, some of it of substance, much of it lighter farce and social comedy. The Catalogue of Welsh Plays produced by Glenys Howells lists a substantial number of published plays from this period; one surmises that there may well be others, acted but unpublished. John Ellis Williams, novelist and playwright, (1901–75) mentions in his autobiography *Inc yn Fy Ngwaed* (Ink in My Blood) of 1963 that he was in touch with over 350 local companies in the period before the Second World War who used to buy his plays. The war devastated those companies— John Ellis Williams calculated that over two hundred had ceased to be active. Often practical considerations such as the blackout curtailed entertainment. Whatever the practical considerations, however, one has the feeling also that a particular style had run its course and exhausted its reserves. One may even surmise that, after the war, will, reason, determinism seemed not to offer a full explanation for man's bestiality or his saintliness.

Our next snapshot is taken in 1948, on 15 and 16 October when Saunders Lewis's *Blodeuwedd* was performed by an amateur group of players under their producer, Morris Jones at the Little Theatre on the Garthewin estate in north Wales. Here, at last, after the debate of the early part of the century, was a verse play with its subject taken from Welsh mythology. The sophistication of the verse and the complex treatment of the myth sets this offering on a totally different level of artistic attainment to the heroic outpourings of Beriah Gwynfe Evans or Pedr Hir. Saunders Lewis (1893–1985), the leading Welsh literary figure in the twentieth century, was born in Wallasey, Liverpool of Welsh parents. After his war service, he returned to his studies in the English Department of Liverpool University, gained a First and later an MA for work subsequently published as *A School of Welsh Augustans.*

There are many formative influences during this period. Within the theatre, there is the influence of Yeats and Synge with their dream of a national drama and a national theatre company who would show the world that Ireland was not, to quote Yeats, 'the home of easy buffoonery'. Philosophically, Saunders Lewis was to be influenced early in his literary life by Maurice Barrès, in particular by *Le Culte du Moi* (1891) and the novel *Collette Baudouche* (1908). In Barrès, Saunders Lewis encountered the concept of community as a celebration of order and ancestry, a concept not dissimilar to Yeats's sense of 'custom and ceremony' in life. It is at this point that he felt, according to his article in the journal *Dock Leaves* (Winter 1955), that Barrès 'had convinced me that Wales for me was not a net but a root'—a sentence which has important repercussions for his later play *Blodeuwedd*. Professor Ioan Williams, in his substantial and important edition of the plays, *Dramâu Saunders Lewis* (1996) traces Saunders Lewis's espousal of *Collette Baudouche* where the individual is at odds with his/her society and yet gains meaning through being true to personal ideals within that society. Professor Williams argues that whereas the idea of the self alienated from society is a theme in nineteenth-century Romanticism, Saunders Lewis, through Barrès, engages with this concept and transforms it. He presents the individual as finding heroic meaning by working from within his/her culture *despite* his/her alienation from its vulgar or philistine manifestations.

In his second play *Gwaed yr Uchelwyr* (Ancestral Blood) of 1922— in which he had made the significant change from writing a play about Wales in English to writing in Welsh—the concept of heroism and honour carries with it the sense of an elite ancestry. The heroine, Luned, talks of emulating her ancestors: 'I would wish to prove myself one of them.' She therefore sacrifices happiness in order to remain true to her personal vision. She departs for Wisconsin; unlike Emrys in *Beddau'r Proffwydi* who leaves to make his fortune, she departs in order to preserve her sense of high idealism:

> That is the difference between us, Arthur. You are a new people; you look forward still, you hope. But I belong to a people who are very old; my roots are far back in my past. And hope has no place in my way of living. I do not fear or hope any longer. I shall wander like the sons of Gruffydd ap Rolant. My life will be an altar to the memories of my nation. I shall be a nun, devoted to my land. And my family will die with me, but it dies without having betrayed its ideals or its traditions.

It is only later that Saunders will have his heroines, and occasional hero, preserve their idealism by working within their existing society. It is at that point also that his literary work and political life will fuse in a common philosophy.

Interestingly, Saunders Lewis is one of the few writers, outside the Renaissance period, who did not choose Yeats's dichotomy of 'perfection of the life or of the art' but somehow managed both. In 1925, Saunders Lewis was part of a small group who founded the Welsh Nationalist Party, Plaid Cymru. In 1936, the British government was preparing for the possibility of war against Germany and had decided to site one bombing school not far from Ynys Enlli (Bardsey Island) on the Llŷn Peninsula. Llŷn and Enlli were on the route of the saints from Ireland, and Enlli itself was reputed to be the final resting place of many saints. All the leading cultural groups in Wales campaigned against the move and cited other venues which the government had rejected because they were areas of cultural or natural interest. But to no avail. In September 1936, therefore, in the company of two other literary figures, the Revd Lewis Valentine and D. J. Williams, Saunders Lewis set fire to the building materials on the site in Penyberth. All three gave themselves up to the police immediately. After two trials, during which Saunders's speeches sound like a rehearsal for some of his later plays, the three were convicted and imprisoned for nine months. The reverberations of this piece of direct action—the first of its kind in Wales despite the example of the Irish 1916 Easter Rising—were to resound for the rest of the century.

The period up to 1936 was a busy one, politically, in which Saunders Lewis found it almost impossible to return to his dramatic writing. After 1936, having been sacked by the University College Swansea for his part in what was to be known as the Fire in Llŷn, Saunders Lewis remains a prolific writer, contributing his influential column to the Welsh-language weekly paper, *Y Faner,* and producing a series of critical studies. His return to play-writing stems from BBC Wales's brave decision to commission a radio play from him from prison. In what must be one of the oddest incidents of prison life, the three prisoners were allowed out of their cells on 2 March 1937 to listen to the broadcast of *Buchedd Garmon.* (BBC Wales was to continue its financial support through radio commissions, e.g. *Siwan* in 1954.) This period also sees his growing acquaintance with R. O. F. Wynne, owner of the estate at Garthewin, and the drama producer Morris Jones. (All of this has been ably chronicled recently by Hazel Walford Davies in her Welsh-language book on Saunders Lewis and Garthewin). It is this connection which led him to return to *Blodeuwedd,* a play started in February 1922, now to be finished and produced in 1948 in Garthewin's Little Theatre.

Blodeuwedd is the story from the Mabinogi of the girl created from flowers to be a wife to Llew Llaw Gyffes. The play opens ambivalently; our sympathies lie with Blodeuwedd: she is rootless, without family, outside society, a woman created for one purpose:

> BLODEUWEDD: I have no root or earth among men.
> There's water to kill these flowers' pain
> And postpone their end; but I was taken
> By an arrogant hand and put here to die
> Without one kind element to keep me young.

Inevitably, her senses are aroused not by her cautious husband but by his noble visitor, Gronw Pebr, whose hunting instinct and wildness spark her desire.

>   . . . Didn't you see
> The wonder of my birth? Before you came to me
> This body was a prison about me,
> Like a dead web about a living chrysalis;
> You came like spring where I lay
> And gave wings to my flesh, put dancing in my blood.
> Among families, I'll not again be lonely;
> To me your smiles are my lineage and my claim
> Upon humanity. There is one will

In leaves and men; no feeble ceremony
Nor custom nor judgement can imprison the heart
That feels the rays of desire beating.

As they deceive Llew, our attitude changes. How can custom and ceremony thrive in the anarchic behaviour which sets self above society? Gronw is torn between his desire for Blodeuwedd and his regret at his betrayal of Llew. In a moment of revelation, Gronw understands that his cuckolding has also betrayed his upbringing, his sense of lineage, his desire to be included in the family of man; he chooses to await Llew's return and his certain death. In a letter to Dr Gwenan Jones, Saunders Lewis compares Llew to Dafydd Nanmor, a fifteenth-century poet redolent of the Welsh poetic tradition with its emphasis (according to Lewis's interpretation of it!) on the preservation of culture through family and social structures. Blodeuwedd he calls the 'Eternal Eve' and insists that her presence still haunts the play at the end, allowing it no easy resolution. Professor Ioan Williams must surely be right in his insistence that this play remained unfinished not through lack of time or inclination, but because Saunders Lewis himself needed to encompass the paradox of the twin desires within humanity. *Blodeuwedd* could have been heroic in following her instincts—a true Romantic heroine in an alien world. Saunders Lewis's own philosophical growth led him to posit against this the need for a structured society based on trust, on tradition, on respect, on the claims of the past which would help create another form of heroism. Professor Williams's contribution is to put Gronw Pebr at the centre of the dilemma; apparently the lesser character, he is ultimately the one to make the all-important decision to stay to meet his end, proclaiming his own guilt against society:

GRONW:
Your love's a grave with no tomorrow; no baby will laugh
On your bosom; there's no cradle in your fort; . . .
I lost the paths of men to chase a flame
And the magic pipes of the fen, and I sank in it,
Embraced a star, had a bat hang on my lips;
Today a bolt struck me and I woke;
I see Penllyn, I see my boyhood there,
And I see myself now, oh loathsome, and I see you—
Better your husband's sword than your kiss.

Blodeuwedd is not the last of Saunders Lewis's heroines. His admiration for Corneille and Racine, for the plays of Euripides (especially as portrayed by Sybil Thorndike: 'It was Mrs Thorndike's *Medea* that gave me the first idea of a kindred character in Welsh legend') leads him to Blodeuwedd and subsequently to Siwan (1954), to Iris in *Gymerwch Chi Sigaret?* (1956), to *Esther* (1960) and to Bet in *Cymru Fydd* (1967). *Siwan* is particularly interesting. It follows the life of Joan, daughter of King John, married to Llywelyn the Great, many years her senior. Again there is the inevitable passion for a younger man, Gwilym de Breos, whom Llywelyn hangs for his adultery like a common thief despite his noble birth. It is at this point that Siwan is led to understand the depth of Llywelyn's passion for her, concealed in politeness and ceremony through the years of their marriage:

LLYWELYN:
Our marriage was statecraft,
Between us lay a gap of twenty years.
Well, that is the custom; it founds alliances
And makes possible true concord between nations.
But four years later when you came to me
A virgin, as slim and graceful as a young silver birch,
My heart bounded as if I had suddenly seen the Grail
And where you walked there was brightness.
But I was afraid of hurting you with my unbounded delight,
And when I held you, here, shaking in my arms,
I never bruised you with clumsy kisses,
Nor stained you with the sweat of barbarous embraces.
I restrained myself with all my will so as not to be loathsome to you:
I was patient, courteous and formal.
And your trembling ceased: this hall became your home,
And I a not altogether distasteful part of the furniture.
So I worshipped you, mutely, and from a distance,
Unwilling to intrude upon a remote image
That burned beyond my reach.

Bruce Griffiths, who has written a study of Saunders Lewis in the Writers of Wales Series, argues forcibly that this is Saunders Lewis's finest play and I share his verdict. On the other hand, whereas he cites the Second Act as a dramatic *tour de force*, I tend to see the disclosure of passion and the reconciliation in the Third Act as a work of singular depth and maturity. Siwan and Llywelyn come together in reconciliation, metaphorically, over the corpse of Gwilym:

> LLYWELYN: Come back to me Siwan.
> SIWAN: If I do, between us in the bed will always be the stench of your love defiled.
> LLYWELYN: If you come, between us in the bed will be another body, a corpse hanged by the neck.
> SIWAN: What shall we do with them Llywelyn?
> LLYWELYN: Stretch out our arms across them towards each other, and accept them as souls accept Purgatory.

Perhaps it is a measure of Saunders Lewis's greatness that whatever is said about him can be challenged by another insight from one of the plays. Thus *Siwan* calls into question the thesis that Saunders Lewis's dramatic structure consists normally of irreconcilable opposites. It is as if Blodeuwedd was to be understood and forgiven her passion. Siwan at her death, however, prefers to be buried alone, thus exploring another theme of the individual's loneliness even within the reconciliation of a mature marriage.

The body of work is immense—nineteen plays, two novels, nine major critical studies, a whole raft of political writing and speechmaking, of which I have only scratched the surface. Saunders Lewis's work is not confined to female characters either: *Brad* (Treason, 1958) explores the attempt to assassinate Hitler by the elite corps of the German army whose sense of honour is destroyed by the Führer's behaviour, and *Gymerwch Chi Sigaret?* (Cigarette? 1956) explores the dilemma of the Communist citizen Marc confronted by the Christian Phugas after Iris's death. Indeed, it can be argued that most of the plays named after a female heroine (with the possible exception of *Esther*) have equally strong and dominant male roles. Whether the role is male or female, however, Saunders Lewis's normal working method is to put his hero or heroine *in extremis*, to make them take the positive Pascalian bet—on the side of life, tradition, religion, society. He tries to make this an existential act; in the face of a mad and hostile, dangerous world, why not bet on the side of structure, of order, of religion, almost as a manifestation of tradition? In *Gymerwch Chi Sigaret?* the platform is set out explicitly:

> PHUGAS: You have been thrown into the casino of your life, here in Vienna. You cannot escape; the doors have been shut on you; and you

cannot remain without placing a bet—that is the rule of the tables. Alright! Bet that there is a God! Chance your life on his existence; you cannot place a smaller bet than that at these tables. The bet is rational, and yet it is a bet because to know is impossible and you cannot believe. You cannot choose not to bet either because that is the same as betting that there is no God. That is why you cannot escape from the need to bet in the casino. Marc, you cannot bet against the existence of God. That would not be a rational act . . . Throw your life on this table and bet that there is a God. Remember, before you know whether you have won or lost, you will already have gained a tremendous inner meaning to your life here in Vienna. After betting, there is no madness, only the waiting to see what happens. It may be that you will win your bet. If so, your reward will be great. If you lose—well, what have you got to lose that you haven't lost already? You mentioned yourself that you had already lost everything . . .

The only play in which this philosophical stance is truly challenged within the dramatic structure is *Cymru Fydd* (1967). Cymru Fydd (A Future for Wales) was the name of the Liberal movement towards Home Rule of which Beriah Gwynfe Evans formed a part and W. J. Gruffydd was a successor. Saunders Lewis too, like Gruffydd before him, portrays a college-educated son returning home. By now the lower-middle class Welsh home is the manse, and the son returns not from America but on the run from prison; this son's evaluation of his country's future is devastating. Unfortunately, whilst his girlfriend Bet (cf. Pascal's bet) bets on the side of life and optimism, *Cymru Fydd* is a classic example of the devil having the best tunes in that Dewi is a more powerful, energetic and engaging character. His suicide is the direct opposite of Emrys's triumphant return in *Beddau'r Proffwydi*. The suicide challenges the liberal optimism of much of twentieth-century drama in which the resolution occurs favourably and relatively painlessly. For Saunders Lewis, the courage to stand up for beliefs, to go against the grain but still to opt to operate within society is never painless. In Dewi, we find someone who cannot believe enough to pay the price in life; instead he pays the ultimate price of nihilism in suicide.

Saunders Lewis's contribution to Welsh letters is breathtaking. His range and energy, the prolific abundance of plays and critical studies, testify to his energy; more importantly, the quality of his writing testifies to a need to reformulate Welsh political thought either through action or through drama. When one looks back at his contribution, one has a sense of awe and also a sense of regret that the Nobel Prize, for which he was nominated, was not awarded. On the other hand, Saunders Lewis's concept of the survival of the language in the context of a spiritual rationalism and a literary classicism had its own problems. Was it too much to ask of any small nation that it should fight for its survival within the context of a conservative classicism in the troubled and rootless times after the Second World War? The route may well have appeared logically desirable, but it could not hold forth against all the turbulent forces of the time. For many nationalists, personal salvation did not seem necessarily the only route for a national reawakening; there were other voices who wanted to revisit the industrial reality of Wales. In Saunders Lewis's literary work too, the arguments appear abstract at times, devoid of characterization, the method manipulative. He himself defined his life as that of one who had dared greatly but had lost the argument. Whatever our individual conclusions, there is no doubt that any thinker or writer engaged in Welsh life also engages himself or herself in defining or refuting the challenges of Saunders Lewis's political, spiritual and literary aspirations for his nation.

One may argue interminably on the philosophical value of Saunders Lewis's contribution to the political and literary life of Wales. What cannot be argued against is his ability to change the mechanical blank verse of the turn of the century into a magnificently versatile tool. In *Blodeuwedd*, and especially in *Siwan*, the verse ranges subtly through a gamut of emotions. As Sir Thomas Parry remarked in his description of *Buchedd Garmon*, it was the birth of a style which transformed Welsh blank verse in the way the greatest of Welsh medieval poets, Dafydd ap Gwilym, had transformed the strict-metre *cywydd* to be his own subtle instrument. There were others too who sought to move away from naturalism into a poetic expression which would allow a greater range and depth of emotion. A naturalistic style of speech suits the small anti-hero in a domestic setting such as Willie Loman in Miller's *Death of A Salesman*, or Dr Stockman in Ibsen's *Enemy of the People*. On the other hand, Eugene O'Neill's treatment of *Mourning Becomes Electra* shows the deficiencies of the style for a more elevated tone. There was, within English as well as Welsh drama, a general dissatisfaction with the domestic confinement of naturalism. Welsh playwrights had one vibrant example of a new elevated style in T. S.

Eliot's *Murder in the Cathedral*, translated by Sir Thomas Parry and played by the students of the University College of North Wales, Bangor in 1949. Even before the war, Robert Speaight who played Thomas à Becket and E. Martin Browne who produced Eliot's play were visitors to Plas Newydd, Llangollen and the drama festival in Garthewin. Saunders Lewis's earlier verse plays preceded or were contemporary with Eliot's, for example *Buchedd Garmon* (1937), *Amlyn ac Amig* (1940) and of course the early unfinished version of *Blodeuwedd*, which precedes them all as far back as 1928. There were other early verse experiments such as *Meini Gwagedd* (1944) and the moving *Sŵn y Gwynt sy'n Chwythu* (broadcast on the BBC in 1953) by Kitchener Davies (1902–52) who had also created a serious naturalistic play (*Cwm Glo*, 1935) exploring in greater depth the issues which had engaged the earlier naturalistic writers.

Whatever the motivation—perhaps a common desire to search for a style capable of containing a spiritual undertone—the period immediately after the war sees a clutch of original verse plays: Sir Thomas Parry's *Llywelyn Fawr* (produced 1951 and published 1954), *Absalom fy Mab* (1957) by the archdruid 'Cynan' (Albert Evans-Jones, 1895–1970), the work of Dyfnallt Morgan (1917–94), F. G. Fisher (1909–70, who founded the Little Theatre in Llangefni) and Tom Parri Jones (1905–80). The National Eisteddfod at Aberdare (1956) and at Llangefni (1957) even offered the Crown for a verse play.

Saunders Lewis's slightly younger contemporary, John Gwilym Jones (1904–88), however, was to conduct his philosophical search in dramatic forms which were linked more closely to the major European influences in the twentieth century. As such, whereas Saunders Lewis's work challenged the age with its new classicism, John Gwilym Jones's work tends to mirror the age in its shifts of style and to explore avenues which are more personal and richer in psychological characterization. The old theme of the 'novus homo', the first of his generation to be sent to university, a theme which emerged in *Beddau'r Proffwydi* in 1913, is explored here in greater depth. In *Y Tad a'r Mab* (Father and Son, 1963), Richard Owen has become so enmeshed in his hopes for his son, that he fails to distinguish the boundaries of their two personalities:

RICHARD OWEN: (*emotionally*) Listen. If you win that scholarship, I shall feel exactly as if I had won it myself, and if you fail, I shall feel

exactly as if I myself had failed. That's how close I am to you.
Everything that happens to you happens to me. I cannot conceive of
myself apart from you. I wanted to know what Elis told you just now
because I felt myself . . . incomplete without that knowledge.
GWYN (his son): But that's sick . . . it's not natural.

Inevitably, into this over-close relationship, a girl enters; not any
girl, but one who will be a precursor for many of John Gwilym
Jones's characters. Pegi has a carefree attitude to sex and fails to
understand the pressures and the aspirations of Richard Owen's
universe. Similarly, Alis in *Ac Eto Nid Myfi* will step into the void
created after the death of the hero's beloved and non-judgmental
grandmother and create a world close to nature, to birth on the
farmyard, to sex without guilt. In both cases, it is the hero himself
who cannot break free. He is too enmeshed in his own upbringing
to find the freedom he desires. Tragically, in *Y Tad a'r Mab*, the
father goes out to kill this siren just as the son is also moving away
from what she has to offer. In *Ac Eto Nid Myfi*, Alis refuses Huw's
offer of marriage after she becomes pregnant because she is able to
realize how detached he is from his physical self and how
judgmental he is about it. Reinforcing this assessment, Huw
addresses the audience about a small incident in his childhood
when he had dared to use a 'dirty' word. (Significantly, John
Gwilym Jones's plays refer to these words by rhymed allusion!):

HUW: That slap on my cheek hurts as if it had happened this instant.
All through my life, it has remained a constant hurt. That hurt is the
hurt of Alis. It was at that point that I imbibed into my unconscious self
that natural things, indeed the most natural things in life, were bad and
disgusting. And that in the end there is no difference between agony and
ecstasy.

In *Beddau'r Proffwydi* Emrys is spared the question of the legacy
of his Nonconformist upbringing on his sexual self; instead, he
finds an adoring, devoted woman from a lower class who will nurse
and sustain him. John Gwilym Jones moves away from the world
of the lower middle class into the working-class world where
aspiration is not aided by devoted servants. Instead, the hero is far
more likely to be challenged for his romanticism and literary
idealism. Whereas the world of *Beddau'r Proffwydi* and *Ephraim
Harris* is relatively privileged, the world of Richard and Gwyn
Owen is that of the hand-to-mouth existence of the north Wales

quarryman or craftsman. The earlier plays of John Gwilym Jones, *Lle Mynno'r Gwynt* (The Wind Bloweth Where It List) and *Y Gŵr Llonydd* (The Still Man) (published together in 1958) and *Y Tad a'r Mab* (1963) take the naturalistic form of W. J. Gruffydd and D. T. Davies and push it towards a seriousness which it had not attained in its former manifestation. Undoubtedly, some hint of melodrama is still retained as in the final scene of *Y Tad a'r Mab*, but the overall intention is one of psychological exploration and a critique of the pressures of the nuclear family.

Even when John Gwilym Jones moved away in *Hanes Rhyw Gymro* (A History of a Welshman, 1964) and *Ac Eto Nid Myfi* (1976) from the naturalistic style into an overtly Brechtian mode, the net result is still to explore the private domain, not the effects of authority or social class on one's happiness. *Hanes Rhyw Gymro* relates the history of Morgan Llwyd's search for salvation. The central character addresses the audience directly and breaks the mould of the fourth wall naturalistic stage where audience and actors conspire to behave as if there is no one present. Morgan Llwyd even breaks away from dramatic dialogues to address the audience. Nevertheless, the storyline remains one of a search for personal salvation; there is no attempt, in my opinion, to place the hero within the social and spiritual pressures of the time. Instead, he is seen as dabbling on an individualistic basis in the religious beliefs on offer. His search is that of the self looking for certainty, not that of a man buffeted by social and historical forces. As such, Jones cannot be said to relate fully to the Brechtian critique although many critics have claimed that his style is Brechtian. It is true that he took the outer trappings of many European styles; but it was to clothe a message which was in the end naturalistic.

The best example of this lies once again in *Ac Eto Nid Myfi*. At first glance, the play does not belong to the naturalistic tradition. Huw breaks away from the opening lines to address the audience directly; from this point on he will address the audience intermittently giving his philosophical or psychological interpretation as the play unfolds. This exposition will be followed by a dramatic reconstruction. Brechtian enough one might say, taking into account plays such as *The Good Person of Setzuan* or *The Mother*. Nevertheless, one has only to dwell on some of the major speeches to show how this can never be a political and social critic at work:

HUW: It's a frightening thing for a man to be born himself and no other . . . a unique individual. There has never been anyone quite like him and there will never be anyone quite like him again, ever. A man is born as Michael Angelo or John Jones, St. John of the Cross or Judas Iscariot. And although one innocently comforts oneself that there is such a thing as free will and the right to choose, you know in your marrow that the little apparent choice, the big choices, are all subject to some dictatorial rules in a merciless and uncaring universe . . . If you have been born with your mother's hooked nose or your father's tendency to die before middle age because cancer ate his bowels, then it also stands to reason that you inherit their . . . well, what do you call it . . . their nature? . . . Each baby is born pregnant, bearing the child of its past born from chance.

Some years ago, arguments like these seemed to belong to a naturalism long since dead with the Ibsen who manifested himself in *Ghosts* or in *Rosmersholm*. More recently, it has seemed a precursor of the scientific arguments of the 1990s born out of genetic experimentation. The geneticist Professor Steve Jones (another Welshman) would have found himself very much at home with these paragraphs of John Gwilym Jones's. What is obvious though is that, despite the Brechtian style, this is not a Brechtian philosophy at work; it does not link birth to social class and social pressures in an overt way.

Despite this, John Gwilym Jones's philosophy is not totally deterministic. There is the possibility of salvation. Not through social evolution or economic assessment as in Brecht but through a reconciliation of the self to its psychological tensions. At the end of *Ac Eto Nid Myfi*, Huw decides to kill himself. He is in his rooms in the lodging house at university and receives the letter telling him that Alis is pregnant. It is the end of his respectability, of keeping up appearances for the sake of his mother. He is too frightened to tell her the truth, so he prepares for death by banishing the draughts underneath the door and feeding the gas meter. The description of his preparation for death is arguably one of the finest pieces of John Gwilym Jones's writing. Instead of an exposition leading to dramatic dialogue, we have a piece of exposition which is drama at first hand; in other words, action and commentary become one. He describes Mrs Williams bringing him his post, with a knowing wink as to the hand on the envelope. As he reads, he vomits. Mrs Williams clears up the mess:

'You are ill', she said. 'It was just something sudden', I said. 'Don't worry, I'll fetch a damp cloth . . .' She tidies me up. 'It didn't go over your ham and eggs anyway,' she said, 'The cat will be glad to have them.' and she laughs heartily. 'You've got something on your nose,' I say. 'Have I? A little water and I'll be alright'.

He then describes himself preparing for death, his conscious mind looking at himself undertaking each act for the last time:

I'm going from the door towards the fireplace for the last time . . . one, two, three, four steps . . . I'm taking off my shoes for the last time. 'Taking off my shoes', I said to myself. 'Why am I taking off my shoes to die?' And a curious burst of laughter swept over me. What odd rationale urged me to leave this world in my stockinged feet?

John Gwilym Jones's immense strength in describing these situations is that he is capable of making concrete each philosophical incident. The abstract is rooted in the concrete; in his own words, in his body of critical essays, he talks about 'primroses not primroseness'. Despite this rootedness in the concrete and the particular, John Gwilym Jones's touch is a little less certain when he tries to move out of the concrete into the world of philosophical revelation. In *Ac Eto Nid Myfi*, at the end of this very powerful passage, Huw stands there at the point of suicide and hears the words of Kathleen Ferrier's great favourite 'I Know That My Redeemer Liveth' wafting from the kitchen:

It came up from the kitchen like an old acquaintance . . . It left the sink and the washing-up bowl . . . It left the cat slurping up the rest of my egg . . . it rose up the stairs . . . and like my father's old nursery rhyme it knocked at the door . . . looked in at the windows . . . it lifted the latch . . . and came in . . . came in . . . came in . . . and I opened my doors to mam . . . to Alis . . . to my little child in her womb . . . and the three filled me . . . filled me. There was no room for anyone else . . . I had been ousted from my own self . . . 'I'll arise' I said to myself, 'I'll arise and I'll go home.'

The mixture in this paragraph of the concrete characterization and the abstract literary mode does not lie happily together. The cat slurping the egg and even Mrs Williams's singing coming up from the kitchen are homely and credible but the rest of the paragraph bears out one's uneasiness at the capability of the naturalistic style to carry heightened emotion. When that emotion is overlayed with a further emotive layer of biblical reference from the prodigal son, then the whole stylistic mode tends to become embarrassing to the audience.

Nevertheless, this paragraph seems to encapsulate much of John Gwilym Jones's personal philosophy. Unlike Saunders Lewis, he was not to develop a national philosophy or to posit one difficult mode of action against the easier. Instead he explored the opposing tensions within human beings: love of life and the existence of the coldness of death (which he describes graphically), the dirt and the beauty, the dung heap on which the beautiful flowers grows, the sex organ set biologically near to that of urine and excrement, and slowly, painfully, he accepts the inevitability of all this. Ever the gentleman, he has his codes for these problems such as the toad and the grift and the rotten apple, but his meaning is explicit enough. In an early play *Lle Mynno'r Gwynt*, Dewi offers us this symbolic vision:

> Eban had just finished clearing out the cowshed and the old cock was pecking in the hot smoke of the dung heap. I saw suddenly that beauty was made up of all these things. The beauty of the river and the moss and the fields are just tinsel-town prettiness and the dung heap by itself is disgusting. Taken together they are part of life and we can share the thrill of this vision by looking at them. (The Old Mill) was beautiful not despite the dung heap but because of it, and not because of the river and the moss but despite them possibly.

So it is when Huw in *Ac Eto Nid Myfi* returns home one day, after his fall from grace to find his mother frying his favourite onions, a vegetable that she cannot stand:

> The smell wafted around me. I couldn't believe what I smelt . . . 'Onions', I said, 'Mam, you've been frying onions for me.' 'Yes,' she said and that was all. But it was like . . . a kiss . . . like a kiss.

What binds together all these plays I have discussed, products of a period of almost eighty years up to the mid 1960s, is that they all belong to an articulate discourse. Within Pedr Hir's play of *Owain Glyndwr*, the hero and his contemporaries articulate their pain, their worries and their ambitions. In the naturalistic plays of the turn of the century and beyond, men and women talk openly about their visions and philosophies whether they belong to an educated class or whether they belong like Dinah and Malachi to a social underclass. When we enter the dramatic world of Saunders Lewis, his plays revolve around the contending philosophies of his characters; he even chooses verse in order to expand the domain of his articulation. In his volume of critical appraisal of Saunders Lewis, Ioan Williams describes his theatre as a straitened stage. It is a narrow theatre space, exquisitely focused upon the philosophical thesis that is clearly articulated by its characters. Similarly John Gwilym Jones's characters *explain* everything to us; there are some additional responses which are left to other means such as the song or the symbolic onions in *Ac Eto Nid Myfi,* but these can be counted on one hand against the explicit exegesis of many of the main speeches.

With the work of Gwenlyn Parry (1932–91) Welsh drama takes on a totally new discursive mode. We find men (mostly men, the women are more articulate and more in command) who live their lives trying to piece together a jigsaw. And there are always gaps in meaning in trying to create a final version. Suddenly, the authentic voice of the inarticulate, the struggling, the defeated is to be heard. Here are characters who cannot analyse their own lives, who cannot articulate a philosophy. Their hopes and despairs are acted out on stage but it is the audience who put together the broken lines and weave them into an articulate whole.

Our third snapshot takes us to the Aberafan Eisteddfod in the first full week of August, 1966. The audience is pouring out of the hall having witnessed the first performance of the commissioned play by Gwenlyn Parry, an author who had just left his teaching post to become the drama script editor of BBC Wales. The play was *Saer Doliau* and according to the reviews in *Y Faner* and *Y Cymro* for that week, audiences were debating hotly for half an hour or more on the meaning of what they had seen. What they had seen of course was one of the first open-ended, unprescribed, ambivalent pieces of theatre which Wales had produced. Furthermore—and possibly more importantly although this was not discussed as fiercely—it was the first play in which the visual served openly as a metaphor of the philosophical theme.

When the curtains opened (this was still the age when the action was revealed as opposed to a later time when the audience would be part of the setting-up) the stage had shelf upon shelf of dolls in all conditions. Ifan, the old doll mender lives in a workshop devoid of modern tools, devoid of electricity. Into this chaotic but comfortable world come two people, the apprentice – a young man in a hurry (and in a leather jacket) the exact opposite of Ifan's painstaking approach, and the woman (unnamed) who turns out to control everything. They are determined to modernize Ifan's workshop but Ifan resists. He has a habit, at times of stress, of going on the phone with his boss, his *Giaffar*. The *Giaffar* (gaffer) never replies and seems to be a figment of Ifan's imagination. Ifan is mocked even more when the apprentice and the woman point out that the phone line is unconnected and that there is no electricity anyway. After a series of tensions and the death of Ifan, the apprentice leaves the workshop only to hear the unconnected phone ring. Does God exist after all? *Saer Doliau* had created a myth open-ended enough to suit other interpretations at other times. The tension between the generations is represented admirably: the workshop is swept clean and the new men enter energetically. In fact, when the play was reproduced twenty years later on BBC Cymru, directed by Gwyn Hughes Jones, he used actress Myfanwy Talog to represent the girl and dressed her in a Thatcherite blue suit with a diamante brooch to emphasize the struggle of labour against capital in old-fashioned industries. This play which resists narrative closure and which can be remythologized by succeeding generations, is one that links Welsh playwrights to the major plays coming from Europe at this time, in particular Beckett's *Waiting for Godot* (1954) and the subsequent work of Harold Pinter in Britain. There were other Welsh playwrights too who had pioneered a new theatre language: Saunders Lewis who wrote a Beckettian play, *Yn y Trên* (In the Train) which he published in the journal *Barn* in 1965; the original, verbally innovative and much-underestimated W. S. Jones, 'Wil Sam' (1920–) some of whose plays were collected in the volume *Dinas Barhaus a Thair Drama Arall* (1968); and during the same year as *Saer Doliau, Pros Kairon*, by Huw Lloyd Edwards (1916–75) also began touring Wales, using a Pirandellian ambiguity of characterization to puzzle and challenge its audience.

Gwenlyn Parry, however, was to build consistently on his methodology to produce a body of work which accepts the impossibility of true narrative closure from the outset. Despite this, there is in *Saer Doliau*, the earliest of his plays to use this methodology, a slight lack of connection between the overall thematic impulse and the image produced by the set. Whereas the play opens to show row on row of dolls, this particular theme is never fully explored. Ifan makes references to throwing some of the dolls into the cellar (hell?), but the full dramatic tension of the piece lies between the blustering old man and the too-knowing young, not between Ifan and the future of the dolls. There is, therefore, to use Eliot's terms about *Hamlet*, a malfunction in the 'objective correlative'. This lack of clarity is tackled more successfully in other work by Gwenlyn Parry. *Y Ffin* (The Border) of 1973 fuses set and theme admirably. Now and Wilias (possibly fugitives from a psychiatric ward) set up house in a disused shepherd's hut high on a mountainside. When the play opens, the hut is merely a series of panels on the floor of the stage. Slowly the two men 'build' their home, taking pleasure in its cosiness and teasing each other by describing its amenities in estate agent terminology, for example the one room is 'open-plan' and the chamber pot a sign of all modern conveniences. Once again, a woman acts as a catalyst to the action or possibly as the eternal Eve in this innocent Eden. Her arrival sparks off a period of immense rivalry culminating in the two men drawing a line (y ffin/the border) along the floor to maintain their territorial rights. In the final assault they make on each other the building collapses, leaving the hut derelict, a mere series of panels thrown about the stage exactly as we had seen them at the very beginning.

Similarly, in a later play *Y Tŵr* (The Tower) of 1979, the set consists of a scaffold or a flight of stairs in the middle of a room. We encounter the two protagonists (who remain unnamed) on the first rung of adult sexuality. Their first encounter is a mixture of joy and hesitation:

GIRL: I've arrived! (*She looks around her with enthusiasm and then goes back to the door and calls down the stairs.*) Hurry! (*She looks around as if she had come across somewhere for which she had been searching for a long time. At last, I've arrived! . . .*
GIRL: What do you think?
YOUTH: (*Looking around him dubiously and still standing by the door.*) I don't know.
GIRL: (*From the middle of the room.*) Come over here.
YOUTH: Eh?

GIRL: (*Extending her arms towards him.*) Over here with me.
YOUTH: (*Without moving*) Do you think we should?

Their second encounter is hedonistic, then as the girl becomes pregnant, they face growing responsibilities and the threshold of their middle years. It is at this point that we become aware of the true significance of the stairs as a gateway into the next level of life. Significantly, it is the woman who chooses to climb first. The middle level is hard and fraught with tensions, the rooms draughty. Their marriage strains under infidelity and job loss. Inexorably, they climb onto the third level. Here the air is tenderer; there is more compassion and warmth. True to biological trends, it is the man who climbs first—towards an after life? The symbolic significance of the set in *Y Tŵr* is enhanced by the fact that the stairs are ever-present. The audience sees not only the protagonists but also their future. A television production by John Hefin struggled hard to find a way of rendering this to a television audience; the inevitable close-ups, the necessary mix of long and medium and close shots meant that the stairs were not always present in the frame. The theatre audience on the other hand has nothing but the long shot. Even when the audience's attention is focused on a particular actor, the whole of the set is also in frame, bringing with it inexorably its philosophical dimension. This method of making use of the set in order to underpin the theme works well also in *Panto* (1986) where the Dame's life in Dressing Room Number One is more of a pantomime than that conducted on stage and where the stage is split in two between the locations.

Another aspect of *Y Tŵr* which made it particularly suitable for a theatre audience is the *tour de force* of the actors ageing in front of the audience. As the actors age, they are given a twenty-minute interval between each act in which to prepare themselves psychologically and physically for the next scene. When the audience of the New Theatre, Cardiff, (this play was once again an Eisteddfod Commission), saw John Ogwen and Maureen Rhys delighting in their physical youth in the First Act and then bent by sickness and old age in the Third Act, they witnessed a piece of theatre which was a showcase for the two actors' skills. They also witnessed a theatre of the emotion; there is no significant abstruse philosophical point in *Y Tŵr*; the meaning is in the journey, in the whole process of living.

OLD WOMAN: (*Dreamily*) It's all gone so fast . . .
OLD MAN: Slipping through one's fingers.
OLD WOMAN: (*After a long pause.*) It was us, wasn't it?
OLD MAN: What?
OLD WOMAN: It was us who came into this room one summer's day?
OLD MAN: (*Smiling*) It was us.
OLD WOMAN: (*Smiling*) We had such fun.

What makes this scene especially poignant is that the author uses our memory of the Second Act; *we* understand that the old woman's final assertion is only partially true, even if she has forgotten.

The increase in theatricality in the works of Huw Lloyd Edwards, Gwenlyn Parry and later in the works of younger playwrights such as Michael Povey (1950–) and Siôn Eirian (1954–), may be partly due to the professionalization of theatre during this period. The years from 1970 onwards were years of great activity in Wales in terms of building new theatres in conjunction with the expanding University Colleges or in partnership with local authorities. Theatr y Werin, Aberystwyth; Theatr Gwynedd, Bangor; Theatr Taliesin, Swansea and the Sherman Theatre, Cardiff opened their doors as part of the campus of the constituent colleges of the University of Wales. Theatr Clwyd in Mold, opened in conjunction with the new and ambitious local authority of Clwyd, following the first local government reorganization in the early 1970s. Some of these theatres were to have resident companies; all had a well-equipped medium-sized theatre with professional lighting and sound operators. Welsh-language theatre had taken immense professional steps since 1965 when Cwmni Theatr Cymru established itself under its director Wilbert Lloyd Roberts. Actors such as John Ogwen and Maureen Rhys, who played *Y Tŵr* so magnificently to a packed Eisteddfod audience in the New Theatre, Cardiff in 1979, had entered the company after graduating in Bangor. For the first time, one saw actors who could spend their entire lives within the profession and make a decent livelihood. There is no doubt in my mind that the playwrights' increasing tendency to use a visual theatrical language owes much to the professionalization of lighting, sound and acting in Welsh theatres.

Our final snapshot is that of two companies, Bara Caws and Brith Gof, who challenged the literary and theatrical assumptions of the 1960s and1970s. At a time when Welsh theatre had increased its professionalism and had developed a literary style which made use of highly developed acting and staging techniques, two particular developments challenged the theatre's whole development. The first, undoubtedly, was the growth of Welsh-language television. BBC Wales throughout the 1970s had developed a high profile drama department, headed by John Hefin with Gwenlyn Parry and Rhydderch Jones (1935–87) as script editors. From this stable emerged memorable single plays, situation comedy such as *Fo a Fe* written by the two playwrights, the first long-running soap, *Pobl y Cwm*, and adaptations (including Daniel Owen once again!). When S4C came on air in November 1982, after a period of considerable political activity and direct action, it was to swallow many talents in providing a minimum of three hours a day of Welsh-language programming. Budding script-writers opted to write for *Pobl y Cwm*; some became involved with a major series: eminent novelists such as Eigra Lewis Roberts and later Wiliam Owen Roberts became fascinated by this opportunity to gain a wider audience. However cynical we may be about authors and mortgages and making ends meet, there were many who wanted the channel to be a success and who were genuinely excited by the autonomy and the airtime. There is no doubt that all this put a severe strain on Welsh theatre. In a population of half a million Welsh-speakers, it is very difficult to find the expertise to maintain an active theatre culture and a television channel.

Fortunately, some writers such as Michael Povey, R. Gerallt Jones and Siôn Eirian still wanted to test their skills against a live audience. They were also concerned to get an audience for a more serious and difficult drama. Michael Povey, who joined Wilbert Lloyd Roberts's company as a very young dramaturge, became a prolific writer as well as a popular actor. His S4C play *Sul y Blodau* (Palm Sunday), remains in my mind the most interesting and significant use of bilingualism within a Welsh play. Despite this, he has reserved his more challenging pieces on attitudes towards outsiders, including those with disabilities or homosexual tendencies, for the theatre. Similarly, Siôn Eirian, who has written a popular urban and sophisticated detective series, *Bowen a'i Bartner* for S4C, reserved his truly challenging work for the theatre. In his his early play *Wastad ar y Tu Fas* (Always on the Outside), which dealt with homosexuality, and in his later *Epa yn y Parlwr* (Ape in the Parlour), which dealt sympathetically with prostitution, there has been a constant desire to shock the audience, to alert it to another side of Welsh culture which it might choose to ignore. Siôn Eirian, who was one of the youngest poets ever to win the National Eisteddfod Crown for non-strict-metre verse, commands his audience through a righteous passion delivered scathingly, originally, and sometimes lyrically.

Individual authors seem to gain a livelihood through television whilst reserving their more experimental or challenging work for the theatre. Or to put it another way, they may well be finding it difficult to deliver the challenging work on screen. Behind S4C's creation was the notion that it had been born as a middle-range, broadly popular channel appealing to many social classes. Its placement on Channel 4 was an accident of history in that it did not share the same philosophical remit; to provide a middle-of-the-road-channel for a linguistic minority is certainly not the same as providing a challenging channel for a minority audience. The only thing the two television companies had in common was the widely diverging use of the word 'minority'. Thus, as far as Welsh-language television was concerned, the more challenging and experimental work still needed a theatre audience.

If we find this latter period in the theatre, however, somewhat devoid of major individual literary figures, the reasons may lie beyond the emergence of S4C. The other factor at work in the death of the individual author on the Welsh stage was the emergence of the idea of the theatre co-operative. John McGrath's company, 7:84, in Scotland had already shown how powerful drama could be in communities normally excluded from elitist theatre. In his Cambridge Lectures under the aegis of Professor Raymond Williams, subsequently published in the volume *A Good Night Out*, McGrath was to define what a working-class audience might appreciate: shorter scenes interspersed with song and stand-up which did not make the sort of demands of concentration of the 2½-hour Ibsenite play, a live performance which tackled a club-like atmosphere in which people downed their pints—and watched intermittently a subject-matter which was relevant to the life of the community. In common with the radical, left-wing thrust of this particular methodology, the co-operative judged that they should have no star performers, no one writer or director; they were co-operatives both financially in sharing profits and artistically in sharing the philosophical and stylistic responsibility. It is this philosophy that imbues the first performance of *Bargen* (1979) by Theatr Bara Caws (Bread and Cheese Theatre). Ironically, just as Welsh theatre had reached a point of satisfactory professionalism, there were many younger actors who believed that the campus theatres were too elitist: they catered for an educated minority; they were run by an establishment mentality in cahoots with the Arts Council; their plays did not reflect the real concerns of the community. Bara Caws was to change all that. Here was a group of actors who had come up through the ranks of Cwmni Theatr Cymru, people like Dyfan Roberts and Valmai Jones, who felt uncomfortable when trying to present a performance of Oedipos Rex to the people of Gwynedd. Bara Caws was to tour small villages; it charged a specific sum; if the local management made a profit that went towards the maintenance of the village hall, so much the better. Their theatre was direct, simple and highly charged.

Bargen (1979) relates the story of the lock-out from the Penrhyn quarries in 1900 when 2,800 men walked out of the quarry in response to the high-handed and intransigent management methods of the second Lord Penrhyn, George Sholto Douglas Pennant (1836–1927). In 1899, a year before the strike his wealth was £133,000 per annum from the quarries and an equal amount from rents. Together with the Assheton Smiths, he owned half the slate industry of Gwynedd and one quarter of the land of Caernarfonshire. The quarryman's wage was at worst, £1 a week and at best £2 a week. The difference between these two figures was made up by the ability to negotiate a good piece of slate. This bargaining procedure was called the *bargen*, the bargain. This negotiation gave the quarryman a degree of autonomy relating to a self-employed status. If he chose to work his bargain flat-out, his profits would increase; if he wished to take a day off to take care of his few acres, his profits would diminish. But he retained his autonomy and self-respect. Douglas Pennant's contribution, together with his new manager, Young, was to force factory working conditions on these men so as to improve general productivity; as such they tried to destroy the 'bargain'. The strike held despite the poverty and the real suffering: one thousand men did not return until November 1903 despite incredible hardship; another thousand never returned having made their way to

America or the coal-pits of south Wales. The strike had been damaging even to the industrialists in that the Penrhyn quarry never regained its capacity after the strike.

Bara Caws is the heir to a long line of *agit-prop* theatre in that it caricatures the opposition. This is its description of Lord Penrhyn:

> LORD PENRHYN: I won't stand for it, I tell you. Damn it! I will not be dictated to in my own quarry. I will not! My father was too soft with them. The old boy, my grandfather, was the one who knew how to deal with them. He had the niggers eating out of his hand.
> LADY PENRHYN: How very unhygienic!
> LORD PENRHYN: Quiet! I tell you he was right to rule them with an iron hand—that Robert Parry and the rest of his unholy rabble. And they call themselves Christians! Don't they know that to go against the master is a sin against God? Rights, indeed! Rights! I'll give them rights. My father was a fool, a cretin, a madman to put up with the so-called Pennant Lloyd Agreements. Why should I put up with it? Why should I? Gertrude, let's abolish it!
> LADY PENRHYN: What dear?
> LORD PENRHYN: Gertrude! Come along!
> LADY PENRHYN: Where are we going, dear?
> LORD PENRHYN: Bed!
> LADY PENRHYN: Oh dear!

Alongside the caricature, there are also highly charged moments when the result of the poverty and the lock-out impinge upon the individual family. Having been brought up in the quarrying valleys of north Wales, I remember sitting in the audience, hearing the lines of *agit-prop* theatre, knowing that I was being deliberately manipulated, and still being moved by the sufferings of grandparent and parent. Such is the strength of community theatre at its best:

> WILLIAM: (*Reading his letter home*):
>
> My Dearest Wife,
>
> I have decided to begin every letter to you from now on with this: My Dearest Wife. You cannot conceive how wonderful it is for me to think about you: wife, mother, children—my family. I miss you so much at times that I want to forget that I ever had a family. Do you know something? I talk so much about you to the boys down the pit that they've all taken to calling me William 'Lovely-family-up-North'.

Bara Caws is the precursor of many companies which have retained their popularity: Theatr Gorllewin Morgannwg still has a strong following; Arad Goch has specialized more of late in young people's theatre; Fran Wen, Harlech, does Theatre in Education work; Outreach in Clwyd and Theatr Iolo in Glamorgan all subscribe to the idea of the devised play and the co-operative. Within this context, Brith Gof (Scattered Memories) has subscribed to the co-operative ethic but not to the ethos of the easily understood, *agit-prop* theatre. Instead, it has tried to revitalize pieces of history and myth, lying underneath the surface of remembrance in Wales. It has done so through the use of images and body language linking it more to the Poor Theatre of Grotowsky than to community theatre as theatre-in-education. There are some theatrical images which are vividly present; I remember being present at the performance of *Branwen* in Harlech. The occasion marked the coming to Wales of the Celtic Film and Television Festival and the fact that Wales was soon to come on air with its own television channel. It is perhaps ironic that this final apotheosis of physical poor theatre was to happen on the eve of the Channel's emergence. As the evening drew in within the castle walls in Harlech in late March, some of the students from my own department at Aberystwyth (students who had pioneered the use of physical imagery instead of declamation under the guidance of the late inspired teacher Emily Davies) joined with Brith Gof in an evocation of the story of Branwen. A table became a stage, a couple of upturned chairs the boat; the imagination reigned supreme. Underlying it all was the knowledge that, in the Mabinogi, this spot was the one from which Bendigeidfran looked over the seas to Ireland. Suddenly, the centuries fused just as the name of the company (Scattered Memories) intended. There was a similar occurrence with *Guernica* in the National Eisteddfod in 1984 when Brith Gof joined with Emily Davies, who had become the director of Cwmni Theatr Cymru. Slowly Picasso's portrayal of physical anguish during the Spanish Civil War came alive before our eyes as the company portrayed the physical stances of that familiar and challenging canvas.

I am still uncertain whether it was this night that triggered the thought that the company could tackle the futility of war on a grander scale. Mike Pearson, who directed the company with Lis Hughes Jones, became convinced that the company should move to large-scale events. He took for this theme Goya's *Images of War* and sought to portray issues of war and peace on a European level, even within the cathedrals of Cologne and Dresden. *Gododdin*, the portrayal of the men of Catraeth who went to battle in the sixth century, moved to Glasgow and met a rapturous response. More than a decade after *Branwen*, a much larger concept, *Pax*, visited St David's Hall Cardiff and took over the old Victorian station building in Aberystwyth. Angels fell from the sky suspended midway, whilst the forces of oppression sought to flay them with fire and water. As in all highly charged performance art, there is sometimes the feeling that the actors have become too engrossed within their own performance to acknowledge the audience; as such, there comes a very fine dividing line between the spectator and the voyeur who looks on the enjoyment of anguish. As the work moved out of the delicate, subtle performance, Lis Hughes Jones left the company and Mike Pearson gained undoubted success internationally with his broader, more Artaud-like canvases. The work since has been tremendously physically challenging; it has also been artistically challenging to various Eisteddfod-attenders who have come round the corner to meet a theatre artist suspended mid-air, providing his or her own physical images.

There is no doubt that Brith Gof's imagery sets up reverberations underneath the threshold of the mind. Unfortunately, however, the area underneath the conscious mind belongs to imagery and not to language. The more imagistic Welsh theatre becomes, the more one wishes to praise it for extending its international significance, for providing a European and all-encompassing passage into the shared complexities of life. It is also possible to appreciate this theatre without understanding Welsh and without having any form of developed literary script at the end. Is it possible that the apotheosis of Welsh theatre is to find a theatre language that does not need Welsh?

Four snapshots, four periods. Yet, in all these different years, voices from other eras persist, complicating the issue. In a hitherto unpublished Ph.D. study, Roger Owen has argued that all voices coexist and overlap and that is undoubtedly the case. Despite this, I have tried to show that there are certain periods in which particular theatre languages emerge and become dominant. Welsh theatre has lived through naturalism into classicism; through the absurd into a shared community theatre; through community theatre into an abstract image. Standing at the crossroads of the millenium, I find myself more than usually uncertain of the path ahead. One can only hope that Welsh theatre will have the energy to reproduce itself in different creative forms. There are positive signals; as television moves into a digital age where more hours are required to satisfy more channels and more airtime, the domestic audience may well find that it has to turn to theatre once again to escape from the wallpaper effect already experienced in most radio. Drama in Wales has, in the past, sloughed off outdated styles and attitudes and adopted others, often at the frontier of that style's adoption in Europe. One can only hope that it will continue to do so. So far, for a small country working against the odds, the theatrical track record has been a remarkable affirmation of the will to live.

Note: The translation of *Blodeuweddd* is by Gwyn Thomas and the translation of *Siwan* by Emyr Humphreys; both translations are published in *Presenting Saunders Lewis.* All other translations from the original are by the author of this chapter.

FURTHER READING

Selected texts

D. T. Davies, *Ephraim Harris* (Caerdydd, 1914).
Kitchener Davies, *Cwm Glo*, adapted by Manon Rhys (Cymdeithas Ddrama Cymru, 1994).
Mair I. Davies (ed.), *Kitchener Davies* (Llandysul, 1985).
Siôn Eirian, *Bob yn y Ddinas* (Llandysul, 1979).
Idem, *Epa yn y Parlwr Cefn* (Dalier Sylw: Aberystwyth: Y Ganolfan Astudiaethau Addysg, 1995).
Beriah Gwynfe Evans, *Glyndwr: Tywysog Cymru* (Caernarfon, 1911).
J. O. Francis, *Change* (London, 1913).
Idem, *Cross Currents* (Cardiff, 1923).
W. J. Gruffydd, *Beddau'r Proffwydi* (Caerdydd, 1913).
Albert Evans Jones (Cynan), *Absalom fy mab* (Lerpwl, 1957).
Idem, *Hen ŵr y Mynydd* (Llandybie, 1949).
Idem, *Hywel Harris* (Wrexham, 1932).
Idwal Jones, *Pobl yr Ymylon* (Abertawe, 1927).
John Gwilym Jones, *Lle Mynno'r gwynt*, In *Lle mynno'r gwynt a gŵr llonydd* (Dinbych, 1957).

Idem, *Y Tad a'r Mab* (Aberystwyth, 1963).

Idem, *Ac Eto Nid Myfi* (Dinbych, 1976).

Thomas Gwynn Jones, *Dafydd ap Gruffydd* (Aberystwyth, 1914).

Idem, *Y Gloyn Byw* (Newtown).

Idem, *Anrhydedd* (Caerdydd, 1923).

Saunders Lewis, *Gymerwch chi Sigarèt?* (Llandybïe, 1956).

Idem, '*Siwan*', in *Siwan a Cherddi Eraill* (Llandybïe, 1955).

Idem, '*Esther*' in *Esther a Serch yw'r Doctor* (Llandybïe, 1960).

Idem, *Cymru Fydd* (Llandybïe, 1967).

Idem, *The Plays of Saunders Lewis*, translated from the Welsh by Joseph P. Clancy, Vol. 1–3, (Llandybïe, Christopher Davies, 1985–86). (Siwan is translated as The King of England's Daughter in Volume One).

Gwenlyn Parry, *Saer Doliau* (Llandybïe, 1966).

Idem, *Y Ffin* (Llandybïe, 1975).

Idem, *Y Tŵr*, (Llandysul, 1976).

Idem, *Panto* (Llandysul, 1992).

Meic Povey, *Perthyn* (Llanrwst, 1995).

Theatr Bara Caws, *Bargen* (Llanrwst, 1995).

Peter Williams, (Pedr Hir), *Owain Gwynedd*, Published in Cyfnodolion a Chyfansoddiadau Eisteddfod Genedlaethol 1912: Wrexham Cymdeithas yr Eisteddfod Genedlaethol, 1912.

Idem, *Owain Glyndwr* (Caernarfon, 1915).

Background

Geraint Bowen (ed.), *Y Traddodiad Rhyddiaith yn yr Ugeinfed Ganrif* (Llandysul, 1970).

Hazel Walford Davies, *Saunders Lewis a Theatr Garthewin* (Llandysul, 1995).

Elsbeth Evans, *Y Ddrama yng Nghymru* (Lerpwl, 1947).

Bruce Griffiths, *Saunders Lewis* (Cardiff, 1979).

Alun R. Jones, and Gwyn Thomas (eds), *Presenting Saunders Lewis* (Cardiff, 1973).

R. M. Jones, *Llenyddiaeth Gymraeg 1936–1972* (Llandybie, 1975).

Owain Llew Owain, *Hanes y Ddrama yng Nghymru 1850–1943* (Lerpwl, 1948).

Thomas Parry, *Hanes Llenyddiaeth Gymraeg* (Caerdydd, 1953).

Dewi Z. Phillips, *Dramâu Gwenlyn Parry* (Caernarfon, 1982).

John Rowlands, *John Gwilym Jones* (Caernarfon, 1988).

Charmian Savill Rabey, *A Critical Study of the History of the Welsh Theatre Company Brith Gof*. Unpublished M.A. Thesis deposited in the National Library of Wales, Aberystwyth.

Elan Closs Stephens, *Y Canol Llonydd, Darlith ar Ddramâu John Gwilym Jones* (Cymdeithas Theatr Cymru, 1988).

Meic Stephens, *The Arts in Wales 1950–1975* (Cardiff, 1979).

Idem, *Y Celfyddydau yng Nghymru 1950–1975* (Caerdydd, 1979).

Idem, *The Oxford Companion to the Literature of Wales* (Oxford, 1986).

Idem, *Cydymaith i Lenyddiaeth Cymru* (Caerdydd, 1986; 1997).

Gwyn Thomas, *Cyfrol Deyrnged John Gwilym Jones* (Abertawe, 1974).

Ioan M. Williams, *Kitchener Davies* (Caernarfon, 1984).

Idem, *A Straitened Stage: A Study of the Theatre of J. Saunders Lewis* (Bridgend, 1991).

Idem, *Dramâu Saunders Lewis: Y Casgliad Cyflawn*, Vol. 1, (Caerdydd, 1996).

In addition, the series *Bro a Bywyd,* published by the Arts Council of Wales, contains a selection of photographs and memorabilia on the life and works of several playwrights. Included in the series so far are volumes on *Albert Evans-Jones (Cynan)*, *John Gwilym Jones* and *Saunders Lewis*.

CHAPTER 9

THE PRESENT SITUATION

R. M. JONES

Welsh literature today seems to be tackling the contemporary situation at a tangent.

Those older writers still active are perhaps more helpful than the younger in trying to define exactly what that tangent is. Perhaps the older writers are not so susceptible to emulation as their younger counterparts. Talent-spotting amongst the younger generation, though necessary and exciting, is often unrewarding, and the propensity for the new generation to search for their own voices can retard the realization of where exactly they intend to go. Surveys of the contemporary situation have ever been notoriously littered with corpses of undeveloped capacity. Surmising potential on the basis of a first work, or even sometimes of a second, is about as rewarding as an assessment of the eventual life-achievement of a person on the evidence of a successful birth. Such failures of judgement from the past, at least for the present, encourage hesitancy.

To a great extent, with the perennial and journalistic emphasis on new writers, the history of the last fifty years in Welsh literature has been the history of a struggle to maintain adulthood. This struggle is the only proper context to perceive what real successes— and there have been some major ones—have resulted. Such a struggle has not been without its failures. This has been as true in verse as in prose fiction, though in both fields we have witnessed some—more than a few—notable conquests. In drama, however, post-Saunders Lewis, we have confronted a slight disintegration followed by a more precipitous one, while fiction and verse have somehow achieved greater consistency in their accomplishment because of the firmer tradition.

Where one does however discover success and with it a vital 'radicalism', it has been somewhat different from the mainstream in more politically powerful European literatures, and has often expressed itself through a consternating Welshness. The more conventional 'radicalism' that often goes by that name is by now, in Wales as elsewhere, usually pretty imitative, the direct contradiction of what radicalism has to be. In such cases, what is usually lacking has been catholicity and intelligence. Now, at the end of the century, the old-fashioned *avant-garde* palls pretty well everywhere, within and without Wales, and tends to become mannerized. Fortunately, in both verse and prose fiction, one frequently encounters in Welsh a preparedness not simply to 'experiment' in the well-worn *avant-garde* manner, but in a way that gets to grips with the contemporary situation in a definite environment, not simply to submit to it, but to wrestle with it, and utilize in its perception an acquaintance with the best of international literature, particularly the relevant European trad- ition which may induce maturation in a fully civilized sense both intellectually and emotionally.

Journalistic attempts at directing literature in Wales towards immediate public acclaim must still be watched warily. Fortunately, the populist oppression within a minority culture, lacking in seriousness, and not really interested in literature at all, has been occasionally punctured by some stubborn artistic talents: Dewi Stephen Jones, Alan Llwyd, Gwyneth Lewis, Emyr Lewis, Twm Morys, Iwan Llwyd, Gareth Alban Davies, Bryan Martin Davies, and the all-too-reticent talents of Elin ap Hywel and Gerwyn Wiliams, these are all poets who have refused the easy path of lazy form and superficial content. In prose fiction the recent quartet of Robin Llywelyn, Wiliam Owen Roberts, Angharad Tomos and Mihangel Morgan, with other shyer but mature talents such as John Emyr and Dafydd Ifans in the background, together with more well-established writers, have provided a firm platform for future development.

Making one interpretation of the present situation in Welsh (particularly for the last ten years), perhaps the most newsworthy items in our literature would seem to present embarrassing similarity to the 'excitement' in the rest of Europe. In criticism, Derridian disciples together with feminists hold sway; lively novelists attempt new territory in magic realism, the unreliable narrator, aporia and intertextuality; while 'new' poets and dramatists often resemble the older ones to a worrying extent.

It is inevitable in a literature positioned as Welsh is, that when post-modernism, feminism, the irony 'boom', ambiguity, absurdism, nihilism and so on eventually reached it in full strength, a great deal of them seemed already shop-soiled and pedestrian. Some of these fashions were curiously inappropriate anyhow in the context of a Welsh nation perpetually in 'terminal' crisis; but there are always susceptible writers in Wales who will long to emulate a big neighbour. There are some refreshing and stimulating exceptions, radical from the roots. Perhaps run-of-the-mill 'radicals' are even more prone to the predictable nowadays (at least to the external observer) than are the more-rooted writers, whose work is more soaked in Welshness, both Welshness of *engagement* and in native formalism—a potent combination that lends originality to the 'traditionalists' not often found amongst the conforming 'radicals'.

In England, certain authorities have recently announced that irony is 'out', 'decadent' and parasitic: ambiguity is at last a bore. In Wales, the dogmas of irony and ambiguity have been suspect for some years for other reasons, not simply as *passé*; indeed, as literary devices (amongst the same timeless resources as metaphor) they were defended by critics who denigrated them as dogma. They were repudiated when they flaunted themselves as inevitable. This was a country where to survive demanded a basic affirmation. Values of commitment, warmth, purpose, universal truths, meaning and even sincere emotion gained a new toughness and could be accepted without a smirk, side by side with a critical sophistication regarding the irony overplay.

The reason for this is not far to seek. It is still painfully difficult in some quarters in Wales to avoid the infection of enthusiastic positivity. The language movement itself is often pervaded with a delightfully unacceptable zest. Sometimes, a visit to Nant Gwrtheyrn or the social warmth of a CYD group can be inspiring. Wales, or at least certain key sectors of Welsh life, can be still irritatingly dynamic. And in the rather cynical and jaded context of post-modernist Europe, it is as if the presence of this language and its appendages has become an anachronistic protest against the insistence on decadence. This rebellious delight in renewal spills over into literature itself. It is in a way an original response to the conventional modernism found amongst more populous literatures.

The present, for the conscious Welsh intellectual, is a vibrant time to be Welsh. Wherever one travels in Wales one feels the ambiguous itch of awakening. There has been an annoying revitalization of affection for things Welsh. Obviously the erstwhile inferiority complex, imperialist tendencies and animosity to the language still remain; but they seem merely to lend an extra tang to what is really going on.

There is certainly a familiar pattern to this revival. It bears a recognizable colonial structure and psychology, and is committed to renewal and restoration in a realistic but dynamic combination that refuses peripherality and decadence. This, were it simply purblind, would obviously narrow literary scope. It is easy for literature to feel satisfied with itself if it merely deals with the burning issues of the day, raises a fracas, puts cats amongst racial, sexual and political pigeons, all fine (if often cosy) journalistic aims, rather than veering towards intelligence and maturity, depth and artistic finish regarding the whole spectrum of human experience. It is easier to get on to the anti-American bandwagon for instance or use the 'jargon' of modernity than to put out feelers towards more profound problems. It is easier too to upset the battered remnants of nineteenth-century respectability than to develop the intellectual subtlety and integrity of a much-maligned civilization that still remains startlingly relevant and insists on affirmation even in the throes of powerful nihilism.

This has resulted in a tension of tone, meaning and energy between three not incompatible tendencies in Welsh literary life.

One group is convinced that it is involved in a joyful struggle, where success though vulnerable is not impossible, to rejuvenate Welsh vigour. For this group, perhaps the most significant secular factor that ties it to language and literature—apart from the more obvious ones encountered elsewhere—is the exciting experience of being in the middle of an original and creative renewal. The Welsh language remains a throbbing instrument, vibrant with suggestiveness, with an immense potential created by tradition, and resplendent with echoes for the future.

Parallel with that group is another more traditional group, more defeatist perhaps though equally and stubbornly involved in the national struggle. Very conservative as regards form, romantically nostalgic and decadent in content, this is rather an anti-intelligence group, betrothed to a narrow vision of what literature can do. The group, some of whom are—because of their inferiority complex—ostensibly anti-academic (though not actually so, as all we who read are academic to varying degrees), is dedicated to finesse and craftsmanship and above all simplicity, and has 'popularity' as its watchword.

The third, perhaps most obvious, group is that of the imitators. This is a gullible group that is anxious to be in the swim. They are somewhat dedicated to irony, nihilism and deconstruction. Rather neurotic about being trendy, they try to transplant American and particularly London fashions and temper into Welsh. Although there is a certain amount of adaptation of these tendencies, this group is not greatly concerned with working out any individual thought within the thrust of Welsh life, and is rather anxious not to be thought of as not knowing the right names or the latest technical terms.

At the end of the twentieth century, Welsh writers within these groups are unable to avoid a dichotomy. The polarity of resurrection and despair, revival and hopelessness, is inherent in the present struggle of identity, not just of Welsh identity, but of having any sort of identity as human beings left at all. In our post-nuclear and pollution-productive age we all ask looking at the smudge on the floor, 'Is that really us?'

For the erstwhile imperialist, irony has for some time been a boost towards the longed-for sophistication that emanates from indulgent class consciousness. With the collapse of Empire it acted also as an inner state of power and authority. Through it the fallen imperialist could attempt to compensate for the immense historical change in international status. To be ironic was the modern way of exaggerating self-esteem. It could keep us in the elite. It meant subtlety in making a class celebration. For the Welsh person on the other hand, conscious or unconscious resistance to irony as a state of being, a norm, a way of life, together with insistence on maintaining it as a device, was linked to the flourishing of the praise tradition. Praise, whether direct, or more significantly indirect, remained a safeguard against the class and imperialist dedication to one-upmanship that is inherent in irony as a state of being. Yet, it seems that, particularly after Saunders Lewis, to be critical of irony and a servant of praise was also more than a way of being non-English: it was a statement about life.

Driven into a corner, confronted by ultimate despair, praise for Welsh poets has always been a most effective weapon. Praise is also a realization of the compulsory presence of affirmation in all creativity. And in a colonialized situation, praise is simply a celebration of survival.

The English stiff upper lip and suspicion of passion that inhibit erstwhile imperialism do not correspond to parallel impediments in the Welsh praise tradition. Native Welsh praise is, of course, a classical discipline, though one that has become more and more passionate. When the Welsh themselves veer from this, the extra-artistic inhibition they formerly experienced from foreign superiority is hardly the main impediment now. Rather, it is the opposing refraction. The contemporary Welsh experience is nothing if it is not international, though not in the big-power sense. We have, up to the present, witnessed the worldwide imperialistic attempt to destroy peoples expeditiously and delete differences. Although the gentler, calmer annihilation of cultural diversity is not as sinister as the sudden physical extermination of a nation, the fact that it is more civilized and more hidden does not make results any the less effective. 'Extirpate' is the diverting term used in the Act of Union of England and Wales, and my dictionary explains this unambiguously as liquidate, however restrained and moderate may be its modern execution. The touchstone is the language. And the effective opposition to annihilation still remains praise.

While English writers were taken up, and rightly so, with the enfeeblement of moral issues, with the waning of hope, with 'liberal' ambiguity, with fragmentation of class and national identity and the ironic longing not to be pretentious in a rather flat intellectual backwater, and of course with sex, Welsh writers were challenging the seemingly incessantly rapid progress to extinction. The inner disintegration experienced in England was here somehow more advanced and had reached more complex and dramatic proportions. And the most important literary works in contemporary Wales are a penetrating expression of this basically universal experience. To be a Welsh-speaker therefore is to be thrust immediately into battle. To write the language is to bleed. Poetry faces the situation instinctively, as did Saunders Lewis in his drama; but fiction and drama nowadays may tag along occasionally with foreign norms.

As regards self-conscious sex as a major topic for literary consumption, Welsh has frequently avoided the cosmopolitan lead, finding a more critical stance in the praise tradition. We too, of course, have our evergreen adolescents. After the collapse (via

humanism) of Christian morality, the immaturity of an
undeveloped secular morality is of course ubiquitously apparent.
Siôn Eirian for instance admits honestly to the manse-syndrome,
although I suspect a more general decadence is often related
(indirectly of course, in Welsh) to commercial fashions. Just as
rational and liberal theology often for a long while seemed
somewhat undigested and adolescent at the beginning of the
century, so too the more recent immaturity of an uncultivated and
unseasoned amorality (taking the place of the wisdom of highly
developed and mature strengths, tried and tested by the rigours of
the centuries) takes some combating. The journalistic knee-jerk
attitude to accepting the 'latest', together with a failure to
discriminate, nurtured under the oppression of deconstruction, are
obviously present. Both are bolstered by a fear of not being
contemporary enough. Both result in a build-up of pressure that
may be resisted only by maturity, and intelligence somewhat scarce
in any period.

The wisdom of the past, however, received an unexpected boost
in the 1960s and 1970s, which has continued unabated to the
present, and that in the form of resurgence of *cynghanedd*. Perhaps,
hidden in this, and even more important, if unconscious, was the
revival of praise.

Verse has the strongest and most consistent of all traditions in
Welsh. Throughout the twentieth century, although the first
flowering between 1902 and 1919 was painfully old-fashioned and
Victorian, the quality and energy of verse-writing have been usually
the stable highlight in Welsh literature. The only exception perhaps
would be the 1950s when drama came to the fore. This was due to
the presence of a brilliant writer, Saunders Lewis, who was able to
branch out from the sophistication of the verse tradition, and with
a bright verbal imagination, a lively sense of form, a sharp intellect,
and moral energy, created the only body of dramatic writing in
Welsh since the eighteenth century that rises far above mere
competence.

Between the 1930s and the 1960s Welsh verse was settling down
nicely to the international norm in tone and form. The remarkable
revival of *cynghanedd* or strict-verse writing had been unexpected.
It is, of course, an unbroken tradition of great intricacy, stretching
back to early poetry. But the tightness of its requirements began to
lose some respect at the end of the last century because of the

dogmas of Romanticism. The rural poet or *bardd gwlad* still maintained these metres, as did some academics as sort of five-finger exercises, but the tone became predictable.

There have been three aspects to this recent vigorous revival. First of all Bois y Cilie, Dic Jones, and others among our rural poets, perhaps given some confidence by Waldo Williams, began to open up in an original and attractive way in the 1950s. Secondly, also in the same decade, Euros Bowen, casting off the stanzaic forms though retaining *cynghanedd*, brought a more intellectual vigour to the use of the tradition, particularly under the influence of imagism, symbolism and surrealism. He was followed by poets like Gwynne Williams (under the influence of Vasko Popa and Christian Morgenstern) and more recently Dewi Stephen Jones. Thirdly, a group of extremely able young poets in the 1970s and 1980s, led by Alan Llwyd, but including that renowned pair of *cynghanedd* magicians, Donald Evans and Gerallt Lloyd Owen, Arfon Williams the prince of *englynion* writers, Peredur Lynch, Gwynn ap Gwilym, Elwyn Edwards, Myrddin ap Dafydd, Twm Morys, Emyr Davies, and Emyr Lewis. Some of these brought *cynghanedd* up to date in their confrontation with modern civilization, and the volumes of *Cywyddau Cyhoeddus* are witness to the fun and public significance of this energy: they were the 'against the grain' poets, not simply with their diction, jargon and terminology but with the emotional throes of the period.

No survey of contemporary literature can ignore the flourishing of *cynghanedd* at the present time. There is always in *cynghanedd* a danger of gravitating back to antediluvian habits and mere conventional mechanics. Many of its practitioners are devoid of even a superficial background in contemporary European literature. But its roots in locality and the real world, its careful craftsmanship, and its closeness to the concrete occasionality of praise, when combined with sharp wit and bright imagination have a permanent contribution to make to the future of Welsh verse. The foremost exponent of *cynghanedd* is indisputably Alan Llwyd. While he and a handful of others, along with *cynghanedd* and the versatility of their traditional bases, also know about Amichai and Holub, Popa and Celan, Quasimodo and Ekelof, the vitality of the craft will remain.

Alan Llwyd has been somewhat of a *bête noire* to one sort of critic in Wales, particularly to such as is enamoured with the

mediocre. He was admittedly in his early period susceptible to neo-
Georgianism and to the pre-modernist and popular perception of
verse; but when we look at his solid achievement, when we consider
the sheer mastery of his medium in such a substantial and diverse
productivity, exemplified in such poems as 'Y Sgrech' (The
Scream), 'Llofruddiaeth' (Murder), 'Merlod mewn storm' (Ponies
in a Storm), 'Yr hebog uwch Felindre' (The hawk above Felindre),
'Gyrrwr ambiwlans' (Ambulance-driver), 'Cymro di-wlad' (The
Welshman without a country), he leaves well behind the Welsh
tendencies to play down to the populace. I would contend that of
the three periods of development in this century's literature,
1902–36, 1936–72, and 1972 to the present, J. Morris-Jones seems
clearly the domineering figure in the first, Saunders Lewis in the
second, and I can see no other figure more central or significant
than Alan Llwyd for the third. As regards the intrinsic value of his
verse and prose, he is not the least of these three substantial figures.
His achievement as editor and critic has been considerable,
although his main right to consideration remains firmly in his
magnificent verse, in particular *Cerddi Alan Llwyd 1968–1990*
(Collected Poems); and fortunately the song continues. His main
critical achievement has been in *Barddoniaeth Euros Bowen* (The
Poetry of Euros Bowen, 1977), *Barddoniaeth y Chwedegau* (The
Poetry of the 1960s, 1986) and the biography *Gwae fi fy myw* of
Hedd Wyn in 1991; but a number of other studies—*Gwyn Thomas*
(1983), *R. Williams Parry* (1984) and his work on Dafydd ap
Gwilym (1980) reveal a critic of great sensitivity. I have scarcely
mentioned half of his original criticism; and his biography of
Goronwy Owen is widely and warmly anticipated. But his
editorship is perhaps what has made him a binding influence and a
sustaining inspiration to his contemporaries, both through the
monthly journal *Barddas*, and through innumerable anthologies
such as *Y Flodeugerdd Englynion* (1978), *Llywelyn y Beirdd* (1984),
Barddoniaeth Gymraeg yr 20fed Ganrif (with Gwynn ap Gwilym,
1987), *Y Flodeugerdd o Ddyfyniadau Cymraeg* (1988), *Gwaedd y
Bechgyn* (1989), and here again I have not mentioned half. Then, if
I were to review his activities as manager of a publishing company
and his organization of a series such as 'Blodeugerddi y
Canrifoedd' (Anthologies of the Centuries), besides his renowned
work in film, I would perhaps just begin to arrive within striking
distance of a catalogue of his activities. If I were asked to

summarize Alan Llwyd's contribution to Welsh literary thinking, I
would say that, at the moment (apart from his aural richness), more
than any other person writing creatively in Welsh, he has
maintained 'Welshness'. He has the greatest hold on the tradition
as a contemporary force of all our writers, and he, more than any
other creative writer of our day, has wrestled with our nationhood.
He has brought professional energy and a highly developed sense of
form and community into everything he writes. As long as he
remains in his present position, and retains his morale (a difficult
task in a country such as Wales racked with jealousy), there will
remain a basic foundation for adapting the living tradition to
modern exigencies.

The renaissance of *cynghanedd* writing in the 1960s, and its
continued flourishing, is an undoubted point of great significance.
Cynghanedd is a beautiful system of verse-craftsmanship
developed—much to the chagrin of some—in the Middle Ages, and
its recent renaissance was due to the national upsurge of the 1960s
combined with the sheer fun of the craft, and a discovery of this
heritage by a number of young talented 'men'. But the pressure is
on, amongst poets as amongst prose-writers, more so in *cynghanedd*
verse than in the more international style, to keep the content of
writing as superficial as possible. After all, the form is difficult
enough. The powerful infantile adult lobby has brought more
pressure in this sector than elsewhere (apart perhaps from prose),
and has had marked success. Besides certain independently minded
individuals like Dewi Stephen Jones, Alan Llwyd and Emyr Lewis,
cynghanedd-writing has often conformed to the demand to remain
intellectually thin. And with that it may eventually forfeit some of
the hopes of becoming centrally influential in forming a
contemporary literature. It is a pity that Emyr Lewis won his first
National chair with one of his less powerful works; but I believe
that is one of the conditions of the competition.

Nevertheless, it seems during the last fifteen years that the
cynganeddwyr have been playing almost an *avant-garde* role. Their
revival coincided with the upsurge of Cymdeithas yr Iaith; and they
consider *cynghanedd* as a sort of language. 'Cynghanedd,' said Alan
Llwyd, 'is like the language itself: it is stubborn, determined to survive
and adapts itself to every age. In this lies its strength: in its flexibility.
It is chameleon: it can change its colour and nature and form as the
need arises.' The radicals of the 1950s seemed to take its demise for

granted: it was accounted 'traditional', 'conservative' and 'lifeless'. And then it surged back. Nowadays, the tone of some 'radicals' is precious and *passé*, and their attitudes and artistic presuppositions painfully predictable, while *cynghanedd* continues to astonish.

The taste for Georgianism took a long time to dissipate itself in Welsh and continued, amongst the older and more sheltered generation, well on into the 1980s. It consisted in a narrow response to a certain sort of mellifluous melody represented by the early Williams Parry, an easy music combined with romantic buzz-words and sharp aphorisms, and an inability to respond to a variety of subjects and a diversity of forms. Before experiencing a significant general change, we had to wait for a new generation whose taste was probably just as narrow but more related to 'political correctness' amongst the 'radicals', and to contemporary topics and journalistic problems amongst the strict-verse practitioners. The real sympathy for a more intelligent and adult taste was however established as a result of the fact that acceptable neo-Georgians such as Waldo Williams had cast off their youthful bad habits, and carried some of their audience with them into more relevant involvement.

We can style the *cynghanedd* revival as the 'new traditional'. The real weakness of this new traditional is that it occasionally imitates the same register and tone as the old traditional and that it relies too often—except in the case of certain poets such as Alan Llwyd, Dewi Stephen Jones and Emyr Lewis—on a minimum of thought and a narrow background in literature. The subject is admittedly nowadays more committed than formerly. The feelings and social content are more intense, but the tune too often can be the same. We have all too often been here before.

The perennial national crisis, however, often enters the stage as a rescuing knight. Welsh verse compared with English has, from its beginnings in the sixth century, been more political and socially involved, a situation not quite artistic 'cricket' in the sheltered English context. The community it writes for, and often about, has always been in danger of utter and seemingly irreversible extinction. The religious consciousness (may one mention it?) has always been much more centrally significant than is considered critically proper in England. And a very conscious concept of general praise, with all its affirmative attributes, even during times of dogmatic irony and absurdity, nihilism and deconstruction, has remained unrespectably virulent.

The other tradition, parallel with *cynghanedd* throughout the centuries, has been free-verse writing, more compatible with international taste, and this since 1936 has become more intellectually demanding. There are six or seven comparatively young poets amongst a host of practitioners who take their craft seriously. They belong to a line that can already boast the continuing originality, urbanity and artistic finesse of Gwyn Thomas, R. Gerallt Jones, Gareth Alban Davies, and Bryan Martin Davies. It is still difficult to prophesy regarding the achievement, though not of the promise, of Iwan Llwyd and Gerwyn Wiliams. Iwan Llwyd has combined a serious muse with pub-songs and successful illustrative tours of the United States for television. But quite apart from this important venture into popularization, he is the most committed to his craft of his generation. Gerwyn Wiliams too has clear and professional potential. 'Hel mwyar duon' reminds one of Heaney's 'Blackberry picking'; and he belongs to the same milieu. Menna Elfyn is much more than the token feminist, although she has been through a thin patch due to being taken advantage of for performance verse. Some of Mihangel Morgan's poems in *Diflaniad fy fi* (Disappearance of my me, 1988) and *Beth yw rhif ffôn Duw* (What is God's telephone number, 1991) remind one of the delightfully wild fancy of the young Gwyn Thomas— 'Ymddiddan' (Conversation), 'Y Ddinas fel Cath—y Fi fel Llygoden' (The City like a Cat—Me like a Mouse), 'Gormod o Egni' (Too Much Energy), and 'Gwyn ap Nudd' in the second volume. I hesitate to prophesy partly because of the fact that the most startling newcomer of the 1990s has been a man in his fifties, writing in seclusion in Ponciau, namely Dewi Stephen Jones, whose slight volume *Hen Ddawns* (Old Dance) is, for me, the book of the decade. He is a poet who reminds me somewhat of Mandelstam, possessing some of his tendencies in creating narrative. Beautifully crafted, sharply imaginative, with freshness of vision and an abundance of spontaneous bubbling life, 'Hen Ddawns' demonstrates Welsh poetry at its highest level. It would have thrilled Saunders Lewis and Waldo Williams. The response to it, however, has been sadly predictable. Gareth Alban Davies, of the older generation, spotted with amazement the marked genius of this writing. But on the whole, his poems have been received with something of the vacant indifference of a people less and less prepared to take poetry seriously. A crowned poet of the younger generation, humbly admitting to being 'old-fashioned', was completely unable to 'rise' to the occasion, and reviewed the volume with a typically blank but stubbornly proud incomprehension. He is inevitably symptomatic. His fellows would now fill the stadium. This is just not simply a lazy intelligence, lack of training in musical imagery, nor just a lack of catholicity of taste narrowing response to the most simple works: it is sheer inability to 'rise' to the occasion, when faced by the extraordinary and exceptional.

A highly sophisticated example of more acceptable 'childhood' writing on the other hand has been the work of Einir Jones. She has adopted the child stance, but done so with subtle maturity—short lines, limited diction, a light lilt, a minimum of content, but accompanied by a well-developed realization of her craft. In a number of remarkable if slim volumes she has developed her own voice, direct, shining, lyrical, and now is one of our most individualistic poets. She is the mature child and stands at the other end of the spectrum from Dewi Stephen Jones, an equally individualistic voice. He is intellectually solid, complex, completely adult: not popular with those who have read no poetry since leaving school. One is tempted in contrasting Dewi Stephen Jones and Einir Jones to fall back on the age-old stereotype—the emotional and non-intellectual female on the one hand and the cerebral and intellectually challenging male on the other. Women writers like the exceedingly gifted pair, Elin Ap Hywel and Gwyneth Lewis, however, would soon prove that such a *cliché* is quite inadmissable.

Women have, with these two, at long last arrived in some force. Poets such as Nesta Wyn Jones, Einir Jones and Menna Elfyn already had a clear achievement to their names in the 1980s. And of course, women in general had since the 1920s been the major force in prose fiction. Now a number of new sensitive poets took centre stage—Nest Llwyd, Elin Llwyd Morgan and others.

In prose fiction the female presence remains even more formidable, particularly amongst the established writers, such as Marion Eames, Marged Pritchard, Jane Edwards, Eigra Lewis Roberts, who now have been joined by one of the most exciting new talents of the last decade, namely Angharad Tomos. Of the generation that established itself in the prose of the 1970s and 1980s—to add some males to the list just mentioned, Aled Islwyn, Alun Jones, Bryan Martin Davies, John Emyr, Dafydd Ifans, John

Rowlands, R. Gerallt Jones, Harri Pritchard Jones—despite great unevenness in one or two and occasionally an unexpected lack of care, certainly one can say they already have a striking body of work to their credit. But the 1990s have seen the emergence of a new formidable quartet: Robin Llywelyn, Wiliam Owen Roberts, Mihangel Morgan and Angharad Tomos. There was some understandable euphoria about this as verse had continued to dominate Welsh literature. At long last, young prose-writers seemed to be becoming intelligent again. But it is still early to predict. The primary stylist of the four, Robin Llywelyn, has published two short novels and a few short stories, but he has demonstrated a vitality of imagery and rhythmic sense, a daring fancy, a sense of thoughtful music that have been most impressive. Wiliam Owen Roberts is the author of perhaps the most significant new development of these years with the novel, *Y Pla*, based on research and (the only possible way for a historical novel to be managed) a maximum of aplomb, creating the history for itself and undoing any literalist chronicling with the full licence of a true novelist, scattering the dreadful inferiority complex so often suffered by creative writers in this *genre*. The first condition for historical fiction is to remake history: otherwise it dies. Wiliam Owen Roberts has a thoughtful perception and generosity of spirit, together with skill, that augur well for the vitality of the Welsh novel in the future. With these two novelists, Robin Llywelyn and Wiliam Owen Roberts, the end of the twentieth century has arrived in the field of the novel with a vengeance. They have a panache that confounds the realism and comfortable style and characterization of their predecessors. They can be gaudy and plain, unpredictable and morally responsible. They need now determination to make time and more time to create a body of mature work alert to the imaginative life of our period.

Angharad Tomos too impresses with her moral experience. She is the most authoritative of her generation in her human awareness. In the fullness of her emotional image of the world she enacts and, in the intelligent realization of profound personal issues, she has maintained the high seriousness and moral integrity of Kate Roberts. Mihangel Morgan too has won deserving praise and is at present the most determined of this group: in his consciousness of technique and salutary emergence out of the photographic realism that has blighted Welsh fiction, he has brought colour and piquancy to the prose scene.

All four delight in the basics of execution—the flair for dialogue, the feeling for character and plot, the structure, the diversity of an energetic style. The men perhaps are stronger regarding originality, intellectual sharpness and boldness; but the woman possesses that high seriousness from which eventually, if she has the time and care, an important novel could emanate. She has the moral maturity and power to embody human experience at its most generalized significance. The men have the diversity, the woman the purpose. But, as I remain rather hesitant in prophesying, by the time a bunch of new novels appears, we may see a complete reshuffling of this situation.

These have all flourished in the teeth of populism where others have floundered. Elsewhere in our fiction (though this is not simply a Welsh difficulty) sexual themes and 'realistic' language are still troublesome for some of our contemporary novelists, particularly for big lads and young ladies from the rural areas and small county towns. The excitement enkindled by the lowering of inhibitions regarding physical functions is known as 'challenging', and regularly described, week by week in the press, by some awakened spirits as 'daring'. The genuine adolescent delight in concentrating climactically on naming genitals, their functions, and so on has far from abated, particularly amongst prose-writers. Nipples are all the vogue; Welsh writers from the valleys or Meirionnydd now want to pose nude in their sentences, want their adverbs to strip off and if possible get an orgasm into their metaphors. Full-stops become a sort of cleavage. The greater poise and maturity of the verse tradition has perhaps avoided this rather innocent sort of decadence. Perhaps it was easier to be adult and 'cure souls' as Henry James might put it when dealing with thimbles and dresses than when wobbling over the daily coition. One cannot but suspect, for instance, that Gide and Mann and James may have managed their humanity, however oriented, with somewhat more intellectual ease than is the wont generally in our Welsh *fin-de-siècle*.

Of three established novelists, John Rowlands, Eigra Lewis Roberts and Jane Edwards, the latter is the most persistent in her dedication to prose narrative. John Rowlands has turned for the moment entirely to criticism, and now is the leading representative of what may be called our central contemporary criticism. Eigra Lewis Roberts, although still fortunately refusing to release her commitment to published prose, has become more involved, and very successfully, in television.

Despite the aforementioned weekly dose of being daring in Welsh, it is still true to say that novel-writing still has little to do with smoking in the school lavatories, or being anti-chapel, using naughty words, even wearing long trousers and so on, and everything to do with maturity and intelligence. On the whole, almost all the narrative written about adolescence between 1960 and 1995, and that is a fair share of Welsh novel-writing, the 'realism' in particular can be written off as pimply catharsis. As regards more rigorous 'realism', Angharad Tomos just simply comes to the fore because of her essentially ethical adult qualification.

Drama is going through a fairly thin patch. This may possibly be a European phenomenon. In Wales one may venture some sort of tentative explanation. Here, more than elsewhere, there has been an ill-thought-through and influential theory of 'theatricality', which simply means 'performance' (the main sector for subsidy in music, opera, and drama). This has diverted attention away from the central need for intelligent, imaginatively visual and linguistic material arising out of a mature and adult vision of life. And again, drama has somehow (perhaps because of the inevitable influence of the visual arts) been more susceptible to the unself-critical diversion of the *avant-garde*. Little reaches publication.

It is easy to understand how the theory of performance has been more influential in drama than in poetry and narrative prose. Performance, even if it is simply mental, always is omnipresent in literature; but it has been, at least from the point of view of developed and versatile imagination, comparatively neglected during recent centuries in verse and story-telling. Pub poems and some light television are the exception rather than the rule. In drama, however, the emphasis has gone all the other way, and so-called 'experimental', sometimes extempore, performers often hold sway. We have an actor-oriented scene. As a result, the technical standard of acting in Welsh has been higher than ever before; but—apart from translation—the theatre itself has failed to attract since Saunders Lewis any major intelligence to take the craft of drama seriously.

Sometimes, the financial pull of television has been blamed for enticing would-be dramatists away from the theatre. But that plausible excuse will hardly hold water. We have fine craftsmen and women in television. But apart from Saunders Lewis riding again,

Emyr Humphreys who has occasionally returned to Welsh as a medium of expression (following an early short novel in 1958) unfortunately very late in his career, and an occasional forage on the part of poets like Caradog Prichard and Alan Llwyd, television drama has seldom been truly substantial and not to be compared with current affairs, sport, nature, or music programmes. In television drama, we are inundated with the ordinary. The media have of late been pretty feeble in general in their service to literature. A regular radio discussion in Welsh on books, for instance, has been notorious for its policy of discussing three English books for every Welsh one, despite the hundreds of Welsh-language books published annually. This represents something of a rift between broadcasting and the vigour of Welsh culture, basically because of a lack of competence on the part of the media. This is also a symptom of a broad ignorance in such circles. Gone are the heady days of Aneirin Talfan Davies, Alun Llywelyn-Williams, Emyr Humphreys and Dyfnallt Morgan, when there was a mutual respect between literature (quite apart from drama) and a number of gifted producers. Intelligence is no longer a positive qualification in such circles.

It seems to me that, as in some of the other arts, drama in Wales has been perverted by inadequate critical thought. Playwriters seem not to have worked through modernism as yet: they have stuck to externals, have succumbed to presuppositions about absurdism and lack of purpose, and—in drama more than elsewhere in literature—have floundered in nihilistic decadence. We have the theatre: what we need is the mind and the imagination to use it.

In Welsh criticism (during Dafydd Glyn Jones's long lexico-graphical fast), the central figure has been John Rowlands, whose positive attitude to the latest trends has fused a number of strands in contemporary ideas as seen in that stimulating collection, *Sglefrio ar Eiriau* (Skating on Words, 1992). One of the most energetic of these trends is of course feminism. Some complain that feminists tend to give feminism a bad name. I prefer to begin with the premise that, though they may be criticized as ridiculous in many of their claims, lacking in humour, immature in their lack of balance, stridently narrow in perspective, and so on, they are just simply right. However other females and well-machoed males feel about their jargon, something obviously had to be done, even in literature. And gradually we are all—fortunately—being reoriented.

Feminism in Wales happily has its own character. The submission of the female is read within the context of Welsh national submission. It is noteworthy that in Welsh, the grammatical term for 'gender' and the common word for 'nation' are homonyms: that is to say, they share the same phonemic home, 'cenedl'. And the most original thoughts about feminism have come from this particular direction. A number of very gifted women have made a singular contribution to our realization of this major issue—Jane Aaron, Ceridwen Lloyd-Morgan, Delyth George, Menna Elfyn, Branwen Jarvis, Marged Haycock, Elin Ap Hywel, Menna Baines and others. The other 'cenedl' for all these women has served as a liberating servitude. Just as black feminism has often been safeguarded by its blackness from being shunted into an enclosed siding, so nationalist feminists have found other troubles to free them, parallel with the business in question. In England a committed feminist may find little of great import to break the mould, though she may be a gardener, a bankrupt, a structuralist, a traveller, even a Christian. Too often in male-dominated university departments, a woman colleague can be 'shunted' to look after feminism: 'so that's settled', while the men get on with the thousand and one tasks of being human in other ways. It is noteworthy that in all Welsh departments of the University of Wales the outstanding women, whatever their undoubted feminist commit-ment, have made their main contribution outside the feminist ambit.

The feminist influence on prose and verse has however gradually become quietly effective. Menna Elfyn, often used as the token feminist, is a stronger poet than her image frequently conveys. After a time of delicate promise (before being put on the band-wagon), she was admittedly used by hack liberals, mostly Anglo-Welsh, and soiled by the syllabuses (called 'working on the buses') and by extra-literary fifth-form discussion on the rights and rights of feminism. She has sometimes been made obvious, been portrayed as doing the things feminists are supposed to do, and saying the things the stock feminists have to say. This is perhaps inevitable. One feels it, with all due respect, an unwarranted sacrifice. The danger of the whole exercise is that feminism, which should not be boring, repetitive, unimaginative and *cliché*-ridden, can be all too easily conveyed as parochial and tired. The cruellest oppression of the female is when she lands up as a stereotype of political correctness, devoid of paradox and wit. Once again, I believe Menna Elfyn's roles as a mother, as wife, as citizen of Wales, as a person sensitive to the fullness of her natural and social environment, together with her delicate imagination and sense of rhythm and imagery, besides her sense of humour, have preserved her from that final enemy of creativity, obviousness. The conventional radical is the cruellest of all ironies, and Welsh literature, male and female, nowadays can suffer a great deal from that particular cruelty.

Theory (both in the journal *Tu Chwith* and *Taliesin*, particularly in the discussion of deconstruction) has inevitably become a recent central feature of criticism. Sometimes, it is somewhat immature and characteristically fickle. More particularly, evaluation as a basic element in criticism now tends to evade almost all if not all critics younger than fifty. The onset of relativism and pluralism (together with the self-contradictory claim that these attitudes are universally true) may be the determining factor in this loss, apart from a prevailing emphasis on the simplistic and popular, or on phonological externals and the journalistic 'relevant'. Few critics younger than Alan Llwyd and Robert Rhys are able to perceive the permanent significance of works of substance with the experienced authority of a Dafydd Glyn Jones, Geraint Gruffydd, Dewi Stephen Jones, J. E. Caerwyn Williams and Bryan Martin Davies. Intelligence, imagination, linguistic sensitivity, a dynamic sense of form, and the energy of a mature and broad response to contemporary life tend to fade due to this growing lack of direction regarding evaluation.

The thrust of the Welsh poetic tradition of praise has left its mark on contemporaries. The praise posture is still so pervasive that, despite regular tendencies to conform to the English—and even the European—post-imperial norm of irony and defensive scepticism, there seems to be a uniqueness about the Welsh stance that even with the younger generation maintains itself despite inevitable pressures. It is to be detected particularly in three fields: in the bias towards praise of people, in the 'green' nationalist function (which has not only opened up themes of universal significance, but given bite to expression), and in the continuity of Christian affirmation (a bias that has maintained seriousness and defended much verse from superficiality). All three would be quite odd from the English perspective.

They sometimes embarrass those Welsh observers who are particularly susceptible to English *mores*. Looking at English verse from the Welsh point of view, our fellow islanders sometimes seem rather parochial, 'up tight', uncritically hesitant even afraid about affirmation, self-defensively ironic to a neurotic degree, over-wary, unable to open out generously (when did one last see a sensible reference to Welsh literature in the *Times Literary Supplement* or the Books section of the *Sunday Times* or for that matter to any national minority in the world?), and they conform to an unquestioning dogma regarding doubt and flatness. They begrudge, therefore, a great deal of the range traditionally permitted within poetry. Comfortable denial and over-scrupulous incredulity often inhibit the spectrum. The Welsh temper is still basically different and for the hurried observer may seem unguarded towards all this. It is frequently more celebratory, and may strike the precipitous reader as both naïve and coy after the emotional constipation and fashion-ridden disavowal in English. Welsh praise can be uncomfortably positive and direct, although in the broad context the modern declension and the negative conscience are fatefully present. But to leave such a contrast simply at that would be to lose the point and to ignore the sharp discipline and the formal complexity that are inherent in contemporary tradition, as well as the fact that praise in Welsh is a belligerent factor within a combative situation. The continuing presence of a consciousness of craft and highly developed artistry has maintained respect towards language and structure. And finally the diffusion of interest in verse amongst the people—beside bringing with it the debit fear of intellectual pretensions—has kept the feet of Welsh metre solidly on the ground.

On the debit side, throughout most of the century, a fair proportion of Welsh readers of poetry has been stubbornly blighted by Georgianism and neo-Georgianism. This has often led to sweet smoothness, *naïveté*, narrow Romanticism, a lack of adventure and an over-rural emphasis. It is not unrelated to the continual threat to Welsh literature from the powerful populist lobby against intelligence, and their concerted and most influential campaign against the use of the brain. This pressure aims at a literature strong on children's books, where the traditionalists insist that survival lies in writing children's verse for adults, specializing in adaptations of Mills and Boon, where rigorous intellectual activity and artistry are considered rather self-indulgent, a literature that gets agitated about being softly pornographic because this is still regarded as venturesome adolescent rebellion against Victorian Noncon-formity, where indigenous originality and maturity are continually submerged beneath imitative trends adventurously imported from London, written in a hurry by a busy people, well-organized and subsidized but gradually losing self-dignity, a *patois* literature satisfied with the mediocre and terrified of uniqueness and continually spying over its shoulder. One does not need to look far to spot the dangers.

All this can be generously supported financially; and fortunately there is a cross-party consensus on this though, in uncertain times, followers of the arts are always nervous. Philistines abound. It is not just a problem for literature. Politicians usually are pretty superficial in the context of cultural values. The questions sometimes arise—can Wales maintain a full national orchestra? Can it afford an opera company? Why should the public subsidize every seat in a performance just for the few? In that context, why permit a rather unpopular book in Welsh? The only reply is to consider the broad scenario. Shall we cross Europe from country to country, each maintaining a high culture (each usually highly subsidized), and then reach the Welsh border: here, relief is at hand, no more of that: civilization steps back? From here, pop music rules OK. That alone pays. Let us allow the natives in Welsh to have more limericks, humorous *englynion*, no challenges to the intellect, no wrestling with the imagination, no orchestra, no snobs. Let us replace the substantial weekly *Y Faner* by the light pictorial *Golwg*. Let us bring pressure for books to be shorter, for journals to forego articles that may be more substantial than snippets. We'll bring out a report on the theme. The establishment will understand.

Despite all this, Welsh periodical literature, where one can usually sniff future developments, is going through a quite vital period at the moment. The solid and reliable *Traethodydd*, the colourful *Barn*, the versatile *Barddas*, and the radical *Tu Chwith* and *Taliesin*, besides the scholarly tomes coming from the University of Wales Press—*Llên Cymru* and *Studia Celtica* incorporating the *Bulletin of the Board of Celtic Studies*, as well as annual volumes of *Ysgrifau Beirniadol*, and the lively series *Llên y Llenor*, all these at present represent a revival in the fortunes of literary discussion. If I had been asked at the end of the 1980s

what about criticism in Welsh?—I probably would have hung my
head. This is the field that in the 1990s (unfortunately when one
considers its supplementary function amongst the *genres*), has now
seen the most dramatic transformation. Such a sea-change
encourages one to be hesitant about considering 'prospects for the
future' in any literary sector. Two or three years can make a world
of difference. The central figure in this renaissance is Professor
John Rowlands, who has not only written some of the most elegant
critical prose of our time, edited *Taliesin*, but has been the lynch-
pin in the revival of interest in critical theory, a field somewhat
neglected since John Morris-Jones. His own *Ysgrifau ar y Nofel*
(Essays on the Novel, 1991) is the standard work on the Welsh
novel; but the essays he edited in *Sglefrio ar Eiriau* recite a roll-call
of the new generation of Welsh critics—M. Wynn Thomas, Menna
Elfyn, Dafydd Johnston, Jane Aaron, Wiliam Owen Roberts,
Delyth George, Gerwyn Wiliams, and Robert Rhys. Simon
Brooks, too, who represents the post-modernist trend has brought
a breath of fresh air into the Welsh critical establishment both with
his own essays and with the publication of *Tu Chwith*. Criticism,
which in Welsh like most languages has been a sober and sensible
activity and somehow survived the eccentricity of Joyce, Kafka,
Mallarmé, Eliot, Breton, Faulkner, Beckett, Apollinaire and
Stevens, is not given like verse, drama, and fiction to surrealism,
absurdism and modernistic frolics. At long last, it has to stand on
its head, and some of its practitioners do not quite fancy the
position. Such an influx of blood to the brain will, however, no
doubt be salutary. One may obviously have reservations regarding
the presuppositions of neo-modernism and deconstruction which
could patently not be properly discussed in the present context; yet
one can accept the method of 'play' for instance without necessarily
condoning dogmas such as the denial of canon or the irrelevance of
the author. To be dismissive of the whole movement is certainly to
miss a great deal. Surely, some of the methodology is at least an
extension of catholicity.

When, therefore, despite our very Welsh tendency to nurse our
frequent pessimism, we consider the general situation in Wales
today: the continued strict-verse revival, the appearance of some
remarkable free-verse practitioners, together with the minor revival
with its great potential in the novel, besides the new confidence in
literary criticism and the study of history through the medium of

Welsh (particularly with the series *Cof Cenedl*), one could make out a strong case for counting the last four or five years as producing a more exciting situation than experienced for some decades. A writer of outstanding promise, author of the surrealist celebration of the virility of being alive *Diogi a Chynhyrfu* (Laziness and Agitation, 1996), is the young Sioned Puw Rowlands, an astounding example of this contemporary renaissance.

Scholarship too, with the formidable contribution of J. E. Caerwyn Williams, doyen of Welsh Letters, and Geraint Gruffydd and a host of other fine scholars is going through a more productive period than ever before. The reason for naming these two will be obvious to Welsh readers. They both possess a wholeness in the scope of their literary scholarship unrivalled by others: Caerwyn Williams, the most knowledgeable of all scholars ever in the literatures of the Celtic countries, author of the standard history of Irish literature, expert in Breton and its literature, and in Wales our major specialist on the Poets of the Princes and medieval religious prose, with standard contributions to his name stretching from the sixth to the twentieth centuries, apart from innumerable linguistic studies, and of course editor of the periodicals and series *Studia Celtica, Y Traethodydd, Llên y Llenor, Ysgrifau Beirniadol*, and advisory editor of the National Dictionary; and Geraint Gruffydd, our main authority on the Welsh Protestant Reformation and Renaissance literature, the first director of the Centre for Advanced Welsh and Celtic Studies, and general editor of its primary series of the Poetry of the Princes, with masterly work on Dafydd ap Gwilym, besides writing original and penetrating studies on all points along the spectrum from the beginnings of Welsh literature to the present day. Surprisingly, work on the nineteenth century by a group of scholars has opened up an oddly undiscovered century—the swashbuckling interpretation by Hywel Teifi Edwards of the philistinism and inferiority complex of the Victorian yuppies, Tudur Jones's magisterial demonstration of the vast structure of Calvinist aesthetic and social thought building on the mature reflections of seventeenth-century divines, on eighteenth- and nineteenth-century inquiry into philosophy and the affections, and on the meditations of a twentieth-century Dutch school of thinkers reaching from Abraham Kuyper through Dooyeweerd on through the Van Tils and Rookmaaker, together with socially oriented studies by E. G.

Millward, E. Wyn James and Kathryn Jenkins on popular literature and hymnology and their contribution to the fuller appreciation of nineteenth-century taste,—all this has proved one of the great new developments. But the nineteenth century is not the only field that has received radical attention in recent years. The study of the Poets of the Princes has been transformed, great strides have been made in the examination of our earliest saga and religious poetry by Marged Haycock, Jenny Rowland and others, solid and novel work particularly on the form and style of our medieval prose by Brynley Roberts, Rachel Bromwich, Christine James, Sioned Davies, and Simon Evans, splendid studies and editions of the *cywydd* poets of the fourteenth and fifteenth centuries by D. J. Bowen, Gruffydd Aled Williams, Enid Roberts, Dafydd Johnston (the most catholic of our younger critics and scholars), and others; sensitive interpretation of the Puritans and Methodists by Tudur Jones and Derec Llwyd Morgan, dramatic progress on the twentieth century by Robin Chapman, John Emyr, Robert Rhys, Dafydd Johnston, Dafydd Glyn Jones and a host of others; and in all other periods steady and substantial inroads. The most significant development in Welsh scholarship has been the establishment of the Centre for Advanced Welsh and Celtic Studies; and generally speaking one could be forgiven for reckoning that academic thinking on Welsh literature is at present in its heyday. But because of the significance of tradition and the difficulty for the Welsh of inheriting that tradition, scholarship with a comparatively small team of workers (though with more substantial materials to work on than most literatures between the sixth and the fifteenth centuries) certainly carries a heavier responsibility for Welsh than for more politically influential literatures.

Just as verse and prose fiction have both forged out in Welsh an original and impressive response to modernity where the realization of form and language, the sensitivity to community (nationally and internationally) and to the social, religious, and literary traditions of Wales are vitally relevant, so too criticism has in Welsh cut out of the native materials and situation an idiosyncratic path that has something of general interest to any intellectuals for whom small countries may not be entirely inadmissible. We therefore approach the end of the millenium with somewhat exhilarating determination and not without a modicum of unfamiliar hope.

INDEX